27

D1348599

CHANGING ASSESSMENTS

Evaluation in Education and Human Services

Editors:

George F. Madaus, Boston College, Chestnut
  Hill, MA, U.S.A.
Daniel L. Stufflebeam, Western Michigan
  University, Kalamazoo, MI, U.S.A.

**National Commission on Testing
and Public Policy**

CHANGING ASSESSMENTS

Alternative Views of Aptitude,
Achievement and Instruction

Edited by

Bernard R. Gifford
University of California, Berkeley

and

Mary Catherine O'Connor
Boston University

Kluwer Academic Publishers
Boston / Dordrecht / London

Distributors for North America:
Kluwer Academic Publishers
101 Philip Drive
Assinippi Park
Norwell, Massachusetts 02061 USA

Distributors for all other countries:
Kluwer Academic Publishers Group
Distribution Centre
Post Office Box 322
3300 AH Dordrecht, THE NETHERLANDS

Library of Congress Cataloging-in-Publication Data

Changing assessments : alternative views of aptitude, achievement, and
  instruction / edited by Bernard R. Gifford and Mary Catherine
  O'Connor.
      p.   cm. — (Evaluation in education and human services)
    Includes bibliographical references and index.
    ISBN 0-7923-9177-2
    1. Educational tests and measurements—United States.   2. Ability-
-Testing.   I. Gifford, Bernard R.   II. O'Connor, Mary Catherine.
III. Series.
LB3051.C448   1992
371.2'6—dc20   91-35093
                                                                    CIP

Contents

Contributors

Ann L. Brown is the Evelyn Lois Corey Faculty Fellow in Instruction at the School of Education at the University of California, Berkeley. She received her Ph.D. in Psychology from the University of London. Since 1978 Brown was professor of Psychology and Senior Scientist at the Center for the Study of Reading at the University of Illinois, Urbana-Champaign. Brown is highly regarded as a leading authority on child development, the psychology of reading, and metacognition. She has well over 100 published articles that are widely cited in the field. Since 1971 she has served as a consultant editor on the boards of six professional journals and is presently an Associate Editor of *Cognition and Instruction*. Dr. Brown has served as President of Division 7 of the American Psychological Society and is currently Vice-President of the prestigious National Academy of Education.

Joseph C. Campione is a professor at the School of Education at the University of California, Berkeley, where he is also the director of the joint program in special education. Dr. Campione received his Ph.D. in Psychology from the University of Connecticut in 1965. Dr. Campione was professor of Psychology and Research Professor at the Center for the Study of Reading and Cognition at the University of Illinois, Champaign, since 1976. Dr. Campione's research and his more than 90 published works focus on learning strategies of educationally at-risk children, transfer of training, metacognition, and issues of assessment and instruction.

Howard Gardner is a research psychologist in Boston. He investigates human cognitive capacities, particularly those central to the arts, in normal children, gifted children, and brain-damaged adults. He is the author of over 250 articles in professional journals and wide-circulation periodicals. Among his ten books are *The Quest for Mind* (1973; second edition, 1981); *The Shattered Mind* (1975); *Developmental Psychology* (1978; second edition, 1982); *Art, Mind and Brain* (1982); *Frames of Mind* (1983); *The Mind's New Science* (1985); and, most recently, *To Open Minds: Chinese Clues to the Dilemma of American Education* (1989). At present, Howard Gardner serves as Professor of Education and Co-Director of Project Zero at the Harvard Graduate School of Education; Research Psychologist at the Boston Veterans Administration Medical Center; and Adjunct Professor of Neurology at the Boston University School of Medicine. In 1981 he was awarded a MacArthur Prize Fellowship.

Bernard R. Gifford, chair of the National Commission on Testing and Public Policy, is Chancellor's Professor of Education in the School of Education at the University of California, Berkeley. He served there as Dean of the Graduate

School of Education from 1983 through 1989. Now on leave from the university, he is currently serving as Vice President, Education, Apple Computer Inc. He received his Ph.D. in radiation biology and biophysics from the University of Rochester. Gifford has published in a number of disciplinary areas, ranging from applied physics to public policy. In recent years he has devoted most of his efforts to writing about the process of educational change and reform. His latest books are *History in the Schools: What Shall We Teacher?* (Macmillan, 1988), *Test Policy and the Politics of Opportunity Allocation: The Workplace and the Law* (Kluwer, 1989) and *Testing Policy and Test Performance: Education, Language and Culture* (Kluwer, 1989).

Kate McGilly is a post-doctoral student at the University of California, Berkeley. Her research interests include children's strategy development and mathematics learning. Dr. McGilly received her Ph.D. in Developmental Psychology from Carnegie Mellon University in 1988.

Mary Catherine O'Connor is an Assistant Professor at Boston University, with appointments in the Program in Literacy, Language and Cultural Studies, and the Program in Applied Linguistics. She received her Ph.D. in linguistics from the University of California at Berkeley in 1987. Funded by a Spencer Postdoctoral Fellowship and by a grant from the Andrew W. Mellon Foundation to the Literacies Institute, she is currently carrying out research on the ways that discourse shapes mathematics learning in middle school. Her research interests include discourse and narrative analysis, the development of school and community-based languages and literacies, and the influences of language and culture on standardized testing and alternative forms of assessment. She also works on the grammar of Northern Pomo, a native language of Northern California, currently supported by a grant from the National Science Foundation.

James W. Pellegrino is a Frank W. Mayborn Professor of Cognitive Studies at Peabody College of Vanderbilt University. Since 1990 he has been co-director of the Learning Technology Center at Vanderbilt. Previously he was Professor of Education and Psychology at the University of California, Santa Barbara. He is widely published in the area of cognitive science research on thinking and learning. Most recently, his research has focused on applications of cognitive theory and computer technology to the assessment and training of quantitative and visual-spatial abilities. His most recent work is being carried out at the Cognition and Technology Group at the Learning Technology Center. Recent publications include work on anchored instruction and its relationship to situated learning, and the use of technology in the design of generative learning environments.

Daniel P. Resnick is Professor of History and Director of European Studies at Carnegie Mellon University. His first scholarly work was in the field of French history, and he has published articles, a monograph, and textbooks in the field of European history and Western development. For more than a decade, his research has dealt with the broad themes of literacy development, schooling, and assessment in American and European settings. A study of public school testing practices, undertaken with Lauren Resnick, was supported by the Carnegie Corporation. He is currently at work on patterns of postsecondary assessment at American colleges and universities, a study supported by the Carnegie Foundation.

Lauren B. Resnick is Professor of Psychology and Education and Director of the Learning Research and Development Center at the University of Pittsburgh. Professor Resnick's primary interest is the cognitive psychology of instruction. Her research focuses on the learning of mathematics and science. She is the founder and editor of *Cognition and Instruction*, a major new journal in the field; coeditor of the *Instructional Psychology Series*; and author of a recent, widely circulated monograph commissioned by the National Academy of Sciences (NAS) entitled *Education and Learning to Think*. She has also authored and edited volumes on *The Psychology of Mathematics for Instruction, The Nature of Intelligence,* and, most recently, *Knowing, Learning, and Instruction*. Dr. Resnick serves on a number of national and international boards and commissions and is active as a consultant to foundations and government agencies. She is a member of the Commission on Behavioral and Social Sciences and Education of the Mathematical Sciences Education Board of the National Research Council, National Academy of Sciences, and has served on various NAS committees. She is past president of the American Psychological Association's Division of Educational Psychology, and a fellow in the Association's divisions of Experimental Psychology, Developmental Psychology, Educational Psychology, and the Experimental Analysis of Behavior. She has also served as president of the American Educational Research Association and vice president of their Division of Learning and Instruction. In addition, Professor Resnick is a fellow of the American Association for the Advancement of Science and a member of the National Academy of Education.

Lorrie A. Shepard is a Professor of Education at the University of Colorado, Boulder. Her research in applied measurement has addressed issues of standard setting and test bias. Her work in educational policy research has focused on the use of tests for special school placements, e.g., identification of learning disabilities, grade retention, and kindergarten screening. Her current work addresses the effects of traditional testing on teaching and learning, and the development of alternative assessments. Shepard has served as President of the National Council on Measurement in Education, and as Vice-President for

Division D of the American Educational Research Association. She has been editor of the *Journal of Educational Measurement* and the *American Educational Research Journal*. She was Vice-Chair of the National Academy of Sciences Panel on the General Aptitude Test Battery, and is currently a member of the National Academy of Education's panel to evaluate the state-by-state version of the National Assessment of Educational Progress.

Robert J. Sternberg is IBM Professor of Psychology and Education in the Department of Psychology at Yale University. He received his B.A. summa cum laude, Phi Betta Kappa from Yale in 1972 and his Ph.D. from Stanford in 1975. Dr. Sternberg has won a number of awards, including the Mensa Education and Research Foundation Award for Excellence (1989), designation in Who's Who in American Education (1989–), the Outstanding Book Award and the Research Review Award of the American Educational Research for Gifted Children (1985), the Cattell Award of the Society of Multivariate Experimental Psychology (1982), and the McCandless Young Scientist Award and the Distinguished Award for an Early Career Contribution to Psychology of the American Psychological Association (1982, 1981). Dr. Sternberg was a John Simon Guggenheim Fellow in 1985–1986 and an NSF Graduate Fellow in 1972–1975. His main interests are in understanding, measuring, and teaching intelligence and related thinking skills.

Lynne S. Webber is a Visiting Assistant Professor in Education at the University of Illinois at Chicago. She received her Ph.D. in Education from the University of Illinois at Urbana-Champaign in 1987. Her research interests include listening comprehension and referential communication in young children, and issues concerning assessment and instruction.

CHANGING ASSESSMENTS

Introduction

Bernard R. Gifford

As we edge toward the year 2000, the information age is a reality; the global marketplace is increasingly competitive; and the U.S. labor force is shrinking. Today more than ever, our nation's economic and social well-being hinges on our ability to tap our human resources—to identify talent, to nurture it, and to assess abilities and disabilities in ways that help every individual reach his or her full potential.

In pursuing that goal, decision-makers in education, industry, and government are relying increasingly on standardized tests: sets of questions — with identical directions, time limits and tasks for all test-takers—designed to permit an inference about what someone knows or can do in a particular area.

CALIBRATING DIFFERENCE

Our emphasis on standardized testing rests on a premise that is so basic it often escapes notice: that we humans are different from each other in ways that are both meaningful and measurable. We differ in terms of cognitive ability; aptitude for performing different kinds of mental and physical tasks; temperament; and interests.

But somehow, without sufficient examination, we have taken a great collective leap from that commonplace to the notion that there are precise, measurable gradations of innate ability that can be used to direct children to the right classrooms, and adults to the right job slots.

Where did this notion come from? As James Fallows has written, "Partly it came from the universal human impulse to put people into hierarchies and to prove that whatever hierarchy exists is fair. But there were some more specific causes too."[1]

Like numerous observers of American assessment practices, Fallows points to the "nativist" reaction in the United States to the overwhelming flow of immigrants at the turn of the century. Alarmed at the numbers and potential impact of new Americans, immigration specialists warned that "races may change their religions, their form of government, and their languages, but underneath they may continue the physical, mental, and moral capacities and incapacities which determine the real character of their religion, government, and literature."[2]

Responding to that kind of rhetoric, experts in phrenology and physiognomy worked overtime to develop a range of tools for classifying and ranking people. Scientists in America and Europe measured feet, skulls, fingers and faces to detect and predict character traits.

Virtually all of these tools have been discredited. As Fallows points out, "...of all the human-classifying devices developed at the turn of the century, mental measurement is the major one to have survived."[3]

ASKING HARD QUESTIONS

Needless to say, psychometrics is not phrenology. Testing has survived for a very good reason: decision-makers need a sound, fair, and reasonably efficient mechanism to help make difficult decisions about the allocation of opportunity among individuals and institutions. In many circumstances, standardized pencil-and-paper tests can and do serve a useful role.

Certainly, people have different abilities and skill levels. Another way to say this is: life is unfair. But that does not relieve us of the burden of being as fair as we possibly can be as we measure differences and assign meaning to them.

We must take care to develop measurement tools that help us pursue both excellence and equity. We must take care to define the limitations of those tools. We must recognize that, as Fallows has written, "the qualities that each society chooses to measure often say more about the society's preoccupations than about the traits that are supposedly being observed."[4]

And finally, we must continue to ask the hard policy questions that cut to the heart of the testing enterprise:

How should a society committed to the ideas of individual merit, equal opportunity, and the free marketplace allocate scarce educational and employment opportunities?

How can that society draw distinctions—fairly and justifiably —among people competing against each other for the same educational or employment opportunity?

These are among the central questions of a democracy. How a society answers them reveals a great deal about its values and its priorities, and determines a great deal about its future course.

In recent decades, we have placed the standardized pencil-and-paper test at the center of these fundamental questions about the nature of opportunity allocation in American life. In more and more areas of our lives—schools, employment, the military—we rely upon the standardized test to rank or classify people, and to assure ourselves that we have done so fairly.

As any baseball fan can tell you, Americans love statistics. Clusters of numbers give us the illusion of precision in situations that might otherwise admit uncertainty. And so it is with tests. But tests are imperfect. No test is a direct measure of aptitude or innate ability. Tests sample only a small portion of what someone knows or can do at a particular time—the time of the test. And no single standard test can illuminate equally well the talents of people from dramatically different ethnic, cultural, and language backgrounds.

THE LIMITATIONS OF TESTING

The popular media often present anecdotal accounts of how tests can misrepresent an individual's abilities or potential. A case in point is Oliver Sacks, the brilliant neurologist who has written with insight and compassion about the cognitive performance of individuals suffering from brain disorders.[5] His own personal experience, as well as his clinical observation of disparities between his patients' test-predicted performance and their actual performance, turned him into a probing critic of the standardized testing enterprise. Says Sacks:

> There's a constraint built into any testing situation that excludes spontaneity, the free function of the person. My own career has been marked by doing incredibly badly in test situations. At Oxford I was given a scholarship on the basis of an essay, but I failed routine exams called prelims three times. The college was bewildered. They said, "We've given you our top science scholarship and now you're failing this stupid exam. What's going on?" I said I don't know. Finally I got it. I think something similar may be happening in patients. A test situation is other people's questions. One is in a rather passive situation. In an active situation, you find your own voice and your own vision.[6]

Tests can underestimate the ability of an individual; they may also be poor predictors of performance by a class of people. Keith Olson made this case persuasively in telling the dramatic story of the G.I. Bill.[7] When, as World War II drew to a close, the U.S. government decided to subsidize the college education of every G.I., many leading educators ridiculed the idea. Robert Hutchins, president of the University of Chicago, warned in 1944 that colleges and universities would become "hobo jungles." James B. Conant, President of Harvard, found the proposal distressing, because it did not distinguish between those who can profit most from advanced education and those who cannot. He and others preferred restricting the program to the most able veterans, "carefully selected..." presumably by means of standardized testing.

If they had been tested, a great many of the 2.3 million people who enrolled in colleges and universities under the G.I. bill would have scored below an arbitrary cutoff, and would have been denied educational benefits. But in fact, these veterans—including about half a million who did not have a traditional "college prep" background—became the most successful group of students American universities had ever seen, taking more than their share of places on deans' lists and honor rolls. Maturity and motivation apparently were more important than skill levels or even academic preparation.

Let me offer one more example of what I think of as "near-miss" classification. An error in the calibration of the 1976 version of the *Armed Services Vocational Aptitude Battery* (ASVAB)—part of the Defense Department's extensive testing program, resulted in the admission of 300,000 recruits who normally would have scored below the cutoff and been rejected. Several studies show that as a group, these enlistees performed "only somewhat less well than those who actually passed the ASVAB. Numerous enlistees fared as well or better."[8]

These three stories all make the same point: whenever people are classified on the basis of cutoff scores on standardized tests, misclassifications are bound to occur. The solution is not to avoid classifying people: such classifications are essential and inevitable in modern society. It is, rather, to avoid making decisions about anyone's future solely on the basis of one imperfect instrument.

Standardized tests are fallible. That much is clear. At best, they are imperfect predictors of real-life performance; at worst—that is, when they are used independently of other relevant information—they are arbitrary and result in the unfair treatment of individuals and groups. Nevertheless, in both employment and education, we continue to rely heavily, and sometimes exclusively, on such tests.

In education, the standardized test now consumes a great deal of our limited resources. Each year, elementary and secondary students take 127 million separate tests as part of standardized test batteries mandated by states and districts. At some grade levels, a student may have to take as many as seven to twelve tests a year. Testing is generally heavier for students in special education or bilingual programs.[9]

Direct costs to taxpayers of purchasing and scoring these tests range from $70 million to $107 million annually. Indirect costs, in terms of teacher and administrator time, are about four times the direct costs.[10]

THE NATIONAL COMMISSION
ON TESTING AND PUBLIC POLICY

Given the complex and onerous role we continue to assign to standardized pencil-and-paper tests, it should not come as a surprise to anyone that the testing enterprise seems to be perpetually embroiled in controversy.

In an attempt to gain a better understanding of the controversies surrounding standardized testing, and more importantly, to examine new possibilities for assessing individual capabilities, the National Commission on Testing and Public Policy was formed in early 1987.[11] It was my pleasure to chair that Commission from its inception until shortly after the publication of its first major public report in 1990.

Over a three-year period, the Commission examined the use of standardized tests and other forms of assessment in schools, the workplace, and the military. We undertook the investigation with a view toward promoting the identification and nurturing of talent, especially among racial, ethnic, and linguistic minorities.

In our deliberations, we were generally more concerned with the policy implications of various tests than their technical characteristics. We reviewed a broad range of tests and testing practices, asking whether they are being used fairly and appropriately. We asked whether they are being used in ways that help our nation fully develop and mobilize the talents of its people. And we asked whether they are being used in ways that strengthen our key social institutions.

Our report, *From Gatekeeper to Gateway: Transforming Testing in America,* summarized the Commission's conclusions. It highlights our central finding: that many current practices in educational and employment testing stand in the way of efforts to identify and develop talent, and to improve the functioning of key social institutions.

The Commission recommended that current testing policies and practices be transformed to help people develop talents and become constructive citizens, and to help institutions become more productive, accountable, and just. It made the following specific recommendations:

1. Testing policies and practices must be reoriented to promote the development of all human talent.
2. Testing programs should be redirected from overreliance on multiple-choice tests toward alternative forms of assessment.
3. Test scores should be used only when they differentiate on the basis of characteristics relevant to the opportunities being allocated.
4. The more test scores disproportionately deny opportunities to minorities, the greater the need to show that the tests measure characteristics relevant to the opportunities being allocated.
5. Test scores are imperfect measures and should not be used alone to make important decisions about individuals, groups, or institutions; in the allocation of opportunities, individuals' past performance and relevant experience must be considered.
6. More efficient and effective assessment strategies are needed to hold social institutions accountable.
7. The enterprise of testing must be subjected to greater public accountability.
8. Research and development programs must be expanded to create and use assessments that promote the development of the talents of all our peoples.

Taken together, these recommendations move us toward a new, broader concept of assessment—one that acknowledges the value of testing as a tool that aids decision-making, but also recognizes the limitations of current testing practices and moves beyond them.

In that spirit, the Commission invited the distinguished authors represented in this volume to elaborate on new or alternative approaches to testing. We asked them to explore new ways of thinking about assessment, based on recent advances in the field of cognitive science. We asked them to lay the theoretical groundwork for new measurement tools and methods, such as dynamic assessment, performance-based assessment, and portfolio assessment. And finally, we asked them to provide a conceptual framework for innovative systems—including computer-based educational strategies—that deeply integrate assessment with instruction.

The result is a collection of articles that helps us move toward the Commission's goal of "transforming testing in America."

ACKNOWLEDGEMENTS

The impetus for the Commission grew out of a series of conversations I had with Lynn Walker, Deputy Director of the Human Rights and Governance Program, and Peter Stanley, Vice President, Programs in Education and Culture, at the Ford Foundation. I would not presume to second-guess Lynn or Peter's reasons for advocating Ford Foundation support of the Commission, but I can note their long-standing commitment to informing public debate about complex public policy issues through disciplined inquiry. Lynn and Peter have proved to be challenging advisors, but they have never sought to channel the thinking of the Commission member (or its many advisors and consultants) in any particular direction.

I also want to acknowledge the tremendous contribution of my co-editor Mary Catherine O'Connor. After I unexpectedly took an extended leave from the University of California, limiting the amount of time I had available to complete work on this volume, Cathy stepped up her role as co-editor. She edited the chapters, with copy-editing and formatting assistance from Mary Lou Sumberg, Alissa Shethar and Randall Roddy. She prepared the overview chapter, which I am sure the reader will find to be extraordinarily thoughtful and comprehensive.

Throughout our collaboration on the work of the Commission, Cathy has worked hard to fill in my knowledge gaps on the connection between language skills and testing outcomes, especially among non-native English speakers, while I have attempted to introduce her to the art and craft of formal policy analysis. It is hard to say who got the best of this exchange, but my guess is that in this case—as happens so often with me—I have learned more from "my student" than I have taught.

I would be remiss if I did not acknowledge the efforts of Linda Wing, who served as the Associate Director of the National Commission on Testing and Public Policy during its formative stage, and on whose shoulders so many of us stood. Commission members Edward E. Potter and Antonia Hernandez also proved to be thought-provoking counselors, especially when they lined up on opposite sides of an issue. George Madaus, who took over the day-to-day operations of the Commission after my leave from Berkeley began, proved to be heaven-sent; he has done extraordinary work under difficult circumstances.

NOTES

1 James Fallows, *More Like Us* (Boston: Houghton Mifflin), 1989, p. 142.

2 Fallows (1989), p. 143.

3 Fallows (1989), p. 143.

4 Fallows (1989), p. 155.

5 See Oliver Sacks, *The Man Who Mistook His Wife for a Hat and Other Clinical Tales* (New York: Harper & Row, 1987), esp. pp. 178-186.

6 Cited in Scott Winokur, "The Extraordinary Case of Oliver Sacks," in *Image: The Magazine of the San Francisco Examiner*, December 16, 1990, p. 14.

7 Keith W. Olson, *The G.I. Bill, the Veterans, and the Colleges* (Lexington, Ky: University Press of Kentucky, 1974), cited in Fallows (1989), pp. 158-159.

8 National Commission on Testing and Public Policy, *From Gatekeeper to Gateway* (Chestnut Hill, MA: Boston College, 1990), pp. 9-10.

9 *From Gatekeeper to Gateway*, pp. 14-15.

10 *From Gatekeeper to Gateway*, p. 17.

11 For more on the origins and purposes of the National Commission on Testing and Public Policy, see the Introduction to Bernard R. Gifford, *Test Policy and the Politics of Opportunity Allocation: The Workplace and the Law* (Boston, MA: Kluwer Academic Publishers, 1989), pp. ix-xii.

OVERVIEW

Rethinking Aptitude, Achievement and Instruction: Cognitive Science Research and the Framing of Assessment Policy

Mary Catherine O'Connor

> If it were not possible to change intelligence, why measure it in the first place?
>
> > Binet, 1905 (Brown, 1985 translation)

> Seems to me we're forcing a lot of kids' talents into this narrow little funnel and hoping that it comes out in reading scores and math scores. And it just ain't fair.
>
> > Elementary school teacher, Northern California

> (P)olicy at best can enable outcomes, but in the final analysis it cannot mandate what matters.
>
> > McLaughlin, 1987: 173

How can assessment be used to foster intellectual development and educational success? Do our educational testing programs encompass progressive views of intelligence and achievement? What is the best fit between test policy, test practice, and what matters most to us, access to enriching instruction for all our students? The trio of epigraphs above contain several themes that are central to the chapters in this volume. The authors of these chapters see assessment in education as a powerful and crucial tool for effective instruction, remediation, and placement. Yet they all struggle, in different ways, with the central problems that testing has presented over the past ninety years: How can we most effectively and fairly identify and nurture talent? How can we best intervene when there are learning problems? And how can we ensure that our assessment tools do not limit us, or even lead us astray, in these goals?

The contributors to this volume are noted for their work in cognitive science and psychology. Their work represents current thinking about intelligence, achievement, and instruction. But these authors have not limited their concerns to the theoretical or academic. All are involved in investigating the real-world consequences of new theories of intelligence, learning and instruction. Changes in test policy may be among these consequences. Testing policy and practice will in turn facilitate or impede new educational approaches. Thus we asked these authors specifically to consider how changes in conceptions of aptitude and achievement would figure in the future of assessment.

Psychologists' theories gradually make their way into general educational practice and policy, but there is a lag of several decades between the forefront of current theory and institutionalized practice. In our view, the public policy community can benefit from getting a clear view of what is on the way. Our intention is to isolate the issues of importance, and to make them available to those whose principal interest is in public policy: its analysis, its creation, its implementation. The volume is intended to reach a wide-ranging audience of people who want to expand their thinking about what it is we measure and why— analysts who inform decision makers, researchers whose applied interests fall into the areas of teaching, learning and assessment; practitioners and clinicians; and any other individual who is concerned with the future of testing and public policy.

What can these chapters offer to policymakers and analysts in particular? Each chapter presents new ways of thinking, ways that are becoming increasingly influential. In thinking about assessment policy, decision makers must be able to evaluate the source of expert opinions, have some sense of what is missing from any particular account, and have a sense of what is new and potentially useful. The chapters here are strongly representative of one particular tradition, a tradition that has been called cognitive science, and will aid readers in making such judgments.

These chapters will be more useful if the reader understands something about previous approaches with which they contrast. In this overview, there are four sections. First, I will discuss an example that contrasts current cognitive science research with more traditional approaches, in a case of particular relevance to policy makers: teachers' attitudes and beliefs about testing. This is not something that the authors of the four core chapters deal with directly. Policy makers, however, are very aware of the importance of beliefs and attitudes. Successful implementation of testing policy stands or falls on the attitudes and beliefs of those who carry out and are directly affected by those policies. Current cognitive science in the area of decision theory provides a new perspective on this, a perspective that may illuminate old problems.

Second, I will provide background for the six papers that follow by comparing two major perspectives on assessment: the cognitive science tradition out of which these papers have emerged, and the longer tradition based within the psychometric and measurement community. As new ways of thinking emerge, it is important to keep a perspective on just which presuppositions and values are being changed, and which maintained. Third, I will briefly overview the ways that standardized tests enter into the public policy cycle, as a way of further contextualizing the chapters in this volume.

Finally, I will give an overview of the chapters themselves, spelling out the specific links between the chapters and general aspects of policy concerns. It will become clear in this section that within policy studies there is a need for an analytic framework, constructed by and for the policy community, to incorporate new conceptualizations about thinking, learning, and assessment into current and future testing policy. The chapters in this volume only present the issues from the field of cognitive science. They begin to make proposals for assessment policy, but the work of incorporating and transforming must be done by policy professionals themselves.

TEACHER BELIEFS ABOUT TESTING:
A COGNITIVE SCIENCE PERSPECTIVE

The chapters in this volume examine scholarly theories of aptitude, talent, learning and achievement, and relate these to current policy concerns. In addition, however, we see people's everyday, non-technical beliefs about learning and achievement as important to the policy process, because of the very nature of policy-induced change: "[C]hange is ultimately a problem of the smallest unit. At each point in the policy process, a policy is transformed as individuals interpret and respond to it. What actually is delivered or provided under the aegis of a policy depends finally on the individual at the end of the line, or the 'street level bureaucrat'. . ." (McLaughlin, 1987: 174). If we see policy implementation as a continual process of bargaining with and transforming the actions of individual actors, we must be concerned with the values and beliefs of those actors. If they do not share the beliefs and assumptions of policymakers, or if they do not see the relevance of the tools chosen by those policymakers, change will be stymied at the critical juncture they inhabit. "(P)olicy at best can enable outcomes, but in the final analysis it cannot mandate what matters" (McLaughlin, 1987: 173).

Teachers, parents, test takers, employers, and district administrators all have views, beliefs, opinions and prejudices, just as do higher-level policy makers and overseers. Their "folk models"[1] of assessment, ability and achievement will in many ways determine the success or failure, acceptance or rejection, of policy that focuses on or uses standardized tests. As the Resnicks suggest in their chapter, effective policy within complex social organizations takes account of all participants' perspectives, and accepts the pragmatic certainty that these cannot be factored out. Thus a predictive policy analytic framework should help us answer questions about human attitudes and motivations as well as institutional and economic variables. From this perspective, attitudes about testing, particularly teacher attitudes, sit squarely in the middle of educational testing policy concerns.

Attempts to use traditional survey methods to gauge teacher attitudes about testing have produced somewhat contradictory results, or at least results that are difficult to interpret and use. Recent surveys by Dorr-Bremme and Herman (1986) and Darling-Hammond and Wise (1985), as well as surveys done before the upsurge in testing in the last two decades (Goslin 1967, Brim et al. 1969), all find that judgments of test fairness are wide ranging and dependent upon context in ways that are difficult to generalize. Some have simply assumed that individuals will favor tests when they see tests as operating to their benefit, and will dislike testing when it threatens their own prospects. Others assume that negative attitudes are the result of poor training in measurement principles. Messick (1988 p. 108) points out that this is not a particularly helpful stance, and that we must rather treat these different viewpoints as "multiple perspectives on the purposes and consequences of testing, as examples of a broader array of differential perspectives on the values of testing in education." The question for policy studies is how to understand and predict the occurrence of these different perspectives, with a view to designing the fairest and most effective test policy.

Certain cognitive science approaches may provide the means for understanding attitudes better. Herbert Simon, one of the researchers most prominently associated with the origins of cognitive science, recently made an argument about economic policy that could usefully be extended to public policy on assessment. He argued that an empirically based theory of choice and decision, grounded in the findings and methods of modern cognitive and social psychology, is essential for "enhancing the explanatory and predictive power of economics" (1986, p. S209). Such a theory would "seek to determine what the actual frame of the decision is, how that frame arises from the decision situation, and how, within that frame, reason operates" (p. S223). In other words, we must ask how actors impose their beliefs and interpretations on a situation— how they frame it—and how that framing determines the way they will think about and act on the situation. The question I will ask in this section concerns how teachers frame the outcomes of testing for their students.

Below, I will briefly describe how two approaches from the constituent disciplines of cognitive science may allow detailed new analyses of policy-relevant choice and attitude in cases such as this. The first approach involves the study of folk models, the second, an analytic framework concerning the process of decisionmaking, developed by Kahneman and Tversky and their collaborators (see for example 1984, and Tversky and Kahneman, 1982). Although this sketch is merely an illustration, not an analysis, it should provide an example of how recent research may provide new ways of conceptualizing and reanalyzing old problems.

The significance of one teacher's beliefs

The study of humans' folk models generally relies upon open-ended, lengthy interviews with subjects, after which transcripts of the interviews are analyzed for content and recurring themes. I have collected such interview protocols from seven teachers[2] and will draw from one to illustrate the kind of understanding this approach might allow.

First let us look at a representative sample from one transcript. This teacher, who has spent more than 15 years teaching in an award-winning elementary school, has been asked why his attitude towards standardized tests of achievement and aptitude is so negative. Among other things, he answers:

> So I have a child, I'm thinking of a particular child, who isn't processing like most kids do. He doesn't read very well, he continually gets shown math concepts and just doesn't get it. SO?? Not everybody in the world is going to be able to do it like everybody else. It's really kind of unfair to say that this child is a failure. But yeah, for some reason the Great Spirit has decided that he's not going to do it like other people. If you really beat him down with that, that's the hard thing, that's the bad thing. That he can't read like most people or do math like most people isn't particularly bad, seen in the long run, if he still has confidence. And he can still have confidence if you know every child is intelligent, and every child is capable, and this child is capable of doing a lot of things. He's really talented, as you might expect, with his hands. He can take a bike apart and put together a bike in no time at all. . . .But everybody has a reservoir of talent and skill in some direction, and it expresses itself in different directions. And thank God for that.

These comments (as well as many others in the interview) reveal that this teacher places equally high value on intellectual, affective and motivational results of schooling for every child. He believes that each individual is important. Good teachers I have interviewed, like this teacher, place a high value on a teacher's ability to intuit a student's needs, to recognize his/her unique talents and problems, and to remember and attend to them throughout the year. In interviews with excellent teachers it is easy to find unhappy discussions about one or another child in the class that the teacher feels she has failed to help for one or another reason. To an excellent teacher, *each* child is a serious responsibility, one that is tracked and accounted for.

So what might these beliefs and values have to do with testing policy? They predict how this teacher frames the outcomes of testing. Kahneman and Tversky, in their (1984) theory of decision making and the perception of risks and benefits,[3] found that traditional views of "rational action" break down in some very predictable ways. Here I'll focus on just one that is relevant to the case at hand.

Decision makers can view potentially negative outcomes in two ways: as *costs*, or as *uncompensated losses*. This framing determines their future choice of action. The key point is whether the actor perceives the situation as providing something in exchange for a negative outcome, or providing nothing in return but the negative outcome itself. For example, Kahneman and Tversky asked subjects whether they would prefer to purchase $50 worth of insurance or run a 25% risk of losing $200. Two thirds bought the insurance, even though they would certainly lose the $50. Then Kahneman and Tversky asked the subjects whether they would prefer a certain loss of $50 or a 25% chance to lose $200. In this case the risks are identical to the first example. Nevertheless, in this second example, 80% would rather run the risk of losing the $200 than the sure loss of the $50. The key is that in the first case, the $50 disadvantage was framed as a cost. In the second case, it was framed as an uncompensated loss.

How does this finding about human decision making and perception of risk help us in understanding the elementary school teacher's negative view of tests, as encapsulated above? Imagine a hypothetical scenario: a teacher, in a classroom of thirty-two students, is confronted with a selection test for placement in a program for the gifted. Let us say that this test is highly reliable, and has been determined to have a correlation coefficient of approximately .7 with grades received by a large sample of children in other gifted and talented programs, comparable to the one for which these students are being selected.[4] By psychometric standards, this is a respectable level of validity.

For purposes of this example, let us assume that the selection ratio is quite high, and that any child receiving a score in the top half of this class's score distribution may enter the program. These parameters might yield a distribution like the following:

	"non-gifted"	"gifted"
low scores	14	2
high scores	2	14

In this example, 16 children will be above the cut-off, and 16 children will score below. Notice that because the test is not perfectly correlated with the criterion, two children with high scores who may not be able to do the work will be admitted to the program. And two other children will be incorrectly rejected—they are likely to be able to do the work, but their low scores will not permit them entry to the program. Now, this level of selection error is not a sign of technical flaws in the test. It is well within the limits of what is considered normal and acceptable. Teachers like the one interviewed above, however, are likely to view it as unacceptable.

This teacher would frame the incorrect categorizations as a loss, an uncompensated loss. The testmaker and the program administrator, on the other hand, are likely to see the incorrect categorization as a cost—a regrettable cost, perhaps, but an unavoidable cost, since no test displays a perfect correlation with any criterion. The teacher, in contrast, will see that potential has gone unrecognized, that a child has been incorrectly evaluated, and is likely to see the entire selection enterprise as insufficient compensation for the "loss" of the two children incorrectly rejected. Similarly, the personal consequences for a child's self-esteem, cited by teachers as extremely important in their view, are also likely to be framed as an uncompensated loss. Measurement professionals (who may be as humanitarian as any teacher) are likely to see such consequences as a cost of testing. Their framing of the situation, like that of the teachers', grows out of their professional role in relation to the situation.

Many discussions of teacher antipathy towards standardized tests focus on the fact that both pre-service and in-service teachers generally possess a low level of psychometric sophistication. These discussions often assume that dislike of tests indicates ignorance. The policy recommendations of this view are obvious: teachers need more training. However, the data I have collected, as outlined above, suggest that for some teachers, for at least some functions of testing, no amount of training in measurement practice would change their views. Their fundamental beliefs and values as teachers (especially so as good teachers) are in direct conflict with some of the normal assumptions of standardized measurement.

This is not to say that the assumptions and values of the measurement community are wrong or maladaptive. It is merely to say that by seriously considering how teachers may view testing within the whole context of instruction, we can see that testing policy may have some very deep conflicts to address at the level of the "street level bureaucrat." The values of the measurement community may never matter to teachers.

What does matter? What do teachers want to use tests for? Here my findings accord with those of large survey studies. Teachers want the ability to diagnose problems and fit instruction to the needs of children. They want each child to get assistance to develop his or her abilities to the fullest. The chapters in this volume can be seen as offering alternatives compatible with those goals. They highlight the diagnostic and identification functions of testing, those that are of most use to teachers and clinicians. They promote recognition of a diversity of talents. This is of great importance to professionals whose task it is to support the growth of each child, all of whom look vividly unique in the classroom. When they do discuss testing for accountability, it is to examine its role in promoting the kind of learning we want to provide for each child.

In the section that follows, as background for the reader of these chapters, I will contrast the tradition out of which these chapters come with the older tradition within which most current standardized testing programs developed.

TWO INTELLECTUAL TRADITIONS: PSYCHOMETRICS/MEASUREMENT, AND COGNITIVE SCIENCE

In comparing the cognitive science perspective on assessment with that of the psychometric and measurement communities, I will necessarily put forth a somewhat idealized picture.[5] Within such a limited discussion, no characterization will be entirely fair, and I will leave out flaws and accomplishments of both traditions. Moreover, idealizations such as these may be rejected by experts in the field as not reflecting the beliefs of the majority of members. Nevertheless, these two characterizations can serve as anchor points that readers of this volume may use in order to evaluate different problem definitions within assessment policy. Each tradition differs in how it views assessment, but each tradition also entails a different perspective on ability, achievement, and instruction. All of these must be sorted out in the process of building sound testing policy.

Before we begin, it's important to distinguish two independent questions: (1) how do we conceptualize the notions we are interested in, like intelligence or aptitude? And (2) how do we measure them after we have decided what they are? We cannot see or measure these things directly. One might have ideas about what mathematics aptitude, or commitment, or vocabulary knowledge is, but in the final analysis all we have as evidence is people's performances on various kinds of visible tasks. Somehow we must get from our ideas and this external evidence to an explicit construct, or abstraction of the notion we're interested in. The first step toward conceptualization (i.e. deciding what it means to say that someone is high in mathematics aptitude or spatial ability) must be followed by attempts to investigate, to refine ideas about the developing construct, and to devise ways to measure its presence in various individuals under various conditions.

After conceptual aspects are first clarified, a construct can be operationalized in numerous ways. The 'best' way of operationalizing is determined in part by the purpose one has in measuring the construct. For example, memory is important in many areas of life. In a traditional psychological paradigm, one might at first conceptualize memory as ability to remember names or numbers; one measure of such a construct might be a digit-span task. However, we would soon find that a different 'version' of memory plays a role in college performance. For this more complex type of memorial ability, we would need very different measures (Cronbach, 1984: 133). We would want these measures to correlate with other criteria, such as grades in school, criteria that we expected this type of memory to clearly influence. In developing these measures, our precise ideas about memory might change. This back and forth process of developing tests to investigate characteristics like aptitudes or intelligence or achievement is called *construct validation*.

Many who are not members of this particular scientific community do not see all of the steps involved in moving from the construct through to an instrument that offers a window onto the construct (the process of construct validation). Instead, they collapse the construct (for example, intelligence) with the test designed to measure it (for example an IQ test). Thus intelligence becomes equivalent to the results of an IQ test. As James Pellegrino discusses in this volume, the conceptualization is replaced by the operationalization.

As the chapters in this volume demonstrate, if we are to develop more illuminating tests and uses of tests within instructional contexts, we cannot simply equate aptitude, learning and achievement with the tests that are used to measure them; we must think actively and carefully about what these constructs mean. Nor can we assume that we can completely separate our understandings of aptitude, learning and achievement themselves from our understanding of how to assess them. In other words, assessment practices are inextricably linked to conceptualizations of what is being assessed.

The psychometric perspective[6]

As described in several of the papers in this volume, much of the intellectual history of the field of measurement and psychometrics is motivated by the philosophical contents of behaviorism. Theorizing about underlying processes or mechanisms was eschewed in favor of psychometric investigation of observable patterns of response, as demonstrated by large samples of subjects. In this tradition, the underlying aspects of intelligent behavior or achievement are *discovered* by establishing the correlations between subjects' performance on different types of tasks. These correlations are then used to buttress a conceptualization of the attribute being measured. For example, an attempt to conceptualize the construct of mathematics aptitude would not consist in theorizing about the precise nature of the mental processes whereby subjects carried out mathematical activities. Rather, hypotheses might be generated about a number of different tasks—specifically, about how relevant they might be to mathematics aptitude.

A psychometric scientist might begin by creating tasks of different types. These would be administered to many subjects. The tests would include, for example, numerical computations, memory for digits, spatial judgments, figural analogies and others. Psychometricians would examine the patterns of performance to see whether certain of the subtests were highly correlated. If some were, this would be preliminary evidence that they shared something in common—that the same cognitive processes or knowledge structures were involved in performing those tasks. If, moreover, performance on these related subtasks was highly correlated with some external criterion, say for example grades in mathematics, or levels of interest in mathematics as a profession, it would be inferred that the construct of mathematics aptitude could likely be tapped by administering these sets of tasks as a test.

Progress in the *theory of aptitude and achievement*, that is, discovery of new knowledge about aptitude and achievement, thus results in this tradition from careful and inventive application of the methods of correlation, including powerful tools such as multiple regression techniques that have only recently been developed.

The *practice of assessment* within this tradition also relies on correlation and comparison of an individual within a group. Without a large sample for comparison, psychometricians cannot discover patterns of correlation between tasks that may reflect an underlying attribute. Concomitantly, without a norm for comparison, a score on a test of performance means nothing. Central to the psychometric perspective is the portrayal of an individual's performance with respect to the performances of others in a group. Within this tradition, a score on a test is transformed in a number of ways into a measure of the test-taker's position relative to other test-takers. Some see this as a pointless and pernicious allegiance to ranking individuals. Others see it as an ingenious way to gain understanding about how intelligence, aptitude, and achievement are distributed in various populations, and to predict how resources may best be allocated to meet the needs of those populations.

The correlational approach, which locates the individual in relation to a larger group, is thus constitutive of the psychometric perspective. Whatever the actual theory of intelligence concurrently viewed as plausible (and there have been many different ones, as the chapters in this volume describe), this use of correlation as a discovery tool is a hallmark of the research and practice of the psychometric community.

Out of this approach we can derive three salient characteristics of psychometric practice. First, its objects are precise and *quantified*. This is a result of the development of mathematical notions such as Pearson's product-moment correlation, which allowed for the quantitative development of what was called an "exact science of the mind" (Irvine 1987, p.8). Second, it views what is measured as *static*: what the psychometrician reasons about are deviations from an average score. An individual score indexes one person relative to a group at a particular moment. This is not to say that the science of psychometrics necessarily excludes the consideration of dynamic aspects such as development of abilities through time. Rather, its characterization of an individual at any point is synchronic, viewed in terms of the position of all other elements of the relevant universe. Third, its investigation of the nature of mental entities is *indirect*. Naturally, all "discovery" of mental phenomena is indirect, but in the psychometric tradition, modeling of the actual processes of cognition does not receive the emphasis found in recent cognitive psychology and cognitive science.

What is the ultimate outcome of such an approach for educational practice? Interpretations vary with allegiance to different traditions. A sympathetic portrayal of traditional psychometric approaches to educational measurement would depict the desired outcome as being the discovery of the relative position of an individual within the relevant larger group. This would facilitate the appropriate educational treatment of that individual. Critics of this tradition see it as necessarily leading to "tracking," which they characterize as a superficially appealing but mistaken way of organizing educational institutions. Tracking is seen as limiting development by segregating students into predetermined ability groups, with some being subjected to predetermined ceilings and low expectations. On the other hand, supporters of the tradition see instead the benefits of identifying talent and diagnosing problems with unparalleled precision, thus allowing teachers to focus their efforts at a level of complexity appropriate for the ability group they are teaching. Virtually all of the contributors to this volume identify with the view that traditional measurement practices have resulted in undesirable educational outcomes.

The cognitive science perspective

Within the psychometric tradition as sketched above, constructs like intelligence, aptitude and achievement are both conceptualized and assessed with respect to distribution of attributes within a group. Within cognitive science, there is a different focus: intelligence and achievement are largely studied as behavior on the part of an individual, sufficient as an object in itself. The goal of many cognitive science enterprises is to accurately and in great detail model the behavior of an individual—to understand and eventually replicate the interplay of knowledge structures and processing strategies and routines. The focus in education-oriented cognitive science research is to better understand the learner (and the variety of learners), and thus to improve the ability of schools to foster learning and development.

Within this tradition, scientists theorize about and model mental processes to a far greater extent than was possible within traditional psychometrics. The decline of behaviorism accompanied a resurgence of theories that postulated mental mechanisms and representations of all sorts. The emphasis is on understanding the processes and knowledge operating within a particular task performance, through a process of modeling what happens in a performance of that task.

Consequently, assessment falls into a different role in this tradition. There is a greater emphasis on testing to diagnose and understand the learner, rather than to predict future performance as against a comparison group. "Tests can predict failure without a theory of what causes success, but intervening to prevent failure and enhance competence requires deeper understanding" (Glaser, Lesgold, and Lajoie 1986: 1). In this tradition, analysis of intelligent behavior for its own sake generally precedes the development of assessment tools. First, the knowledge or action domain must be understood; only then will there be time for development of diagnostic tools. Because the domain of behavior must be understood first in terms of a small number of intensely analyzed individual performances, the correlational approach is not as important. Thus, the characterization of ability or achievement generally does not take a quantitative form. Nor is it static. Rather, there is a concern with characterizing skill and knowledge within a framework of development. Below I will give several examples of recent work in cognitive science, each of which represents a different characteristic aspect of that field.

Brown and Burton (1978) conducted a famous study concerning the assessment of subtraction knowledge in early elementary school. They showed that simply counting errors reveals nothing about the knowledge structures underlying those errors. Children who fail a subtraction test may suffer from one or more of many simple misconceptions, or "bugs" in their subtraction algorithm. Instead of counting errors, the emphasis is on *accounting for* errors. (However, even in the relatively simple domain of subtraction, the complexity and number of possible misunderstandings has impeded progress towards the development of an efficient diagnostic assessment tool.)

One preoccupation of cognitive science is with the characterization of *expert behavior*. In the development of expertise, we see changes in organization of the student's knowledge base itself, as well as changes in the ways that knowledge is accessed. By closely studying expert and novice performances, researchers have found that growing expertise also affects the *mental representation* of the problem. That is, the way an expert recognizes and mentally embodies a problem, and then does the cognitive operations needed to solve the problem, differs systematically from the approach of the novice (Glaser 1987, Chi, Glaser and Farr 1989). The overriding concern with the mental processes of problem solving, not just the products, is characteristic of cognitive science as opposed to psychometrics.

Another distinctive aspect of the cognitive science approach to these issues is a deep concern with the *context-specificity* of thinking and learning. To what extent do the subject matter, the context of performance and the context of learning itself determine the outcome, over and above the learner's individual characteristics? Instead of the static measurement of a particular trait or skill relative to the skills possessed by a norming sample, we have a serious consideration of the problem contexts within which the thinking is embedded. This leads to very careful and detailed accounts of the problem context, and what the subject does in solving the problem. One example notable for its detail is

Ohlsson, 1987. Ohlsson provides forty pages of description and analysis of a single subject working through a single, relatively simple spatial reasoning task. He then goes on to argue for the theoretical and practical desirability of reforming our notions of testing to encompass the kind of knowledge his analysis seeks to characterize.

Other works link learning and teaching with assessment. Frederiksen and White (1988) see the tasks of teaching and assessment as requiring the same kind of understanding. We must understand the interaction of basic knowledge, problem-solving abilities, and learning strategies. For them "[T]he goal of measurement should not be the creation of a quantitative scale, for such a construct obscures the underlying mental models that account for students' problem-solving performance. The goal is, rather, to create representations of students' mental models for reasoning within a domain and of their strategies for applying those models in solving problems" (1988, p. 351). They point out that when we have an explicit model for a particular student, we can presumably diagnose problems more easily, get a clearer picture of where the student is in terms of mastery, and thus develop more useful pedagogical insights.

The use of computer technology within cognitive science-oriented assessment is driven by the same concern with creating a detailed model of a student's learning processes and knowledge structures, and tying the model in with instruction and assessment. In the work of Fredericksen and White, as well as others (see, for example, Glaser, Lesgold and Lajoie 1986), computer technology is used to create intelligent tutoring systems that will model the domain to be learned, as well as the possible paths through problem spaces in that domain. The assessment function of these tutors is not separated from their teaching function, either practically or theoretically.[7]

All of these works, to the extent that they touch directly on assessment, call for the integration of instruction with assessment. As we will see in the core chapters of this volume, the integration of assessment with instruction may be a profoundly disruptive process. As notions of ability and achievement are rethought, and as we learn more about how learning really happens, there will be an increasing call to develop assessment tools that reveal how learning is progressing throughout the school year. The views developed in this volume call for a move away from summative testing at the end of the year, and a move towards truly diagnostic testing throughout the year (see especially Brown et al. and Gardner, this volume).

LINKING THEORIES OF ASSESSMENT
WITH POLICY CONCERNS

In order to make use of the chapters in this volume, theoretical and methodological points must be tied to the realities of testing policy. By and large, the contributors to this volume do not make this their primary task.

Nevertheless, those inside and outside the policy community must have a clear notion of the many and varied ways that tests enter into public policy in order to put into perspective the contributions of the following chapters. Therefore, in this section I will briefly review some of the basic parameters of testing and public policy.

The subject is complex, largely because of the many functions tests may specifically be designed to fulfill, and because of the many different roles they may come to play in the policy process. The functions of testing can be parcelled out in a number of ways. (For informative discussions see Mehrens 1989 and Messick 1988.) For the purposes of this chapter I will distinguish between the *design* function of a test, its *policy* functions, and its *unofficial* functions.

The design function of a test concerns the kind of information that an administration of the test yields at the most local level. What are the test questions about? For example, one test may have the design function of testing basic skills in mathematics and language arts. The policy functions of a test are those uses the test results may play within school policy or public policy. For example, the results of the basic skills test might be used (very controversially) to evaluate teacher competence. Or they might be used to evaluate a bilingual education program, or even as a diagnostic tool for curriculum planning. Or they might be used for placement of students in next year's classes. All these I will call policy functions because they are the product of decisionmakers' considered judgments about how the test results are to be used. The unoffical functions of tests include all those that are not publicly admitted: the exclusion of members of some groups from opportunities (whether intended or not); the provision of an unofficial index of school quality for real-estate purposes; as a political 'hobby-horse' or rallying symbol, and so forth. The policy professional must keep these three test functions distinct in considering how the perspectives in this volume might affect assessment policy.

How do these three levels of test functions interact with stages in the policy process? Briefly, and in general terms, we can outline the stages of public policy making as follows. First, a problem is brought to the attention of a public body of some sort, prototypically governmental, a body that has some authority to find a solution. After a set of commonly accepted facts is acknowledged to constitute the core of the problem, problem definition can proceed. The agreed-upon set of facts is incorporated into some framing of the problem such that goals can be considered, goals that will constitute a problem solution.

Depending upon the goals deemed necessary to solve the problem, and depending upon the resources and characteristics of the policy-making body, choices about the implementation of a solution will be made. An institution may be chosen to carry out the solution. A policy implement will be chosen. There are four generic classes of policy instruments: *mandates* (control devices aimed to produce compliance across the spectrum of target participants); *inducements* (use of resources to elicit compliance or change); *capacity building* (the investment of resources in the present to increase system capacity to solve problems in the future); and *system change* (assignment of responsibility for the problem solution or implementation to a new social or political institution) (McDonnell and Elmore 1987).

Where do tests enter into these stages? It is difficult to make conceptual progress in talking about testing and public policy, partly because tests can enter into this sequence in so many different guises. Test scores, seen as an indication of educational achievement, may be perceived as the problem which triggers the policy debate. If they play a crucial role as part of the problem definition, they may also play a role as an indicator in the course of problem solution. In this role, test scores often become proxies for the processes they index, garnering attention at the expense of real change. In this capacity, they also tend to play a highly charged symbolic role, a focal point for symbolic posturing on the part of politicians and administrative figures (Baker 1989, Haertel 1989).

Testing may not enter into a policy problem until implementation of solutions is considered. Then they may be part of a remedy for another problem, either as indicator of compliance to a mandate, or as a performance measure to determine allocation of inducements. They may be used unofficially to build consensus and concern about a policy problem, particularly in education.[8]

Clearly, any statement about testing and public policy will be highly contingent on factors such as those just discussed. In assigning a role to standardized tests within public policy, we assume a shared understanding of what it is that tests do, and how it is they do it. We also make assumptions about what their relationship should be to instruction. What these chapters question is the underpinnings of these assumptions. They suggest that as long as the goal of public effort is simply to "raise test scores" we will produce frustrated and beleaguered teachers, parents, students and administrators. Instead, to improve education in the largest sense, we must question our tacit understandings of learning, development, instruction, and the measurement of all of these. Not all of these chapters are pertinent to all functions of testing as described above, and it is difficult to see how our conceptions of intelligence, achievement and so on are relevant at every stage of the policy process. Nevertheless, a consideration of these chapters against a background of the many uses of tests in public policy may open a window on unexpected solutions to old problems.

CONTENTS OF THE CHAPTERS

Several issues emerge from these chapters, though they are treated differently in each. First and perhaps most important is the direction of influence between tests, curriculum and instruction. Many have observed that in recent years, the "testing tail" is wagging the "instructional dog" (although not all agree, compare Ruddell 1985, and Suhor 1985). The chapters in this volume go beyond that observation. They assume that, human nature being what it is, tests will continue to drive instruction and curriculum; we must accept this as a fact and make use of it. The logic of their position, whether tacit, as in Sternberg's chapter, or explicitly discussed, as in the Resnick's chapter, is as follows: our society wants its students to develop broader, more powerful and more encompassing knowledge, skills and abilities. Therefore, we need to be able to assess these things. If we develop means to assess them, and then use those assessment tools widely, we will be forced to find ways to teach these forms of knowledge, skills and abilities more effectively than we are now doing. Similarly, many segments of our society want greater consideration given to the diversity of human talents and gifts. When our assessments of ability and aptitude consider a fuller range of talents, beyond simply mathematical and verbal skills, we will be forced to regard school or job applicants as repositories of many different skills. This in turn may lead us to reconsider the nature of schooling or employment in a more humanistic vein.

The implementation of these broadening views of aptitude, achievement, and the relation between instruction and assessment, may have a salutary effect on those students who are now to a large extent shut out of many educational opportunities due to their lower levels of performance on standard tests of ability and achievement. On the other hand, the application of these new ideas is not trivial or easy, with respect to any group of students. All of the chapters in this volume deserve a careful reading with a view to how issues of access and equity might be usefully advanced by the notions discussed within them. The methods and approaches discussed by Brown et al. and by Gardner seem particularly likely to support advancement in this area. As the ideas are laid out, it remains to pursue their implications for equity and access in education.

Finally, to some extent, the chapters all share the observation that assessments should be carried out in a way that allows test givers and interpreters to keep clear sight of the appropriate functions of the tests they are using. The major functions of tests should be kept separate. The Resnicks advise against using accountability tests for diagnosis. Brown et al. advise against using diagnostic tests for accountability. Gardner restricts his view to how portfolio assessment can be used for individual diagnosis and program evaluation at a very local level. Sternberg is clear that the function of his comprehensive abilities test is necessarily only that associated with traditional ability tests. Its value lies in the far more comprehensive notions of ability and intelligence that underlie its contents.

Resnick and Resnick

This chapter boldly asks testmakers and policymakers to take a leading role in educational reform of a particular kind. The effort to improve higher-level thinking abilities, or "critical thinking" as it is sometimes called, is hampered, say Lauren and Daniel Resnick, by the nature of the standardized tests we now use for accountability. These tests are used widely for certification of student achievement and they test mathematics, English, language arts, reading, science, and so forth. But they test these skills in a decontextualized way, in a fashion that does not allow the assessment of mastery of the whole activity. The Resnicks cite recent research demonstrating that "we cannot teach a skill component in one setting and expect it to be applied automatically in another. That means, in turn, that we cannot validly assess a competence in a context very different from the context in which it is practiced or used" (p. 43, this volume).

The Resnicks propose that testing should function as a key policy instrument in this sort of educational reform, but not the usual sort of implement. Their suggestion is not to use testing as an index of compliance with a mandate, or as a monitoring device for the progress of a program, or even as the target of a policy goal ("let's raise test scores"). Rather, they propose that by changing the primary content of tests of accountability, (that is, by changing their design function, what they actually test for) we will drive instruction in the direction we want it to go. In some sense, they are suggesting an unusual type of capacity building, unusual in that it takes into account a tendency, "teaching to the test," that has widely been regarded as something we must eradicate. In the Resnicks' proposal, research results are driving reconsideration of practice, and the key policy instrument is testing. This is quite different from another proposal, "measurement-driven-instruction" (Popham et al. 1985), which purports to make a virtue of teaching to traditional standardized tests.

The Resnicks' proposal is timely in that several other instructional reform movements are highlighting the need for new and appropriate assessment measures. "Writing across the curriculum" has provoked a new interest in the problems associated with writing assessment. A grass-roots philosophy within the language arts, sometimes called "whole language," seeks to bring children to the highest levels of literacy by surrounding them with enriching, enabling experiences with oral and printed language. These activities are the antithesis of the decontextualized approach to language skills found in current standardized tests, and, as might be expected, teachers who are committed to the values of "whole language" face a tremendous problem when their students are evaluated in traditional ways. The California Department of Education, whose "State Framework for Language Arts" prominently features notions central to the "whole language" philosophy, is currently grappling with the mismatch between their state-mandated achievement tests and the curricular and instructional implications of their innovative new framework.

A similar dilemma is implied by the recent report of the National Research Council on the subject of reform in mathematics instruction. "Skills are to mathematics what scales are to music or spelling is to writing. The objective of learning is to write, to play music, or to solve problems—not just to master skills. Practice with skills is just one of many strategies used by good teachers to help students achieve the broader goals of learning" (National Research Council 1989: 57).

One principal benefit of the Resnicks' approach is the potential for upgrading the quality and status of thinking about instruction and performance: For decades, professional discourse on educational objectives has been so shaped by the assumptions of standardized testing—decomposition of domains of skill and knowledge into independent components; decontextualized measurement of these components; correct responses defined in advance—that terms for discussing the nature of complex, coherent, and contextualized academic performance barely exist. We need a new discourse, shaped by the demands of choosing performance contexts for assessment and developing judgment criteria" (p. 70, this volume).

Gardner

In comparison to the previous chapter, this contribution by Howard Gardner is likely to strike the reader as fairly utopian. Gardner's applied work in the area of assessment grew out of his investigations of giftedness and the multiple kinds of intelligence found in human cultures, broadly surveyed. Even individuals with unimpressive linguistic or logical-mathematical capacities may possess a broad range of other kinds of intelligence. In Gardner (1983), there are hypothesized to be seven kinds of computations or analyses: those involving language; logical-mathematical analysis; spatial representation (for instance, the painter, sculptor, architect, sailor, geometer, or engineer); musical analysis; bodily-kinesthetic thinking (for example, that found in the mime, surgeon, craftsman, or actor); and two forms of personal understanding—interpersonal knowledge (the ability to reason creatively and insightfully about others, as in a salesperson, teacher, therapist, or political leader); and intrapersonal knowledge, "the ability to know one's own desires, fears, and competences, and to act productively on the basis of that knowledge."

For both ethical and scientific reasons, Gardner sees the crucial challenge as providing opportunities for students whose cognitive and personal strengths do not center on those intelligences traditionally tested—language intelligence and mathematical/analytic intelligence. Gardner and his colleagues sought ways to assess this wider range of intelligences. They carried out the search, called Project Spectrum, in a preschool setting, trying to develop ways to identify particularly talented individuals. As the work progressed, Gardner reports that he discovered how deeply and inextricably the classroom learning context must be connected to the assessment process in order to engender real understanding of student abilities. The detection of giftedness without a concomitant involvement in the context of performance and learning is uninformative.

The Project Spectrum researchers came to believe that there is no "pure potential" apart from some experience in working with a domain or symbol system. He suggests that if one is truly interested in assessing potential in some area, the best way to get the true distribution of that ability within a particular sample is to expose the sample to the activity or domain over an extended period of time. Of course, this is more costly and more time-consuming, but it is not subject to the same concerns about reliability and ecological validity as are many standardized instruments. And particularly in the early years of school, when abilities are relatively unfixed, exposure to a wide range of activities and types of endeavor is a positive by-product.

All of the chapters suggest to some extent that instruction must be integrated with assessment in new ways to attain the greatest educational benefits for all. Gardner's chapter spells out many details about an assessment-curriculum amalgam that seeks to fully develop all of the students' abilities in a particular domain.

This approach has potential for a fairer and perhaps more culture- and class-neutral type of assessment than the heavily linguistic assessments that now take place. The point is strengthened by Gardner's description of the middle school and high school program of development and assessment in the visual arts, "Arts Propel." Here there was heavy reliance on "process-folios," work in progress, evaluated and kept in portfolio form throughout the year. His account of the Arts Propel program spells out even more clearly how his approach entails a well-developed notion of the most important abilities and skills underlying a curriculum, a curriculum that must be integrally linked with assessment.

Gardner sees the constant interplay between assessment and instruction as critical in an education system that embodies learning as apprenticeship, rather than as the uniform, unmotivating experience described so often in studies of our schools.

The policy functions of testing that Gardner addresses are local, in that they involve diagnosis, identification of talent, and certification of achievement. Gardner presents his model as one designed to help, not rank, students. These functions are to be served by the rich, detailed performance assessments found in collected portfolios. It is clear that the main beneficiaries are those who can take the time to view and reflect on the contents of a child's work over an extended period of time. Thus, this approach to assessment finds its idealized future realization in a type of school, an "individual-centered school," which will require several new participant roles. The assessment specialist would have a far more critical presence in the classroom than any testing specialist might now have. The student-curriculum broker takes the conclusions of the assessment specialist and translates them into concrete suggestions. The school-community broker surveys the educational opportunities available in the community and finds ways to bring the students to them, for vocational and avocational experiences to augment classroom learning. While these positions may be superficially similar to some found in traditional schools, it is clear that the overall conception of the school as an individual-centered system is quite different.

Brown, Campione, Webber, and McGilly

Ann Brown and her colleagues also depict an idealized learning and teaching situation, centered on the integration of instruction and assessment. Again, the goal is the most beneficial diagnosis and remediation for each child. The resources they rely on to build such an ideal world, however, are somewhat different than those proposed by Gardner. In this chapter we gain an in-depth perspective on the origins and motivations for dynamic assessment. Dynamic assessment aims to build an understanding of far more than the current knowledge state of a particular child. The child's capacity to learn in a socially supported, or scaffolded situation is investigated, as well as how ready the child is to learn a particular set of data and procedures. Brown et al. give a detailed history of the two strands of thought that led to the current variants of dynamic assessment, explicating the differences and commonalities between the research of Vygotsky and Feuerstein.

   In contrast to Gardner, Brown et al. discuss the contributions of Binet in their historical overview, but portray him as a fellow traveler, concerned with issues of metacognition and the corrigibility and dynamicity of intelligence and learning potential. From reading their account of Binet's real (and ambivalent) attitudes toward the notion of intelligence, one gets a flavor of how difficult it is to use appealing but elusive notions like metacognition and dynamic assessment in designing real classroom instruction and assessment materials—and how easy it will be for users of such materials to reify and overinterpret them in just the way that standard IQ scores are reified and overinterpreted.

   Both the process-folios discussed by Gardner and the dynamic assessment tools discussed by Brown et al. capture performance in assisted situations. By allowing children to learn in the process of assessment, they reason, we get deeper insights into the capacities that interest us: the ability to learn new things and transfer knowledge and strategies from one domain to another. And although both Gardner and Brown et al. began their investigations with a concern for assessing specific aptitudes and ability to learn, both ended up with a deep involvement in developing curricula for the content areas. Thus the underlying principles that inform the dynamic assessment approach welcome an extension from aptitude testing to achievement testing. These underlying principles, discussed briefly at the beginning of Brown et al.'s chapter, also naturally extend to ways of thinking about instruction.

As assessment becomes an integral part of instruction, the principles of socially mediated learning and scaffolding are seen to be central to instruction also. Brown et al. describe their own approach to guided instruction, exemplified by the method they call reciprocal teaching.

Unlike Gardner, however, Brown et al. are able to envision the use of their approach as a part of accountability testing programs, although this is not their primary interest. The different functional possibilities, however, are not due to differences in principle; rather, Brown et al. see a major role for computers, in the form of intelligent tutors and intelligent assessors. Thus, in the most utopian version of their vision, the power of computers is harnessed to provide learning (and constantly assessing) environments that can calibrate their offerings to a student based on that student's immediate and remote past performance.

What would the implementation of their vision require? At the end of the chapter Brown et al. spell out the kinds of investments that need to be made. First, in order to design a finely detailed and truly diagnostic dynamic assessment of some content area, we must have richly detailed and insightful accounts of the interplay, within that content area, of knowledge structures and processing strategies and routines. Moreover, we need an account of how normal learning and development proceed in the domain. Then we may design instruction and assessment tools to be used in computer worlds or in face-to-face interaction with teachers and other professionals.

Thus a large amount of capacity building is called for. Basic research in the content areas is necessary, and Brown et al. suggest that there must be general agreement on what areas of the curriculum to study in this way, so as to most efficiently use the resources available. The task is tremendously large; yet there have been other tasks of comparable scope, such as the mapping of the human genome, which yielded striking discoveries very quickly when resources and human will were directed in concert. The goals Brown et al. spell out seem sufficiently important to warrant consideration of large-scale capacity building.

Sternberg

One of the most frequently cited abuses or misuses of standardized tests of intelligence is the reification of a single score into a cognitive entity. Another is the use of only a single score to make decisions about selection or placement. Robert Sternberg's chapter confronts both of these misuses in a fashion that is implicitly parallel to that suggested by the Resnicks. He argues for an assessment battery for a comprehensive, well-described set of abilities, an assessment device that he hopes will make it much more difficult for users to be unaware of the range of abilities being assessed, or to use and reify only a single score. By rethinking the ways that intelligence and general abilities of various kinds are measured, he forces a reconsideration of what abilities play a role in what kinds of life successes.

At the present time, Sternberg is developing a test of intellectual functioning for The Psychological Corporation. The test includes a broad range of measures, and he claims that it is superior to current tests. It is substantially broader than the tests of intelligence and ability now extant and allows separate scores for componential information processing, coping with novelty, automatization, and practical-intellectual skills. Each of these is evaluated with respect to three different content areas: verbal, quantitative, and figural. Sternberg aims to be able to diagnose strengths and weaknesses, but in keeping with the interests of recent cognitive psychology, he also wishes to assess strategies and processes in interaction with a particular type of knowledge representation.

However, this test does not include everything that Sternberg envisions in his version of the utopian future. In particular, the complete multidimensional abilities test would take cognizance both of intelligence defined broadly, and of intellectual styles. It would also take into account the context of measurement. In this chapter, Sternberg shares with us his current approach to developing assessments of intellectual style. He contrasts three individuals, all high in intelligence as depicted above, but who differ in the ways they govern and participate in their own mental lives. Using a metaphor of mental "self-government," he claims that different forms of intellectual style, or mental self-government, are differentially rewarded in particular fields, and thus may predict success in those fields.

Sternberg sees such a test as useful for placement, diagnosis, and selection. Some readers will have a problem with viewing his test as diagnostic. (He points out that the Intellectual Styles questionnaire should probably not be used for selection, since there are no right or wrong answers. It is unlikely that all test users will be able to resist this, however.)

Like Brown et al. and Gardner, Sternberg does not view abilities as fixed, and echoes Binet (as cited in Brown et al.). Sternberg asks, "What good is a score to an individual if he or she does not have the possibility of modifying it?" Although far less embedded in the classroom than any of the other chapter authors, he sees his program of assessment as incomplete without an accompanying program of teaching the intellectual skills and abilities he measures. His test will be distributed in two forms, so as to be available to function as both a pretest and a posttest in a training program. Like the others in this volume, he sees the goals of assessment as assisting people in capitalizing on their strengths, and identifying and remediating their weaknesses.

One of the values of Sternberg's chapter is the overview it presents of the recent history of thought on notions of ability and intelligence. Sternberg is a central member of the field of information-processing psychology; nevertheless, he is not entirely divorced from the psychometric tradition. He supports his case for the wide variety of tasks and approaches he describes with correlational evidence from many experiments. However, he sees his test as having a far more elaborate theoretical base than other tests currently available. The contrasts and distinctions sketched in the second section of this overview are analyzed and elaborated upon at length in Sternberg's review of literature. Finally, he resolves the conflicts between the single factor and multifactor theories of intelligence, between the contextualists and the cognitivists. His framework offers a comprehensive accounting of many of the most important factors thought to contribute to successful performance in school and work.

Many will find his analysis of the contexts of intelligence most illuminating to the educational issues that concern the authors of the other chapters here. The importance of discovering how the mainstream school environment sees intelligence, what is rewarded and what is presumed most valuable in the way of intellectual activity, cannot be overestimated. In the same vein, Sternberg's introduction of data regarding the divergence of informal or tacit views of intelligence, where those views sort by profession, age, and so forth, is invaluable in getting us to think about the fact that there are many expressions of intellect and many ways to direct those expressions.

Pellegrino's commentary

James Pellegrino, a scholar in the field of cognitive science, adds his perspective on how we can secure better tests, and better uses of tests. For Pellegrino, the key lies in deeper understanding of aptitude and achievement. He argues that in our thinking about these areas, tests often substitute for deeper understandings of the phenomena. Since test items are often far removed from a theory of the knowledge that underlies the test performance, test scores may provide little that is directly useful for guiding instruction or placement. A primary goal of his chapter is to consider how contemporary thinking, as illustrated by the chapters in this volume, can provide for a richer understanding and analysis of individual differences in learning and cognition. Since these are our primary concerns, a better understanding of them is a prerequisite to solving the "interpretive dilemma"--What does a test score really mean? Pellegrino's chapter echoes many of the themes in the four core chapters, but he adds something to them: concrete examples of findings cognitive science has produced, drawn from the instructional domain of early mathematics. These are intended to give the general reader a sense of how such knowledge might be useful for assessment and instruction.

Shepard's commentary

Finally, Lorrie Shepard, an influential member of the research community in measurement, speaks frankly and plainly to policy makers. She suggests that this volume may be somewhat inaccessible to those it purports to address. Yet policy makers must be aware, she warns, that their decisions about public policy concerning schools, testing, and funding for educational reform are based on their implicit theories about learning, instruction and intelligence. Therefore she undertakes to translate for policy makers the most important findings from the "new psychology" of intelligence and learning in her review of the four core chapters.   Drawing from these chapters she highlights the most important consensus views of the cognitive science community, and relates them to assessment issues, including classroom assessment, tracking and placement, and accountability testing. Her contribution is an invaluable addendum to the highly theoretical core chapters.

SUMMARY

From these chapters, the following observations emerge: our notions of talent, aptitude, learning and achievement are expanding. This expansion has consequences far beyond the quiet world of the academy. If we develop tests that reflect these changing notions, entire educational and job placement systems will be affected. The links between testing and instruction will change, perhaps drastically. The public will change their views of how tests can be used as goals of public policy, or as instruments of public policy. And the measurement community itself will no doubt come to view things in a somewhat new light.

These chapters may add to the clarity and sophistication with which the policy community frames its problems. Some readers may find the lack of a univocal conclusion distressing, having expected that by now the research community of social and cognitive scientists would have assembled a majority position on assessment in relation to aptitude, achievement and instruction. Disagreement, however, is productive within scholarly discussion, and leads to novel exploration. It is hoped that disagreement provoked by chapters in this volume will lead to such exploration on the part of the policy studies and decisionmaking community.

NOTES

* I wish to thank all the individuals who assisted in various ways in the preparation of this chapter and this volume. None are responsible for errors found herein, nor do any necessarily agree with the opinions expressed here. Each paper was read by three anonymous referees, whose careful responses are gratefully acknowledged. Helpful comments and responses to various aspects of the volume were generously given by Ann Brown, Joe Campione, the Chases, Ann Jungeblut, George Madaus, Sarah Michaels, Jim Pellegrino, Bill Rohwer, Lauren Resnick, Matthew Robert, Marty Rutherford, Bonnie Schwartz, Lorrie Shepard, Alissa Shethar and Amy Strage. Completion of the final stages of the volume was facilitated by support from the Andrew W. Mellon Foundation to the Literacies Institute, for which I am very grateful.

[1] The term "folk model" or sometimes "cultural model," is used to denote the belief systems which individuals use to guide their decisions, judgments, and actions. These belief systems may or may not be organized and internally coherent. They are distinct from theoretical models in that they are generally not axiomatized, and do not support strong inference. Rather, they seem to consist of loosely coupled general principles, rules of thumb, and working definitions that are based in experience, and are local, that is, relativized to a small corner of experience. Stemming from earlier efforts in anthropology to characterize the knowledge of members of other cultures, the study and characterization of folk models has increased substantially in the last decade. A number of cognitive scientists, linguists and anthropologists have studied a wide range of phenomena from this perspective. See Holland and Quinn, 1987.

[2] Surveys and questionnaires do not establish the crucial link between what a teacher says and what he or she does in daily practice. Similarly, the investigation of folk models must be augmented with long-term observation of teacher practice. I have observed only two of the seven teachers I have interviewed at this point, thus, my conclusions are limited in scope, and the example used is only suggestive of what might emerge from the full analysis.

[3] For further reference, Kahneman, Slovic and Tversky 1982 contains a number of studies carried out within this general framework.

[4] This hypothetical table was constructed to exemplify a Phi coefficient of approximately 0.7. The Phi coefficient is a measure of association between two dichotomous variables.

[5] This comparison should not be taken to preclude the existence of researchers who are central members of both traditions. A significant number of researchers integrate aspects of the two approaches in their work. A good example is Snow, Federico and Montague 1980.

[6] There are many ways to characterize these two perspectives. A full review would include the dimensions of methodology, central organizing concepts, accepted inference procedures and goals, and so forth. This overview draws the boundaries more simply than others might. For those desiring more technical content, an informative work is Irvine 1987.

[7] This is not to say that all uses of computers in assessment are by definition aligned with a cognitive science perspective. More traditional measurement programs use computers as support devices, to assist, for example, in sampling a domain of items, graded for their difficulty. A test taker can then be tested more efficiently, being given only those items that are in his or her range of competence. These systems adapt to the test taker, but they do not reflect a fundamentally different view of learning than that found in traditional paper-and-pencil tests.

[8] This list does not exhaust the policy-related functions of tests. There are some concerns that are relevant at any stage in the policy process, such as technical quality of tests and differential performance by ethnolinguistic minorities. Neither of these issues is dealt with in this volume.

REFERENCES

Baker, E. 1989. Mandated tests: Educational reform or quality indicator? In *Test policy and test performance: Education, language, and culture*, ed. B. Gifford, 3–24. Boston, MA: Kluwer.

Brim, O. G., Jr., D. C. Glass, J. Neulinger, and I. J. Firestone. 1969. *American beliefs and attitudes about intelligence*. New York: Russell Sage.

Brown, A. L. 1985. Mental orthopedics: A conversation with Alfred Binet. In Vol. 2, *Thinking and learning skills: Current research and open questions*, ed. S. Chipman, J. Segal, and R. Glaser, 319–37. Hillsdale, NJ: Erlbaum.

Brown, J. S., and R. R. Burton. 1978. Diagnostic models for procedural bugs in basic mathematical skills. *Cognitive Science*, 2. 155–92.

Chi, M. T. H., R. Glaser, and M. Farr. 1989. *The nature of expertise*. Hillsdale, NJ: Erlbaum.

Cronbach, L. J. 1984. *Essentials of Psychological Testing*. Fourth Edition. New York: Harper and Row.

Darling-Hammond, L., and A. Wise. 1985. Beyond standardization: State standards and school improvement. *Elementary School Journal* 85:315–36.

Dorr-Bremme, D. W., and J. L. Herman. 1986. Assessing student achievement: A profile of classroom practices. Monograph no. 11. Center for the Study of Evaluation, Monograph Series in Evaluation. Los Angeles: UCLA Center for the Study of Evaluation.

Fredericksen, J. R., and B. Y. White. 1988. Implicit testing within an intelligent tutoring system. *Machine-mediated learning*, Vol. 2, 351–72. New York: Basic Books.

Gardner, H. 1983. *Frames of mind*. New York: Basic Books.

Glaser, R. 1981. The future of testing: A research agenda for cognitive psychology and psychometrics. *American Psychologist* 36 (9): 923–36.

Glaser, R. 1987. Thoughts on expertise. In *Cognitive functioning and social structure over the life course*, ed. C. Schooler and W. Schaie, 81–94. Norwood, NJ: Ablex.

Glaser, R., A. Lesgold, and S. Lajoie. 1986. Toward a cognitive theory for the measurement of achievement. Manuscript. To appear in *The influence of cognitive psychology on testing and measurement*, ed. R. R. Ronning, J. Glover, J. C. Conely, and J. C. Witt. Hillsdale, NJ: Erlbaum.

Goslin, D. A. 1967. *Teachers and testing*. New York: Russell Sage.

Haertel, E. 1989. Student achievement tests as tools of educational policy: Practices and consequences. In *Test policy and test performance: Education, language, and culture*, ed. B. Gifford, 25–50. Boston, MA: Kluwer.

Holland, Dorothy, and Naomi Quinn, Eds. 1987. *Cultural Models in Language and Thought*. Cambridge: Cambridge University Press.

Irvine, S. H. 1987. Functions and constants in mental measurement: A taxonomic approach. In *Intelligence and cognition: Contemporary frames of reference*, ed. S. H. Irvine and S.E. Newstead, 1–25. NATO ASI Series D: Behavioural and Social Sciences — No. 38. Dordrecht, The Netherlands: Nijhoff.

Kahneman, Daniel and Amos Tversky. 1984. Choices, values, and frames. *American Psychologist*. 39.4 pp. 341-350.

Kahneman, Daniel, Paul Slovic, and Amos Tversky. 1982. *Judgment under uncertainty: Heuristics and biases.* Cambridge: Cambridge University Press.

McDonnell, L. M., and R. F. Elmore. 1987. Getting the job done: Alternative policy instruments. *Educational Evaluation and Policy Analysis* 9 (2): 135–53.

McLaughlin, M. W. 1987. Learning from experience: Lessons from policy implementation. *Educational Evaluation and Policy Analysis* 9 (2): 171–78.

Mehrens, W. A. 1989. Using test scores for decision making. In *Test policy and test performance: Education, language, and culture,* ed. B. Gifford, 93–114. Boston, MA: Kluwer.

Messick, S. 1988. Assessment in the schools: Purposes and consequences. In Jackson, P.W. (Ed.) *Contributing to Educational Change: Perspectives on Research and Practice.* Berkeley, CA: McCutchan. 107-125.

National Research Council. 1989. *Everybody counts: A report to the nation on the future of mathematics education.* Washington, DC: National Academy Press.

Ohlsson, S. 1987. Trace analysis and spatial reasoning: An example of intensive cognitive diagnosis and its implications for testing. Technical Report no. KUL-87-02. Pittsburgh, PA: Learning Research and Development Center, University of Pittsburgh.

Popham, W. J., K. L. Cruse, S. C. Rankin, P. D. Sandifer, and P. W. Williams. 1985. Measurement-driven-instruction: It's on the road. *Phi Delta Kappan* (May): 628–34.

Ruddell, R. B. 1985. Knowledge and attitudes towards testing: Field educators and legislators. *The Reading Teacher* (February): 538–43.

Simon, H. A. 1986. Rationality in psychology and economics. *Journal of Business* 59 (4): S209–24.

Snow, R. E., P-A Federico, and W. E. Montague. 1980. *Aptitude, learning, and instruction,* vols. 1–3. Hillsdale, NJ: Erlbaum.

Suhor, C. 1985. Objective tests and writing samples: How do they affect instruction in composition? *Phi Delta Kappan* (May): 635–39.

Tversky, Amos and Daniel Kahneman. 1982. Introduction. In *Judgement under uncertainty: Heuristics and biases.* Cambridge: Cambridge University Press. Pp. 3-20.

Assessing the Thinking Curriculum: New Tools for Educational Reform

*Lauren B. Resnick and Daniel P. Resnick**

In America, educational reform and testing are intimately linked. Test scores signal the need for reform, as evidenced by the attention paid to declining scores on college entrance exams and standardized tests, to Americans' weak performances on international comparisons, and to the percentages of students failing certain kinds of items on our national assessments. Tests are also widely viewed as instruments for educational improvement. Calls for better performance by American schools are almost always accompanied by increases in the amounts of testing done in the schools. New tests, or more active scrutiny of tests already in place, are frequently prescribed, both as a source of information for a concerned public and as a form of "quality control" and an incentive to better performance by educators and students. This link between testing and efforts at educational reform is not new—it has been a feature of efforts to improve American schools since at least the end of the nineteenth century (D. P. Resnick 1982). In each new round of reform, testing theory and practice have been refined and elaborated. Tests are so ubiquitous in this country's educational life, however, and the test instruments we use are often so technically elegant, that it is difficult to imagine proceeding in a different way. Complaints about testing and tests, from those who claim that tests block opportunities for certain social groups and those who point to the limited range of human competence assessed by the tests, bubble up whenever the amount and visibility of testing increase. These complaints sometimes lead to modifications of tests, but there is rarely sustained or widespread consideration of the possibility that the very idea of using test technology as it has developed over the past century may be inimical to the real goals of educational reform.

In this chapter we consider that possibility in depth. Our argument hinges on three analyses: first, of the nature of current educational reform goals and what they imply for the kinds of activities that must permeate the schools; second, of the assumptions about the nature of knowledge and competence built into standardized tests; and third, of the ways in which assessments function as elements in social systems. These three analyses lead us to conclude that the tests widely used today are fundamentally incompatible with the kinds of changes in educational practice needed to meet current challenges. We will suggest

* We wish to thank Allan Collins, Lee Cronbach, John Frederiksen, Robert Glaser, and Loretta Shepard for their critical comments on an earlier draft of this chapter.

alternative forms of assessment, forms currently within reach, that can adequately reflect today's educational goals and, if properly used, serve as positive tools in creating schools truly capable of teaching students to think.

THE CHALLENGE OF THE THINKING CURRICULUM

In the past several years, a new vision of education has emerged, fueled partly by the needs of a changing economy and partly by recent research on learning and cognition. According to this view, education must focus on "higher-order abilities," on problem solving and thinking, on ability to go beyond the routine and to exercise personal judgment. Analyses of how technology is affecting both the workplace and communication point to the need for workers at all levels who understand the technical systems they use and can participate in dispersed management systems requiring judgment and decision making (L. B. Resnick 1987; Scribner 1984; Zuboff 1988). Furthermore, conditions of work are likely to change several times during an individual's work life, requiring a capacity for adaptive learning on the job. Employers are finding that students now leaving high school are not prepared to function well in the work environments they enter. Employers, like colleges, are calling on the schools to provide educational programs that enable graduates to reason and think, not just to perform routine operations.

The educational system we have inherited was not, by and large, designed to prepare people for such adaptive functioning in a technically complex environment. Although there have always been proponents of a more challenging intellectual program in the schools, we have not previously heard so many calls for thinking and reasoning as goals for all students, not just an elite. Like other industrialized countries in the nineteenth century, America developed two educational systems—one designed for an elite, the other for the mass of our population. The mass system was intended to teach routine skills: simple computation, reading predictable texts, reciting civic or religious codes. Its goals for students did not include the ability to interpret unfamiliar texts, construct convincing arguments, understand complex systems, develop approaches to problems, or negotiate problem resolutions in a group. Those goals were reserved for the elite, originally in separate schools, more recently within our comprehensive schools. Despite the tremendous increase in the number of years people now spend in school, the curriculum most Americans are exposed to focuses mainly on the routinized basics of the old mass school system. They learn—or sometimes do not—the "old basics," but they have little chance to learn the new basics of thinking, reasoning, and learning how to learn.

A thinking-oriented curriculum for all constitutes a significant new educational agenda. While it is not new to include thinking, problem solving, and reasoning in *some* students' school curriculum, it is new to include it in *everyone's* curriculum. It is new to seriously aspire to make thinking and problem solving regular aspects of the school program for the entire population, even minorities, even non-English speakers, even children of the poor. Developing educational programs that assume all individuals, not just an elite, can become competent thinkers is a new challenge (L. B. Resnick 1987).

One of the most important findings of recent research on thinking is that the kinds of mental processes associated with thinking are not restricted to an advanced or "higher-order" stage of mental development. Instead, thinking and reasoning are intimately involved in successfully learning even elementary levels of reading, mathematics, and other school subjects. Cognitive research on children's learning of basic skills reveals that reading, writing, and arithmetic— the three Rs—involve important components of inference, judgment, and active mental construction. The traditional view that the basics can be taught as routine skills, with thinking and reasoning to follow later, can no longer guide our educational practice.

A good example to consider is reading. A large body of research on reading comprehension now shows that comprehension is *always* based on processes of inference in which readers use their prior knowledge to interpret and give meaning to the written words (see Just and Carpenter 1987; Perfetti 1985). The reason for this is that normal, well-written texts are by their nature incomplete expressions of the author's ideas. The texts omit some essential elements because the writer assumes that readers will supply them. If this assumption is not realized, comprehension fails, even if the reader has understood every individual word. This process of supplying missing elements through inference normally goes on so automatically that people are unaware of doing it. Yet studies of eye movements during silent reading, of pause patterns as texts are read aloud, and of the disruptions in comprehension that can be caused by minor modifications at key points in texts provide convincing evidence of inferential work in readers' efforts to make sense of even simple texts. Research shows that children who are poor readers do not do this inferential work, often do not know when they have failed to comprehend, and are generally unaware that they are expected or allowed to do any personal mental interpreting as part of the reading process. In writing, too, many children treat the process as a mechanical one of writing down everything they can think of that might be relevant to a topic, and not as a process of solving the problem of shaping a communication to an audience.

There is now abundant evidence that young children, even before attending school, develop robust, although simple, mathematical concepts and that they are able to apply these concepts in a variety of practical situations (see L. B. Resnick 1989). Yet school mathematics is decidedly difficult to learn for many children. In large part, the difficulty comes from children's failure to recognize and apply the relations between formal rules taught in school and their own independently developed mathematical intuitions. Encouraged by the way math is often taught, they treat school math as a matter of memorizing rules and manipulating symbols. Many children remain unaware that they can make sense of the rules by drawing connections between symbols and the mathematical principles they apply intuitively in practical situations. Evidence for this claim comes from detailed analyses of the kinds of errors children make in doing calculations together with observations and interviews with children about topics in the elementary school curriculum. According to this evidence, failure to engage in higher-order reasoning about quantities causes failures in learning the basic skills of calculation and number usage.

Much the same story about the importance of reasoning, judgment, and inference, even in apparently simple or basic performances, can be told about the rest of the school curriculum (see Bransford 1979; Bransford and Vye 1989). Research on memorizing, for example, shows that, even in "learning the facts," mental elaboration and judgment are required for success (Brown 1978). How much children remember is dramatically affected by how they organize their knowledge of a topic. Simply rehearsing a list, for instance, is better than doing nothing at all, but it is the least effective of all ways of learning information. The basic skills of studying and remembering information require one to organize and interpret information actively—even in first grade. What is more, learning new information often requires constructing theories about why things work the way they do. Learning a new science principle—for example, how electric current works in a circuit—may require confronting prior contradictory beliefs. Such learning requires students to build a mini-theory to explain new facts and observations. Otherwise, evidence shows, they will mouth the taught principle on tests but quickly forget it and apply their older, often nonscientific ideas to everyday problems (for example, Driver, Guesne, and Tiberghien 1985).

To summarize, one cannot effectively memorize without organizing knowledge. Facts acquired without structure and rationale will disappear quickly. Children cannot understand what they read without making inferences and using information that goes beyond the written text. They cannot become good writers without engaging in complex planning and self-evaluation processes. Basic math skills will not be learned well if children only memorize rules for manipulating written numerical symbols. Science learning requires that students build explanatory theories they can believe. All of this means that the skills we are accustomed to calling *higher-level* are involved in the most basic competencies.

To achieve today's educational goals, then, requires that thinking pervade the entire school curriculum for all students from the earliest grades. The thinking curriculum is not a course to be added to a crowded program when time permits. It is not a program that begins after the basics have been mastered or the facts memorized. It is not a program reserved for a minority of students, such as the gifted or the college bound. The thinking curriculum calls for recognition that all real learning involves thinking, that thinking ability can be nurtured and cultivated in everyone, and that the entire educational program must be reconceived and revitalized so that thinking pervades students' lives beginning in kindergarten.

The thinking curriculum does not imply that instruction in processes of reasoning should substitute for insistence on students acquiring substantial knowledge. Indeed, recent cognitive research teaches us to be highly respectful of knowledge as a requirement for good thinking. Study after study shows that people who know more about a topic reason more profoundly about that topic than people who know little about it. But the knowledge required for good thinking can only be acquired through processes of thinking. For concepts and organizing knowledge to be mastered, they must be used generatively—that is, they have to be called upon over and over again as ways to link, interpret, and explain new information. Education requires an intimate linking of thinking processes with important knowledge content. This in turn calls for a reorganization of schooling so that thinking suffuses the curriculum and is demanded in every subject matter. Turning the entire educational system into one that pursues the thinking curriculum thus poses a major challenge for American education.

CURRENT TESTING PRACTICE: INIMICAL TO THE THINKING CURRICULUM

To a large extent, we have inherited only the tools of the routinized curriculum to meet the challenges of the thinking curriculum. Our testing theory and practice, in particular, are firmly rooted in the mass educational system of routinized rather than thinking aspirations. Two key assumptions of standardized testing technology, which we term the *decomposability* and the *decontextualization* assumptions, were compatible with the routinized skill goals of the mass educational system and with the psychological theories of the first part of this century. They are, however, incompatible with thinking goals for education and with what we know today about the nature of human cognition and learning. Nevertheless, as we shall show in an analysis of some widely used achievement tests, these assumptions pervade current assessment practice.

Underlying Assumptions

Decomposability

Psychological theories of the 1920s assumed that thought could best be described as a collection of independent pieces of knowledge. That assumption can be clearly recognized in the work of Edward L. Thorndike, a psychologist whose work profoundly influenced instruction and testing from the 1920s onward. In 1922 Thorndike published *The Psychology of Arithmetic* in which he showed how the content of the elementary school arithmetic curriculum could be analyzed as a collection of "bonds" between stimuli and responses. In keeping with the exercise psychology that he and his colleagues had initially developed in work on animal learning, Thorndike proposed that the task of arithmetic instruction was to exercise all of the bonds that constitute arithmetic, rewarding correct responses and "stamping out" incorrect ones. Students who acquired all of the bonds could be said to know arithmetic completely. Students who acquired fewer bonds, or who learned them to a less reliable criterion of performance, could be said to have measurably less arithmetic knowledge.

With this analysis of the nature of arithmetic knowledge and skill, constructing efficient, objective tests posed little problem. It would be impractical to test all possible bonds, but samples of the bonds could easily be tested on any given occasion. Provided that neither students nor teachers knew exactly which arithmetic facts or procedures would appear on a given test, they would need to practice all of them, or all in a given subsection of a curriculum, in order to perform well. Thus, according to Thorndike, performance on a collection of specific items would constitute a valid indicator of how much of the whole body of arithmetic a child knew.

Built into the decomposability assumption is a metaphor that likens thought to a simple machine. One can build a machine by separately constructing each of the parts. When the parts are put together, if the design is proper, the machine will run. This view suggests that in teaching mental competencies it will suffice to teach each of the components. It supports a notion of teaching and testing separate skills, reserving their composition into a complex performance for some indeterminate later time. For a domain such as arithmetic computation, this analysis into components, practice of the components, and testing by sampling components seems reasonable. However, for thinking skills dependent on complex knowledge (for example, understanding a written passage, writing a composition, solving a mathematics problem, or interpreting the results of a science experiment), analysis into components fails to capture the organic whole that we recognize as true competence.

Thorndike himself struggled with this problem. In *The Psychology of Arithmetic*, he reached for ways to deal with the problem of how students would understand the arithmetic performances they were exercising. But his theory of bonds and exercise provided no theoretical terms in which he could explain why individual bonds seemed to form naturally into groups that "go together" and should, therefore, be exercised together. Although Thorndike and many other associationist and behaviorist psychologists tried to account for intelligence, thinking, reasoning, and creativity, they were largely forced to limit their work to problems that could be subjected to analysis as collections of bonds and simple associations.

The decomposability assumption has been seriously challenged by recent cognitive research, which recognizes that complicated skills and competencies owe their complexity not just to the number of components they engage but also to interactions among the components and heuristics for calling upon them. Complex competencies, therefore, cannot be defined just by listing all of their components. Information-processing theories of cognition (Anderson 1983; Newell and Simon 1972), for example, analyze cognitive performances into complexes of rules, but performances critically depend on interactions among those rules. Each rule can be thought of as a component of the total skill, but the rules are not defined independently of one another. The "competence" of a problem-solving system thus depends on how the complex of rules acts together. Other cognitive theories, which stress the role of structured knowledge and organizing principles in learning and thinking, move even further from the decomposability assumption.

All of this suggests that efforts to assess thinking and problem-solving abilities by identifying separate components of those abilities and testing them independently will interfere with effectively teaching such abilities. Assessing separate components will encourage exercises in which isolated components are practiced. But since the components do not "add up to" thinking and problem solving, students who practice only the components are unlikely to learn to do real problem solving or interpretive thinking.

Decontextualization

This is the second major assumption built into standardized tests. Closely linked to the decomposability assumption, decontextualization asserts that each component of a complex skill is fixed, and that it will take the same form no matter where it is used. According to this assumption, if students know how to distinguish a fact from an opinion, for example, they know how under all conditions of argument and debate, in all knowledge contexts. If this assumption were valid, it would be sensible to select key critical thinking skills for decontextualized practice in school. But the assumption no longer appears valid. Recent developments in the epistemology and philosophy of science (for example, Lakatos 1978; Toulmin 1972) show there is no absolute line to be drawn between fact and theory, data and interpretation. Instead, what is counted as fact depends on a complex of tools and instruments that have theories built into them and on communally accepted methods for deciding among competing assertions. Thus, not only history and literature, but also science and mathematics must be understood as interpretive domains in which knowledge and skill cannot be detached from their contexts of practice and use. Educationally this suggests that we cannot teach a skill component in one setting and expect it to be applied automatically in another. That means, in turn, that we cannot validly assess a competence in a context very different from the context in which it is practiced or used.

An example is writing. An important part of writing a good essay is being able to edit one's own work. This fact is sometimes used to justify teaching editing and then testing it as a component of writing skill, usually on passages in which students must detect errors and choose corrections from among several given alternatives. Such exercises measure copyediting ability reasonably well, but they are poor ways to practice composition. Editing one's own work is not just a matter of detecting errors; it is also a matter of crafting phrases and sentences to convey intended meanings. Decontextualized editing exercises, whether in class or on tests, do not reveal what people do when they edit their own work. If our educational goal were to train a community of copyeditors for publishing houses, editing tests would be entirely appropriate. But if we are trying to educate people to compose a good essay or a clear memorandum, editing tests set a false direction. Such decontextualization does violence to the kinds of abilities we seek.

Analysis of Widely Used Achievement Tests

The decomposability and decontextualization assumptions, remnants of the routinized curriculum, permeate today's achievement tests, the very tests often used to energize and monitor school reform. To gauge the character of today's tests, we examined the standardized test batteries widely used in educational assessment by individual school districts and, as part of mandated testing programs, in state assessments of educational quality.[1] The structures of the standardized achievement batteries are similar. Each of the widely used batteries is broken into several sections, typically mathematics (often with subsections for computation and reasoning, concepts, or problem solving); reading comprehension; listening comprehension; language (often with subsections on spelling, grammar and usage, and vocabulary); science; social studies; and perhaps a library skills or study skills section. Of these, the reading, language, and mathematics tests are the most widely used; we examine them here.

Reading Comprehension

The five widely used standardized reading tests use similar approaches in assessing reading comprehension. The standard reading-comprehension test format consists of a passage to be read, followed by a series of questions about the passage. The questions are always in multiple-choice form. There is a certain face validity to this way of assessing reading ability. Being able to answer questions about the content of a passage is certainly part of what we mean by understanding the passage. Furthermore, there is a generality built into these tests. Assuming the test has been held secure as intended, the passages are fresh to the students; they cannot memorize the answers to the questions in advance but must do their comprehension work during the testing period. So to a considerable extent, the test measures a process skill rather than specific memorized knowledge.

Yet there are serious limitations to the standard reading tests when considered in terms of a curriculum aimed at cultivating thinking. Two primary features of the tests are striking when examined from this perspective. First, the passages are short, and the questions favor choppy reading, searching for information in bits rather than interpreting an extended passage with many sections. This testing style reflects the decomposability assumption, treating knowledge and skill as accumulations of isolated pieces of information and not as coherent, interactive systems.

We examined in some detail the reading-comprehension subtests of two of the most widely used tests. In one, the test form intended for grades eight through eleven contains ten passages on which fifty-five separate questions are asked. The entire test must be completed in fifty minutes. Students thus have an average of five minutes to read a passage and answer five or six questions about it—hardly a situation that invites reflection and elaboration on a text. The passages on this test are quite brief. The longest passage in the set contains only 410 words; the average, not counting a poem, has less than 250 words. The second test examined was very similar in this respect. Its comprehension test for grades eight and nine contains seven passages and fifty-eight questions to be answered in forty-two minutes, giving students an average of just over six minutes to read a passage and answer approximately eight questions. The prose passages on this test are slightly longer, averaging 350 words; the longest passage in the set contains 545 words.

The second striking feature of the tests is that the questions are tilted toward superficial processing of the passages. We examined the items on two major tests, classifying them under the rubrics of *literal, stylistic,* and *interpretive* comprehension. These classifications are based on our own judgments; we began with, but modified, the test publishers' categorizations of the questions on their tests. We judged as *literal comprehension* those items asking who, what, and when questions or questions of factual detail and description, those asking for meanings of particular words in the text, and those asking for cause-effect relationships already stated in the text. Almost 30 percent of the questions on one test and 40 percent of the questions on the other were of this type. We judged as *stylistic comprehension* those items focused on knowledge of genre or language used in the passage—for example, questions about the structure of a story (for example, its turning point), those asking for the meaning of a figurative phrase, or those calling for attention to particular techniques of persuasive language. About 25 percent of the questions on one test, but only 10 percent of those on the second were of this type.

We judged as *interpretive comprehension* those questions asking for inferences beyond the stated language of the text. Overall this category accounted for about 50 percent of the questions on both tests; however, the category itself was extremely varied. The two most popular kinds of questions asked about the main idea of a passage (about 11 percent of all questions on the two tests combined) or for a conclusion based on the information given (15 percent of all questions). Each of these types of questions requires a degree of textual interpretation of the kind that the thinking curriculum demands, although such separate, isolated questions do not really examine how students interrelate various parts of the text or the kinds of justifications and arguments they might develop to support their interpretations.

Other questions in the interpretive comprehension category are even less demanding in these terms. A significant number (about 6 percent) of questions about characters' motives and feelings require a general knowledge of how people act and feel in certain circumstances rather than inferences from the text passage itself. Others (nearly 12 percent) ask questions about the tone and mood of a piece, the author's apparent purpose, or fact/opinion distinctions, but do not ask the students to use these judgments to carry forward a line of reasoning about the passage. Again we see the influence of the decomposability assumption: pieces of knowledge, even when based on some degree of inference beyond the statements of the text, need not be related to one another.

These tests tacitly convey a definition of reading as perusing short passages to answer other people's questions. Furthermore, the test format suggests that the answers to these questions are already known by the person asking them. Under these conditions, reading comprehension appears to be a matter of finding predetermined answers, not interpreting the written word. Children who practice reading mainly in the form in which it appears on the tests—and there is good evidence that this is what happens in many classrooms—would have little exposure to the demands and reasoning possibilities of the thinking curriculum.

Language

The other standardized subtests devoted to language engage students in even less contextualized and extended thinking than the comprehension tests. Vocabulary tests present decontextualized words in questions that must be answered at a rate of two or three per minute if the whole test is to be completed. Spelling tests usually contain items in which the student selects a word's proper spelling from among a set of misspellings—again at a rate of two or three per minute. There are various subtests on language usage, mechanics, expression, and punctuation. The items involve recognizing errors and choosing (not producing) corrections, usually at the rate of two or three items per minute. Students who practiced exercises like those that fill the standardized language tests would not learn to write coordinated, coherent prose. They might not even learn to write locally correct prose or to use a wide range of vocabulary in their writing, for there is good evidence that recognizing other people's errors and choosing the correct alternatives are not the same processes as those needed to produce good written language. These tests carry the decontextualization assumption to the extreme.

Mathematics

On the whole, the mathematics portions of the standardized tests fare even worse than the reading portions on the criteria we have laid out in this chapter. All the tests contain major sections in which arithmetic computations are to be performed at the rate of one or two problems per minute. These are, perhaps, reasonable assessments of computational fluency; in any case, they do not claim to assess aspects of mathematical reasoning. Much more disturbing are the subtests aimed at assessing mathematical concepts and problem solving. These, too, consist of many short items, usually presenting problems to be solved at the rate of about one per minute. Recent publications of the National Council of Teachers of Mathematics (1989) and the Mathematical Sciences Education Board (National Research Council 1989) establish standards for a conceptually oriented thinking curriculum in mathematics and call for extended mathematical reasoning on problems that can be attacked by several different methods. None of the standardized mathematics tests that we examined even approximates these standards. Students who practiced mathematics in the form found in the standardized tests would never be exposed to the kind of mathematical thinking sought by all who are concerned with reforming mathematics education, ranging from people involved with practical mathematics to those interested in more academic forms of mathematical activity.

In summary, all of the standardized tests we examined fare badly when judged against the standard of assessing and promoting a thinking curriculum. They embody a definition of knowledge and skill as a collection of bits of information. They demand fast, nonreflective replies. The tests, and the classroom practices that might prepare for them, suggest to students a view of knowledge counter to what the thinking curriculum seeks to cultivate: If you do not know an answer immediately, there is no way of arriving at a sensible response by thought and elaboration. Although some items on the reading-comprehension sections of the tests demand interpretation of and inference from the text, questions are usually presented as isolated and unconnected with each other, with no hint that interpreting a text might involve an extended line of reasoning. The multiple-choice format, furthermore, reinforces the idea that someone else already knows the answer to the question, so that original interpretations are not expected; the task, then, is to find or guess the "right" answer rather than to engage in interpretive activity.

THE FUNCTIONS OF TESTING

In evaluating standardized tests we have assumed that tests influence classroom teaching and the activities in which students engage. Is this assumption necessary? How important to educational reform is the mismatch of current tests with the goals of the thinking curriculum? To answer these questions sensibly, we must first distinguish among several different functions that tests and assessments play in education. No analysis of testing or set of recommendations for its future can be understood without first specifying which of the several functions of testing is in question and then considering what kinds of social constraints operate on and through the tests in use. We have identified three main classes of educational testing: (1) public accountability and program evaluation; (2) instructional management and monitoring; (3) student selection and certification. Each has different sets of audiences, and each places different demands on the assessment system. In each, the interplay between test results and curriculum and instruction is different.

Public Accountability and Program Evaluation

A major function of standardized achievement testing—indeed, its earliest function historically—is to permit those in positions of public oversight and responsibility for the education system to monitor the schools' performance. Accountability tests are intended to provide those responsible for the funding and the civic supervision of education with information on how the school system as a whole is performing. Program evaluation can be considered a special kind of accountability testing meant to provide information on whether a particular instructional or support program is succeeding in its academic goals. In both cases, the primary audience for assessment results is people at some distance from the day-to-day educational process who require a disinterested evaluation of the overall effects of educational programs, but not detailed information on individual students or, usually, on the details of instructional practice. As we shall see later, these characteristics of accountability testing create opportunities for forms of assessment very different from those now widely used for accountability purposes.

A principal requirement of accountability and program evaluation tests is that they permit detached and impartial judgments of students' performance, that is, judgments by individuals other than the students' own teachers, using assessment instruments not of the teachers' devising. On the other hand, because the focus in accountability is on how target *groups* of students, considered as a population experiencing a particular program of instruction, are performing, accountability assessments do not need to provide detailed information on individual students. Indeed, global performance descriptors that give a broad sense of what students are learning are more informative to the public than the kinds of detailed reports on individual students or specific skills that educators need to guide their instructional work. Furthermore, accountability assessments, because they are meant to track performance of a system over time, need not be administered frequently or scored quickly, since educators do not depend on them for information to guide details of the instructional process. Finally, to track the performance of the system, it is not necessary to test and grade every individual in the system; a properly chosen sample is adequate.

Accountability tests do, however, bear a close relationship to the school curriculum. In many instances, they are used as instruments of school reform, intended to motivate educators to greater instructional effort and to shape the direction of that effort. Even when there are no explicit incentives for performing well or disincentives for performing badly on accountability tests, educators tend to use activities in their teaching that they believe will produce high scores for their students. Later in this chapter, we provide evidence for this claim and elaborate on its implications. For now, we simply want to stress that accountability tests, by virtue of their place in a complex social system, exercise an important influence on the curriculum of the school. Those designing and adopting accountability assessment instruments, therefore, have a responsibility to consider the kinds of instructional practices their tests are likely to invoke and the kinds of messages about educational goals the tests implicitly or explicitly convey.

Selection and Certification of Students

A second function of testing in the educational system is selection of students for particular educational institutions or programs. The intended users of selection tests are those making admissions decisions in higher education or assigning individuals to special education programs. In both cases, the test data are typically used in conjunction with other student information, although the extent to which tests constrain selection and assignment is a matter of debate and public concern (for example, Wigdor and Garner 1982). The fundamental requirements for selection tests are that they provide information on *individuals* and that the test scores predict future performance in the institution or program for which the student is being considered. Since selection directly affects students' educational futures, there is substantial public concern that selection tests not be systematically biased against any particular groups of students, for example, minorities or females. Selection tests could, however, be based on teachers' judgments or on grades, as long as these predicted future performance effectively and were not systematically biased against any group.

This country's dominant practice is to base college selection on curriculum-neutral tests. The Scholastic Aptitude Test (SAT), introduced in 1926, but widely used only after World War II, was originally thought to measure a general ability to learn that was not a function of educational experience. Today we recognize that the SAT measures learning, but learning of a very general kind, not associated with particular curriculum content. In the description of those who have directed and administered this testing program, "The SAT is intended to go into the broadest sources of education, beyond any academic curriculum" (Angoff 1971). The American College Test (ACT), introduced in 1959, although organized by the four headings of natural science, social studies, mathematics, and English, correlates strongly with the SAT (despite some internal discrepancies) and measures a similar kind of general learning. According to a technical report published by ACT, "The ACT assessment seems to reflect long-term factors rather than short-term learning and is more like an aptitude test in this way" (American College Testing Program 1973, 19).

The relationship of selection tests to school curricula is more open to choice and preference than most discussions in the United States acknowledge. Selection tests do not *need* to be related to past studies, but they *can* be. Indeed, in most countries, selection for higher education is not based on curriculum-independent tests but on examination performance on an established course syllabus (see Resnick and Resnick 1984). Such examinations also serve to certify that individual students have completed a course of study and reached a certain criterion of performance in that course. The British Public Examinations, the French Baccalaureate exams, and similar examination programs in many other countries are examples of certification assessments. The only similar certifications widely used in the United States are the Advanced Placement tests. The test-certified high school diplomas used in a few states differ significantly from the examinations used in other countries. Except for the New York State Regents examination program, the tests for high school diplomas certify only *minimal* competence—usually basic arithmetic and language skill—whereas examinations in other countries set a high standard of performance tied to a specific course of study.

Selection and certification tests differ sharply from accountability in that they must focus squarely on individuals. In other important respects, however, selection and accountability testing requirements are quite similar. Like accountability tests, selection and certification tests must be impartial. The public function of certification would not be met if teachers were to grade the performance of their own students; and for selection it is important to be able to compare students from different schools on a common standard. In both cases, too, detailed assessments, quick scoring, and frequent testing are not needed, and the primary audience for test results is at some distance from the classroom.

Instructional Management and Monitoring

Tests can also be used for functions much closer to the actual conduct of instruction. These include assigning students to classes, diagnosing particular strengths and weaknesses in individual students' performances, and monitoring the effects of small units of instruction—as small as a daily lesson or, in the case of certain forms of computer-assisted instruction, portions of lessons. Tests—including informal assessments designed and administered by teachers—can also serve as motivators and organizers of students' study time. Testing for instructional management and monitoring purposes functions very differently from accountability or selection testing. It has a very different audience and, as a result, rather different requirements with respect to frequency, timing of testing, and level of detail in reporting results.

The audience for instructional management tests is the people closest to the instructional process: school staff and the students themselves. Unlike accountability and selection tests, instructional management tests must yield their data quickly, because they measure human beings in the process of changing, and their diagnostic information is instructionally useful only if acted upon quickly. They must yield data on individual students, the targets of instructional adaptation, and they must, in most cases, yield rather fine-grained analyses of performance in order to help instructors shape teaching to individual needs.

The purpose of instructional management tests is not external evaluation of students, teachers, or educational programs, but rather assistance to teachers and students in their classroom work. For this reason, there is less need for detached and disinterested judgments here than there is in accountability and selection testing. The judgments of the students' own teachers can properly serve as part of the assessment. However, for instructional management tests to work effectively, they must be tied directly to the curriculum in use, providing information about exactly what aspects of a syllabus individual students know or do not know and which problem-solving and reasoning processes they can or cannot manage.

Comparison of Functions

Table 1 summarizes the similarities and differences among the three classes of testing functions. We have discussed several dimensions of variation: the audience for test results; the extent to which evaluations of individual students are required; the extent to which it is necessary to develop measures independent of teachers' judgments; how quickly data must become available to users; and the degree of detail required in the assessment. We have also discussed at some length the appropriate relationships between tests and curriculum for the different test functions. Accountability and selection/certification testing are similar in many respects, but differ in one key matter: accountability testing does not require scores for individual students; selection testing does. In that respect, testing for selection is more like that for instructional management. The many differences between instructional management and accountability testing make it highly unlikely that a single testing program can be effectively used for both functions—as some states and school districts seek to do and as many test publishers recommend.

These contrasts argue for a public discourse on assessment that maintains a clear separation among the three functions of testing. Discussions of testing that fail to specify clearly which function is under consideration, or that move from one function to another without clearly signaling the shift, are unlikely to help us reach clear, sensible decisions about testing policy. Of the three functions, selection testing has received the most intense and continuing public scrutiny.[2] Although still largely a hope for the future, systematic testing for instructional management and monitoring is a major concern of many educational researchers and test developers, many of whom see new possibilities for testing integrated with instruction (for example, Glaser 1987; Frederiksen and

TABLE 1
Requirements for Three Testing Functions

	Public Accountability/ Program Evaluation	Instructional Management/ Monitoring	Selection/ Certification
Audience			
At a distance	Yes	No	Yes
School staff	No	Yes	No
Characteristics			
Evaluate individual student	No	Yes	Yes
Impartial	Yes	No	Yes
Results needed quickly	No	Yes	No
Detailed assessment needed	No	Yes	No
Closely related to curriculum	Yes	Yes	Open
Frequent testing needed	No	Yes	No

Collins, in press; Nitko 1989). Accountability testing, usually imposed by legislators or other public bodies outside the educational and technical community, has received less systematic attention from the scholarly community and has rarely been discussed as a category in its own right. Yet it can be argued that, at present, accountability testing has a more profound influence on educational practice and possibilities than testing for either selection or instructional management. That influence derives from the growing pervasiveness of accountability testing in American education and the control—direct and indirect—that mandated accountability tests exert over curriculum and teaching practice at all levels of the school system. We consider this influence in the next section.

ACCOUNTABILITY TESTS AND CURRICULUM: AN INTIMATE RELATIONSHIP

Origins of Accountability Testing

The origins of accountability testing are firmly rooted in the mass educational system of routinized rather than thinking aspirations. The elite school system had little need for accountability tests or other standardized testing instruments. It was a system in which teachers and parents understood each other, students were expected to be interested in learning, and the colleges that accepted the students knew the teachers in the high school academies. Standardized accountability systems were not necessary. Accountability lay in the system of social relationships among different parts of the educational system and society at large. As schooling became a mass undertaking in which the people involved did not know each other personally and often mistrusted one another, a need arose for public, nonpersonal knowledge of how well this vast system was performing.

The press for accountability and program review testing began early in the United States. In the 1890s, Joseph Mayer Rice, educational reformer, medical doctor, and publicist, introduced the prototype of the first standardized tests for these purposes. In two school systems, he used tests he had designed to measure, in several subject areas, the impact of different amounts of instructional time on student performance. In spelling, for example, the first subject area he examined, his principal finding was that, at different grade levels, instructional time varied from fifteen to thirty minutes each day but made no difference in the performance of school children.[3] Rice's goal was to use testing to review the effects of different patterns of instruction on school learning and to establish how well the schools were doing. He was not interested in the analysis of individual student performance. Rice did not have the technical tools of modern psychometrics, but he shared the concern for objectivity and freedom from human judgment that was to drive the later standardized testing movement.

By the time that America entered World War I, more than two hundred standardized achievement tests were available for use in the primary and secondary schools. Different tests met different criteria for standardization. Responses were often self-generated short answers; multiple-choice forms were just beginning to gain favor. Some, like the Cleveland Survey and Courtis Standard, imposed stated times for completion, but not all did this. Median scores were often reported for different test populations, but graded tests providing norms for performance by specific grade levels began to appear only in the last half-dozen years before the war. Edward L. Thorndike and his students at Columbia University were pioneers in the development of these scaled achievement tests. A study of the market by Walter Monroe, published in 1918, indicated that there were eleven standardized achievement tests available in arithmetic alone. Subjects for these tests ranged from geography to handwriting and mirrored the curriculum of the schools. They were marketed principally by the publishers of school textbooks, like Houghton-Mifflin and World Book Company, whose sales representatives were already a visible presence in the local school districts.

The achievement tests, however, were not intended to map onto a particular curriculum or to advance any one approach to a course of study. This indifference to the particular content of a curriculum has two principal sources. One derives from the structure and values of the local school districts; the other from the marketing concerns of the publishers of tests. Within the districts, which had numbered 100,000 at the turn of the century and were gradually consolidating, there was no predisposition to yield to imposed curricula, and no state education agencies, except for a few like New York's Board of Regents, had any inclination to work in this direction. From the standpoint of the test publishers, there was no disposition to dovetail tests to textbooks because of the way in which this would restrict sales. Marketers of the tests had a strong interest in presenting them as independent of any curriculum, even though they dealt with school-taught subjects. The adoption of pencil-and-paper intelligence tests by school districts after the war, following the well-known experiment with the Army Alpha Test (Chapman 1989; Kevles 1968), reinforced the focus on tests that were free of the curriculum (D. P. Resnick 1982).

School administrators, caught up in the efficiency drive of the early part of this century, found themselves increasingly under pressure to improve the cost-effectiveness of school operations in a period of rapidly growing enrollments (Callahan 1962; Wise 1979). In so doing, they used tests to deal with the costly problem of school failure and grade repeating. To resolve the problem of failure, leading educators called for homogeneous grouping of students in tracked programs. To classify students for grouping or to support teacher judgment in establishing those groups, school administrators turned to standardized achievement and ability tests. In the decade from 1912 to 1922, nearly sixty testing and measurement bureaus were set up within local school districts, establishing a presence in almost every major city. This was the period of the most rapid concentrated growth in staffing of district testing offices before the 1960s. Administration of tests to place students in homogeneous groups was the major function of these offices (Deffenbaugh 1926).

State agencies did not develop a capacity to monitor local school districts until the 1930s. Their role as it then emerged was to offer a range of backup and advisory services to the local school districts, occasionally taking testing initiatives in programs for the gifted and the disabled and supporting new forms of testing for guidance purposes at the district level. Guidance was a central interest of the 1930s, growing out of a concern for both youth unemployment and the large numbers of able young people not attending college. The state departments and boards of education were not engaged in developing testing programs that would impact intentionally on the curriculum (the action of the New York Board of Regents, begun much earlier, was an exception). The role of state agencies did not change radically until the early 1960s.

In the early 1960s, accountability testing became a more important concern of the states. At that point, too, testing began to develop the potential for impacting more directly on the curriculum. One impetus to state-level testing came from federal legislation, and that in turn was a response to the civil rights movement. The Congress moved after the 1964 elections to actively promote compensatory education in the public schools. The Elementary and Secondary Education Act of 1965 (ESEA), Title I, called for financial assistance and special services for low-income students and districts (Jeffreys 1978). Performance data on students receiving assistance from these programs had to be gathered and forwarded at regular intervals to state boards. The federal government also primed the states for a role in evaluation by contracting in 1969 with the Education Commission of the States to create the National Assessment of Educational Progress (NAEP) to "examine achievement in ten learning areas, to spot changes in level of achievement over the years and to apply the implication of those changes to national educational policy" (Wise 1979, 9). Other developments, like the assumption by the states of a larger portion of school expenses in local districts and grass-roots interest in access to test scores for purposes of public accountability, help to explain the transformation of the testing enterprise in this period.

Today, accountability testing is a vast enterprise in the United States, touching the educational lives of students and teachers in every classroom. Almost every state has some form of state-mandated testing program—either a state-administered test or a requirement that districts administer standardized tests of their own choosing. The states vary considerably in how frequently they test. In many states, students are tested every school year, but in many others, every two or three years. In most states, students are tested at least once in elementary school, in middle school, and in high school. In addition, many local districts administer the tests for their own accountability purposes more frequently than their state. Many states use one of five nationally marketed, commercial, standardized tests as all or part of their testing program.[4] Six states use portions of the National Assessment of Educational Progress (NAEP) tests as part of their state assessment programs, and the number of NAEP-related state programs will probably increase. Thirty states supplement the standardized tests with one or more customized tests, and thirteen use only customized tests in their programs.

How Accountability Tests Influence the Curriculum

Regardless of the form or frequency of testing, to the extent that test performances of classrooms, schools, or districts are made visible and have consequences (ranging from prestige and shame to economic resources and management constraints), the nature of tests tends to shape teachers' practice. This fact is often masked by the rhetoric surrounding the introduction and interpretation of assessment programs. Assessment programs are often announced and discussed as if they were not meant to influence curriculum and teaching directly. This rhetoric of curriculum-neutral tests accords well with American traditions of local control over education, which produce a profound and continuing resistance to any attempt (or even the appearance of an attempt) to impose a curriculum from outside the local school district. If tests and assessments are considered curriculum-neutral—not geared to any particular instructional program and not imposing any particular set of goals or practices— they can be incorporated easily into the ideology of local educational control. If tests are recognized as guiding or constraining the curriculum, however, they become problematic within our educational ideology. For this reason, educators have long been discouraged from "teaching to the tests."

In keeping with this constraint, we often speak of test scores as *indicators* of how well schools are performing (for a set of discussions of educational indicators, see Fuhrman 1988; see also Murnane and Raizen 1988), rather than as *direct samples* of what students have learned. The term *indicator* suggests a system in which the measurements correlate with what we care about, but the behaviors measured are not necessarily themselves important. Indicators are used in many domains. For example, to obtain an indicator of the amount of ambient heat in the air and thus how comfortable a room is for its occupants, we examine the height of mercury in a confined column and take a numerical temperature reading. We do not really care about the height of the mercury, however. What we normally care about is the physical comfort of people in the room. If we were to take a *comfort sample* instead of using the temperature indicator, we would examine to what extent people were sweating, shivering, or showing other signs of physical discomfort or ask them to rate their degree of comfort. Clearly, using the temperature indicator is more convenient, but it provides no direct information about discomfort due to heat or cold.

One reason for using the temperature indicator is its unobtrusive character; taking a thermometer reading does not change the degree of comfort in the room. Educational tests, however, do not share this characteristic of unobtrusiveness. We cannot place a "test thermometer" in a classroom without expecting to change conditions in the classroom significantly. This is because tests are used in a *social* rather than a physical system, a system in which measurements that are made known to actors in the system can be expected to affect their future actions. The molecules of air are not motivated to produce a temperature reading in a specific range. Teachers and school principals *are* motivated to produce test scores in an acceptable range. Any educational assessment that receives publicity will produce efforts on the part of educators to have their students perform well on that assessment.

This power of tests and assessments to influence educators' behavior is precisely what makes them potent tools for educational reform. In imposing public accountability programs, it is the *intention* of state education departments and legislatures to influence what is taught and the standards of performance. In other words, tests have become instruments of school reform. They are introduced not just to provide neutral *indicators* of the education system's performance, but also in the hope of upgrading curriculum, teaching, and academic performance.

There is considerable evidence that this strategy works, in the sense that it produces a rise in test scores. When test scores for a school or school district are charted over time, it is not uncommon to see scores rise in the first few years after introducing a particular test. Even in school districts where official policy is against "teaching to the test," if considerable attention is paid in the press or elsewhere to test scores, teachers will gradually adapt their teaching to the tests. Although many tests are held secure and the items varied from year to year, a teacher who administers the tests yearly has an opportunity to see what is being tested and to adjust class practice to match the test. This process is often exaggerated in school districts with knowledgeable testing directors and curriculum specialists who encourage—even if only implicitly—adaptation to the test in order to demonstrate publicly students' rising academic performance. Often the effects of this adaptation process become visible only when a new test, with different emphases, is adopted by or imposed on the district. Test scores in grade equivalent or other comparative terms then drop.

In sophisticated discussions of the relationship between testing and curriculum, there is usually considerable attention to the question of "overlap," the extent to which test items and curriculum activities are the same. When overlap is high, test scores are high; when overlap decreases, so do test scores (for example, Leinhardt and Seewald 1981). School districts and teachers try to maximize overlap between the tests they use and their curriculum by choosing tests that match their curriculum. When they cannot control the tests—which is increasingly the case when states mandate the tests—they strive for overlap by trying to match curriculum to the tests, that is, by "curriculum alignment." In the first few years of a test's use, overlap increases as the curriculum is aligned to the tests. When a new test is imposed, overlap suddenly decreases, because the curriculum cannot change as quickly as the test.

Some educators have argued that the process of curriculum alignment is a favorable one that should be publicly encouraged and supported with tools to make teaching to the tests easier and more reliable. A major advocate of this process, James Popham (1987), calls for what he terms *Measurement-Driven Instruction* (MDI), a cost-effective way of improving education. According to Popham, effective MDI would give teachers prototype test items in advance and invite them to prepare all students to pass these item types. Popham argues that an effective MDI program should focus on a small number of objectives, and that guidelines and even instructional materials should be provided to help teachers teach exactly what the tests will assess. Measurement-Driven Instruction carries to its logical extreme the idea of using tests as instruments of school reform. It creates the ultimate in curriculum alignment by directly matching what is taught to what is tested.

The adoption of MDI in certain parts of the country has provided evidence that it is possible to focus instructional attention on a small set of desired objectives and thereby to improve performance on a particular set of test items. But can we conclude that educational standards have been raised? We can only if we can assume that the test used adequately measures *all* that we want children to achieve in school. If the test measures only part of a school's or a state's goals for its children, a rise in scores on that test means, at best, only an increase in some limited aspect of the desired achievement. If, for example, we would like students to be able to solve mathematical problems and also be proficient at calculation, but we test calculation skill only, we cannot say that *mathematics* achievement has risen as test scores go up, but only that *calculation* achievement has risen. At most then, a rise in test scores signals a rise only in some portion of achievement.

Raising a portion of achievement by the introduction of testing would be a favorable outcome, *unless, in raising the part of achievement that is tested, we produced some negative effect on other portions of achievement that are valued as much or more*. Is this the case? Is it possible that we might actually lower problem-solving achievement by testing for calculation while leaving problem solving out of the math test?

Popham and other advocates of MDI deny that this will happen. They argue that teachers in an efficient test-driven system will "waste far less of their students' time with irrelevancy and busywork. Creative teachers can *efficiently* promote mastery of content-to-be-tested and then get on with other classroom pursuits" (Popham 1987, 681–82). Two potential objections to this claim must be considered. First, it may not be true that teachers in a high-stakes situation will quickly attend to teaching what is tested and then go on to other pursuits. Second, it may be a poor educational idea to leave the "other classroom pursuits" to chance. If MDI is such a good idea, why is it not a good idea for all of our educational goals?

Evidence has been accumulating that teachers do not, in fact, quickly attend to tested objectives and then go on to other things. Instead, when the stakes are high—when schools' ratings and budgets or teachers' salaries depend on test scores—efforts to improve performance on a particular assessment instrument seem to drive out most other educational concerns. Shepard (1988) has studied this process in Texas, where materials suggesting instructional strategies for each of the objectives on the state assessment were provided for teachers. The strategies are specific to the test item form and promise teachers who use them high test performance for their students because their curriculum will be perfectly aligned with the test. Commercially sold programs to help students learn test-taking skills, Shepard found, are also closely tied to specific item *forms* that appear on the major standardized test batteries. Under these conditions, not only is the range of skills taught restricted, but also slight variants in format that might be equally valid ways of exercising a skill are ignored in favor of drilling students on the precise forms they will encounter on the tests. Other investigators (for example, Cohen 1987; Kellaghan, Madaus, and Airasian 1980; Romberg, Zarinnia, and Williams 1989) further document the tendency of high-stakes tests to progressively restrict curricular attention to the objectives that are tested and even to the particular item forms that will appear on the tests.

Whether we like it or not, what is taught and what is tested are intimately related. No serious possibility exists for creating accountability tests that will not eventually influence what is taught and how it is taught in the schools. This means that there is no way to create accountability tests that will be curriculum-neutral. We must think of every test or assessment used for public accountability or program evaluation purposes as an instrument that will affect the curriculum. With this in mind, the following three principles may serve as guidelines for accountability assessments.

1. *You get what you assess.* Educators will teach to tests if the tests matter in their own or their students' lives. This is what makes tests potential tools in educational reform. It also means that the tests must be carefully crafted to sample directly those educational performances that are valued. *Indicators* of desired goals, no matter how well they may correlate with the truly desired outcome, do not make good accountability measures. For example, multiple-choice tests can be designed to correlate very highly with written composition grades. Such tests are good indicators of composition skill. But if we put many multiple-choice tests into the testing system, we must expect children to practice answering multiple-choice questions—as required by so many of today's workbooks in every school subject. In contrast, if we put debates, discussions, essays, and problem solving into the testing system, children will spend time practicing those activities.

2. *You do not get what you do not assess.* What does not appear on tests tends to disappear from classrooms in time. If the goals of solving complex problems or writing extended essays are educationally important, those activities need to be sampled directly in an assessment program aimed at encouraging improved instruction. This means it is not sufficient to test "the basics" (a common strategy in today's assessment programs), assuming that preparing for the tests will take minimal time and that teachers will then go on to other "higher-order" abilities.

3. *Build assessments toward which you want educators to teach.* This principle follows directly from the first two, and lies at the heart of the matter. Assessments must be designed so that when teachers do the natural thing—that is, prepare their students to perform well—they will exercise the kinds of abilities and develop the kinds of skills and knowledge that are the real goals of educational reform. This principle assumes that what is in the assessment will be practiced in the classroom, in a form close to the assessment form. For any proposed assessment exercise, it directs us to pose one central question: "Is this what we want students to be doing with their educational time?"

ALTERNATIVE ASSESSMENTS FOR THE THINKING CURRICULUM

The principles just outlined place curriculum at the heart of assessment decisions. They assert that the problem of assessment is really a problem of curriculum and of educational goals. They point us toward direct observation of the kinds of performances the thinking curriculum values rather than toward indicators and probes that are not meant to be taught to. Can such direct assessments be developed and used within the constraints of mass assessment systems?

One way to begin answering this question is to examine practices in a few states that have adopted alternative assessments to the standardized tests. About 75 percent of the states supplement or supplant standardized tests with customized assessments of their own design. Although many of these customized state assessments are criterion- rather than norm-referenced,[5] almost all follow the pattern of the standardized tests in terms of the kinds of items and test formats used. A few states, however, have stepped outside the model of numerous short questions and precoded answers. To date, alternative assessments have been mainly of writing skills.

Several states have recently added to their assessment batteries a writing examination in which students produce essays that are graded by panels of judges to yield quantitative scores. A similar writing assessment is now included in the National Assessment of Educational Progress. These writing assessments begin to meet the criteria laid out in this paper for educationally appropriate assessment. If students engaged regularly in the activities found in the assessment, they would be practicing writing in an authentic form. These tests can be "taught to" without destroying their educational validity. They represent potentially powerful tools of educational reform because their presence in the assessment system will actively encourage educators to provide significant amounts of writing practice in the curriculum.

Current writing assessments vary significantly in the length of the essay to be written (some request no more than a paragraph) and in the degree to which the essay is prestructured by the questions posed. Thus, they do not yet all represent perfect instruments for promoting the thinking curriculum. Despite these limitations, the adoption of open-ended writing assessments by several states and by the NAEP marks an important change in assessment policy. National and state testing agencies are now recognizing that students' open-ended responses can be scored with sufficient reliability to provide data on the quality of learning to the public and the educational system. The use of writing assessments has thus shown the feasibility of using complex, integrated performances, rather than series of isolated questions, in a public accountability system. Their use has also shown that it is possible to derive reliable, publicly believable quantitative measures from judgments of these products rather than from precoded "correct" answers. The successful use of writing assessments as part of public accountability testing opens the way for a much wider variety of new assessment methods, methods that are more compatible with the nation's aspiration to education for thinking.

The essay assessments are an example of a broader category of assessments often called *performance assessments*. A performance assessment is one that uses direct judgments and evaluations of performances rather than indirect indicators of competence. Performance assessments are widely used in the arts and in athletics. At the Olympics, for example, performances in sports with no direct competition against an opponent (such as diving and gymnastics) are rated by judges, and the pooled ratings used to decide who wins medals. In music competitions, pianists or violinists perform a prescribed or self-selected repertoire; these performances are rated by judges, and again pooled ratings determine the winners of the competition. Ratings are often made on several separate dimensions as well as on overall, global performance, and there may be complex formulas for weighting the different judgments. A variant of the performance assessment is the *portfolio assessment*. In this method, frequently used in the visual and plastic arts and other design fields, individuals collect their work over a period of time, select a sample of the collection that they think best represents their capabilities, and submit this portfolio of work to a jury or panel of judges.

Although best developed in the arts and athletics, performance and portfolio assessments are adaptable to other domains of knowledge and skill. The simplest form of performance assessment is the written essay. Essay questions can be used not only to assess writing skill, but also as a vehicle for assessing knowledge of issues and ideas within a subject matter. Special forms of essay examinations also yield evidence of students' ability to carry out investigations and analyses of data. For example, the Advanced Placement (AP) Test in History contains a Document-Based Question in which students must analyze a set of documentary sources to answer an interpretative question. Figure 1 shows a sample page from the 1979 AP American history test. In addition to the materials shown, students received fifteen additional documents. These included statistical tables; newspaper cartoons; excerpts from government reports, the *Congressional Record*, and Supreme Court opinions; political speeches; and resolutions of citizens' organizations. A report on grading for this exam (Niven 1978/1979) describes the process of arriving at reliable scores on this question. An analysis of the documents and questions from the historian's point of view provided the basis for describing a set of scoring standards. Graders (teachers from schools in which advanced placement courses are given, along with college faculty in those disciplines) worked in groups, with opportunity to discuss and change (by consensus) scoring standards, as they studied various student answers. Thus, the applied standards emerged from inspection and analysis of students' work rather than having been fully prescribed in advance by those who prepared the examination questions.

Performance assessments need not be limited to written essays. In England, where open-ended essay examinations have always been part of the

FIGURE 1
Document-Based Question from
the Advanced Placement Test in American History[*]

AMERICAN HISTORY
SECTION II
Part A
Time—60 minutes

Directions: The following question is based on the accompanying Documents A-Q.
You will have 60 minutes to read and analyze the documents and answer the question.
You may make notes and plan your answer on the green insert or on the printed pages
of the pink, free-response booklet. Write your answer to the question on the lined
pages of the free-response booklet.

This question tests your ability to work with historical documents. Your answer
should be derived mainly from the documents. You may also refer to historical facts
and developments not mentioned in the documents and may assess the reliability of
the documents as historical sources where relevant to your answer.

1. To what extent and for what reasons did the policies of the federal
government from 1865 to 1900 violate the principles of laissez faire,
which advocated minimal governmental intervention in the economy?
Consider with specific reference to the following three areas of policy:
railroad land grants, control of interstate commerce, and antitrust
activities.

Document A
"Economically, it will ever remain true, that the government is best which governs
least. The wants of a people are the sole proper, the sole possible, motives for
production. Nothing can be substituted for them. Anything that seems to take their
place is merely a debasement of them. The interests of producers, whether laborers or
capitalists, secure, better than any other possible means, the gratification of such
wants."

Amasa Walker, an American economist,
The Science of Wealth: A Manual
of Political Economy (1866)

Document B
"Let us inquire for a moment what are the proper functions of government, and how
far, if at all, it may interfere with the natural laws governing commerce, manufactures,
and agriculture. Legitimate functions of government I conceive to be to maintain
domestic tranquillity, defend the people from invasion, and protect them when

---

[*] Source: J. Niven (1978/1979), from Grading the Advanced Placement Examination
in American History by J. Niven. Copyright © 1979 by College Entrance
Examination Board. Reprinted by permission.

traveling . . . to which may be added a few other functions of kindred nature, leaving the individual enterprise untrammeled. For that purpose we maintain an Army, Navy, and civil courts. When these general functions are exceeded the result is generally injurious to the Government. It is better always to leave individual enterprise to do most that is to be done in the country."

> Daniel Knowlton, a New York City merchant,
> testimony before the Senate Committee on
> Education and Labor (September 27, 1883)

school-leaving examinations taken by students at sixteen and eighteen years of age, there have been recent experiments with the use of extended project reports as part of the formal assessment system. The Manchester Joint Matriculation Board's Engineering Science Examination, for example, includes both experimental investigations and extended applied projects as part of the assessment portfolio (Joint Matriculation Board 1982). Candidates conduct experiments or investigative projects (on topics such as measuring strain in a model suspension bridge, estimating the volume of water flowing in a river, designing and building a device for evaluating sound-insulating properties of common building materials) over several months and submit reports on their plans, execution, outcome, and interpretation to the examining board. These reports are rated on each of several criteria (for example, theoretical understanding, planning, design, use of procedures and equipment, possible alternative solutions considered, quality of the written report), and ratings are averaged to yield an overall grade for each candidate.

Project examinations of this type approach the kinds of portfolio assessments discussed in Gardner's chapter in this volume. In England, a system of *moderation,* in which examination questions, scoring criteria, and samples of graded exam papers are checked by individuals from associated institutions who are expert in the field but have no stake in the outcome of a particular examination, is a regular part of the assessment process. This, together with the practice of publishing reports on examinations and grading standards, serves to maintain consensus on standards within an open-ended system (Christie and Forrest 1989).

The Advanced Placement Tests and the Engineering Science Examination just described are equivalent to first-year college course examinations and are intended for only a fraction of the secondary school population. Performance assessments are, however, equally suitable for younger and broader populations of students. In this country, the National Assessment of Educational Progress has studied the feasibility of using open-ended exercises to assess higher-order thinking in science and mathematics at grades three, seven, and eleven (Blumberg et al. 1986; NAEP 1987). These assessment exercises included written responses to problems; "station activities" in which individual students used equipment to investigate a phenomenon and then answered open-ended questions about it; and complete experiments that students designed, carried out, and reported orally. Figures 2 and 3 show examples of some of the exercises used with the third- and seventh-graders. Some of the exercises could be graded on the basis of students' written answers—their *products*. Others required observers to rate the *processes* students revealed as they worked. In both cases, graders had to be trained to apply common criteria and standards.

FIGURE 2
A Science Performance Exercise with Sample Responses

Activity Identification: Whirlybird
Grade(s): 3, 7
Method of Administration: Group Activity
Content Area: Science-Physics
Apparatus Required: "Whirlybird" apparatus, 6 ball bearings of equal mass and volume, spare rubber bands and a spare ball bearing.

Group   Activity- 3, 7
        (to be read by the *A*)

The piece of equipment in front of you is called a Whirlybird. This part of it is called the Whirlybird arm (*A* should point towards the arm). If you look at the arm closely you will see that it has three holes on each side.

I am going to put the steel balls on different holes to see what happens when I wind the arm three times and let go.

When I have finished, I will ask you to answer the question on the paper in front of you. "What was different about the way the Whirlybird arm moved when the steel balls were in the different holes?"

Look what happens when I put the steel balls in the outside pair of holes and wind the arm three times. Now I am going to let go of the arm. Watch carefully.

Now I am going to move the steel balls to the middle pair of holes and wind up the arm three times. Watch what happens as the arm unwinds.

Now I'm going to move the steel balls to the inside pair of holes. Watch carefully as the arm unwinds.

I am going to do the experiment all over again. You may want to jot down some notes about what you see happen when the steel balls are moved to different holes.

(*A* should repeat the experiment and then give the following instructions.)

Now answer the question in front of you. The question is "What was different about the way the Whirlybird arm moved when the steel balls were in the different holes?" Think back on how the Whirlybird arm acted.

Score 3 pts. for a response that accurately describes how the Whirlybird moved in relation to the positioning of the ball bearings in the holes.

Score 2 pts. for a response that describes how the Whirlybird moved but doesn't specify the relationship between the position of the holes and the speed of the Whirlybird arm (e.g. It moved faster the second time.).

Score 1 pt. for an incorrect or irrelevant statement about what happens as the ball bearings were moved to different holes.

Score 0 for no response.

Skills involved: In this exercise students need to infer a relationship between two variables based on their observations.

Sample Response Sheet

1. Watch as the teacher does the experiment.
   Watch the "Whirlybird" arm carefully each time until it stops.

   (1) The ball bearings were put in the two outside holes. The "Whirlybird" arm was wound up *exactly* three times and let go.
   (2) The ball bearings were put in the next two holes. The arm was wound up *exactly* three times and let go.
   (3) The ball bearings were put in the next two holes. The arm was wound up *exactly* three times and let go.

   > What was different about the way the Whirlybird arm moved when the steel balls were in the different holes?

   (A)   Use this space to jot down notes about what you see happen when the steel balls are moved to different holes.

   (B)   Use this space to write down your answer to the question in the box.

   _____

   _____

   _____

   _____

Sample Third Grade Answers
Score Point 3

   (B)   Use this space to write down your answer to the question in the box.

   _____

   _____

(B)   Use this space to write down your answer to the question in the box.

Sample Third Grade Answers (continued)

(B)   Use this space to write down your answer to the question in the box.

Source: F. Blumberg et al. (1986).

Figure 3
A Math Performance Exercise with Sample Responses

3. Joe, Sarah, José, Zabi, and Kim decided to hold their own Olympics after watching
   the Olympics on TV. They needed to decide what events to have at their Olympics.
   Joe and José wanted a weight lifting and a frisbee toss event. Sarah, Zabi, and Kim
   thought a running event would be fun. The children decided to have all three events.
   They also decided to make each event of the same importance.

   One day after school they held their Olympics. The children's mothers were the
   judges. The mothers kept the children's scores on each of the events.

   The children's scores for each of the events are listed below:

Child's Name	Frisbee Toss	Weight Lift	50-yard Dash
Joe	40 yards	205 pounds	9.5 seconds
José	30 yards	170 poinds	8.0 seconds
Kim	45 yards	130 pounds	9.0 seconds
Sarah	28 yards	120 pounds	7.6 seconds
Zabi	48 yards	140 pounds	8.3 seconds

   (A)   Who would be the all-around winner?

   (B)   Explain how you decided who would be the all-around winner.

Be sure to show all your work.

_____

_____

_____

Sample Seventh Grade Answers
Score Point 4

(A)   Who would be the all-around winner?

_____

(B)   Explain how you decided who would be the all-around winner.
Be sure to show all your work.

_____

_____

_____

_____

(A)   Who would be the all-around winner?

_____

(B)   Explain how you decided who would be the all-around winner.
Be sure to show all your work.

_____

_____

_____

_____

(A)   Who would be the all-around winner?

_____

(B)   Explain how you decided who would be the all-around winner.
               Be sure to show all your work.

               _____

               _____

               _____

               _____

Source: F. Blumberg et al. (1986).

Videotaping of performances, a technology now inexpensive and reliable enough
for widespread use, could in the future substantially simplify grading when direct
observation is necessary. Indeed, the ease of videotaping makes it possible to
imagine a wide variety of assessments in which one examiner interviews a
student in a manner designed to probe understanding and thinking abilities, and a
different set of graders scores the performances. We are experimenting with this
form of assessment in a primary grades mathematics project (Resnick, Bill, and
Lesgold 1989). In one kind of assessment interview, a child is asked to solve an
arithmetic problem and to explain its solution. Figure 4, at the top, shows a
multiplication solution worked out by a seven-and-a-half-year-old who had not
yet been taught the multiplication tables. He explained that since three 3s make
9, taking the result of 3 x 6 three times would yield the answer to a 9 x 6
problem. In some of our interviews, the child is next shown an alternative
solution procedure, such as the one at the bottom of the figure, and asked
whether it too could be correct and how it is that two different solutions could
yield the same answers. Performances of this kind can be graded on multiple
criteria. For example, we rate performances on the sophistication of the
procedure,[6] the completeness of the explanation, whether the child explains the
solution conceptually or only procedurally, and whether the child produces the
explanation spontaneously or needs to be questioned or prompted by the
examiner. A very rich picture emerges from these multiple codings, which is
what we need for our current research work. But these multiple ratings could
easily be reduced to reliable single scores in order to use these interview results
for public accountability purposes.

      If widely adopted as part of the public accountability assessment system
in education, performance assessments (including portfolio methods) could not
only remove current pressures for teaching isolated collections of facts and skills,
but also provide a positive stimulus for introducing more extended thinking and

FIGURE 4
Two Problem Solutions in an Arithmetic Performance Assessment

Solution Generated by Child

$9 \times 6 = ?$

––––––––––––

$3 \times 6 = 18$
$18 \times 2 = 36$
$36 + 18 = 54$

––––––––––––

$9 \times 6 = 54$

Alternative Solution

$9 \times 6 = ?$

––––––––––––

$6 + 6 = 12$
$12 + 12 = 24$
$24 + 24 = 48$
$48 + 6 = 54$

––––––––––––

$9 \times 6 = 54$

reasoning activities in the curriculum. A decision to adopt performance assessment methods would require educators to describe more precisely what kinds of thinking performances are desired and what the criteria of excellent performance are in each case. The first critical step in developing performance assessments is to decide what kinds of performances are valued. This has been relatively easy to do for writing assessments because a broad (although not unanimous) consensus on the nature of well-crafted essays exists among educators and the general public. In other fields—such as mathematical and scientific thinking, reasoning in the social sciences, or the language arts other than written composition—defining the critical performances that should be assessed is more difficult, largely because educators have had little practice in such educational goal definition. For decades, professional discourse on educational objectives has been so shaped by the assumptions of standardized testing—decomposition of domains of skill and knowledge into independent components; decontextualized measurement of these components; correct responses defined in advance—that terms for discussing the nature of complex, coherent, and contextualized academic performance barely exist. We need a new discourse, shaped by the demands of choosing performance contexts for assessment and developing judgment criteria. At least one state has begun this process, with positive effects on the ways in which task forces of educators now discuss criteria for thinking performances in different subject matters.

Once introduced, performance assessments will also assure a continuing forum for refining objectives and criteria for the thinking curriculum. There is good evidence for this in the experience of states that have used writing assessments for a few years. In those states, educators are beginning to discuss whether the kinds of essays students are asked to write adequately reflect educational goals for writing. They are questioning, for example, whether the current assessments adequately sample the range of writing genres, whether extended writing assessments should be tied to social studies or science curricula, and whether students' abilities to revise and rewrite for different audiences can be assessed. These debates make it clear that current writing assessments are only first steps toward reform. What is most striking, though, is that the debates are primarily about curriculum and learning goals, not about techniques of assessment. For example, in one instance, the main problem encountered in introducing an essay assessment in social studies was not the difficulty of setting topics or grading students' work in the context of public accountability, but that there had been little or no writing practice in social studies classrooms, so students performed at distressingly low levels on essay assessments in social studies. Those engaged in these discussions had no doubt that, within a few years of instituting essay assessments in social studies, the amount of time spent writing in those classrooms would be increased. What was under debate was whether that would be a profitable way of spending limited social studies instructional time. This case illustrates the ways in which performance and portfolio assessments would positively affect discussions of curriculum and educational goals.

Using performance assessments as part of public accountability programs would require that students' performances be evaluated by panels of judges other than the students' own teachers. These judges must, of course, be trained to apply agreed-upon criteria for performance; this training would ensure adequate degrees of agreement among the judges and make it possible to derive reliable, unbiased scores from a set of individual judgments. Strategies for training judges, assessing interjudge reliabilities, and maintaining reliabilities through periodic sessions in which judges review and discuss each others' ratings have been developed by various groups that have long used open-ended performance assessments in education. These include the several Public Examination Boards in England and Wales and the Advanced Placement Testing program of the Educational Testing Service in the United States, along with the NAEP and states that have introduced open-ended writing assessments. Experiences of these groups suggest that if the judging panels are composed of teachers (as is likely), the training and continuing review sessions can serve as important sites for ongoing staff development. Teachers who have served on judging panels often report finding the training and review sessions very important in their professional lives. Many find that the experience helps them develop and refine criteria for their own classroom work. Recognizing this, some school districts involved in performance assessment programs are discussing possibilities for using the training sessions as part of their staff development programs. Although it is too early for definitive evidence, experience to date suggests that participation in judging and grading performance assessments can serve an important role in the general upgrading of educational standards.

One objection to performance assessments that is frequently raised is their high cost relative to the machine-scorable tests now in use. For each student assessed, performance assessments undoubtedly are more costly than current precoded tests. This is because multiple judges are needed every time the assessment is given. In the case of public accountability assessment, the costs of a full assessment *program* can be kept within tolerable bounds by testing less frequently and sampling more lightly than is the case in many current, mandated testing programs. As we have noted in our discussion of the various functions of testing, accountability testing need not be frequent or examine every student. An educational *system*, not individual students, is being evaluated in accountability assessment.

Various schemes for light sampling have been developed in which only some students are examined, or in which all students in a given grade are examined but individuals take only a portion of the examination. Considerable technical, statistical sophistication is needed to determine what justifiable inferences about student competencies can be made from different sampling procedures. These issues are receiving continuing attention from certain states, from the NAEP, and from commissions and study panels devoted to questions of assessment practice. Thus, a scientifically sound basis exists for controlling costs by reducing the amount of testing, rather than by insisting on cheap-to-administer, precoded forms of testing. To benefit from light sampling methods, states and other educational authorities will have to resist the temptation to combine accountability assessment with other testing functions requiring data on individual students, such as instructional monitoring, or student selection and certification. Accountability assessments should not attempt to offer diagnostic or other instructional management information. Such efforts will drive up the costs of open-ended performance assessments, creating pressures to return to multiple-choice tests. In any case, as we have noted, large-scale assessments cannot be expected to provide the kind of quick turnaround that teachers require for test-based information to be useful to them in guiding instructional decisions.

Although attempts to combine several functions in a single testing program are not advisable, performance assessments can also be used for selection/certification and instructional management. Selection and certification testing, although it requires examination of individual students, needs to be done only once or twice in a student's educational career, keeping costs of performance assessment within bounds. For college selection, the additional costs might even be included in the usual testing fee. In the case of instructional management testing, it is perfectly acceptable—even desirable in many cases—for the students' own instructors to grade and interpret their performances. While this may take more of an instructional staff's time than sending multiple-choice tests through a machine-scoring process, the time spent is directly relevant to the instructional process and should, as we have suggested, help to focus instructional efforts on the quality of students' thinking and reasoning.

Performance assessments are, then, a feasible and attractive solution to the problems we have laid out in the course of this chapter. Properly developed and implemented, they allow for reliable measurement of thinking and reasoning in school subject-matters. They offer a way to release educators from the pressures toward fractionated, low-level forms of learning rewarded by most current tests. They can also set positive standards for an educational system that aims to cultivate thinking. In an earlier paper based on comparative studies of testing and examination systems in three countries, we made a distinction between *tests* and *examinations* (Resnick and Resnick 1984). *Tests* are instruments only loosely linked to what is taught in school; *examinations* are instruments tied to the curriculum that guide and channel teachers' and students' efforts in school, and provide incentives for particular forms of academic work. We concluded then that American students are over-tested and under-examined. The performance assessments advocated here represent a move toward examinations that can profitably shape school activity. Tied to curriculum and designed to be taught-to, performance assessments can become essential tools in educational reform.

NOTES

1. We would like to thank Jennifer Walter, research assistant, for her help in making this analysis. Ramsay Selden, Director, State Education Assessment Center, Council of Chief State School Officers, helped us to survey the state-level assessment programs and collect specimen assessment instruments.

2. In the past ten years, two major studies of the National Research Council have examined selection testing in education. In one (Wigdor and Garner 1982), issues in selection for higher education were considered alongside selection testing for jobs in both the public and private sectors. In the second (Heller, Holtzman, and Messick 1982), the use of tests for placement in special education was reviewed.

3. On Rice, see Patricia Graham (1966); G. L. Noble (1970); and R. Venezky (1980). Rice's articles on spelling began to appear in the *Forum* in 1897.

4. Eight states use the Stanford Achievement Test, five use the Iowa Test of Basic Skills, four the Metropolitan Achievement Test, six the Comprehensive Test of Basic

Skills, and four the California Achievement Test. Most other states use tests they developed; these customized tests, with some exceptions to be discussed later, are modeled on the standard batteries.

5. That is, they do not provide scores that compare students with one another, but rather describe students in terms of the number and type of specific instructional objectives that they can meet, as represented in test items.

6. The performance at the top of the figure is more sophisticated because it composes multiplications, whereas the one at the bottom composes additions only.

REFERENCES

American College Testing Program. 1973. *Assessing students on the way to college.* Vol. 1. Iowa City: ACT Publications.

Anderson, J. R. 1983. *The architecture of cognition.* Cambridge, MA: Harvard University Press.

Angoff, W. H., ed. 1971. *The College Board Admissions Testing Program: A technical report on research and development activities relating to the Scholastic Aptitude Test and Achievement Tests.* New York: College Entrance Examination Board.

Blumberg, F., M. Epstein, W. MacDonald, and I. Mullis. 1986. *A pilot study of higher-order thinking skills assessment techniques in science and mathematics.* Final report. Princeton, NJ: National Assessment of Educational Progress.

Bransford, J. D. 1979. *Human cognition: Learning, understanding, and remembering.* Belmont, CA: Wadsworth.

Bransford, J. D., and N. J. Vye. 1989. A perspective on cognitive research and its implications for instruction. In *Toward the thinking curriculum: Current cognitive research. 1989 ASCD Yearbook,* ed. L. B. Resnick and L. E. Klopfer, 173–205. Alexandria, VA: Association for Supervision and Curriculum Development.

Brown, A. L. 1978. Knowing when, where, and how to remember: A problem of metacognition. In *Advances in instructional psychology,* ed. R. Glaser, vol.1, 77–165. Hillsdale, NJ: Erlbaum.

Callahan, R. 1962. *Education and the cult of efficiency.* Chicago: University of Chicago Press.

Chapman, P. D. 1989. *Schools as sorters: Lewis M. Terman, applied psychology, and the intelligence testing movement, 1890–1930.* New York: New York University Press.

Christie, T., and G. M. Forrest. 1980. *Standards at GCE A-level: 1963 and 1973.* London: Macmillan Education.

Cohen, S. A. 1987. Instructional alignment: Searching for a magic bullet. *Educational Researcher* 16 (8): 16–20.

Deffenbaugh, W. S. 1926. *Uses of intelligence and achievement tests in 215 cities.* U.S. Bureau of Education, City School Leaflet No. 20. Washington, DC: U.S. Department of the Interior.

Driver, R., E. Guesne, and A. Tiberghien. 1985. *Children's ideas in science.* Philadelphia: Open University Press.

Frederiksen, J. R., and A. Collins. In press. *A systems theory of educational testing.* Cambridge, MA: BBN Laboratories.

Fuhrman, S. 1988. Educational indicators: An overview. *Phi Delta Kappan* 69 (7): 486–87.

Glaser, R. 1987. The integration of instruction and testing: Implications from the study of human cognition. In *Talks to teachers*, ed. D. C. Berliner and B. V. Rosenshine, 329–41. New York: Random House.

Graham, P. 1966. Joseph Mayer Rice as a founder of the progressive education movement. *Journal of Educational Measurement* 3:129–33.

Heller, K. A., W. H. Holtzman, and S. Messick, eds. 1982. *Placing children in special education: A strategy for equity*. Washington, DC: National Academy Press.

Jeffreys, J. R. 1978. *Education for children of the poor: A study of the origins and implementation of the Elementary and Secondary Education Act of 1965.* Columbus, OH: Ohio State University Press.

Joint Matriculation Board, Examinations Council. 1982. *General Certificate of Education: Engineering science (advanced) instructions and guidance for centres*. Manchester, England: Author.

Just, M. A., and P. A. Carpenter. 1987. *The psychology of reading and language comprehension*. Rockleigh, NJ: Allyn and Bacon.

Kellaghan, T., G. F. Madaus, and P. W. Airasian. 1980. *The effects of standardized testing*. Dublin/Boston: St. Patrick's College/Boston College.

Kevles, D. J. 1968. Testing the army's intelligence: Psychologists and the military in World War I. *Journal of American History* 55:565–81.

Lakatos, I. 1978. The methodology of scientific research programmes. In *Philosophical papers,* ed. J. Worrall and J. Currie, vol. 1. New York: Cambridge University Press.

Leinhardt, G., and A. M. Seewald. 1981. Overlap: What's tested, what's taught? *Journal of Educational Measurement* 18 (2): 85–96.

Monroe, W. S. 1918. Existing tests and standards. *Seventeenth yearbook of the National Society for the Study of Education*. Part 2. Bloomington, IN: Public School Publishing Company.

Murnane, R. J., and S. A. Raizen, eds. 1988. *Improving indicators of the quality of science and mathematics education in grades K–12*. Washington, DC: National Academy Press.

National Assessment of Educational Progress. 1987. *Learning by doing: A manual for teaching and assessing higher-order thinking in science and mathematics*. Report 17-HOS-80. Princeton, NJ: Educational Testing Service.

National Council of Teachers of Mathematics. 1989. *Curriculum and evaluation standards for school mathematics*. Reston, VA: Author.

National Research Council. 1989. *Everybody counts—A report to the nation on the future of mathematics education*. Washington, DC: National Academy Press.

Newell, A., and H. A. Simon. 1972. *Human problem solving*. Englewood Cliffs, NJ: Prentice-Hall.

Nitko, A. J. 1989. Designing tests that are integrated with instruction. In *Educational measurement*. 3d ed., ed. R. L. Linn, 447–74. New York: American Council on Education/Macmillan.

Niven, J. 1978/1979. *Grading the advanced placement examination in American history*. Princeton, NJ: College Entrance Examination Board.

Noble, G. L. 1970. Joseph Mayer Rice: Critic of the public schools and pioneer in educational measurement. Ph.D. diss., State University of New York (SUNY) at Buffalo.

Perfetti, C. A. 1985. *Reading ability*. New York: Oxford University Press.

Popham, W. J. 1987. The merits of measurement-driven instruction. *Phi Delta Kappan* 68 (9): 679–82.

Resnick, D. P. 1982. History of educational testing. In *Ability testing: Uses, consequences, and controversies. Part II: Documentation section*, ed. A. K. Wigdor and W. R. Garner, 173–94. Washington, DC: National Academy Press.

Resnick, D. P., and L. B. Resnick. 1984. Standards, curriculum, and performance: A historical and comparative perspective. *Educational Researcher* 14 (4): 5–20.

Resnick, L. B. 1987. *Education and learning to think*. Washington, DC: National Academy Press.

Resnick, L. B. 1989. Developing mathematical knowledge. *American Psychologist* 44 (2): 162–69.

Resnick, L. B., V. Bill, and S. Lesgold. 1989. Developing thinking abilities in arithmetic class. Paper presented at the Third European Conference for Research on Learning and Instruction, September, Madrid.

Romberg, T. A., E. A. Zarinnia, and S. Williams. 1989. *The influence of mandated testing on mathematics instruction: Grade 8 teachers' perceptions*. National Center for Research in Mathematical Science Education, University of Wisconsin-Madison.

Scribner, S. 1984. Studying working intelligence. In *Everyday cognition: Its development in social context*, ed. B. Rogoff and J. Lave, 9–40. Cambridge, MA: Harvard University Press.

Shepard, L. A. 1988. Should instruction be measurement-driven: A debate. Paper presented at the meeting of the American Educational Research Association, April, New Orleans.

Shepard, L. A. 1989. Why we need better assessments. *Educational Leadership* 46 (7): 4–9.

Thorndike, E. L. 1922. *The psychology of arithmetic*. New York: Macmillan.

Toulmin, S. E. 1972. *Human understanding*. Princeton, NJ: Princeton University Press.

Venezky, R. 1980. From Webster to Rice to Roosevelt: The formative years for spelling instruction and spelling reform in the USA. In *Cognitive processes in spelling*, ed. Uta Frith, 10–30. New York: Academic Press.

Wigdor, A. K., and W. R. Garner, eds. 1982. *Ability testing: Uses, consequences, and controversies. Part II: Documentation section*. Washington, DC: National Academy Press.

Wise, A. E. 1979. *Legislated learning: The bureaucratization of the American classroom*. Berkeley and Los Angeles: University of California Press.

Zuboff, S. 1988. *In the age of the smart machine: The future of work and power*. New York: Basic Books.

Assessment in Context:
The Alternative to Standardized Testing

Howard Gardner *

CONTRASTING MODELS OF ASSESSMENT

A familiar scene almost anywhere in the United States today: Several hundred students file into a large examination hall. They sit nervously, waiting for sealed packets to be handed out. At the appointed hour, booklets are distributed, brief instructions are issued, and formal testing begins. The hall is still as students at each desk bear down on number two pencils and fill in the bubbles which punctuate the answer sheets. A few hours later, the testing ends and the booklets are collected; several weeks later, a sheet bearing a set of scores arrives at each student's home and at the colleges to which the students have directed their scores. The results of a morning's testing become a powerful factor in decisions about the future of each student.

An equally familiar scene in most pre-industrial societies over the centuries: A youth of ten or eleven moves into the home of a man who has mastered a trade. Initially, the lad is asked to carry out menial tasks as he helps the master to prepare for his work or to clean up the shop at the end of the day. During this initial phase, the lad has the opportunity to watch the master at work, while the master monitors the youth to discover his special talents or serious flaws. Over the months the apprentice slowly enters into the practice of the trade. After initially aiding in the more peripheral aspects of the trade, he eventually gains familiarity with the full gamut of skilled work. Directed by tradition, but also guided by the youth's particular skills and motivation, the master guides his charge through the various steps from novice to journeyman. Finally, after several years of supervised training, the youth is ready to practice the craft on his own.

---

* Research described in this chapter has been supported by the Grant Foundation, the Lilly Endowment, the Markle Foundation, the McDonnell Foundation, the Rockefeller Foundation, the Spencer Foundation, the Van Leer Foundation, and the U.S. Center for Technology in Education of the Bank Street College of Education. For their comments on earlier drafts of this manuscript, I am indebted to Bernard Gifford, Drew Gitomer, Catherine O' Connor, Robert Sternberg, and Joseph Walters.

While both of these scenes are idealized, they should be readily recognizable to anyone concerned with the assessment and training of young people. Indeed, they may be said to represent two extremes. The first "formal testing" model is conceived of as an objective, decontextualized form of assessment which can be adopted and implemented widely, with some assurance that similar results will be obtained. The second "apprenticeship" model is implemented almost entirely within a naturally occurring context in which the particularities of a craft are embedded. The assessment is based upon a prior analysis of the skills involved in a particular craft, but it may also be influenced by subjective factors, including the master's personal views about his apprentice, his relationship with other masters, or his need for other kinds of services.

It should be evident that these two forms of assessment were designed to meet different needs. Apprenticeships made sense when the practice of various crafts was the major form of employment for non-rural youths. Formal testing is a contemporary means of comparing the performance of thousands of students who are being educated in schools. Yet these forms of assessment are not limited to the two prototypical contexts described above. Despite the overwhelmingly agrarian nature of Chinese society, formal tests have been used there for over two thousand years in selecting government officials. And, by the same token, in many art forms, athletic practices, and areas of scientific research (Polanyi 1958), apprenticeships and the concomitant ongoing, context-determined forms of assessment continue to be used in our highly industrialized society.

Thus, the choice of "formal testing" as opposed to "apprenticeship" is not dictated solely by the historical era or the primary means of production in the society. It would be possible in our society to utilize the apprenticeship method to a much greater extent than we do. Most observers today (myself included) do not lament the passage of the obligatory apprenticeship system, with its frequent excesses and blatant sexism; from several points of view, contemporary formal testing represents a fairer and more easily justifiable form of assessment. And yet, aspects of the apprentice model are consistent with current knowledge about how individuals learn and how their performances might best be assessed.

Our society has embraced the formal testing mode to an excessive degree; I contend that aspects of the apprentice model of learning and assessment—which I term "contextualized learning"—could be profitably reintroduced into our educational system (see Collins, Brown, and Newman, in press). Following an account of the origins of standardized testing and the one-dimensional view of mentation often implied by such testing methods, I review several lines of evidence from the cognitive, neural, and developmental sciences which point to a far more capacious view of the human mind and of human learning than that which informed earlier conceptions.

Our task here is to envision forms of education and modes of assessment which have a firm rooting in current scientific understanding and which contribute to enlightened educational goals. In the latter half of the chapter I describe in general terms the characteristics of these novel forms of assessment. I then introduce educational experiments in which my colleagues and I have become engaged, at levels from preschool to college admissions. These educational experiments demonstrate alternative ways in which information relevant to guidance and selection could be obtained. I conclude with a description and endorsement of a possible "individual-centered" school-of-the-future, in which the lines between assessment and curriculum, students and disciplines, school and community are newly drawn. Such a school can be fashioned within a society that spurns standardized-testing-in-isolation and favors assessment-in-context.

BINET, THE TESTING SOCIETY, AND THE "UNIFORM" VIEW OF SCHOOLING

The widespread use of formal testing can be traced to the work on intelligence testing carried out in Paris at the turn of the century by Alfred Binet and his colleagues. Binet was asked by city educational leaders to assist in determining which students would succeed, and which would likely fail, in elementary school (Binet and Simon 1905; Block and Dworkin 1976). He hit upon the inspired idea of administering a large set of items to young school children and identifying which of the items proved most discriminating in light of his particular goal. The work carried out by the Binet team ultimately led to the first intelligence tests, and the construct of intelligence quotient, or IQ.

So great was the appeal of the Binet method that it soon became a dominant feature of the American educational and assessment landscape. To be sure, some standardized tests—ranging from the California Achievement Tests to the Scholastic Aptitude Test—are not direct outgrowths of the various intelligence tests. And yet it is difficult to envision the proliferation of these instruments over just a few decades without the widely esteemed examples of the Stanford-Binet, the Army Alpha, and the various Wechsler intelligence instruments (Brown and Herrnstein 1975).

In the United States especially, with its focus on quantitative markers and its cult of educational efficiency, there has been a virtual mania for producing tests for every possible social purpose (Gould 1981; Hoffmann 1962). In addition to standardized tests for students, we have such tests for teachers, supervisors, soldiers, and police officers; we use adaptations of these instruments to assess capacities not only in standard areas of the curriculum but also in civics and the arts; and we can draw on short-answer measures for assessing personality, degrees of authoritarianism, and compatibility for dating. The United States is well on the way to becoming a "complete testing society." We could encapsulate this attitude thus: If something is important, it is worth testing in this way; if it cannot be so tested, then it probably ought not to be valued. Few observers have stopped to consider the domains in which such an approach might *not* be relevant or optimal, and most have forgotten the insights which might be gained from modes of assessment favored in an earlier era.

It is risky to attempt to generalize across the thousands of "formal instruments" which are described in books like the Buros's (1978) *Mental Measurements Yearbook*. Yet, at the cost of doing some violence to certain instruments, it is worth indicating the features which are typically associated with such instruments.

There is within the testing profession considerable belief in "raw," possibly genetically based potential (Eysenck 1967; Jensen 1980). The most highly valued tests, such as IQ tests and the SATs, are thought to measure ability or potential performance. There is no necessary reason why a test cannot assess skills which have been learned, and many "achievement" tests purport to do this. Yet, for tests that purport to measure raw ability or potential, it is important that performance cannot be readily improved by instruction; otherwise, the test would not be a valid indicator of ability. Most authorities on testing believe that performance on ability and achievement tests reflects inherent capacities.

Adherents of testing also tend to embrace a view of human development which assumes that a young organism contains less knowledge and exhibits less skill than a more mature organism, but that no qualitative changes occur over time in human mind or behavior (Bijou and Baer 1965). Making such assumptions enables the testmaker to use the same kinds of instruments for individuals of all ages; and he or she can legitimately claim that descriptions of data at a certain point in development can be extended to later ages, because one is dealing with the same kind of scale and the same property of mind or behavior. Thus the makers of a test called the QT (Quick Test) claim in a regularly run advertisement that their instrument "handles two-year-olds and superior adults within the same short series of items and the same format."

Reflecting general American technological pressures, as well as the desire for elegance and economy, most testmakers and buyers place a premium on instruments which are efficient, brief, and can be readily administered. In the early days of testing, assessment sometimes took hours and was individually administered; now, group-administered instruments are desired. Virtually every widely used test has spawned a "brief" version. Indeed, some of the staunchest supporters of formal intelligence tests hope to strip them down even further: Arthur Jensen (1987) has embraced "reaction time" measures, Michael Anderson (1987) looks to sensory discrimination, and Hans Eysenck (1979) has called for the examination of patterns of brain waves.

Accompanying a fealty to formal testing is a view of education which I have termed the "uniform view of schooling." This view does not necessarily entail the wearing of uniforms, but it does call for homogenized education in other respects. According to the uniform view, as much as possible students should study the same subject matter. (This may include a strong dosage of the values of the dominant culture or subculture—see Bloom 1987; Hirsch 1987;

Ravitch and Finn 1987). Moreover, as much as possible that subject matter ought to be conveyed in the same way to all students.

In the uniform view, progress in school ought to be assessed by frequent formal tests. These tests should be administered under uniform conditions, and students, teachers, and parents should receive quantitative scores which detail the student's progress or lack thereof. These tests should be nationally normed instruments, so that the maximum comparability is possible. The most important subject matters are those which lend themselves readily to such assessment, such as mathematics and science. In other subjects, value is assigned to the aspects which can be efficiently assessed (grammar rather than "voice" in writing; facts rather than interpretation in history). Those disciplines which prove most refractory to formal testing, such as the arts, are least valued in the uniform school.

In putting forth this picture of Binet, the testing society, and the uniform view of schooling, I am aware that I am overemphasizing certain tendencies and lumping together views and attitudes in a way which is not entirely fair to those who are closely associated with formal testing. Some individuals intimately involved with testing have voiced the same concerns (Cronbach 1984; Messick 1988). Indeed, had I put this picture forth fifteen or twenty years ago it might have seemed an outrageous caricature. However, the trends within American education since the early 1980s bear a strong resemblance to the views I have just sketched. At the very least, these views serve as a necessary "contrast case" to the picture of contextualized and individualized assessment and schooling which I present later in the chapter; they should be taken in that contrastive spirit.

SOURCES FOR AN ALTERNATIVE APPROACH TO ASSESSMENT

While the testing society has responded more to pragmatic needs than to scientific dictates, it does reflect a certain view of human nature. The scientific ideas on which the testing society has been based derive from an earlier era in which behaviorist, learning theoretical, and associationist views of cognition and development were regnant (see Gardner 1985 for a summary). According to these views, it made sense to believe in "inborn" human abilities, in a smooth, probably linear curve of learning from infancy to old age, in a hierarchy of disciplines, and in the desirability of assessing potential and achievement under carefully controlled and maximally decontextualized conditions.

Over the past few decades, however, the various assumptions on which this testing edifice was based have been gradually undermined by work in developmental, cognitive, and educational studies, and a quite different view has emerged. It is not possible in this chapter to review all of the evidence on which this shifting psychological conception has been based. But because my alternative picture of assessment builds on the newly emerging picture of human development, it is important to highlight the principal features of this perspective and to indicate where it may clash with standard views of testing.

The Necessity for a Developmental Perspective

Owing to the pioneering work of Jean Piaget (1983), it is widely recognized that children are not simply miniature versions of adults. The infant or the toddler conceives of the world in a way which is internally consistent but which deviates in important particulars from a more mature conception. Here are some of the most familiar instances from the Piagetian canon: the infant does not appreciate that an object continues to exist when it has been removed from view; the toddler does not understand that material remains constant in quantity, even when its physical configuration has been altered (for example, squashing a ball of clay); the young school child is unable to reason solely from the implications of one proposition to another but instead proceeds on the basis of knowledge of concrete instances and perceived empirical regularities.

According to Piaget's view, children pass through a number of qualitatively different stages called sensori-motor, pre-operational, concrete operational, and formal operational. A child at one stage in one area of knowledge will necessarily be at the same stage in other domains of experience. Few investigators hold any longer to a literal version of this "structured-stage" perspective; there have been too many findings which do not support it (Brainerd 1978; Gelman 1978). But most developmental psychologists continue to subscribe to the point of view that the world of the infant or toddler has its own peculiar structures; many developmentalists believe that there are stage sequences within particular domains of experience (for example, language, moral judgment, understanding of physical causality); and nearly all emphasize the need to take into account the child's perspective and level of understanding (Case 1985; Feldman 1980; Fischer 1980).

Another feature of this approach is its assumption that development is neither smooth, nor unilinear, nor free of perturbations. While details differ among theorists, most researchers believe that there may be critical or sensitive periods during which it is especially easy—or especially difficult—to master certain kinds of materials. Similarly, while youngsters tend to improve in most areas with age, there will be periods of more rapid growth and periods of stasis. And a minority of researchers believes that in some domains there may actually be regressions or "U-shapes," with younger children performing in a more sophisticated or integrated fashion than students in middle childhood (Strauss 1982).

It is possible to construct measurement instruments which reflect the developmental knowledge recently accrued. In fact, some batteries have been devised which build specifically on Piagetian or allied notions (Uzgiris and Hunt

1966). For the most part, however, American tests have been insensitive to developmental considerations.

The Emergence of a Symbol-System Perspective

At the height of the behaviorist era there was no need to posit any kind of mental entity, such as an idea, a thought, a belief, or a symbol. One simply identified behaviors or actions of significance and observed these as scrupulously as possible; so-called thoughts were simply "silent" movements of musculature.

Over the past few decades, however, there has been increasing recognition of the importance in human cognition of the capacity to use various kinds of symbols and symbol systems (Gardner, Howard, and Perkins 1974; Goodman 1976; Langer 1942). Humans are deemed the creatures par excellence of communication, who garner meanings through words, pictures, gestures, numbers, musical patterns, and a whole host of other symbolic forms. The manifestations of these symbols are public: all can observe written language, number systems, drawings, charts, gestural languages, and the like. However, the mental processes needed to manipulate such symbols must be inferred from the performances of individuals on various kinds of tasks. Unexpectedly potent support for the belief in internal symbol-manipulation has come from the invention and widespread use of computers; if these human-made machines engage in operations of symbol use and transformation, it seems ludicrous to withhold the same kinds of capacities from the humans who invented them (Newell and Simon 1972).

Considerable effort has been expended in the relevant sciences to investigate the development of the human capacity for symbol use. It is widely (though not universally) agreed that infants do not use symbols or exhibit internal symbolic manipulation and that the emergence of symbol use during the second year of life is a major hallmark of human cognition. Thereafter, human beings rapidly acquire skill in the use of those symbols and symbol systems which are featured in their culture. By the age of five or six most children have acquired a "first draft" knowledge of how to create and understand stories, works of music, drawings, and simple scientific explanations (Gardner 1982).

In literate cultures, however, there is a second level of symbol use. Children must learn to utilize the *invented symbol* (or *notational*) systems of their culture, such as writing and numbers. With few exceptions, this assignment is restricted to school settings, which are relatively decontextualized. Mastering notational systems can be difficult for many students in our society, including students whose mastery of "practical knowledge" and "first-order symbol systems" has been unproblematic. Even those students who prove facile at acquiring notational systems face a non-trivial challenge: they must mesh their newly acquired "second-order" symbolic knowledge with the earlier forms of "practical" and "first-order" symbolic knowledge they brought with them to school (Bamberger 1982; Gardner 1986; Resnick 1987).

Nearly all formal tests presuppose that their users will be literate in the second-level symbol systems of the culture. These tests thus pose special difficulties for individuals who, for whatever reason, have had difficulty in attaining second-level symbol knowledge or cannot map that knowledge onto earlier forms of mental representation. Moreover, it is my belief that individuals with well-developed second-level symbolic skills can often "psyche out" such tests, scoring well even when their knowledge of the subject matter which is ostensibly being assessed is modest (Gardner 1983). At any rate, what the exact relations are which exist among "practical," "first-order," and "second-order" symbolic knowledge and the best way to assess these remain difficult issues to resolve.

Evidence for the Existence of Multiple Faculties or "Intelligences"

When intelligence tests were first assembled, there was little attention paid to the underlying theory of intelligence. But soon the idea gained currency that the different abilities being tapped all fed into or reflected a single "general intelligence." This perspective has remained the view-of-choice among most students of intelligence, though a minority has been open to the idea of different "vectors of mind" or different "products, content, and operations" of intellect (Guilford 1967; Thurstone 1938). This minority has based its conclusions on the results of factor analyses of test results; however, it has been shown that one can arrive at either unitary or pluralistic views of intellect, depending upon which assumptions guide factor analytic procedures (Gould 1981).

In recent years, there has been a resurgence of interest in the idea of a multiplicity of intelligences. Mental phenomena have been discovered that some researchers construe as evidence for mental *modules*—fast-operating, reflex-like, information-processing devices which seem impervious to the influence of other modules. The discovery of these modules has given rise to the view that there may be separate analytic devices involved in tasks like syntactic parsing, tonal recognition, or facial perception (Fodor 1983).

A second source of evidence for a multiplicity of intelligences has been the fine-grained analysis of the mental operations involved in the solution of items used in intelligence tests (Sternberg 1977, 1985). These analyses have suggested the existence of different components which contribute to success on any standard intellectual assessment. Individuals may differ from one another in the facility with which the different components operate, and different tasks may call upon a differential use of the various components, meta-components, and sub-components.

My proposal for a set of "multiple intelligences" (Gardner 1983, 1987a) has been prompted by a different set of considerations. Initially I was impressed in my research by two lines of findings: (1) normal children can distinguish themselves in one or two areas of performance with no predictive value about how they will perform in other areas and (2) brain-damaged individuals may lose capacities in one or two areas but otherwise appear to be as competent as before (Gardner 1975).

I subsequently surveyed research on the development of different capacities in normal children; the breakdown of these capacities under different varieties of brain damage; the existence in special populations of highly jagged cognitive profiles (prodigies, idiot savants, autistic children, individuals with learning disabilities); the sets of abilities found in individuals from different cultures; the evolution of cognition over the millenia in humans and in infra-human species; and two kinds of psychological evidence—correlations among psychometric tests and the results of studies of transfer and generalization of skills.

Pulling together the results of this massive survey, I isolated the existence of seven different mental faculties or intelligences. As outlined in *Frames of Mind: The Theory of Multiple Intelligences* (Gardner 1983), humans have evolved as a species to carry out at least seven kinds of computations or analyses: those involving language (linguistic intelligence, as exemplified by a poet); logical-mathematical analysis (in a scientist, mathematician, or logician); spatial representation (for instance, the painter, sculptor, architect, sailor, geometer, or engineer); musical analysis; bodily-kinesthetic thinking (for example, the dancer, athlete, mime, actor, surgeon, craftsman); and two forms of personal understanding—interpersonal knowledge (of other persons, as in a salesman, teacher, therapist, leader) and intrapersonal knowledge (the ability to know one's own desires, fears, and competences and to act productively on the basis of that knowledge).

According to my analysis, most formal testing—whatever the area that is allegedly being tested—engages primarily the linguistic and logical-mathematical faculties. If one has high linguistic and logical-mathematical intelligences, one is likely to do well in school and in formal testing. Poor endowment or learning in one or both of these intelligences is likely to result in poor standardized scores.

If life consisted solely of schooling, most formal tests would serve their purpose well—though last year's grades would fulfill the same predictive purposes equally well. Schooling, however, is supposed to be a preparation for life, and there is ample evidence that formal testing alone is an indifferent predictor for success once a student has left school (Jencks 1972).

I therefore call for assessment which is "intelligence-fair"—which looks *directly* at an individual's skills in areas such as music, spatial knowledge, or interpersonal understanding, rather than looking through the "window" of linguistic and/or logical-mathematical prowess. It is the desire for modes of assessment that can detect capacities in the other intelligences, even in the face of indifferent linguistic or logical-mathematical capacities, which animates much of the applied research program described below.

While my research documents that individuals differ from one another in the profile of intelligences which they exhibit, it is not clear how particular intelligences are distributed in the population. Indeed, in the absence of adequate measures of nonscholastic intelligences, quantitative questions about strength and distribution of intelligences cannot be answered at the present time. It cannot, therefore, be maintained a priori that each individual stands out in one or more intelligences or that every person has clear deficiencies as well as strengths. There may be individuals with potency in every intelligence, as well as others who have only "relative strengths" or "relative weaknesses." Still there is reason to think that, given a broader gamut of indexes, more individuals will emerge as competent on at least some measure and that such competence in turn can have beneficent effects on self-concept and on productivity.

Recognition of Vast Individual Differences

A consequence of the "multiple intelligence" perspective is the recognition that instead of a single dimension called intellect, on which individuals can be rank-ordered, there are vast differences among individuals in their intellectual strengths and weaknesses and also in their styles of attack in cognitive pursuits (Kagan and Kogan 1970). Our own evidence suggests that these differences may be evident even before the years of formal schooling.

The literature on different individual strengths, as well as the findings on diverse cognitive styles, has crucial educational implications. To begin with, it is important to identify strengths and weaknesses at an early point so that they can become part of educational planning. Striking differences among individuals also call into question whether individuals ought to all be taking the same curriculum and whether, to the extent that there is a uniform curriculum, it needs to be presented in the same fashion to all individuals.

Formal tests can be an ally to the recognition of different cognitive features, but only if the tests are designed to elicit—rather than mask—these differences (Cronbach and Snow 1977). It is particularly important that instruments used in "gatekeeping" niches (like college admissions) be designed to allow students to show their strengths and to perform optimally. Until now, little effort has been made in this regard and tests are more frequently used to point up weaknesses than to designate strengths.

A Search for Human Creative Capacities

During most of the first century of formal testing interest fell heavily on assessment of individual intelligence, and there was relatively little concern with other cognitive capacities. In the post-Sputnik era, when scientific ingenuity was suddenly at a premium, American educators became convinced of the importance of imaginativeness, inventiveness, and creativity. They called for the devising of instruments which would assess creativity or creative potential (Guilford 1950).

Regrettably (from my perspective), in their search for creativity measures they repeated most of the mistakes that had been made throughout the history of intelligence testing. That is, they tried to devise short-answer, timed measures of the abilities they thought central to creativity—the capacity to come up with a variety of answers to a question (divergent thinking) or to issue as many unusual associations as possible to a stimulus (ideational fluency).

While the field of intelligence testing is currently filled with controversy, there is consensus that creativity tests have not fulfilled their potential (Wallach 1971, 1985). These instruments are reliable, and they do measure something other than psychometric intelligence, but they cannot predict which individuals will be judged as creative on the basis of their productions within a domain. Rather than attempting to devise more and better "creativity tests," researchers have instead begun to examine more closely what actually happens when individuals are engaged in problem-solving or problem-finding activities (Gruber 1981; Sternberg 1988).

These recent studies have yielded two major findings. On the one hand, creative individuals do not seem to have at their disposal mental operations which are theirs alone; creative individuals make use of the same cognitive processes as do other persons, but they use them in a more efficient and flexible way and in the service of goals which are ambitious and often quite risky (Perkins 1981). On the other hand, highly creative individuals do seem to lead their lives in a way different from most others. They are fully engaged in and passionate about their work; they exhibit a need to do something new and have a strong sense of their purpose and ultimate goals; they are extremely reflective about their activities, their use of time, and the quality of their products (Gruber 1985).

Except rhetorically, the quest for creativity has not been a major goal of the American educational system. However, to the extent that the fostering of creative individuals is a desirable goal for an educational institution, it is important that this goal be pursued in a manner consistent with current analyses of creativity (Gardner 1988a). In some of the programs described in this chapter, an attempt is made to foster the kinds of personal habits which appear to be associated with creative individuals—rather than to engender the kinds of fluency which have typically been monitored in so-called creativity tests.

The Desirability of Assessing Learning in Context

When standardized tests and paradigmatic experimental designs were first introduced into non-Western cultural contexts, they led to a single result: pre-literate individuals and others from non-Western societies appeared to be much less skilled and much less intelligent than Western control groups. An interesting phenomenon was then discovered. Simple alterations of materials, test setting, or instructions frequently elicited dramatic improvements in performance. The "performance gap" between the subjects from another culture and the subjects from our own culture narrowed or even disappeared when familiar materials were used, when knowledgeable and linguistically fluent examiners were employed, when revised instructions were given, or when the "same" cognitive capacities were tapped in a form which made more sense within the non-Western context (Laboratory of Comparative Human Cognition 1982).

Now a huge body of experimental evidence exists to indicate that assessment materials designed for one target audience cannot be transported directly to another cultural setting; there are no purely culture-fair or culture-blind materials. Every instrument reflects its origins. Formal tests that make some sense in a Western context do so because students are accustomed to learn about materials at a site removed from the habitual application of such materials; however, in unschooled or lightly schooled environments, most instruction takes place in situ, and so it only makes sense to administer assessments which are similarly in context.

Building upon this cross-cultural research, there is also an accumulation of findings about the cognitive abilities of various kinds of experts. It has been shown that experts often fail on "formal" measures of their calculating or reasoning capacities but can be shown to exhibit precisely those same skills in the course of their ordinary work—such as tailoring clothes, shopping in a supermarket, loading dairy cases onto a truck, or defending one's rights in a dispute (Lave 1980; Rogoff 1982; Scribner 1986). In such cases, it is not the person who has failed but rather the measurement instrument which purported to document the person's level of competence.

Locating Competence and Skill
Outside the Head of the Individual

The research just reviewed has yielded another novel conceptualization. In many cases it is erroneous to conclude that the knowledge required to execute a task resides completely in the mind of a single individual. This knowledge can be "distributed": that is, successful performance of a task may depend upon a team of individuals, no single one of whom possesses all of the necessary expertise but all of whom, working together, are able to accomplish the task in a reliable way (Scribner 1984). Relatedly, it is too simple to say that an individual either "has" or "does not have" the requisite knowledge; that knowledge may show up reliably in the presence of the appropriate human and physical "triggers" but might be otherwise invisible to probing (Squire 1986).

It makes sense to think of human cognitive competence as an emerging capacity, one likely to be manifest at the intersection of three different constituents: the "individual," with his or her skills, knowledge, and aims; the structure of a "domain of knowledge," within which these skills can be aroused; and a set of institutions and roles—a surrounding "field"— which judges when a particular performance is acceptable and when it fails to meet specifications (Csikszentmihalyi 1988; Csikszentmihalyi and Robinson 1986; Gardner and

Wolf 1988). The acquisition and transmission of knowledge depends upon a dynamic which sustains itself among these three components. Particularly beyond the years of early childhood, human accomplishment presupposes an awareness of the different domains of knowledge in one's culture and the various "field forces" which affect opportunity, progress, and recognition. By focusing on the knowledge that resides within a single mind at a single moment, formal testing may distort, magnify, or grossly underestimate the contributions which an individual can make within a larger social setting.

The foregoing research findings point to a differentiated and nuanced view of assessment, one which, in at least certain ways, might more closely resemble traditional apprenticeship measures than formal testing. An assessment initiative being planned today, in light of these findings, should be sensitive to developmental stages and trajectories. Such an initiative should investigate human symbolic capacities in an appropriate fashion in the years following infancy and investigate the relationship between practical knowledge and first- and second-level symbolic skills. It should recognize the existence of different intelligences and of diverse cognitive and stylistic profiles, and it should incorporate an awareness of these variations into assessments; it should possess an understanding of those features which characterize creative individuals in different domains. Finally, a new assessment initiative should acknowledge the effects of context on performance and provide the most appropriate contexts in which to assess competences, including ones which extend outside the skin of the individual being assessed.

It is a tall order to meet all of these needs and desiderata. Indeed, an attraction of formal testing is that one can bracket or minimize most of the features which I have just outlined. However, if we seek an assessment which is both true to the individual and reflective of our best understanding of the nature of human cognition, then we cannot afford to ignore the lines of thinking which I have just outlined.

GENERAL FEATURES OF A NEW APPROACH TO ASSESSMENT

If one were to return to the drawing board today and lay out a fresh approach to assessment, one might attempt to incorporate the following principal features:

Emphasis on Assessment Rather Than Testing

The penchant for testing in America has gone too far. While some tests are useful for some purposes, the testing industry has taken off in a way which makes little sense from the point of view of a reflective society. Many who seek to understand the underlying theoretical or conceptual basis of findings of validity are disappointed. It seems that many tests have been designed to create, rather than to fulfill, a need.

While I have ambivalent feelings about testing, I have little ambivalence about assessment. To my mind, it is the proper mission of educated individuals, as well as those who are under their charge, to engage in regular and appropriate reflection on their goals, the various means to achieve them, their success (or lack thereof) in achieving these goals, and the implications of the assessment for re-thinking goals or procedures.

I define assessment as the obtaining of information about the skills and potentials of individuals, with the dual goals of providing useful feedback to the individuals and useful data to the surrounding community. What distinguishes assessment from testing is the former's favoring of techniques which elicit information in the course of ordinary performance and its general uneasiness with the use of formal instruments administered in a neutral, decontextualized setting.

In my view, those in the psychological and educational communities charged with the task of evaluation ought to facilitate such assessment (see Cross and Angelo 1988). We ought to be devising methods and measures which aid in regular, systematic, and useful assessment. In some cases we would end up producing "formal tests." But not in most cases, I expect.

Assessment as Simple, Natural, and Occurring on a Reliable Schedule

Rather than being imposed "externally" at odd times during the year, assessment ought to become part of the natural learning environment. As much as possible it should occur "on the fly," as part of an individual's natural engagement in a learning situation. Initially, the assessment would probably have to be introduced explicitly; but after a while, much assessment would occur naturally on the part of student and teacher, with little need for explicit recognition or labeling on anyone's part.

The model of the assessment of the cognitive abilities of the expert is relevant here. On the one hand, it is rarely necessary for the expert to be assessed by others unless engaged in competition. It is assumed that experts will go about their business with little external monitoring. However, it is also true that the expert is constantly in the process of assessing; such assessment occurs naturally, almost without conscious reflection, in the course of working. When I first began to write, I was highly dependent upon the detailed criticism of teachers and editors; now most of the needed assessment occurs at a preconscious level as I sit at my desk scribbling, or typing a first draft, or editing an earlier version of the material.

As assessment gradually becomes part of the landscape, it no longer needs to be set off from the rest of classroom activity. As in a good apprenticeship, the teachers and the students are always assessing. There is also no need to "teach for the assessment" because the assessment is ubiquitous; indeed, the need for formal tests might atrophy altogether.

Ecological Validity

A problem for most formal tests is their validity, that is, their correlation with some criterion (Messick 1988). As noted, creativity tests are no longer used much because their validity has never been adequately established. The predictive validity of intelligence tests and scholastic aptitude tests is often questioned in view of their limited usefulness in predicting performance beyond the next year of schooling.

Returning to our example of the apprenticeship, it would make little sense to question the validity of the judgments by the master. He is so intimately associated with his novice that he can probably predict his behaviors with a high degree of accuracy. When such prediction does not occur reliably, trouble lies ahead. I believe that current assessments have moved too far away from the territory that they are supposed to cover. When individuals are assessed in situations which more closely resemble "actual working conditions," it is possible to make much better predictions about their ultimate performance. It is odd that most American schoolchildren spend hundreds of hours engaged in a single exercise—the formal test—when few if any of them will ever encounter a similar instrument once they have left school.

Instruments Which Are "Intelligence-Fair"

As already noted, most testing instruments are biased heavily in favor of two varieties of intelligence—linguistic and logical-mathematical. Individuals blessed with this particular combination are likely to do well on most kinds of formal tests, even if they are not particularly adept in the domain actually under investigation. By the same token, individuals with problems in either or both linguistic and logical-mathematical intelligence may fail at measures of other domains, just because they cannot master the particular format of most standard instruments.

The solution—easier to describe than to realize— is to devise instruments which are "intelligence-fair," which peer directly at the intelligence-in-operation rather than proceed via the detour of language and logical faculties. Spatial intelligence can be assessed by having an individual navigate around an unfamiliar territory; bodily intelligence by seeing how a person learns and remembers a new dance or physical exercise; interpersonal intelligence by watching an individual handle a dispute with a sales clerk or navigate a way through a difficult committee meeting. These homely instances indicate that "intelligence-fairer" measures could be devised, though they cannot necessarily be implemented in the psychological laboratory or the testing hall.

Uses of Multiple Measures

Few practices are more nefarious in education than the drawing of widespread educational implications from the composite score of a single test—like the

Wechsler Intelligence Scale for Children. Even intelligence tests contain subtests and, at the very least, recommendations ought to take into account the "scatter" on these tests and the strategies for approaching particular items (Kaplan 1983).

Attention to a range of measures designed specifically to tap different facets of the capacity in question is even more desirable. Consider, for example, the admission standards of a program for gifted children. Conservatively speaking, 75 percent of the programs in the country simply admit on the basis of IQ—a score of 129, and you are out, 131, and you are in. How unfortunate! I have no objection to IQ as one consideration, but why not attend as well to the products which a child has already fashioned, the child's goals and desire for a program, performance during a trial period with "gifted" children, and other unobtrusive measures? I often feel that enormous educational progress would be made simply if the Secretary of Education appeared in front of the television cameras, not accompanied by a single "one-dimensional" wall-chart, but against the backdrop of a half-dozen disparate graphic displays, each monitoring a distinctly different aspect of learning and productivity.

Sensitivity to Individual Differences, Developmental Levels, and Forms of Expertise

Assessment programs which fail to take into account the vast differences among individuals, developmental levels, and varieties of expertise are increasingly anachronistic. Formal testing could, in principle, be adjusted to take these documented variations into account. But it would require a suspension of some of the key assumptions of standardized testing, such as uniformity of individuals in key respects and the penchant for cost-efficient instruments.

Individual differences should also be highlighted when educating teachers and assessors. Those charged with the responsibility of assessing youngsters need to be introduced formally to such distinctions; one cannot expect teachers to arrive at empirically valid taxonomies of individual differences on their own. Such an introduction should occur in education courses or during teaching apprenticeships. Once introduced to these distinctions, and given the opportunity to observe and to work with children who exhibit different profiles, these distinctions come to life for teachers.

It then becomes possible to take these differences into account in a tacit way. Good teachers—whether they teach second grade, piano to toddlers, or research design to graduate students—have always realized that different approaches will be effective with different kinds of students. Such sensitivities to individual differences can become part of the teacher's competence and can be drawn upon in the course of regular instruction as well as during assessment. It is also possible—and perhaps optimal—for teachers to season their own intuitive sense of individual differences with judicious occasions of assessment, crafted with the particular domain of practice in mind.

Use of Intrinsically Interesting and Motivating Materials

One of the most objectionable, though seldom remarked upon, features of formal testing is the intrinsic dullness of the materials. How often does *anyone* get excited about a test or a particular item on a test? It was probably only when, as a result of "sunshine" legislation, it became possible for test takers to challenge the answer keys used by testing organizations, that discussion of individual test items ever occupied space in a publication which anyone would voluntarily read.

It does not have to be that way. A good assessment instrument can be a learning experience. But more to the point, it is extremely desirable to have assessment occur in the context of students working on problems, projects, or products which genuinely engage them, which hold their interest and motivate them to do well. Such exercises may not be as easy to design as the standard multiple-choice entry; but they are far more likely to elicit a student's full repertoire of skills and to yield information that is useful for subsequent advice and placement.

Application of Assessment for the Student's Benefit

An equally lamentable aspect of formal testing is the use made of scores. Individuals receive the scores, see their percentile ranks, and draw a conclusion about their scholastic, if not their overall, merit. In my own view, psychologists spend far too much time ranking individuals and not nearly enough time helping them. All assessment should be undertaken primarily to aid students. It is incumbent upon the assessor to provide feedback to the student that will be helpful at the present time—identifying areas of strength as well as weakness, giving suggestions of what to study or work on, pointing out which habits are productive and which are not, indicating what can be expected in the way of future assessments, and the like. It is especially important that some of the feedback take the form of concrete suggestions and indicate relative strengths to build upon, independent of rank within a comparable group of students.

Armed with findings about human cognition and development, and in light of these desiderata for a new approach to assessment, it should be possible to begin to design programs which are more adequate than those which exist today. Without having any grand design to create a "new alternative to formal testing," my colleagues and I at Harvard Project Zero have become engaged in a number of projects over the last several years which feature new approaches to assessment. In the following sections of this chapter, I describe our two principal efforts at the present time. I then attempt to place these efforts within a broader picture of assessment in the schools and in society as a whole.

PROJECT SPECTRUM:
ASSESSMENT AT THE PRESCHOOL LEVEL

Project Spectrum is a collaborative project undertaken by several researchers at Harvard Project Zero in conjunction with our colleague David Feldman at Tufts University and the staff and students of the Eliot-Pearson Children's School in Medford, Massachusetts. The project was originally designed to assess the different intellectual strengths or "intelligences" in a representative group of three- and four-year-old children. As I will indicate, however, it has evolved over its four-year history into a preschool curriculum, with assessment aspects folded in at various points (see Hatch and Gardner 1986; Malkus, Feldman, and Gardner 1988; Sherman, Gardner, and Feldman 1988 for further details).

When we first undertook Project Spectrum, we were interested in whether the cognitive profiles of children three or four years old could be distinguished from one another. Stated differently, we were searching for early indices of the seven intelligences identified in *Frames of Mind*. It soon became apparent, however, that far more than seven intellectual capacities wanted examination; moreover, it was also clear, at least for that age group, that it is important to examine cognitive or working styles (such as attention, planfulness, ability to reflect upon a task) as well as "sheer" cognitive strengths. Thus, at the present time, we monitor in our population approximately fifteen different cognitive strengths as well as a dozen stylistic features (see table 1).

Even as we had to broaden the ensemble of skills at which we were looking, we also came to reconceptualize the nature of our assessment project. Like many others in the assessment field, we had initially assumed that one could assess "potential" or "gifts" directly, without the need for involvement in curriculum or teaching. We have come to believe, however, that this assumption is flawed. There is no "pure potential" apart from some experience in working with a domain or symbol system. As soon as one assesses, one is assessing some form of prior learning, whether or not it has been deemed relevant to the particular target domain. And so, if one wants any assurance that one is assessing the domain of interest, it is advisable to present individuals with an ample set of experiences in that domain.

Let me use an example. Suppose that one is interested in assessing talent at chess. One could see how quickly the person can respond to a light bulb, or one might examine the size of the person's vocabulary. It is conceivable that these two measures might correlate with chess talent, though I would not be surprised if neither did. One could also try to break down chess into its components and assess an individual's spatial imagery or logical reasoning skills or interpersonal skill in outwitting an opponent. Conceivably one or more of these measures might foretell chess wit or wisdom.

TABLE 1
Dimensions Examined in Project Spectrum

Activities which sample different cognitive strengths:

Music	Production Measures:	Happy Birthday New Songs–Up in the Air –Animal Song
	Perception Measures:	Montessori Bells Incidental Music Task
Language	Narrative Measure:	Storytelling Board
	Descriptive Measure:	Reporter Task
Numbers	Counting Measure:	Dinosaur Game
	Calculating Measure:	Bus Game
Science	Hypothesis-Testing Measure:	Water Table Activity
	Logical Inference Measure:	Treasure Hunt Game
	Mechanical Measure:	Assembly Task
	Naturalist Measure:	Discovery Area
Visual Arts	Drawing Measures:	Art Portfolios Farm animal, person, imaginary animal
	3-D Measure:	(Clay Activity)
Movement	Creative Movement Measure:	Biweekly Movement Curriculum
	Athletics Measure:	Obstacle Course
Social	Social Analysis Measure:	Classroom Model
	Social Roles Measure:	Observations of children's interactive styles

Measures of Working Style:

Child is	easily engaged/reluctant to engage in activity confident/tentative playful/serious focused/distractible persistent/frustrated by task reflects on own work/impulsive apt to work slowly/apt to work quickly conversational/quiet
Child	responds to visual/auditory/kinesthetic cues demonstrates planful approach brings personal agenda/strength to task finds humor in content area uses materials in unexpected ways shows pride in accomplishment shows attention to detail/is observant is curious about materials shows concern over "correct" answer

focuses on interaction with adult
transforms task/material

What is clear is that, in both of these examples, one is assessing something, whether or not it turns out to be related to facility in chess. One could simply give a chess board to children and see how well they play; but in the absence of knowing the rules of chess, the children are as likely to play chess as the proverbial monkeys are likely to pen the plays of Shakespeare.

This presentation of the chessboard does, however, point to the path that I would endorse. If you want to assess chess potential, you should teach your subjects the rules of the game and let them play chess with one another over a period of months. I have little doubt that the students would sort themselves quite reliably in terms of "chess aptitude" and that the distribution of chess talent in this population would emerge after thirty or forty games.

My colleagues and I have followed this line of thinking in surveying a variety of intellectual domains, including those which utilize linguistic, musical, and/or bodily intelligences. In each case our approach has been to expose students to experiences in the particular domain of interest and to observe the way in which they become engaged in that domain. The ensuing record provides a powerful indication of how much talent or potential the students exhibit in the domain of interest.

Having said a bit about the general philosophy and approach of Project Spectrum, let me indicate how it operates in practice. A Spectrum classroom is equipped with a rich set of materials. There are musical instruments, a fantasy play area, puzzles and games which stimulate numerical and logical thinking, a naturalist area in which students can examine different kinds of biological preparations, and the like, all of which are designed to engage the interest of students and to encourage them to play with these materials. There are also regular activities—like "Weekend News"—which give observers the opportunity to observe the child's oral language skills. A careful observer, watching children interact with these materials and participate in the activities over a semester or a year, gains considerable information about the profile of interests of each child and should also be able to perceive the degree of sophistication with which the materials have been plumbed.

Complementing these enriched classroom materials and activites is a set of tasks and measures which we have designed to look specifically at different intellectual spheres. These tasks are engaging to children and can be introduced in the course of a natural classroom interchange. In the area of number, for example, we feature two games. The dinosaur game pits the child against the experimenter in a race to escape from the dinosaur's mouth to his tail. The number and direction of moves is determined by two dice: one bearing numbers, the second featuring plus and minus signs. The players shake their dice and, at times, the child is allowed to "fix" his or her own or the experimenter's dice.

The child's success at this game can be fully quantified, and the score provides a "user-friendly" index of the child's numerical sophistication.

For children who "ceiling" on the dinosaur game, there is the bus task. In this game the child plays the role of busdriver while the experimenter is "the boss." The bus proceeds on its route and, at each stop, some children and adults mount the bus and some depart. Every once in a while "the boss" telephones and asks the driver for a count of how many adults and children are currently on the bus. Tokens are available to aid in the counting. Children of this age do not ordinarily have written numbers or other tally systems at their disposal, but sheer involvement in this game stimulates the most able among them to develop "on-line" a system whereby they are better able to keep track of the comings and goings on the bus.

In other areas analogous games and exercises have been devised (see table 1). Some of these exercises feature a fully quantifiable scoring system; others include more holistic and subjective scoring, as appropriate. In certain areas, it is not necessary to devise special exercises: for example, we evaluate talent in the visual arts by rating a collection of "spontaneous" drawings made by the child; and we evaluate social strengths through a checklist which probes how children respond to certain "charged" situations which arise in the ordinary course of events (for example, a new child coming to school, a fight breaking out, a bossy child throwing his weight around). While we wish for our scoring systems to be as precise and reliable as possible, we recognize that rough-and-ready measures can be useful as well.

The school year is divided into biweekly intervals during which a particular set of measures is taken on the children. When the classroom is an experimental one, the exercises are administered and assessed by the experimenter; in an ordinary classroom each teacher decides how to approach the targeted assessments. It is our expectation that most teachers will not wish to administer most tasks formally, nor will they generally assess them using our score sheets. Instead, they will monitor children's activities in an informal way, using our tests and sheets chiefly in instances where there is uncertainty about the child's competence. (I believe that the same philosophy should be followed in the case of standardized instruments, such as intelligence tests, which can be helpful when children appear to be "at-risk.")

By the end of the year, the teachers or experimenters will have amassed a great deal of information about the intellectual strengths and working styles of all the children in the classroom. This material becomes the basis of Spectrum Reports, brief essays which describe the particular pattern exhibited by the child: strengths, weaknesses, stylistic features, and the like. This information is presented relativistically; that is, each child's strengths are described with reference to the child's other strengths and weaknesses. In the less frequent case in which the child stands out in comparison to the entire population of pre-schoolers, an "absolute" strength or weakness is indicated.

As important as the trajectory of strengths illustrated in the Spectrum Report is the list of recommendations which are offered. Consistent with our belief that psychologists should help rather than rank students, we include in the report concrete suggestions about what might be done at home, in school, and/or in the community, in light of a particular profile of competences and proclivities.

With its detailed assessments and its year-end reports, Project Spectrum raises a number of questions, including the advisability of such an undertaking. Is such detailed assessment really necessary and might it in some way be injurious? Recall that our initial goal was to find out whether individual differences do exist and can be documented at this early age. However, we posed this question not only out of curiosity but because of our belief that such information can be educationally beneficial. The mind of the preschooler is both flexible and trainable; thus, if difficulties can be identified at an early age, they are much more likely to be remediable. By the same token, if our scales identify unusual strengths that have somehow been missed before, the parents or teachers gain the option of seeking special help or training.

However, there is a clear risk to the early labeling by Spectrum, particularly in view of our current practice of describing child abilities in terms of readily recognizable adult "end-states" (for example, dancer, naturalist, mediator). The danger is of premature billeting, by which an early attempt at description ends up by engendering a self-fulfilling prophecy. This risk is best mitigated by two procedures. The first is to stress to consumers of Spectrum Reports that these are descriptions at a particular historical moment; especially when children are young and active, the profile of abilities and disabilities can change dramatically from one year to the next. The second is to maintain Spectrum-like procedures each year. So long as students continue to be exposed to a variety of inviting materials and exercises, and so long as assessment is not a one-shot affair, there is every reason to believe that the cognitive profile will evolve—not remain static—and that subsequent reports will capture the new profile accurately.

Another question concerns the ultimate purpose of Project Spectrum. Is it simply an assessment program, or can it fulfill a broader and more integrative function? The explicit purpose of Project Spectrum has always been assessment, and the bulk of our efforts have been directed at the production of tasks and instruments which are reliable and which can be used by classroom teachers. For these reasons we are both adapting the instruments to varying degrees of fineness and planning a set of handbooks with varying degrees of detail. Note, however, that Spectrum can constitute a valuable intervention even apart from any formal assessment. That is, the range of exercises provided and the number of intellectual spheres touched upon compare favorably with offerings in most preschool programs. Even if teachers were to decide that they were not primarily interested in the Spectrum assessment materials but simply in the games, or if they used the assessment tools only in cases of children with special problems, these materials could still fulfill an important educational goal.

Indeed, this potential for curricular as well as assessment use is consistent with our belief that the line between curriculum and assessment ought ordinarily to be blurred, particularly at the younger age levels. Moreover, it is our expectation that teachers who regularly use the Spectrum materials would develop that "sixth sense" of individual differences which would allow them to make on-line assessments without necessarily having to use our formal procedures. Thus the Spectrum materials can be seen as potentially shaping teacher understandings and consequently affecting teacher practices in ways that we hope will foster the development of individual potential.

In the current political climate in America, there is tremendous pressure for good programs for preschool children. Most programs either serve as extensions upward from homecare (attachment and social ties) or as extensions downward from school (pre-literate skills). Only a few programs, like the Montessori approach, seem to be fashioned with the particular strengths and needs of the "typical" preschooler in mind. Thus another potential purpose of the Spectrum materials may be to aid in the development of innovative, developmentally sensitive, and student-centered preschool curriculum. We feel that our program speaks to the wide range of potentials in the preschool child and fosters creative growth and imaginativeness without constraining development in artificial ways. No matter how well conceived, however, our program is unlikely to be adopted if its efficacy cannot be demonstrated. The existence of an extensive battery which assesses student growth in several areas of competence can document whether a Spectrum program achieves its stated goals.

Even if the majority of teachers do not employ our full paraphernalia, we feel that it is important to have developed these materials for research purposes. Indeed, we are currently carrying out a longitudinal study with Marc Bornstein which examines the relationship between standard measures of infant cognition and attachment and the results of assessment at age four with our array of instruments. This study should broaden our knowledge of the relationship between early measures of infant competence and the range of skills exhibited by preschool children.

ARTS PROPEL:
ASSESSMENT AT THE MIDDLE AND HIGH SCHOOL LEVELS

Like Project Spectrum, ARTS PROPEL is a collaborative project. The partners are Harvard Project Zero, the Educational Testing Service, and the Pittsburgh public school system. As with Project Spectrum, the original aim was to develop new means of assessing intellectual competences, particularly in the arts; over the years there has been a gradual evolution toward curriculum, so that the line between assessment and curriculum has become almost invisible (see Gardner 1989c; Zessoules, Wolf, and Gardner 1988 for further details).

The initial impetus that brought the partners together was the desire to identify youngsters who possessed intellectual strengths which are not detected by standard scholastic aptitude tests. Because the arts are an area of intellect not usually or readily tapped through standard instruments, they were selected as the arena for the collaboration.

Traditionally, arts education in our country has focused almost exclusively on artistic production. When students are assessed at all, the assessment takes place as a holistic, and often subjective, judgment about the merits of student work. Occasional objective tests sample knowledge of art history or criticism, but these are unusual.

Our desire to keep production central in arts education but to tie it more closely to other forms of artistic knowledge has colored our approach to this project. The name ARTS PROPEL captures the thinking which underlies our approach. Artistic education ought to feature at least three activities: *Artistic Production*—the creation of art objects and the gaining of facility in "thinking in" particular artistic symbol systems; *Artistic Perception*—the ability to make fine and appropriate discriminations in one's own art works and in art works produced by others, including artistic masters; and *Artistic Reflection*—the capacity to step back from works of art, to think about their purpose, the extent to which and the manner in which they have been achieved, and to clarify the nature of one's own productions and perceptions.

In embracing this trio of goals, our ARTS PROPEL team is possibly at odds with the approach called Discipline-Based-Arts Education (DBAE). The DBAE perspective, developed by the Getty Center for Education in the Arts, calls for a kindergarten through twelfth grade sequential curriculum in art history, art production, art criticism, and aesthetics (Eisner 1987; Getty Center 1985). While we share the Getty belief that arts education should not be limited to artistic production, we believe that artistic production ought to remain central in arts education at the pre-collegiate level. In effective arts education, perceptual and reflective activities ought to be ubiquitous; but they should grow naturally out of one's own productions, particularly during the early years of formal education. Historical, critical, and analytic work ought to be directly tied to one's own art work and should not ordinarily be presented as separate disciplines.

As in Project Spectrum, we initially hoped to devise a battery of assessment instruments which would bring to the fore those students possessing talents or potentials in a number of art forms—specifically, creative writing, graphic arts, and musical performance. We wanted these instruments to be useful for all students in an ordinary school system, not just for those who were members of an elite school population or had special training in the arts.

We soon discovered, however, that the likelihood of assessing potential, in the absence of previous training, is as remote in high school art programs as in the preschool classes in which we are working. And so we found ourselves working directly in the region of curriculum development—not in the sense of developing a full-scale curriculum, but rather becoming deeply involved in the curricular concerns which daily preoccupy teachers. Also, our desire to pick out "stars" gave way gradually to a wish to develop means of assessing growth and learning in all students.

Our approach in the curricular area is worth chronicling. We develop our materials through an extensive and intensive collaboration among a large number of individuals: skilled artists, dedicated classroom teachers, researchers in developmental psychology, experts in testing and assessment, and arts supervisors and students. Each of our exercises and concepts is reviewed by these various individuals; those which cannot be justified are revised or dropped. At the end of this extensive collaborative process, we expect to have materials that satisfy each of the partners in our project.

The core of our program is the devising of two kinds of instruments, both of which span the region between curriculum and assessment in a way that makes sense to us.

Domain-projects are sets of exercises designed to present an idea, concept, or practice which is central within a particular artistic domain. Thus, a specimen domain-project in the visual arts presents the notion of graphic composition, while such a project in imaginative writing deals with character and dialogue in the crafting of a play, and a sample project in music involves the learning which accrues from rehearsing a section of a piece. Each domain-project can be carried out in a few sessions. It is deliberately designed to be flexible: flexible in that it can be fit into different junctures of the standard curriculum and flexible in that teachers can substitute their own examples or questions for those in our specimen projects. We speak of the domain-projects as being curriculum-compatible—capable of being slipped into a variety of standardized (or tailor-made) curricula in a number of ways. The domain-projects each feature several assessment components, some to be used by the students themselves, some by teachers or others charged with assessing student learning.

As an example, let me describe in more detail the current version of the aforementioned domain-project in graphic composition in the visual arts. In an initial session, each student is given a piece of white paper and ten oddly shaped black cutouts. The opening assignment is to drop these cutouts randomly on the background paper and then glue them on—a so-called random composition. Next, the students are given identical sets of the same materials, but this time they are asked to put together a composition to their liking—a deliberate composition. Then they are given work sheets on which they compare the properties of the two compositions. It should be noted that this domain-project, like most others, begins with production but contains ample opportunities for perception (comparing the two compositions) and reflection (articulating the reasons for the differing impact of the two compositions). In a second session, most likely to occur the following week, students are introduced to sets of paintings executed by well-regarded artists. They are asked to describe in their own words the different compositional patterns which they see—balanced, lop-sided, symmetrical, dynamic, and so on. Literal as well as metaphoric descriptions are welcome. The teachers are provided with a discussion of compositional facets of these paintings prepared by an artist consultant. The teachers can make as much use as they like of this accessory material, adapting it to introduce ways of discussing composition, balance, and harmony.

At the conclusion of the session, students are shown some additional pairs of slides and asked to contrast them using the concepts and vocabulary which have been introduced. They are also asked to be on the lookout during the next week for examples of interesting compositions—instances in art work which come to their attention as well as instances in their natural environment which they may have to "crop" on their own. These observations can become the basis for future discussions and can be included in the students' notebooks or portfolios (see below).

In the third session, attempts are made to build upon and integrate the lessons of the first two sessions. There is discussion of what students have collected during the previous week. Then students are asked to plan a second *deliberate composition* and to anticipate what it will look like. They are asked to make the composition which they planned and are allowed to move the cutouts around. Their final assignment is to evaluate their new deliberate composition along the same lines as the earlier compositions but also in light of their newly acquired vocabulary and conceptual understanding. The teacher then fills out score sheets; these evaluate the different compositions produced by the students as well as any enhancement of the students' perceptual and reflective capacities over the course of the exercise.

It is our goal to produce a set of domain-projects for each of the artistic areas in which we are working. Taken together, an ensemble of domain-projects should survey important concepts (for example, style, composition, expressiveness), techniques, procedures, and background knowledge. These allow students to appreciate the full context of a work. The domain-projects are so devised that they can be used more than once a year and also carried over from one year to the next. And of course teachers are encouraged to alter them in whatever way makes sense to them.

Student performance can also be assessed in a developmental scheme. That is, for each domain-project we are defining levels which span the range of performances from novice to student-expert. All teachers will be exposed, during the period of their training, to this full gamut of possible responses and conceptualizations. Scoring then places the students somewhere along this continuum on as many dimensions as are being assessed. Some of the scoring focuses on explicit dimensions which are readily quantified (for example, correct notes in a performance), while some of the scoring calls on more holistic or subjective judgments (the quality of the interpretation in a performance).

Special attention is paid in the assessments to individuating features of students' productions. Thus in domain-projects of poetry writing, it is possible to secure measures of each student's command of imagery, figurative language, rhythmic sensitivity, thematic development, and other aspects of poetic skill. By the same token, in musical performance, the scales which accompany domain-projects are sensitive to technical mastery, fingering, pitch control, rhythmic expertise, interpretive skills, and so on. In reviewing the assessment with students, the teachers can assess more than overall improvement in developmental level; in addition, both students and teachers can discuss the students' progress with reference to particular features of the artistic medium.

The second curriculum-cum-assessment device with which we have been working is called a *portfolio* (or, perhaps more accurately, a *process-folio*). Portfolios are familiar in the arts as repositories of the best works fashioned by a student. Portfolios are the basis of decisions made regarding admission to art school, prizes in a competition, or display in an art gallery.

Our process-folios, however, are instruments of learning rather than showpieces of final accomplishment. A PROPEL process-folio contains full process-tracing records of a student's involvement in one or more art works. A typical process-folio contains initial plans, drafts, early self-evaluations, feedback on the part of peers, teachers, and other experts, collections of works which students like or dislike, together with comments on the reasons for the reaction, a record of the final work, together with any relevant comments, and plans for subsequent projects, whether or not these are ever carried out.

Process-folios can fulfill several purposes. They serve as convenient means of collecting information which may be relevant to the growth of individual students over a significant period of time. Process-folios can document the biography of a specific work or domain-project but can also span much longer periods of time and document growth over a year or more. Process-folios focus on students' artistic productions, where they are free to go in a direction which has meaning to them; these stand in contrast to classroom assignments, which may (however unintentionally) be confining.

Process-folios can be extremely valuable to present as well as future teachers, for they serve as complete records of the students' growth. Teachers can assess process-folios on a variety of dimensions: number of entries, richness of entry, degree of reflection shown, improvement in technical skill, achievement of one's goals, interplay of production, perception, and reflection, use of art-historical and art-critical materials, responsiveness to internal and external feedback, development of themes, and the like. Though the PROPEL team has yet to develop prototype scoring mechanisms for the process-folios, such scoring procedures are likely to include some of the dimensions that I have just listed.

We are planning to produce specimen process-folios for use and study by both students and teachers.

But, in my view, the process-folio is most important as an aid and even "silent mentor" to the students. Productive individuals in any domain must go through—at least tacitly—a process of self-monitoring: observing their skills, reassessing their missions, noting their growth or regression. Ultimately, these processes can take place implicitly, but in early education it is advisable to assemble a tangible record in a notebook or some other convenient format. By asking students to keep and review process-folios regularly, we hope to involve them in constant reflection on their activities and to allow them the opportunity to monitor and to learn from their own growth and even their own setbacks. Ultimately, we hope that these process-folios can become rewards in themselves as well as a tangible record of an artistic apprenticeship.

In this way, too, PROPEL parallels our experience with Spectrum. While our own research goals center on the development of powerful and valid assessment tools, the procedures and techniques may prove useful to individuals whose interest is remote from assessment. The domain-projects can be viable classroom exercises, independent of their utility in assessment. By the same token, the process-folios can serve an important educational goal, irrespective of whether they are explicitly tied to assessment by the students, their teachers, or their school districts.

In my view, process-folios have a special role to play in the educational environment of today. At the time of apprenticeships in artistic ateliers, a portfolio or process-folio was perhaps less necessary; after all, the involvement of the master in his own work was completely evident, and students soon became at least accessories to the master's current project. But in the contemporary educational environment, where so much attention is directed toward the inculcation and the testing of particulate knowledge, students may have a pressing (though often unrealized) need: to become involved in significant, long-term projects, where they can reflect upon their development and use their skills in productive ways. As I have noted, such a course has often been the choice of individuals who have become established creative masters; it is only proper to expose young students to this way of thinking, acting, and being.

As currently devised, PROPEL is a pilot project in the area of artistic education for children from ages eleven to seventeen. The required assessment tools are still in the stage of development and formative evaluation; we cannot yet say how successful they will be. It is our belief, however, that our orientation might prove valuable beyond the particular bounds of our current assignment. The completion of domain-projects and the keeping of process-folios could be extended both to younger pupils and to students who are already in college. By the same token, while these procedures have been developed for use in the arts, they may well prove adaptable and welcome in other areas of the curriculum. Some of the critiques which have been leveled at standard teaching and assessment in the arts can be extended to other areas of the curriculum as well, ranging from science and social studies to mathematics.

The projects which we feature in the arts may be applicable across the full high school curriculum. Such is the belief of Theodore Sizer who, as part of his Coalition of Essential Schools, calls for more intensive involvement in a few basic areas of the curriculum and recommends that graduation occur, not upon achievement of sufficiently high test scores or sufficiently numerous Carnegie units, but rather when students can "exhibit" their accomplishments at a satisfactory level of expertise (Sizer 1984). It may seem ironic that two projects which began with narrow assessment goals at opposite ends of the age spectrum now "have designs" across the curriculum and at all ages. I hope that this growth in aspiration is not merely a reflection of arrogance or grandiosity. I prefer to think that educational problems and opportunities extend across the curriculum and that effective pedagogical ideas might be useful across different ages.

There is another, more pragmatic reason for assuming this active stance. In America, the current modes of assessment cast a powerful shadow on what goes on in the classroom and have motivated the large-scale study of which this chapter is part. If the "assessment tail" is going to wag the "curricular dog," it is important for those who are interested in school curriculum to become involved in assessment issues and to join forces with those whose primary expertise lies in assessment and testing.

As should be evident, our assessment experiments are designed largely as a means of improving the quality of education in America (and possibly elsewhere). The use of these instruments for purposes of selection has been a secondary consideration. In principle, of course, the materials developed for Spectrum and for ARTS PROPEL could be employed by elementary or high school teachers for placement purposes, and in the case of PROPEL process-folios, for college admissions. I am comfortable with such usages because I think that these forms of information could usefully supplement—and perhaps even replace—the more common standardized testing instruments. In addition, and not incidentally, the assessment techniques on which we are working can provide useful feedback to students, independent of their selection or non-selection. They have valuable educational purpose in themselves.

ASSESSMENT AT OTHER AGES

Our major research efforts have been devoted to the two projects which I have just described. It is certainly feasible to envision parallel assessment projects for other ages and in other subject domains. Here I would like to mention briefly a number of related assessment efforts, focusing on those in which our research group has had some involvement. I will organize the discussion around the areas of assessment not explored above. Of course, the entire program of research and implementation sketched in this chapter is not comprehensive; we have, however, set down some of the major issues that must be explored further in a wide range of teaching and assessment contexts.

Early Childhood

In my view there is no pragmatic reason to assess the intellectual proclivities or styles of infants or young toddlers. Children of that age have little experience with most materials used in assessment, and the results of such assessments could well be misused or overinterpreted.

For research reasons, however, it could be extremely instructive to sample a broader survey of human abilities than are tapped by standard psychological or psychometric measures. One could examine the capacities of one- and two-year-olds to habituate to (or to distinguish among) different kinds of sensory information—linguistic sounds, musical sounds, musical rhythms, abstract pictorial patterns, numerical configurations, and so on. Skill at learning various kinds of motor or sensori-motor sequences could also be assayed. While one should guard against attaching undue significance to such early cognitive markers, it would be informative to trace continuities, or lack thereof, between such early signs and the later profile of abilities detected in Project Spectrum. Indeed, in addition to the work mentioned above, the Project Spectrum team is hoping to undertake just such a set of studies with our collaborator Marc Bornstein.

The Early Elementary Years

The methods used with three- and four-year-olds in Project Spectrum might well be extended upward to kindergarten and to the early years of school. Providing environments for rich exploration, offering tasks with which children can become engaged, devising unobtrusive means of assessing growth, and preparing detailed Spectrum-style reports for parents are all activities which could easily be implemented at the older levels and which might well provide information of use to parents and teachers. Indeed, a chief value of the Spectrum approach is the possibility that it can be carried over from one year, or perhaps even from one quinquennium, to another.

Just as the Project Spectrum ideas could "trickle up" to the primary grades, the ARTS PROPEL approach might profitably "trickle down" to elementary school. Domain-projects, process-folios, and other kinds of reflective activities might be useful tools for teachers working with students aged eight to twelve. A record of student growth extending across annual boundaries is as valuable for older children as it is for younger ones (Carini 1987).

In Indianapolis there is a Key School which is based in significant part on the Theory of Multiple Intelligences. Planned by Patricia Bolanos and seven other teachers and underwritten in the early stages by the Indianapolis public schools and the Lilly Endowment, the school is now functioning as an inner city "option" school, with racially balanced enrollment and an active parent support group (Olson 1988).

The goal of the Key School is to nourish the whole spectrum of human intelligences. To this end, teachers offer regular instruction in such areas as music, dance, visual arts, computing, and Spanish, as well as the "basic" subjects of reading, math, and social studies. But what distinguishes the school as well are a number of special offerings and organizing schemes.

To begin with, each child participates in the "flow area," a rich Spectrum-like corner of the school, where youngsters can play with games and engage in activities appealing to their specific profile of intelligences and interests. Students also participate on a daily basis in small cross-age groups called "pods," in which they have the opportunity to carry out an apprenticeship in an area of special interest, ranging from architecture to astronomy to Hispanic culture. To help tie together the disparate strands of the school, there is also a school-wide theme which changes every nine weeks—initial themes have included "connections" and "changes in time and space."

Thus far, the kinds of assessment which take place in the Key School occur chiefly during the course of regular class activities. As in other elementary schools, the teachers intervene when a problem or difficulty arises. One special feature of the school, however, is the involvement of all children in an individual project during each nine-week period. These projects give the children a chance to mobilize their abilities in the service of the "school theme." Children then present, and record on videotape, the results of their project. The videotape becomes part of the archival material maintained by the school; these visual records should prove of use to future teachers and of considerable interest to the students themselves at a subsequent time.

Other schools, like the Putney School in Vermont, have featured major student projects over the years; and a few selected schools, like the Prospect School (also in Vermont), have maintained student portfolios indefinitely. There is little question that this activity has intrinsic value for the school and the students, emphasizing as it does that learning is intensive as well as extensive, and it accrues gradually over long periods of time. The portfolios at the Prospect School also help teachers to think about student work and about the special characteristics of individual students.

Surprisingly, little assessment of these records themselves, or of their use by students and teachers, has taken place, to my knowledge, probably due to the considerable expense of such assessing activities and the other competing interests of the school staffs. However, these already assembled materials provide a repository of invaluable information which could be drawn on for many purposes and which might be assessed by techniques now being developed in ARTS PROPEL. The utility of such methods of learning and documentation was demonstrated in the 1930s by the Eight Year Study, a blue-ribbon investigation undertaken to determine the efficacy of nontraditional methods of education (Aiken 1942). I suspect that if this study were replicated today, these educational procedures would once again be vindicated.

Computer Support for Domain-Projects

At Project Zero, we are developing an additional set of domain-projects for use with computer software. According to our analysis, there is much powerful software available for use by individuals with pre-existing expertise in a domain. Just to mention a few instances, there is software which allows musicians to compose, artists and architects to draft, programmers to solve problems, and the like.

We have found that novices are typically unable to make use of this software, even if they are motivated to engage in the activities for which the software has been designed. The novices lack the prerequisite skills and concepts, while the software itself does not provide sufficient clues as to its possible uses. We are therefore devising "computer domain-projects"—sample problems and solutions which are provided as databases accompanying the software, as well as manuals which instruct the novices in how to use these problem sets to "educate themselves."

The computer domain-projects have been used only on a pilot basis, but the results are encouraging. Individuals with a moderate amount of musical knowledge and with the desire to compose music have been able to compose and "orchestrate" limericks after just a few hours at the computer terminal. The computer domain-projects provide enough support so that the novice can perform at a journeyman, if not a master, level. Similar domain-projects are being created in the areas of computer programming (aiding students in learning to use PASCAL) and social studies (allowing students to recreate and solve the problems faced by Boston immigrants in the mid-nineteenth century).

Once again, we find that an ingenious curriculum approach can engage students and bring them directly into contact with the "stuff" of a culturally valued domain. And once again, the border between curriculum and assessment becomes blurred, if not irrelevant. In the case of the computer domain-projects, there is no need for extensive separate assessment. Assessment of progress and evaluation of products can be built directly into the use of the domain-project itself. The research can therefore focus directly on the questions of which factors allow some domain-projects to operate successfully and how the domain-projects, as a class of educational vehicles, can be improved.

College Admissions

A final area of interest to our group is the process of college admissions, particularly as it is practiced at selective colleges. At present there is a disjunction between the actual practices of these schools and the public perception of how one gains admission to them. Most students and parents place undue emphasis on the scores received on college admissions tests. This emphasis is unwarranted because (1) so few colleges are actually selective enough to call for the use of the tests, (2) the tests have little predictive value beyond freshmen year, and (3) selective colleges now recognize the importance of extracurricular activities and long-term engagement and follow-through as powerful predictors of success in and beyond college (Willingham 1985).

I sense a shift from the apparent reliance on the results of formal testing to a greater concern with student involvement in long-term projects and to a willingness to consider the kind of record which can be presented in effective portfolios or process-folios. Now what is needed are two coordinated events. First, students and guidance counselors must be apprised of the potential importance of submitting such ancillary materials as part of the college admissions packet. Second, individuals interested in rounded assessment must develop economical means for assessing such projects and process-folios; after all, with thousands of students competing for spaces at selective colleges, it is not practical to devote many hours to each dossier. We hope that the procedures being devised by ARTS PROPEL can be streamlined for such purposes.

AN INDIVIDUAL-CENTERED SCHOOL

Earlier in this chapter I outlined the assumptions of the "uniform school" where students encounter an identical curriculum, all subjects are taught according to the same procedures, and students are evaluated according to the same formal "standard" instruments. Even though current research throws each of these assumptions into question, they still constitute an ideal in our society.

At one time when the amount of formal knowledge to be conveyed was considerably smaller and when less was known about individual differences in human beings, the uniform school might have made sense. Nowadays, however, it is evident that no individual can learn even an infinitesimal percentage of extant knowledge; choice is inevitable and it might as well be informed. Moreover, now that we know something of the many differences among individuals, it is increasingly indefensible to treat them (to treat ourselves) as if no such differences exist.

On the basis of our foregoing analysis, it is possible to imagine a different school—one which I have termed the "individual-centered school." Such a school recognizes the need for certain basic skills and certain bodies of common knowledge for all students. At the same time, however, this school takes seriously the need for choices in education and the documentable differences among students and strives to make these factors central to the educational process (see Gardner 1987b, 1988b, 1989a, 1989b).

In implementing such a school, one would be advised to delineate three distinct roles which can be realized in a number of ways: (1) the assessment specialist, (2) the student-curriculum broker, and (3) the school-community broker.

The Assessment Specialist

It is the job of this individual to carry out regular and appropriate forms of assessment of the children in the school, to document these assessments, and to make the results available in appropriate form to teachers, to parents, and (eventually) to students themselves. The assessments would cover a range of materials, procedures, and instruments. Because assessments would be regular and ongoing in such a school, the descriptive reports should be constantly updated to provide current information. Of course, in cases where there are special problems, needs, or skills, a more aggressive intervention may be necessary.

Our projects have suggested a number of forms that assessment might take in an individual-centered school. But even when "formal standard assessment techniques" are utilized, the emphasis should always fall on making the results of the assessment useful to the consumers—in other words, on the formulation of concrete suggestions about what the student ought to do next .

The Student-Curriculum Broker

The student-curriculum broker takes the results of the observations and analyses carried out by the assessment specialist and translates them into concrete suggestions for students. These suggestions include courses and electives which the student might take, given his or her particular strengths and weaknesses, as well as which versions (or sections) of a course the student ought to take, in light of his or her particular style of learning.

I am sympathetic to the idea of course electives. These choices might as well be informed ones, and the student-curriculum broker is in an excellent position to guide students to courses that they would find interesting and from which they might profit. However, I would certainly not endorse the *assignment* of students to particular electives—in fact, this would be a contradictory notion. Students should be given options and allowed to make their own choices. If students bypass courses which ought to be of interest to them or elect courses for which they apparently have little aptitude, this practice is perfectly acceptable. Indeed, many individuals—myself included—are energized by the challenge of studying areas for which they apparently have little natural talent. Obstinacy is fine so long as it has been properly put "on notice."

Of course in any school, including this "idealized" one, there will be required courses. The issue is whether these required courses need to be taught in the same manner to all students. To the extent that there are teachers who favor different teaching styles or who themselves can offer instruction in more than one way, information about these options ought to be used to guide students to the appropriate "section." Most subjects in a core curriculum can be presented in a variety of ways, and there is no reason why this should not happen.

Even where "custom-teaching" cannot take place, it is still possible to help individual students learn in the most effective way. Many educational and technological inventions can aid students who exhibit a characteristic learning style to deal with information or to carry out analyses which might otherwise cause difficulties. To take just one example, students with deficient or limited spatial imagery have often encountered difficulties with geometry and physics. Now the existence of software which can supplement imagery by providing it "on-line" should make these subjects easier and far more palatable to these students. The task of the student-curriculum broker is to increase the chances that such salubrious student-software matches can be effected.

The School-Community Broker

Even though it would be optimal if all educational needs could be met within the walls of each school, this is not feasible. Schools can do a good job in covering the traditional curriculum and in developing some of the intelligences, but it is unrealistic to expect them to meet all needs and to cover all subjects.

Here the school-community broker comes in. It is this person's job to survey the educational opportunities which are available in the community—apprenticeships, mentorships, clubs, professions, art forms, big sisters, big brothers, and so on—and to organize them in a database. Information about print and media resources ought to be incorporated as well. This information can then be made available to students who will have the option of broadening their learning in after-school programs or, perhaps, during the school day itself. If the broker is successful, the students are more likely to develop a range of intelligences and to find an appropriate vocational and avocational niche within their community.

In truth, I do not worry about those students who are excellent in linguistic and logical pursuits. They will likely find their rewards within the school, in standard gifted programs, or in special advanced sections or honors groups. The educational challenge is to provide comparable opportunities for students who have cognitive and personal strengths which are not well-addressed by the standard school curriculum.

In the past, these students "found themselves"—if they did at all!—by accident or happenstance. The crystallizing experiences which can be so crucial in helping an individual to discover a life-long vocation or avocation were rarely brought about through planning (Walters and Gardner 1986). To my mind, the most important educational event in a student's life is the discovery of some situation or material which excites and motivates the student to make a commitment to master the materials necessary for a deeper grasp of this area. It is the job of the school-community broker to engender more frequent cystallizations in more different fields, and most especially those crystallizations which are valued in the community-at-large but are often invisible in the school.

The question may be raised about the advisability of promoting matches in domains which do not appear to be viable vocational options for students. Certainly, efforts should be made to locate options which are both compatible with the student's proclivities and relevant for careers. Yet, I do not feel that the danger of "useless" matches need concern us much. First of all, it is better for a student to have some kind of engagement than none at all; the very feelings of competence and experience of mastering a domain may turn out to have considerable transfer value. Second, the scholastic matches which are currently valued in school do not necessarily forecast vocational success in later life; the personal intelligences may well be more important for such success. Third, it is short-sighted to try to calculate in advance just which combinations of intelligences will be valued in the future or which amalgam can be drawn upon profitably by a specific individual. Finally, even if a match cannot point the way directly to a career choice, it can at least delineate an area in which the individual can expect to gain satisfaction of a personal or avocational sort in the future.

I have described these curricular, assessment, and educational opportunities in terms of individual roles only as a convenience. School systems can evolve comfortable means of realizing these roles, perhaps by drawing on guidance counselors or other existing personnel or by creating centralized sources of information.

Implementing these roles, however, is of little avail if the school and the surrounding community are not dedicated to education across a broad spectrum of areas and abilities. Taken in combination with a supportive educational community, these roles ought to aid in the realization of a school in which individual differences are taken seriously, cherished, fostered, and mobilized to worthwhile personal and community ends.

My description of one school of the future should lay to rest any lurking fears that I am out to abolish the role of testing and assessment in the schools. If anything, the program I have laid out would call for the development of a cadre of specialists that does not now exist and that would be called on to carry out work which is even more pivotal than that now being carried out by psychologists, guidance counselors, and testing experts. I am not lobbying for the decimation of testing but for a broadening and a deepening of the assessment roles.

At the same time, I have no aim to minimize the role of teachers. Indeed, it is my hope that this scheme will free teachers to teach as expertly as possible in the ways that they find comfortable. This kind of education can only take place if teachers are highly professionalized and have responsibility for planning their curricula and for running their classes. (The model of the Indianapolis Key School is relevant here.) The improvement of teaching conditions and the upgrading of the quality of teacher-training programs central to this enterprise are topics of signal importance in our society but fall beyond the scope of this chapter.

TOWARD THE ASSESSING SOCIETY

This chapter has been an extended essay in favor of regular assessment occurring in a natural fashion throughout the educational system and across the trajectory of life-long learning. I have reviewed a sizeable body of theoretical innovations and experimental evidence, which, by and large, point up problems with standard formal testing as an exclusive mode of assessment. Many of these findings suggest that it would be more fruitful to create environments in which assessments occur naturally and to devise curricular entities, like domain-projects and process-folios, which lend themselves to assessment within the context of their production. It would be an exaggeration to say that I have called for a reintroduction of the apprentice method. Yet I do claim that we have moved too far from that mode of assessment; contemporary assessment might well be informed by some of the concepts and assumptions associated with traditional apprenticeships.

Indeed, if one considers "formal testing" and "apprentice-style assessment" as two poles of assessment, it could be said that America today has veered too far in the direction of formal testing without adequate consideration of the costs and limitations of an exclusive emphasis on that approach. Even outside the realm of physics, an excessive action calls for a reaction—one reason why this chapter stresses the advantages of more naturalistic, context-sensitive, and ecologically valid modes of assessment. Standard formal tests have their place—for example, in initial screening of certain "at-risk" populations—but users should know their limitations as well.

Some objections to the perspective introduced here can be anticipated. One is the claim that formal testing is, as advertised, objective and that I am calling for a regression to subjective forms of evaluation. I reject this characterization for two reasons. First of all, there is no reason in principle to regard the assessment of domain-projects, process-folios, or Spectrum-style measures as intrinsically less objective than other forms. Reliability can be achieved in these domains as well. The establishment of reliability has not been a focus of these projects; however, the conceptual and psychometric tools exist to investigate reliability in these cases. Moreover, these assessment measures are more likely to possess "ecological" validity.

A second retort to this characterization has to do with the alleged objectivity or non-bias of standard formal tests. In a technical sense, it is true that the best of these instruments avoid the dangers of subjectivity and statistical bias. However, any kind of instrument is necessarily skewed toward one kind (or a few kinds) of individual and one (or a few) intellectual and cognitive styles. Formal tests are especially friendly to those individuals who possess a certain blend of linguistic and logical intelligences and who are comfortable in being assessed in a decontextualized setting under timed and impersonal conditions. Correlatively, such tests are biased against individuals who do not exhibit that blend of intelligences, those whose strengths show up better in sustained projects or when they are examined in situ.

I believe that, especially when resources are scarce, every individual ought to have the opportunity to show her or his strength. There is no objection to a "high scorer" being able to show off a string of eight hundreds to a college admissions staff; by the same token, individuals with other cognitive or stylistic strengths ought to have their day as well.

There are those who might be in sympathy with the line of analysis pursued here and yet would reject its implications because of considerations of cost or efficiency. According to this argument, it is simply too inefficient or expensive to mobilize the country around more sustained forms of assessment; and so, even if formal testing is imperfect, we will have to settle for it and simply try to improve it as much as possible.

This line of argument has a surface plausiblity, but I reject it as well. To be sure, formal testing is now cost-effective, but it has taken millions, perhaps billions of dollars expended over many decades to bring it to its current far-from-perfect state. Nor do I think that more money spent on current testing would improve it more than marginally. (I do believe that it is worthwhile to spend money on diagnostic and interactive forms of testing, but those are not topics which I am treating in the present chapter.)

Our current pilot projects, while dependent on research funds, are modest by any standard. In each instance we believe that the main points of the approach can be taught readily to teachers and made available to interested schools or school districts. We subscribe to Theodore Sizer's estimate that a move toward more qualitative forms of education (and perhaps also to higher-quality education) might increase costs by 10 to 15 percent but probably not more.

The major obstacle I see to assessment-in-context is not availability of resources but rather lack of will. There is in the country today an enormous desire to make education uniform, to treat all students in the same way, and to apply the same kinds of one-dimensional metrics to all. This trend is inappropriate on scientific grounds and distasteful on ethical grounds. The current sentiment is based in part on an understandable disaffection with some of the excesses of earlier educational experiments but, to a disturbing degree, it is also based on a general hostility to students, teachers, and the learning process. In other countries, where the educational process is held in higher regard, it has proved possible to have higher-quality education without subscribing to some of the worst features of one-dimensional educational thinking and assessment.

It is not difficult to sketch out the reasons for the tentative national consensus on the need for more testing and more uniform schools. Understandable uneasiness with poor student performance in the early 1980s resulted in a general indictment of contemporary education, which was blamed for a multitude of societal sins. Government officials, especially state administrators and legislators, entered the fray; the price paid for increased financial support was simple—more testing and more accountability based on testing. The fact that few students of education were entirely comfortable with the diagnosis or the purported cure was not relevant. After all, political officials rarely pore over the relevant literature; they almost reflexively "search for scapegoats" and call for the "quick fix."

It is unfortunate that few public officials or societal leaders have put forth an alternative point of view on these issues. If significant forces or interest groups in this country were to dedicate themselves to a different model of education, which subscribes to the assessment-and-schooling philosophy outlined here, I have every confidence that they could implement it without breaking the bank. It would be necessary for a wider gamut of individuals to "pitch in"; for college faculty to examine the process-folios that are submitted; for community members to offer mentorships, apprenticeships, or "special pods"; for parents to find out what their children are doing in school and to work with them (or at least encourage them) on their projects. These suggestions may sound revolutionary, but they are daily occurrences in excellent educational settings in the United States and abroad. Indeed, it is hard to imagine quality education in the absence of such a cooperative ambience (Grant 1978, 1988).

To my way of thinking, the ultimate policy debate is—or at least should be—centered on competing concepts of the purposes and aims of education. As I have intimated above, the "formal standard testing" view harbors a concept of education as a collection of individual elements of information which are to be mastered and then spewed back in a decontextualized setting. On this "bucket view" it is expected that individuals who acquire a sufficient amount of such knowledge will be effective members of the society.

The "assessment view" values the development of productive and reflective skills, cultivated in long-term projects. The animating impulse seeks to bridge the gap between school activities and activities after school, with the thought that the same habits of mind and discipline can be useful in both kinds of undertakings. Especial attention is paid to individual strengths. On this view, assessment should occur as unobtrusively as possible during the course of daily activities, and the information obtained should be furnished to gatekeepers in useful and economical form.

The "assessment view" fits comfortably with the vision of individual-centered schooling that I have outlined above. Some individuals sympathetic to a focus on assessment might still object to the individual-centered view, seeing it as an impractical or romantic view of education; they would prefer more naturalistic modes of assessment in the service of a rigorous curriculum. To these individuals I would respond, perhaps surprisingly, by unequivocally endorsing the importance of rigor. There is nothing in an "individual-centered" approach which questions rigor; indeed, in any decent apprenticeship, rigor is assumed. If anything, it is the sophomoric "multiple-choice-cum-isolated-fact" mentality that sacrifices genuine rigor for superficial conformity. I fully embrace rigorous curricula in an individual-based school; I simply call for a broader menu of curricular options.

I obviously think that the assessment approach and the individual-centered school constitute a more noble educational vision. Both are more in keeping with American democratic and pluralistic values (Dewey 1938). I also think that this vision is more consistent with what has been established in recent decades by scientific study of human growth and learning. Schools in the future ought to be so crafted that they are consistent with this vision. In the end, whatever the forms and the incidence of "official assessments," the actual daily learning in schools, as well as the learning stimulated long after "formal" school has been completed, should be its own reward.

REFERENCES

Aiken, W. 1942. *The story of the Eight Year Study*. New York: Harper and Brothers.
Anderson, M. 1987. Inspection time and the development of intelligence. Paper delivered to British Psychological Society Conference, Sussex University.
Bamberger, J. 1982. Revisiting children's drawings of simple rhythms: A function for reflection-in-action. In *U-shaped behavioral growth*, ed. S. Strauss. New York: Academic Press.
Bijou, S., and D. Baer. 1965. *Child development*. New York: Appleton Century Crofts.
Binet, A., and T. Simon. 1905. Methodes nouvelles pour le diagnostique du niveau intellectuel des anormaux. *L'annee psychologique* II:245–336.
Block, N., and G. Dworkin. 1976. *The IQ controversy*. New York: Pantheon.
Bloom, A. 1987. *The closing of the American mind*. New York: Simon and Schuster.
Brainerd, C. 1978. The stage question in cognitive-developmental theory. *The Behavioral and Brain Sciences* 2:173–213.
Brown, R., and Herrnstein, R. 1975. *Psychology*. Boston: Little Brown.
Buros, O. 1978. *The eighth mental measurements yearbook*. Highland Park, New Jersey: Gryphon Press.
Carini, P. 1987. Another way of looking. Paper presented at the Cambridge School Conference, Weston, Massachusetts, October.
Case, R. 1985. *Intellectual development: Birth to adolescence*. New York: Academic Press.
Collins, A., J. S. Brown, and S. E. Newman. In press. Cognitive apprenticeship: Teaching the craft of reading, writing, and mathematics. In *Cognition and instruction: issues and agendas,* ed. L. Resnick. Hillsdale, NJ: Lawrence Erlbaum.
Cronbach, L. 1984. *Essentials of psychological testing*. New York: Harper and Row.
Cronbach, L., and R. Snow. 1977. *Aptitudes and instructional. methods*. New York: Irvington.

Cross, K. P., and T. Angelo. 1988. *Classroom assessment techniques: A handbook for faculty*. Ann Arbor: National Center for Research to Improve Postsecondary Teaching and Learning (NCRIPTL).

Csikszentmihalyi, M. 1988. Society, culture, and persons: A systems view of creativity. In *The nature of creativity*, ed. R. Sternberg. New York: Cambridge University Press.

Csikszentmihalyi, M., and R. Robinson. 1986. Culture, time, and the development of talent. In *Conceptions of giftedness*, ed. R. Sternberg and J. Davidson. New York: Cambridge University Press.

Dewey, J. 1938. *Experience and education*. New York: Collier.

Eisner, E. 1987. Structure and magic in discipline-based arts education. In *Proceedings of a National Invitational Conference*, Los Angeles: The Getty Center for Education in the Arts.

Eysenck, H. J. 1967. Intelligence assessment: A theoretical and experimental approach. *British Journal of Educational Psychology* 37:81–98.

Eysenck, H. J. 1979. *The nature and measurement of intelligence*. New York: Springer-Verlag.

Feldman, D. 1980. *Beyond universals in cognitive development*. Norwood, NJ: Ablex.

Fischer, K. W. 1980. A theory of cognitive development. *Psychological Review* 87:477–531.

Fodor, J. 1983. *The modularity of mind*. Cambridge: MIT Press.

Gardner, H. 1975. *The shattered mind*. New York: Knopf.

Gardner, H. 1982. *Art, mind, and brain*. New York: Basic Books.

Gardner, H. 1983. *Frames of mind*. New York: Basic Books.

Gardner, H. 1985. *The mind's new science*. New York: Basic Books.

Gardner, H. 1986. The development of symbolic literacy. In *Toward a greater understanding of literacy*, ed. M. Wrolstad and D. Fisher. New York: Praeger.

Gardner, H. 1987a. Developing the spectrum of human intelligence. *Harvard Education Review* 57:187–93.

Gardner, H. 1987b. An individual-centered curriculum. In *The schools we've got, the schools we need*. Washington, DC: Council of Chief State School Officers and the American Association of Colleges of Teacher Education.

Gardner, H. 1988a. Creative lives and creative works: A synthetic scientific approach. In *The nature of creativity*, ed. R. J. Sternberg. New York: Cambridge University Press.

Gardner, H. 1988b. Mobilizing resources for individual-centered education. In *Technology in education: Looking toward 2020*, ed. R. Nickerson. Hillsdale, NJ: Lawrence Erlbaum.

Gardner, H. 1989a. Balancing specialized and comprehensive knowledge. In *Schooling for tomorrow: Directing reforms to issues that count*, ed. T. Sergiovanni. Boston: Allyn and Bacon.

Gardner, H. 1989b. The school of the future. In *The reality club*, ed. J. Brockman. New York: in press.

Gardner, H. 1989c. Zero-based arts education: An introduction to ARTS PROPEL. *Studies in Art Education* 30 (2): 71–83.

Gardner, H., and C. Wolf. 1988. The fruits of asynchrony: Creativity from a psychological point of view. *Adolescent psychiatry* 15:106–23.

Gardner, H., V. Howard, and D. Perkins. 1974. Symbol systems: A philosophical, psychological and educational investigation. In *Media and symbols*, ed. D. Olson. Chicago: University of Chicago Press.

Gelman, R. 1978. Cognitive development. *Annual Review of Psychology* 29:297–332.

Getty Center for Education in the Arts. 1985. *Beyond creating: The Place for art in American schools.* Los Angeles: J. Paul Getty Trust.

Goodman, N. 1976. *Languages of art.* Indianapolis: Hackett.

Gould, S. J. 1981. *The mismeasure of man.* New York: Norton.

Grant, D., ed. 1978. *On competence.* San Francisco: Jossey-Bass.

Grant, G. 1988. *The world we created at Hamilton High.* Cambridge: Harvard University Press.

Gruber, H. 1981. *Darwin on man.* 2d ed. Chicago: University of Chicago Press.

Gruber, H. 1985. Giftedness and moral responsbility: Creative thinking and human survival. In *The gifted and talented: developmental perspectives,* ed. F. Horowitz and M. O'Brien. Washington: American Psychological Association.

Guilford, J. P. 1950. Creativity. *American Psychologist* 5:444–54.

Guilford, J. P. 1967. *The nature of human intelligence.* New York: McGraw Hill.

Hatch, T., and H. Gardner. 1986. From testing intelligence to assessing competences: A pluralistic view of intellect. *The Roeper Review* 8:147–50.

Hirsch, E. D. 1987. *Cultural literacy.* Boston: Houghton Mifflin.

Hoffmann, B. 1962. *The tyranny of testing.* New York: Crowel-Collier Press.

Jencks, C. 1972. *Inequality.* New York: Basic Books.

Jensen, A. R. 1980. *Bias in mental testing.* New York: Free Press.

Jensen, A. R. 1987. Individual differences in the Hick paradigm. In *Speed of information processing and intelligence,* ed. P. Vernon. Norwood, NJ: Ablex.

Kagan, J., and N. Kogan. 1970. Individual variation in cognitive processing. In *Handbook of child psychology,* ed. P. Mussen. New York: Wiley.

Kaplan, E. 1983. Process and achievement revisited. In *Toward a holistic developmental psychology,* ed. S. Wapner and B. Kaplan. Hillsdale, NJ: Lawrence Erlbaum.

Laboratory of Comparative Human Cognition. 1982. Culture and intelligence. In *Handbook of human intelligence,* ed. R. J. Sternberg. New York: Cambridge University Press.

Langer, S. K. 1942. *Philosophy in a new key.* Cambridge: Harvard University Press.

Lave, J. 1980. What's special about experiments as contexts for thinking? *Quarterly Newsletter of the Laboratory of Comparative Human Cognition* 2:86–91.

Malkus, U., D. Feldman, and H. Gardner. 1988. Dimensions of mind in early childhood. In *The psychological bases of early childhood,* ed. A. D. Pelligrini. Chichester, U. K.: Wiley.

Messick, S. 1988. Validity. In *Educational measurement.* 3d ed., ed. R. Linn. New York: Macmillan.

Newell, A., and H. A. Simon. 1972. *Human problem-solving.* Englewood Cliffs, NJ: Prentice-Hall.

Olson, L. 1988. Children flourish here: 8 teachers and a theory changed a school world. *Education Week* 7 (18): 1,18–19.

Perkins, D. 1981. *The mind's best work.* Cambridge: Harvard University Press.

Piaget, J. 1983. Piaget's theory. In *Manual of child psychology,* ed. P. Mussen. New York: Wiley.

Polanyi, M. 1958. *Personal knowledge.* Chicago: University of Chicago Press.

Ravitch, D., and C. Finn. 1987. *What do our seventeen-year-olds know?* New York: Harper and Row.

Resnick, L. 1987. The 1987 presidential address: Learning in school and out. *Educational Researcher* 16 (9): 13–20.

Rogoff, B. 1982. Integrating context and cognitive development. In *Advances in developmental psychology*, vol. 2, ed. M. Lamb and A. Brown. Hillsdale, NJ: Lawrence Erlbaum.

Scribner, S. 1986. Thinking in action: Some characteristics of practical thought. In *Practical Intelligence*, ed. R. Sternberg and R. K. Wagner. New York: Cambridge University Press.

Sizer, T. 1984. *Horace's compromise*. Boston: Houghton Mifflin.

Squire, L. 1986. Mechanisms of memory. *Science* 232:1612–19.

Sternberg, R. 1977. *Intelligence, information processing, and analogical reasoning*. Hillsdale, NJ: Lawrence Erlbaum.

Sternberg, R. 1985. *Beyond IQ*. New York: Cambridge University Press.

Sternberg, R., ed. 1988. *The nature of creativity*. New York: Cambridge University Press.

Strauss, S. 1982. *U-shaped behavioral growth*. New York: Academic Press.

Thurstone, L. 1938. *Primary mental abilities*. Chicago: University of Chicago Press.

Uzgiris, I., and J. McV. Hunt. 1966. *An instrument for assessing infant intellectual development*. Urbana, IL: University of Illinois Press.

Wallach, M. 1971. *The intelligence/creativity distinction*. Morristown, NJ: General Learning Press.

Wallach, M. 1985. Creativity testing and giftedness. In *The gifted and talented: Developmental perspectives*, ed. F. Horowitz and M. O'Brien. Washington, DC: American Psychological Association.

Walters, J., and H. Gardner. 1986. The crystallizing experience. In *Conceptions of giftedness*, ed. R. Sternberg and J. Davidson. New York: Cambridge University Press.

Wexler-Sherman, C., H. Gardner, and D. H. Feldman. 1988. A pluralistic view of early assessment: The Project Spectrum approach. *Theory into Practice* 27 (1): 77–83.

Willingham, W. 1985. *Success in college*. New York: College Entrance Examination Board (CEEB).

Zessoules, R., D. Wolf, and H. Gardner. 1988. A better balance: ARTS PROPEL as an alternative to discipline-based art education. In *Beyond discipline-based art education*, ed. J. Burton, A. Lederman, and P. London. North Dartmouth, MA: University Council on Art Education.

Interactive Learning Environments: A New Look at Assessment and Instruction

Ann L. Brown, Joseph C. Campione, Lynne S. Webber, and Kate McGilly

INTRODUCTION

Among the major creations of psychological theory in this century has been the notion of an individual intelligence quotient (IQ) and the means for measuring it. Enthusiasm for this invention, however, has been less than universal (Gould 1981); some regard it as a crowning accomplishment of psychological theory, while others see IQ tests as instruments for reinforcing social injustice.

Despite the increasing sophistication of both psychological and psychometric theories, there has been little change in the naive theory of intelligence that motivates the use and interpretation of intelligence tests in schools and clinics. The implicit, underlying assumptions about mental testing and the uses to which these tests should be put have remained unchanged. However, these assumptions differ greatly from those emerging from new work in mental testing, work that is the topic of our chapter.[1] Briefly, there are four main orientations or assumptions that we can usefully contrast in laying out the differences between traditional "common wisdom" and the new perspectives on assessment currently developing:

1. *Generality versus domain specificity.* Common wisdom assumes that individuals "possess" a *general* factor of learning, to which the only exceptions may be special abilities, such as artistic or musical ability. If a certain child is "diagnosed" as having an IQ of 75, common wisdom would assume that the child would perform similarly poorly in mathematics, reading, spelling, and so on. IQ is largely seen as stable across contexts.

New work we will discuss instead stresses *domain specificity*: a child is seen as a different kind of learner within various academic domains depending upon interest, aptitude, and knowledge.

2. *Stability versus malleability.* Traditional views assume that the general intelligence quotient is stable across time as well as context. And in line with these beliefs, the cognitive processes commonly thought to be responsible for the IQ score in the first place, such as learning ability, memory, and so forth,[2] are thus also seen as fairly constant and unchanging. This view also implies that the *static measurement* of a child's intelligence quotient is unproblematic. The

assumptions of generality and stability together imply that measurements of current competence will provide information appropriate across time and different contexts of learning.

In contrast, new views of assessing ability and aptitude focus on the changeability of learning and intelligence. Learners are corrigible; they can learn to be more efficient learners; and tests should measure this flexibility *dynamically*. Thus this view implies that assessment must accompany the learner throughout development and should ideally be designed in such a way as to track both that development and the capacity for growth.

3. *Isolated versus socially embedded learning*. Traditionally, school learning has been viewed as an isolated, individual accomplishment. Teachers teach and students learn, the students working independently to acquire the knowledge and skills needed for success. (As we review below, this approach to learning has strongly influenced the way instruction is typically structured in schools.) Given this view, it makes sense that testing procedures should also involve students working alone and unaided: the contexts of assessment and instruction are matched. In the traditional view, a child comes to school with a relatively fixed academic potential, which can be measured via an IQ test, and compared with that of other children. While the quality of that intelligence will substantially determine the amount of the child's learning, the focus is on the assumed intellectual endowment itself rather than on the interaction with possible variations in the school environment.

In the new views we are exploring, much greater importance is given to the social context in which learning takes place and the relation between ability and response to various forms of *cooperative* and *guided learning*. Teachers and students work collaboratively to influence and determine student performance. The sociocultural context in which the child develops before school, as well as the social contexts of learning found in school, fundamentally influence the learning process. But if learning is seen in large part as a social accomplishment, it follows that assessment should also take place in a social context. The interaction between the individual's capacities and the characteristics of the learning environment must be included in any assessment.

4. *Prediction versus prescription*. The common wisdom instantiated in the points above entails a particular view of the *use* of IQ tests. The function they assume for these tests is one of *prediction*. The tests are used, implicitly or explicitly, as a method of selection, at best specifying those deemed in need of additional help in navigating their school careers and at worst excluding those regarded as unlikely to succeed at all. It is believed that IQ scores can predict both present and future academic performance. As such, these scores are used to predict a student's trajectory through school rather than to provide information that would inform methods of instruction. This in itself is not surprising. Recall that Binet's original charge from the French government was to identify those children who were predicted to experience school problems so that remedial

instruction could be provided. And in current use in schools in the United States, the same task exists. Special-education resources are limited, and there is a need for an objective method of identifying students who should be afforded those services. However, it is still the case that current tests do not inform instruction. Knowing that a particular child has an IQ of 75—or even knowing additionally that she is two years behind on standardized tests of mathematics—tells us only that she is a candidate for additional help in mathematics; it tells us little about what or how to teach her.

In contrast to these views, the new work we discuss entails a view of the function of such testing that centers on *prescription*. Tests that provide information about what a child does not know now but is just about ready to learn would be invaluable to a classroom teacher or clinician. If a sufficient battery of such tests existed, and if the tests were truly sensitive to readiness within domains, schools could bypass the "select and label" routine altogether.[3]

The contrasts described above are necessarily oversimplified. Yet they point to tendencies and assumptions that differentiate traditional from newer views of testing. In this chapter we will begin by going back to the early history of mental testing to uncover the roots of the traditional assumptions described above. We will discuss data that do support these views and draw out surprising continuities between certain traditional views of the psychometric community and the newer views we discuss. In the last section of this chapter we will discuss recent work that centers on and supports the new assumptions we briefly described above. First we describe the general properties of the modern research in dynamic assessment and its instructional implications, with a brief description of the theoretical frameworks within which this work developed (Vygotsky and Feuerstein are its two principal antecedents). Then we review a number of studies that investigate the psychometric properties of dynamic assessments of children's ability to reason inductively. We conclude that these methods provide superior insights into learning potential. We then delve into the issue of dynamic assessment within the content-rich realm of early mathematics. This area allows us to go more deeply into the question of how the results of dynamic assessment can be translated into suggestions for instruction. The assessment-instruction link is central to many policy-oriented considerations of testing and is pursued in the final section of the chapter, in which we discuss interactive instruction in general and illustrate it with one approach, reciprocal teaching, that we have explored in depth. Finally, we will discuss the brave new world of assessment implied by this new work in terms of what we know now, how far we need to progress, and what practical resources it would take to make that progress possible. We will attempt to draw together what we see as the most important findings for policymakers, and we will make a fairly ambitious proposal for what needs to be done next.

A BRIEF HISTORY OF IQ AND LEARNING

We will review three of the main issues that motivated the testing movement and that remain controversial today. The first two have to do with theoretical views about the nature of intelligence, the third with the clinical uses and interpretations of test scores. The first theoretical issue is the search for a framework within which to specify the underlying mental processes that determine intelligence; of primary concern here is the generality versus specificity of those processes. Also in this context, we consider the extent to which there is a stable relationship between measures of intelligence and learning—that is, to what degree are learning ability and intelligence interchangeable? And third, we address the enduring problems of selection, labeling, and cultural bias. In all three areas we reach the same conclusion. To achieve our goals of understanding and using assessment devices, we need better measures of learning, better methods of instruction, and a closer link between the two. To achieve these goals, we also argue for situating assessment in specific academic domains. Attempts to meet these goals will be the subject of the succeeding section of the chapter.

Underlying Processes: Domain Specific or Domain General?

A major theoretical controversy for the inventors of mental testing was the time-honored problem of domain specificity and domain generality. All were committed to finding a few (if not one) underlying key processes that resulted in the multiplicity of human talent. Binet's theoretical speculations are prototypical. Although his approach to test development was strongly empirical—he tried many items and retained only those that distinguished children of different ages—he did outline a process theory to capture the differences revealed by the test. His initial attempts reflect the tension between the general and the specific. On the one hand, he identified attention as the key to intelligence (Binet 1903), but on the other hand, he emphasized the "complexity of mental life" (Binet and Simon 1908). Binet reached an uneasy compromise: while paying lip service to specific knowledge, to which he attributed great powers, he settled on "four general factors as common to all intellectual activities. 'Comprehension, invention, direction and criticism—intelligence is constrained in these four words' " (Binet [1911] 1962, 118).

Three of Binet's four general factors, "direction and persistence of thought, autocriticism, and invention," tally with current metacognitive or metacomponential theories of intelligence (Brown 1974, 1978; Brown and Campione 1981; Campione and Brown 1977, 1978; Campione, Brown, and Ferrara 1982; Sternberg 1984, this volume). Briefly put, several contemporary research groups have pinpointed metacognition as a central aspect of higher-order thought and hence of intelligence. Metacognition refers to the knowledge one has of one's own mental processes. It sometimes also refers to the ability to allocate one's mental efforts efficiently, to plan, monitor, oversee, orchestrate, and control one's own learning (Brown 1975, 1978; Brown et al. 1983; Campione, Brown, and Ferrara 1982; Flavell and Wellman 1977). Sternberg's metacomponents consist of similar planning and overseeing functions (see Sternberg, this volume). Among others who have theories featuring an emphasis on metacognition are Borkowski (1985), Bransford (1979), and Feuerstein (1980). It is notable that, with the exception of Sternberg, these researchers were all working with academically at-risk populations when they came to the conclusion that metacognition was crucial to intelligence.

Binet was also particularly impressed by the lack of understanding and self-regulation in the thought of slow-learning children:

> I am repeatedly struck by the lack of these skills in children in the face of school tasks. The child's power of self-criticism is very weak. He is not well aware of the appropriateness of what he says or does. He is awkward with his mind as well as with his hands. He is known for using words without realizing that he does not understand them.

> It is easy to test this lack of adequate self-criticism; it appears as a problem on tests in general, but we have an excellent exercise intended to demonstrate failures of autocriticism, i.e., sentences to critique. We tell the child that we are going to read a sentence in which something is wrong, and he will have to say what it is. These are some examples: 1) An unfortunate cyclist fractured his skull and died at once; he has been taken to the hospital and we are afraid that he won't be able to recover; 2) Yesterday there was a train crash, but nothing serious; only 48 people died; 3) I have three brothers, Pierre, Ernest and me; 4) Yesterday we found a woman's body sliced in 18 pieces; we believe she killed herself. You would be surprised at how many of the "thoughtless young" are quite happy with this nonsense. (Binet 1909, from Brown 1985, 321)

In describing the characteristic learning mode of the retarded child, Binet ([1911] 1962) claims, "The child is unreflective and inconstant; he forgets what he is doing. . . . He lets himself be carried away by fantasy and caprice. . . . He lacks direction" (pp. 119–20). Similarly on autocriticism: "The power of *criticism* is as limited as the rest. *He does not know that he does not understand*" (p. 122, emphasis added).

Another founding father, Spearman (1904, 1923, 1927), had less internal conflict than Binet in deciding in favor of general factors. Although formally he does accord influences to specific, or *s*, factors, his heart lies with his general factor, the ubiquitous *g*. In the ensuing arguments, prompted mainly by measurement issues, we have tended to lose sight of Spearman's definition of *g*. Interestingly, Spearman's general factors are not unlike Binet's, the three principal components of *g* being (a) educing relations, (b) educing correlates, and (c) self-recognition, or the "apprehension of one's own experience." Spearman claims that people have "more or less" the power to observe what goes on in their own minds. "A person cannot only feel, but also know that he can feel; not only strive, but know that he strives; not only know, but *know that he knows*" (Spearman 1923, 342; emphasis added). Similarly: "Any active knowing process, no less than any passive feeling one, belongs to lived experience, so that it can equally well evoke an awareness of its own occurrence and character. I can know, not only *that* I know, but also *what* I know" (Spearman 1923, 52).

Spearman does not claim scientific priority with such notions of metacognition. Indeed, he observes:

> Such a cognizing of cognition itself was already announced by Plato. Aristotle likewise posited a separate power whereby, over and above actually seeing and hearing, the psyche becomes aware of doing so. Late authors, as Strato, Galen, Alexander of Aphrodisias, and in particular Plotinus, amplified the doctrine, designating the processes of cognizing one's own cognition by several specific names. Much later, especial stress was laid on this power of "reflection," as it was now called by Locke. (Spearman 1923, 52–53)

Spearman did, however, contribute the identification of such metacognitive-sounding elements as essential elements of *g*, agreeing with Binet that self-awareness and autocritical skills are fundamental to intelligence.

The alternative position, that intelligence consists of many specific faculties, abilities, or skills, was championed by Thorndike, Cattell, Guilford, and others. This position too is alive today (see Gardner, this volume; Sternberg, this volume). But as the main thrust of this chapter is on the assessment and instruction of learning, we will concentrate on the metacognitive position.

If figures as influential as Binet and Spearman identified metacognition as central to intelligence, why did the concept have to be reinvented in the 1970s? We believe this is because metacognition was conceived of so generally. Such amorphous processes are very difficult to instruct, much less to assess. Even though Binet believed autocriticism to be fundamental to intelligence, it is quite unclear how his standardized test items were intended to tap that ability. To illustrate this point, the above examples of comprehension-monitoring tests (sentences to be evaluated) did *not* occur in Binet's intelligence scale.

Binet also noted problems of self-regulation in his observations of classroom behavior, here, for example, with arithmetic:

Some students can perform the four operations perfectly, but are unable to use them in a problem; they use a multiplication when a division is required; they find, for instance, that a salesman has more merchandise after the sale than before, and other fantastic results that they omit judging. They have been taught to calculate, not to reason. Everyone knows schools where the instruction became nothing but routine. The teacher develops their memory, but doesn't do anything to develop their judgment, their spontaneity, in other words their intelligence. (Binet 1909, from Brown 1985, 322)

Ahead of his time at the turn of the century, Binet believed strongly in the modifiability of intelligence:

I have always believed that intelligence can, to some extent, be taught, can be improved in every child, and I deplore the pessimism that this question often evokes. There is a frequent prejudice against the educability of the intelligence. The familiar proverb which says "When we are stupid, it is for a long time" seems to be taken for granted by unscrupulous teachers. They are indifferent to children lacking intelligence; they don't have any sympathy for them, or even respect, for their intemperancy of language is such that they would say "this is a child who will never do anything . . . he is not gifted, not intelligent at all." I have too often heard this uncautious language. . . .

Some contemporary philosophers seem to have given their moral support to such lamentable verdicts, asserting that intelligence is a fixed quantity, a quantity that cannot be increased. We must protest and react against this brutal pessimism and show that it has no foundation.

If it were not possible to change intelligence, why measure it in the first place? *After the disease, the remedy*. Diagnosis is crucial but remedy must follow. (Binet 1909, from Brown 1985, 323)

Given these beliefs, Binet turned his attention to the design of remediation. Here, in contrast to his standardized test, he did concentrate on comprehension-monitoring activities. Binet's curriculum, Mental Orthopedics (Binet 1909; Brown 1985), is full of interesting ideas about such remediation but contained few specifics; it is for this reason that it has not stood the test of time. But his main claims have been much in keeping with contemporary thinking about cognitive instruction.

Binet's main point was that by exercise and training we can improve attention, memory, and judgment and "literally become more intelligent than before" (Brown 1985, 324). He argues that his program does not strengthen mental faculties as such, but teaches children how to use more effectively the resources they already have. Yet he fails to specify how this might be done, except to point out such generalities as bringing the material to the child's level, increasing motivation to learn, giving the child "the pleasure of self-confidence," and so forth.

Binet also introduced a notion similar to Vygotsky's zone of proximal development, which we will deal with in detail later. This refers to the child's "region of sensitivity to instruction" (Wood and Middleton 1975):

> The teacher, with only a few students to work with, is able to know each of them. The teacher looks after them, making sure that the students understand. If not, he would start over, instead of keeping going. He would ask each student for a little effort, always proportional to his ability, and make sure that it was accomplished. He would teach them only a few things, but they were well learned, well understood, and well assimilated. *To ask a child only what he is really able to do*—what is more right, more simple? (Binet 1909, from Brown 1985, 326)

The most explicit statement of Binet's method stresses again his key notions of autocriticism, judgment, and reflection.

> Having to deal with children who don't know how to listen, how to watch or stay quiet, we guessed that our first goal wouldn't be to teach them what we think would be useful for them, but first to teach them how to learn. Thus, we created, with Mr. Belot and all our other collaborators' help, what we called exercises of mental orthopedics. The words are expressive and have become famous. One can guess the meaning. As physical orthopedics give remedy to a bent spine, mental orthopedics cultivate and reinforce attention, memory, perception, judgment, and will. We don't try to teach the child content or memory, we shape his mental faculties by exercise and practice in attention, perception, and self-control. For example, we train him to answer questions about what he saw in the street, in the class, then on the board, in books, etc. But it is important that the child be active, be the participant, be the leader. The teacher encourages and guides.

> There is no doubt that these methods are excellent, for home practice and in class, for the training of the child's mind. Instead of explaining some ideas to him, it is better to have him discover them. Instead of giving him orders, it is better to let him be

spontaneous, and just control him when necessary. It is excellent to have him form the habit of judging for himself, whether it be a book, a conversation, the event that everybody is talking about; excellent that he learns how to speak, how to explain, how to relate what he has seen; to defend his own opinion clearly, logically, methodically. (Binet 1909, from Brown 1985, 326–28)

Although the philosophy is compatible with contemporary ideas, the lack of specificity in how to *instruct* judgment and, even more seriously, how to *measure* such improvement, contributed to the decline of this program. Few people today are even aware that Binet engaged in remedial education. And it is surprising that these instructional activities did not penetrate his testing program more thoroughly. The link between Binet's testing program and his instructional program was weak to nonexistent, a common problem to which we shall return.

The interesting point is that Binet's underlying theory was used to *explain* performance on the test, although the theory did not play a role in determining the content of the test. In contrast, the theory did guide *directly* his attempts at remediation. That is, even though the theory is not readily discernible from the structure of the test itself, it did lead to a "metacognitive" kind of remedial program, featuring attention to students monitoring and regulating their own learning activities. As Binet's theory was supplanted, so too were the suggestions for instruction.

With the reinvention of metacognition as a central tenet of intelligence, contemporary researchers still face the crucial questions Binet raised: (1) how domain general or domain specific are processes like planning, monitoring, judging, and reflecting? (2) how do we measure effectively a child's learning potential within and across domains? and (3) how do we instruct children to become more effective learners—how do we teach them to learn how to learn? We will return to these issues in our discussion of contemporary work on guided assessment.

The Relation of IQ to Learning

Another of the debates that has continued from the inception of the testing movement concerns the relation between IQ and learning. Conclusions about the existence of such a relation have fluctuated over time, due in part to changes in the way in which learning has been treated theoretically at different junctures throughout the century. The shifts have influenced both the ways in which students, particularly academically at-risk students, have been viewed and the kinds of instruction they have received. Recall how Binet's emphasis on learning and his theory about the skills of learning influenced his mental orthopedics program. As the centrality of learning processes to views of intelligence changed, and as theories of learning changed, so too did the kinds of instructional programs afforded marginal students. Here we summarize briefly some of the changes that took place and the views that held sway in the middle third of the century.

In the early 1900s, it was commonly believed that IQ tests measured the ability to learn; indeed, this is what they were designed to do. But controversy over this belief was also widespread. Many early theorists claimed that intelligence *was* the ability to learn (Peterson 1925). For example, at an influential 1921 conference concerned with definitions of what intelligence tests actually measured, Buckingham (1921, 273) claimed directly that "intelligence is the ability to learn." Colvin (1921, 136) described intelligence as "equivalent to the capacity to learn." Pintner (1921, 139) defined it as "the ability to adapt adequately to relatively new situations" and as "the ease of forming new habits." Henman (1921, 195) described the intelligent man as "one who is capable of readily appropriating information or knowledge—intelligence involves two factors—the capacity for knowledge and knowledge possessed." And Dearborn (1921, 210) explicitly dubbed intelligence as "the capacity to learn or profit from experience."

The stronger claim that the *best* indexes of intelligence would be those that actually measured learning directly was also prevalent in the 1920s. For example, Dearborn argued that "measurement of the actual process of learning would furnish the best test of intelligence" (Dearborn 1921, 211), and Thorndike stated that "estimates of it (intelligence) are, or at least should be, estimates of the ability to learn. To be able to learn harder things, or to be able to learn the same things more quickly, would then be the single basis of evaluation" (Thorndike 1926, 17–18). In short, Woodrow (1946), who was to attack this position later, complained that "statements identifying learning ability with intelligence are found so frequently that a careless reader might form the opinion that such identification is beyond dispute" (p. 149).

Woodrow later renounced the 1921 consensus. What caused his skepticism? Primarily Woodrow's own work. He began by defining intelligence as "the capacity to acquire capacity" and set out to test this view through a series of studies that asked whether learning and transfer efficiency were related to standard IQ measures. For example, in 1917, Woodrow published two papers concerning the learning (Woodrow 1917a) and transfer (Woodrow 1917b) performance of "normal" and "retarded" students matched for a mental age of nine to ten years. The learning tasks required that the students sort five geometrical forms (stars, triangles, and so on) into different boxes. They sorted five hundred of these a day for thirteen days, with the order of the boxes being changed every two days. The main metric was the increase over time in the number of forms sorted. Transfer tests consisted of two new sorting tasks (lengths of sticks and colored pegs) and two cancellation tasks (letters and geometric forms). The normal and retarded children did not differ on any of the tests, and Woodrow concluded that IQ and learning proficiency were *not* related.

As another example, in later work with college students (Woodrow 1938a, 1938b), learning was assessed on tasks such as backward writing, reproduction of spot patterns, horizontal adding, canceling letters, estimating lengths, and speed in making gates (making four horizontal lines and one diagonal slash in each square of a page divided into a thousand squares). Transfer measures were not included because, by the 1930s, learning theorists, indoctrinated by Thorndike and Woodworth (1901), were quite convinced that transfer hardly ever happens! Again Woodrow found no intelligence-learning relation at all. Reviewing the contemporary literature, Woodrow (1946) denied the intelligence-learning position so popular in 1921: "Intelligence, far from being identical with the amount of improvement shown by practice, has practically nothing to do with the matter" (p. 151). This conclusion became doctrine for decades, although those citing it soon lost sight of the flimsy data base on which it was predicated.

Woodrow's tasks, and those of others working at the same time, reflected the prevailing conception of learning as "improvement shown by practice," a very general skill or faculty indeed. As such, the type of task on which that improvement was founded did not matter. There was no detailed process analysis of *what* was changing with practice. There were no systematic rules *shared* between learning problems that could be induced during the course of practice and no *principled transfer gradient* to which such rules could be applied. Furthermore, the conditions under which learning was to occur were simply those of "practice unguided save for knowledge of results" (Cronbach 1967, 26). In a very real sense, there was no opportunity for students in these experiments to learn. What were they to learn? What were they to remember? What were they supposed to transfer? Why should people with high general ability sort stars and circles, make gates, and so on, any more quickly than those with putatively lower ability? In short, the tasks do not appear to represent the most fertile ground for seeking a relation between learning and ability.

The dominant theory of learning had strong implications for the way in which students were treated. Intelligence became viewed as comprising a set of skills, abilities, or processes that students "possessed" in varying degrees. Following a medical model, weak students were seen as "lacking" or "deficient" in the operation of some, maybe many, of those skills. Remedial programs were then designed to strengthen the operation of those skills. Following the learning theory of the times, the programs featured simple drill and practice on skill execution. As we have argued in more detail elsewhere (Brown and Campione 1986), both the skills thus targeted and the contexts in which they were practiced had relatively little to do with actual academic tasks such as reading and mathematics.

Current Approaches to Learning

In contrast to earlier work, contemporary learning theories are theories of understanding that admit privileged classes of learning and cede a special place to the learner's understanding and control of the learning process—metacognition, if you will (Brown, Bransford, Ferrara, and Campione 1983). Contemporary work is guided by a view of learning as an active, socially mediated process. Great care in task analysis is seen as a necessary condition for evaluating learning and transfer, assumed to operate within limited fields (Glaser 1988). In current research, the problems to be learned are set in nonarbitrary domains, that is, ones in which there are rules for the students to learn and it is possible for those students to come to understand why certain approaches are appropriate in some situations and not in others (Brown 1978). This understanding then serves as a basis for subsequent use of the newly acquired information; that is, principled transfer is possible. The preferred metric of learning is a change in the processes of learning rather than an increase in speed of production over time. Often, this change in process is socially mediated via a supportive context that involves relatively direct instruction.

Guided by such a learning theory, in a series of studies on inductive reasoning, we have consistently found a clear relation between psychometric IQ and learning or transfer efficiency (Campione and Brown 1984, 1987). The settings involved rule-based IQ-like tasks, such as progressive matrix and series completion problems, that permit principled transfer; that is, problems could differ in surface formats but still rest upon the same underlying set of basic rules (details of such tasks will be given later). Unlike earlier testing procedures, we provided assistance if independent solution was not obtained. In comparative studies of normal and educable retarded children, matched for a mental age of nine to ten years (as were Woodrow's), normal children outperformed retarded learners, and the magnitude of this difference increased as the similarity of the learning and transfer contexts decreased. In other studies involving a wide spread of normal ability (IQs ranging from 85 to 140), learning and transfer metrics were again significantly correlated with IQ. Our findings are diametrically opposed to Woodrow's. We will discuss these studies in the section on guided (dynamic) assessment.

We argue that the differences between Woodrow's results and later work on guided assessment reflect disparate theoretical conceptions of what learning is, conceptions that dictate the type of learning that is examined. Woodrow's theory led him to concentrate on increased speed of production following practice on any learning task. Our theory led us to consider the amount of guidance and aid needed for the acquisition and application of a set of rules, rather than the number of trials required for learning to appear.

Another feature of contemporary work on dynamic assessment is the concentration on current learning, rather than the fruits of past learning, a development recommended in the 1921 conference by Colvin, Dearborn, Haggerty, Woodrow, and others, all of whom made the point that IQ tests, as a measure of past learning, were only indirectly a measure of current learning ability. Such tests provide a good measure of learning ability only if one makes the tenuous assumption that all examinees have had "common opportunities for past learning" (Colvin 1921, 137). All argue that better yet would be a measure of learning as it is actually occurring, a theme picked up in the section on guided assessment.

Selection and Labeling

A third recurrent issue in the development of the testing movement was the problem of selection and labeling. From the start Binet had warned against the enormous potential for abuse inherent in mental testing. He feared that teachers would reason that "here is an excellent opportunity for getting rid of all children who trouble us" (Binet 1905, 169, from Binet and Simon 1916) and that reification of a score into an entity would lead to the kind of self-fulfilling prophecy that indeed did emerge: "It is really too easy to discover signs of backwardness in an individual when one is forewarned" (1905, 170, from Binet and Simon 1916).

Binet's task, set by the ministry of education in Paris, was to identify children in need of special education in order to select those who could be helped by enriched experience. Mental testing, for Binet, should have the positive effect of enhancing learning potential through education tailored to special needs. As we have seen earlier, he practiced what he preached and spent a considerable amount of time developing a special curriculum for slow-learning children.

Historically, however, widespread mental testing was developed as a means of selecting individuals for educational, industrial, and military placement to achieve a maximal return on a given training investment. The aim was efficiency and economy in placement, *not* Binet's idea of helping the needy by providing additional enrichment. The classic example of such mass testing was the Army Alpha and Beta tests used to select and place recruits in World War I. The Army Alpha, demanding reading, was given to literate recruits; the Beta test, consisting of pictorial material, was given to those failing the Alpha and those deemed illiterate. Those failing the Beta were then to be brought back and tested individually on selected Binet scales. This retesting hardly ever occurred because of time pressures and the fact that many scoring low on the Beta were minorities, especially from the South, and it was deemed that they could not benefit from further testing. Indeed, the comments made about them were so intemperate that we will not repeat them here; the interested reader is referred to Yerkes's (1921) contemporary report and Gould's (1981) devastating synopsis of it.

All recruits were graded on a scale from A to E. Men of D grade were designated as "not expected to understand written directions," "rarely suited for tasks requiring special skill," "lacking in initiative and responsibility." That they could not read is a reification of their illiteracy, but how one could reach the other conclusions on the basis of these tests is hard to imagine, especially given the widespread lack of opportunity for formal education before the World War I.

Obviously, however, the tests were not used to select those for remedial training but to label and place human material efficiently. For example, no man receiving a score of C or below could be considered for officer training.

An interesting sideline of this first emergence of mass testing is the publicity that followed the finding that the average white American male had a mental age of thirteen. As the learned ones of the day had declared that any adult with a mental age of between eight and twelve was a moron, "then we are a nation of nearly half-morons" (Yerkes 1921, 791). This claim led to laments about America's declining intelligence because of the unconstrained breeding of the poor, and the presence of feebleminded, unpopular minorities and certain less desirable immigrant groups. Not, you will note, a call for better education. The potential biasing effect against the poor due to differential exposure to both informal and formal educational opportunities did not seem to worry anyone. For example, the Army Beta, although not requiring reading, did require a recognition of numbers and how to write them. As Gould reports, an examiner admitted to being touched by the "intense effort put into answering the questions, often by men who never before had held a pencil in their hands" (Gould 1981, 204). Still a D man is a D man and must be assigned accordingly, often with short shrift to active combat.

A concern for equal opportunities developed late. Culturally fair tests began to appear after World War II, but these, on occasion, actually increased the difference in scores between minority and majority cultures (Jensen 1980). Culturally fair tests were standardized versions of Army Beta-like items, consisting of pictorial sequences, analogies, and so forth, and requiring no verbal content. The idea was to equate all for background knowledge by their lack of it: supposedly, no one had been exposed to such tests before, and, therefore, they were fair to all. Yet this notion presupposes that all had equal exposure to academic-type tests, taken in academic settings, under time pressure. It also completely overlooks the concept of learning to learn; different cultural groups supposedly differ in terms of how much help they have had becoming independent academic learners, comfortable with timed tests of, for example, spatial puzzles such as the Cattell or the Raven Progressive Matrices. So it should not be surprising that cultural differences in school readiness would continue to be found on so-called culturally fair tests as well as those that directly tap prior verbal knowledge.

Such "culture-fair" tests as the Cattell, the Raven, and subitems of the Wechsler Scale (such as the coding item) were intended to measure new learning and, therefore, be a better index of "the ability to learn." However, a major feature of such tests is that performance is unguided: students do not even receive information as to the correctness of their answers; they certainly receive no instruction that could form a basis upon which to learn. As we shall see, several recent approaches to assessment involve attention to these issues. Students are explicitly taught how to take the test, the argument being that such instruction will minimize the role of extraneous factors having to do with test-taking sophistication, test anxiety, and so forth. The counterclaim, of course, is that teaching students how to take the test will destroy its predictive validity. This is an empirical, not theoretical, issue and we will review some of the relevant evidence in the section on guided assessment.

It is important, therefore, to note that a central concern of those interested in the development of guided assessment methods is that efforts to assess children's competence should provide mediation and guidance so that they can show their *potential for learning*. The two principal proponents of guided assessments began to think this way when faced with severely disadvantaged populations. For both Vygotsky (1978) and Feuerstein (1980), a major motivation for their attempts to develop alternative assessment methods was the need to work with individuals who had been exposed to suboptimal learning environments. Vygotsky, in his role as the director of the Institute of Defectology in Moscow, dealt with children raised in the aftermath of the Russian Revolution. Feuerstein worked with children who were refugees from displaced persons camps in the wake of World War II. In both cases, it is safe to say that those students' opportunities for learning had been severely restricted and that performance on standard tests would provide virtually no valid information to guide either classification or instruction. Both Vygotsky's and Feuerstein's approach was to observe students as they were actually learning to deal with novel problems and to use their performance as the basis for prediction *and remediation*.

THEORETICAL FOUNDATIONS

Vygotsky and Feuerstein provide the historical underpinnings of most modern research in the area of dynamic assessment and its role in instruction. Therefore, before proceeding to a review of relevant research, we will give a thumbnail sketch of their theories.

Vygotsky

We begin with a brief description of Vygotsky's theory concerning assessment and instruction. Vygotsky's theory of psychological processes has as its central tenet the notion of development in social contexts and, as such, it is not surprising that he had a special interest in developing methods of observing cognitive processes "undergoing change right before one's eyes." His is a complex theory and we will concentrate here only on those aspects pertinent to the main theme of creating methods of looking at learning potential and interactive instruction.

A key concept in Vygotsky's theory was that of a *zone of proximal development* (ZPD) through which a child can navigate with and without aid. Vygotsky intended the notion of a ZPD to capture the widely recognized fact that "learning should be matched in some manner with the child's developmental level" (Vygotsky 1978, 85). But he went further, arguing that one cannot understand the child's developmental level unless one considers both the *actual developmental level* and the *potential developmental level.* "The zone of proximal development is the distance between the actual developmental level as determined by independent problem solving and the level of potential development as determined through problem solving under adult guidance, or in collaboration with more capable peers" (Vygotsky 1978, 86). The actual developmental level is the result of "already completed developmental cycles." Static tests reveal "already completed development"; what is still needed is some estimate of the potential for future learning.

An example of a static test of actual developmental level would be a one-shot test of an average five-year-old's performance on a task purportedly measuring a particular cognitive process. Many researchers and clinical assessors stop here. But what if one does not stop here, and like Piaget in his clinical interviews, "offers leading questions" or, like Vygotsky, demonstrates "how the problem is solved" or "initiates the solution and the child completes it." In short, what if the child "barely misses an independent solution of the problem" (Vygotsky 1978, 85) and is helped by a supportive other to achieve a greater level of competence? This is the situation that the ZPD was meant to capture.

Vygotsky addressed this point by posing the following thought experiment:

> Assume that we have determined the mental age of two children to be eight years. However, we do not stop with this. Rather, we attempt to determine how each of these children will solve tasks that were meant for older children. We assist each child through demonstration, through leading questions, and by introducing the initial elements of the task's solution. With this help or collaboration from the adult, one of these children solves problems characteristic of a twelve year old while the other solves problems only at a level typical of a nine year old. This difference between the child's actual level of development and the level of performance that he achieves in collaboration with the adult, defines the zone of proximal development. In this example, the zone can be expressed by the number 4 for one child and by the number 1 for the other. Can we assume that these children stand at identical levels of mental development, that the state of their development coincides? Obviously not. (Vygotsky [1934] 1986, 203–4)

Luria, a disciple of Vygotsky's, added an additional methodological point to Vygotsky's classic comparison of the two children with different learning potential, an addition that has important ramifications for issues of assessment. Luria (1961) suggested that Vygotsky's notion of the ZPD might prove useful in distinguishing between truly "feebleminded" children and those who have been underestimated in some way. To test his theory he introduced the superficially trivial modification of the Vygotsky anecdote of the two eight-year-olds. He asked his readers to imagine *three* children with IQs of, say, 70. Asked to work collaboratively with an examiner, one shows little gain, while the remaining two show marked improvement. Upon being asked *again to perform unaided*, one of the children reverts to her initial low level while the other maintains his gain. This example contains two important differences from Vygotsky's original: (1) the introduction of a *pre*test and *post*test to measure improvement, and (2) the difference between those who maintain their improvement when working independently and those who do not. It is interesting that the introduction of a pretest and posttest to look for "individual" gain occurred to most research groups tackling this problem empirically. It is a source of some advantage, some disadvantage, and considerable controversy (Griffin and Cole 1984; Guthke 1982; Minick 1987; Wertsch 1984), which we will review later. But, as we will see, many programs of guided assessment have stressed the importance of posttest status as a better predictor of a child's developmental level.

Regardless of how it is estimated, Vygotsky believed that the fundamental principle of a ZPD was essential to an understanding of learning and development. He argued:

> For the child . . . development based on collaboration and instruction is the source of all the specifically human characteristics of consciousness. Development based on instruction is a fundamental fact. Thus, a central feature of the psychological study of instruction is the potential the child has to raise himself to a higher intellectual level of development through collaboration. . . . The zone of proximal development . . . *determines the domain of transitions that are accessible to the child.* . . . What lies in the zone of proximal development at one stage is realized and moves to the level of actual development at a second. In other words, what the child is able to do in collaboration today he will be able to do independently tomorrow. (Vygotsky [1934] 1986, 206)

The zone of proximal development, then, marks ever-changing boundaries of competence within which a child can perform with and without aid. At the lower boundaries are those "fruits of developmental cycles already completed," a conservative estimate of the child's status. At the upper boundary are the estimates of just-emerging competences that are actually created by interactions in a supportive context. By considering both levels, one has a better estimate of a child's potential and, in addition, by observing the process of change as it occurs "right before one's eyes," one learns a great deal about development in general as well as about the particular development of the child in question (Brown and Reeve 1987).

It is important to note that what the child can do now in social interaction becomes, in time, part of his or her independent repertoire of learning activities. Social interaction creates zones of proximal development that operate initially *only* in these collaborative interactions. But, gradually, the newly awakened processes "are internalized, they become part of the child's *independent developmental achievement*" (Vygotsky 1978, 90). "What is the upper bound of competence today becomes the springboard of tomorrow's achievements" (Brown and Reeve 1987).

The implications of this theory for assessment and instruction occurred to Vygotsky; indeed, it was in part to address these issues that the theory was developed. As director of the Institute of Defectology in Moscow, he was intimately involved in classification and remediation at a time when standardized tests were ideologically impermissible. Furthermore, Vygotsky viewed assessment and instruction as inextricably related; Vygotsky *always* discussed the concept of the ZPD in connection with the relation between instruction and development. Unfortunately, Vygotsky himself left behind no accessible empirical description of what was actually done at the institute.

Feuerstein

Feuerstein's theory of learning bears a striking family resemblance to Vygotsky's, also placing great weight on assisted instruction as essential for adequate assessment of learning potential. According to Feuerstein, cognitive growth is the result of incidental and mediated learning. Incidental learning occurs as a result of the child's exposure to a changing environment, but mediated learning is seen as the more important shaper of human growth. "Mediated learning is the training given to the human organism by an experienced adult who frames, selects, focuses and feeds back an environmental experience in such a way as to create appropriate learning sets" (Feuerstein 1969, 6). Mediated learning refers to experiences in which a supportive other (a parent, teacher, peer) intervenes between the individual and environment and serves to influence the nature of their interaction. Feuerstein believes that these experiences are an essential aspect of development, beginning when the parent selects significant objects for the infant's attention and proceeding throughout development, with the adult systematically shaping the child's learning experiences. In Feuerstein's model, this is the principal means by which children develop the cognitive operations necessary for learning independently. By interacting with an adult, who guides problem-solving activity and structures the environment, the child gradually comes to adopt problem-solving and structuring activities as his or her own.

Feuerstein has taken as his major research focus the intellectual development of deprived students, and it is in the context of his mediated theory of learning that Feuerstein describes their basic learning problems. Feuerstein argues that the culturally deprived child should not be confused with the culturally different child. Cultural deprivation is "an *intrinsic* criterion of specific culture" (Feuerstein et al. 1979, 39); that is, the culture to which the individual belongs has not been successfully transmitted; therefore, the child does not have the cognitive mechanisms necessary to function within his own, or any other, culture. Cultural difference on the other hand is an *extrinsic* criterion; the individual's original culture has been successfully transmitted so that she can function well within her own culture and, as a result, she has the cognitive mechanisms necessary to adapt to a different culture (she has learned how to learn). The culturally deprived individual lacks such adaptability because his own culture has not been successfully transmitted. The culturally deprived individual has "a reduced capacity to modify his intellectual structures in response to sources of stimuli. The inability to modify, on his own, his intellectual structures implies impaired and absent cognitive structures" (Feuerstein 1980, 19).

Feuerstein argues that the principal reason for the poor performance of many disadvantaged students is the lack of consistent mediated learning in their earlier developmental histories due to many factors, including parental apathy, ignorance, or overcommitment. But poor performance under such circumstances must be regarded as an underestimate of the level that could be achieved if disadvantaged students were subjected to intensive, remedial mediated learning experiences. Feuerstein predicts that retarded performers, who do poorly because of inadequate early learning environments, will show improvement if supported and guided by an adult tester or a supportive learning environment. By contrast, truly retarded individuals, for example, those with organic brain damage, would be expected to show less benefit from intensive intervention aimed at supplying the missing mediated learning experience. Feuerstein's basic position seems to be that, to the extent that children's prior histories have been suboptimal, dynamic assessment procedures will be better indicators of learning potential.

GUIDED ASSESSMENT

We turn now to empirical attempts to design *assessments* of mental functioning aimed at revealing learning potential masked by static tests of ability. In response to widespread concern about the existing nature of static tests, several investigators have developed testing approaches that involved guided learning sessions to test a child's learning potential. *Dynamic assessment*, a term used initially by Feuerstein (1979), is the general term used to encompass a number of distinct approaches (see Lidz 1987, for an overview). Others have used different descriptors, Budoff (1987a) referring to *learning potential* assessment, Guthke (1982) and a number of German researchers to *learning tests*, Carlson (Carlson and Wiedl 1978) to a *testing-the-limits approach*, the Vanderbilt group (see, for example, Vye et al. 1987) to *mediated assessment*, Vygotsky and Luria to evaluation of the *zone of proximal or potential development*, and the Illinois group (see, for example, Campione 1989; Campione and Brown, in press) to assessment via *assisted learning and transfer*. The common feature of all these approaches is an emphasis on evaluating the psychological processes involved in learning and change. This contrasts with standard methods of assessment that rely on product information. The argument is that individuals with comparable scores on static tests may have taken different paths to those scores and that consideration of those differences can provide information of additional diagnostic value. The clearest example is of individuals who have not experienced a full range of the opportunities needed to acquire the skills or information being tested. And it is in this context—testing children either from atypical backgrounds or who were experiencing school-related problems—that most of the above researchers have conducted their work.

Different workers have concentrated on different aspects of the problem. In the case of students considered likely to perform poorly in school, there are issues associated with both identification of those in need of special help and the development of the means for providing that help. Those who have emphasized different goals have tended to opt for different methods. Generically, the two approaches can be said to involve *normative* or *threshold* models. Normative approaches are highly standardized and aspire to produce strong quantitative data that can be used to compare individuals and thus provide the basis for determining who needs assistance. The goal is to increase the predictive validity of the assessment procedure and thus inform the general referral process, for example, in special education. This normative approach is seen as necessary, as the distribution of limited services to subsets of students must be defended on scientifically defensible grounds. (In the "brave new world" we envision at the end of this chapter, it would be possible to minimize the selection and classification problem.)

In the threshold case, the goal is not one of comparing individuals, but rather finding the instructional approach that will help each student reach an acceptable level of performance. In this system, assessment is embedded in instruction and, because there is no intent to compare individuals directly, the assessment process does not have to be standardized and hence allows the tester considerable flexibility. Although the ideal assessment procedure would serve both needs, there are trade-offs that result in some procedures being more appropriate in one case than in the other. Across the approaches we review here, however, the common feature is an emphasis on an individual's *potential for change*. In the next section, we outline a taxonomy of the various approaches, highlighting the similarities and differences that exist among the alternative formats.

Taxonomy of Approach to Guided Assessment

It is useful to classify the various approaches to guided assessment by considering their stances along three general dimensions. The first, which we refer to as *focus*, looks at the competing ways in which potential for change can be assessed. One is by observing or measuring the actual improvement that takes place following intervention. The alternative is to try to specify the processes that underlie any improvement and assess the operation of those processes directly. By *interaction*, we mean the nature of the social interaction involving the examiner and subject. That interaction can be conducted in either a standardized or clinical fashion. And finally, by *target*, we indicate that dynamic assessment attempts can be geared to either general or domain-specific skills.

Focus

There are two general ways in which potential for change has been assessed. One is to concentrate on the *product* of assisted assessment; that is, how much change has occurred or how much aid was needed to effect meaningful change. The other is to concentrate on the *processes* that are changing.

Product

In the product approach, the idea is to provide an opportunity for students to learn to deal with the test items and then to generate quantitative estimates of the effects of that intervention. The most common product approach involves some form of test-train-test procedure. Students take a particular test, are given some practice and/or instruction on typical test items, and then take a posttest. This procedure yields (1) the pretest score, that is, the static test score that would normally be the primary vehicle for prediction or classification; (2) data available from the instructional interaction itself; (3) the change score, or the degree of improvement that took place from the pretest to the posttest; and (4) the posttest score. Each of these scores is a candidate predictor, and the empirical question is, which is the most predictive of future performance? This is the general procedure used by, among others, Budoff (see, for example, 1974), Soviet psychologists influenced by Vygotsky and Luria (Egorova, Lubovskii, and Rozanova; see Brown and French 1979), the Illinois group (see Campione and Brown 1984, 1987, in press), Carlson and his colleagues (see, for example, Carlson and Wiedl 1978, 1979), and Embretson (1987). In the next section, we indicate some of the differences among these researchers.

Process

The alternative approach to measuring potential for change is to attempt to specify the processes involved in change in more detail and to evaluate their operation. That is, rather than looking at how much learning takes place in a given situation, we can try to specify the skills that underlie learning and evaluate them directly. Toward this end, Feuerstein highlights a group of deficient cognitive functions that are evaluated through a battery of instruments. In some of our own work on reading (for example, Palincsar and Brown 1984), we have highlighted a number of comprehension-fostering and comprehension-monitoring activities (questioning, summarizing, predicting, and clarifying) that serve as the focus for instruction and assessment. The goal here is a description of an individual that reveals which skills are functioning smoothly and which are not being appropriately used. This profile can then be used as the basis for designing enrichment activities or for structuring teacher decisions. In this approach, pretests and posttests are not necessary, although they could be incorporated. Feuerstein and his followers prefer this second approach.

Interaction

For some, the goal is to devise a standardized protocol to govern the provision of help to students during the training portion of the intervention. That is, given a test-train-test sequence, the training experiences should be as standardized and consistent across students as possible. Others resort to a less structured, clinical interview approach in which the examiner is given latitude in selection of both the tasks to be presented and the way in which to respond to the test-taker statements and actions.

Standardized Procedure

For those who choose to standardize the procedure (for example, Budoff 1987b; Campione and Brown 1987, in press; Carlson and Wiedl 1978, 1979; Embretson 1987), one goal is to generate psychometrically defensible quantitative data that can be used for description and classification; the approach is normative. Even here, however, there are differences. Budoff is concerned primarily with a gain score, the difference between the initial and final test performance (taking into account the pretest score). His argument is that how much a student gains from instruction ("gainer" versus "nongainer" status) will provide diagnostic information beyond that afforded by the pretest or other standardized scores. Carlson and his colleagues, as well as Embretson, focus more directly on the posttest score. They believe that the intervention provided between testing sessions will improve performance by minimizing the effects of extraneous factors (motivational, misunderstanding of instructions, and so on) that artificially reduce performance. The higher, less contaminated levels of performance obtained on the final test should then provide more accurate characterizations of subjects and should result in greater predictive validity.

In the work of the Illinois group (Campione and Brown 1974, 1987, in press), we have taken still another approach which concentrates on *transfer efficiency* as a major metric of learning. Students are asked to learn new rules or principles, and we provide titrated instruction, beginning with weak, general hints and proceeding through much more detailed instruction. We ask not how much improvement takes place, but rather how much help students need to reach a specified criterion with regard to rule use and then how much additional help they need to begin to transfer those rules to novel situations. The idea is that these assisted learning and transfer scores will provide more information about individuals than competing static scores, for example, general intelligence or entering competence.

Clinical Evaluation

In designing the interaction between examiner and student, the alternative method, championed by Feuerstein (1979), is to resort to a more clinical evaluation. The group at Vanderbilt (see, for example, Bransford et al. 1987; Burns 1985; Vye, Burns, Delclos, and Bransford 1987) has devised a compromise method. The overall procedure is scripted, but occasionally the interviewer is allowed considerable latitude in addressing student difficulties. The argument is that the most sensitive assessments result when the examiner, rather than being restricted by a standardized protocol, has the flexibility to follow promising leads as they arise during the interview. A crucial feature of the interview is the examiner's ability to take advantage of the student's cues and use them as an opportunity to probe in more detail the student's strengths and weaknesses. The goal here, rather than generating quantitatively useful data, is to paint a rich clinical picture of an individual learner, one that can be used to guide remediation attempts. It is also argued that this is an efficient way to merge assessment and instruction. When the examiner perceives a problem, he or she can select examples and provide instruction designed to build on existing strengths, clarify misconceptions, or show the student how to improve his or her reasoning. Here the overriding goal is to maximize student performance, and the approach reflects a threshold, rather than normative, approach to testing.

Target

The goal of assessment can be either evaluation of relatively domain-general or domain-specific skills and processes. Some (for example, Feuerstein 1979) have concentrated on general skills (deficient cognitive functions, in Feuerstein's terminology), whereas others (for example, Bransford et al. 1988; Brown et al., in press; Campione, Brown, and Connell 1988; Ferrara 1987) have been concerned with assessments situated within a particular content area. The competing assumptions are in terms of whether one wishes to assess and eventually modify problems associated with intelligence or more domain-specific cognitive skills (Brown and Campione 1986; Campione 1989; Campione and Brown 1987).

It is important to point out that these different emphases represent just that—emphases—and several of the research groups we review below have combined more than one focus. Similarly, the programs should be seen as representing points on a continuum rather than reflecting dichotomous points of view. With these caveats in mind, we will now review in more depth some of the leading programs.

Major Programs of Research and Practice

In this section we will describe some of the major programs of research in which dynamic assessment procedures have been developed. We will begin with the two major programs that have opted for a primarily clinical approach: Feuerstein's Learning Potential Assessment Device (LPAD) and work from the Vanderbilt group. We will then proceed to programs which have taken a more standardized approach and have relied heavily on the pretest-posttest format: Budoff, Carlson, and the Illinois group.

Clinical Approaches

Feuerstein

Like most proponents in the field, Feuerstein was motivated by skepticism concerning the suitability of traditional psychometric measures as indices of an individual's capacity to *acquire* skills strategies and knowledge. He therefore developed the *Learning Potential Assessment Device* (LPAD) to measure low-achieving individuals' ability to benefit from instruction. In the words of Feuerstein et al. (1987), the goal of the LPAD is to "produce changes in the very structural nature of the cognitive processes that directly determine cognitive functioning" (p. 42), or to "modify the cognitive style characteristics of an individual, or his or her preferential mode of functioning" (p. 43).

The philosophy driving the LPAD is that *structural change* is possible regardless of etiology, stage of development, and degree of severity of condition (Feuerstein et al. 1987). Further, Feuerstein et al. argue that "*new* cognitive structures" can be produced in the individual by the instructional component of the LPAD that is not restricted to building up cognitive structures already within the child's repertoire (p.44).

Feuerstein et al. claim that change in cognitive structures is brought about through the intervention component of the LPAD, which serves a dual purpose. One purpose of the intervention is to produce changes in the child's performance in order to be able to *assess* the child's degree of "modifiability." The second purpose of the intervention is to *remediate* problems in the child's problem solving and to serve as the basis for the intervention program following assessment.

To achieve this end, Feuerstein's model of dynamic assessment incorporates four major changes from traditional testing approaches. First, he claims to select tasks that tap "higher mental processes" that are susceptible to change and in which meaningful change can be detected. The tasks are also meant to reflect "complex real life experience"; however, Feuerstein, like many others in this field, uses primarily common IQ-like items in his battery, such as matrices problems, tests of analytic perception, span tests, and embedded figure tasks. Presumably, the tests are not as important as the clinical judgment concerning the child's mental processes as she attacks them.

Second, Feuerstein fundamentally changes the testing situation. Rather than standardized and static, the testing situation is flexible, individualized, and highly interactive. Feuerstein views the examiner as a teacher/observer and the examinee as a learner/performer. Crucial is the role of affect. A neutral, unresponsive stance from the examiner will, Feuerstein feels, essentially reinforce the examinee's already negative view of herself. Simply offering encouragement or praise will be viewed as only lip service. To counteract such feelings and produce a more positive attitude, the examiner must adopt the role of teacher: a role that necessitates active involvement on the part of the examiner. "Thus, the examiner constantly intervenes, makes remarks, requires and gives explanations whenever and wherever they are necessary, asks for repetition, sums up experiences, anticipates difficulties and warns the child about them, and creates reflective insightful thinking in the child not only concerning the task but also regarding the examinee's reaction to it" (Feuerstein 1979, 102).

Third, Feuerstein argues for a process rather than a product orientation. For example, he is not interested in how many items a child can complete but in how a child receives information from the environment (input), how she deals with that information (elaboration), and how she communicates what she has processed (output). The goal is not, as it is in traditional assessment, to predict future behavior on the basis of a static score. Feuerstein's approach to dynamic assessment seeks to assess just how modifiable the individual's structures are and where the individual's deficits lie. The result of Feuerstein's analysis is a *cognitive map*. Briefly, this map is composed of seven parameters (see Feuerstein 1980, chapter 5, and Feuerstein et al. 1979, 123–25; see also Bransford et al. 1987), by which a mental act can be analyzed, categorized, and ordered. The seven parameters of the map are (1) *content*: it is important to estimate the familiarity of the content or material in determining the success of the child; (2) *modality*: different children have different patterns of strengths and weaknesses within disparate modalities, such as the verbal, pictorial, aural, and tactile modes; (3) *phase*: the three phases of mental operations—input, elaboration, and output—are distinct, and efficiency in each phase should be estimated; (4) *operation:* it is important to evaluate the skills or strategies that the children apply; (5) *level of complexity*: one must consider the level of complexity of material that the examinee can handle; (6) *level of abstraction*: similarly, it is important to assess the level of abstraction of the task; and (7) *level of efficiency*: efficiency may be impaired by lack of familiarity, fatigue, anxiety, and so on, and this should be taken into account when evaluating the child.

Finally, Feuerstein has a great deal to say about *interpretation*. Using the cognitive map of a child's "deficient cognitive functions," the interpreter tries to pinpoint the child's principal problems. Is the deficit occurring during the input, elaboration, or output phase? Is it the result of a content deficit, inefficient behavior on the task, the complexity or level of abstraction of the task? Interpretation centers on a *profile of modifiability* that outlines performance in three areas: "the domain in which the change has occurred, the quality of the achieved change, and the change in the amount and nature of the intervention required for the production of the structural modification" (Lidz 1987, 47).

The primary sign that a structural change has occurred is a decrease in dependence on the adult's help. This can be defined in a quantitative way or, more satisfactorily, as "the distance between the intervention and the achieved product" (Lidz 1987, 48), that is, in terms of the amount of help and the type of help the mediator provides. Is the mediator guiding the hand of the examinee or simply providing general instruction? In other words, the examiner specifies the *type* and *amount* of change qualitatively. Assessment and instruction are intermingled; improvement in a client *is* the measure of successful assessment because it implies that the mediator did assess the child well enough to effect change.

The inherent potential for circular reasoning here could pose a problem for interpretation, but essentially Feuerstein aims to divide people on a clinical continuum of those who are more or less modifiable and to draw a cognitive map of their strengths and weaknesses. Note that Feuerstein does seek to classify learners, specifically in terms of the amount and quality of help they need to acquire new skills. This goal is quite similar to our own (see below). The important difference is that Feuerstein attempts to get that information as a by-product of instruction: his examiners teach and generate the cognitive map as they go, and the questions concern the accuracy of the resulting description and the extent to which all learners are afforded equal opportunities to demonstrate their abilities (see Mehan 1973, for a discussion of tester bias effects even with noninteractive testing conditions). We standardize the test administration procedure and seek to assess individual readiness by asking how little instruction we need to provide to generate change.

Feuerstein and colleagues have used the LPAD with below-average adolescents, and they claim great success for the methodology. Supporting evidence for Feuerstein's approach with this population has been found by other researchers working in the area of cognitive intervention (for example, Ballester 1984; Frankenstein 1979; Haywood et al. 1975; Hobbs 1980; Meltzer 1984; Narrol and Bachor 1975; Scott 1978). In addition, Ballester and Lidz (cited by Lidz 1987) examined "nonexceptional" urban black preschool boys from low socioeconomic backgrounds as they worked on a series of cognitive tasks. They noted that the cognitive deficiencies highlighted by Feuerstein et al. (1979) were also observed in preschool children. And there was a significant association between cognitive deficiencies and academic performance for these young children.

The Vanderbilt Group

One of the major programs of research in America aimed at testing and extending the Feuerstein model of assessment was developed at Vanderbilt University (see, for example, Bransford et al. 1986, 1987; Burns, Delclos, and Vye, in press; Burns et al. 1987; Vye et al. 1987). In contrast to Feuerstein's work, which is primarily with adolescents, the Vanderbilt group has developed a series of procedures for assessing learning potential in young, intellectually handicapped children.

The Vanderbilt group has conducted several studies to examine the predictive validity of their dynamic assessment procedures (for representative studies see Burns et al. 1987; Vye et al. 1987). The major findings are that (a) static measures of IQ do not predict performance well; (b) both standardized and clinical dynamic assessment methods produce learning; and (c) clinical methods produce more transfer than standardized assistance. This latter finding highlights one of the contrasts between clinical and standardized methods. Mediated dynamic assessment, as developed by the Vanderbilt group, involves intensive instruction, and the standardized assistance method provides as little instruction as possible to diagnose readiness (see discussion below of Illinois group). Given these differences, the two procedures would be expected to yield different results and hence would be useful in different situations (Bransford et al. 1987).

We do not have space to do justice to this work, but the Vanderbilt group has, independent of Feuerstein, produced an impressive body of work suggesting that clinical assessment of learning potential, in the spirit of Feuerstein, is a viable method of assessing the hidden competence of underachieving students. In more recent research, the Vanderbilt group has begun extending its investigations to academic domains, such as mathematics and reading, an extension we will return to in the section on instruction. Their principal finding is that, indeed, traditional IQ tests do a grave disservice to disadvantaged children, underestimating their capacity to learn and thereby potentially assigning students to learning environments that would not capitalize on their true potential.

Before leaving the Vanderbilt group we would like to mention one extremely important finding about teacher expectation effects. Teachers are the intended consumers of information derived from dynamic assessment, and their impressions of a learner's potential have a great deal to do with academic success or failure. A rather depressing finding is that even though teachers have been informed of their students' impressive learning potential, this information has little effect on teachers' behavior toward them. Information to teachers, however, has usually taken the form of verbal reports on progress. In an important and creative study, the Vanderbilt group had teachers watching videotapes of children's performance before and after intervention (Vye et al. 1987). Teachers were asked to view both a segment of a standard static assessment and of a dynamic assessment on the same child. After viewing the excerpts, the teachers' opinions of the child were elicited. Teachers who viewed only static assessment consistently gave lower estimates of children than those who saw both static and dynamic assessment episodes. After dynamic events, teachers viewed the child as more competent and more strategic than they had thought. This positive influence has important implications for potential practical uses of dynamic assessment information by classroom teachers.

Standardized Approaches

The programs to be reviewed here all use a format that involves an attempt to optimize performance on some test. One approach features a test-train-test approach in which guided assessment of some form is interspersed between a pretest and a posttest. Across approaches, there are differences in the nature of the training, but in each, there is an attempt to standardize it in some way. Indeed, the need for standardization in order to convey progress in systematic ways has led the Vanderbilt group to modify its original clinical method in favor of a more scripted approach than that advocated by Feuerstein. In another variation, the testing procedure itself is modified. The goal is again to optimize performance, for example, by providing test takers with additional feedback about their performance, explanations about why some answers are right and some are wrong, and so on. The programs we will review also differ in their goals: Budoff and his colleagues ask whether gain occurs and, if so, whether it is predictive (see also Guthke 1982). Carlson and his colleagues ask whether the type of intervention matters and whether the resultant modified level of performance is more predictive than that obtained from the canonical form of the test. The Illinois group asks how much help (and what quality of help) is needed, and if this is predictive of future change. All work primarily with IQ-type deductive reasoning tasks, notably the Raven Progressive Matrices, although the Illinois group has extended the work to content domains of reading (Campione, Valencia, and Palincsar, work in progress) and mathematics (Brown et al., in press; Ferrara 1987) for reasons that will be discussed below.

Budoff

Budoff and colleagues were among the first in the United States to develop systematic learning-potential assessments, although there was a long prior history of work on coaching on IQ tests (see Lidz 1987, for a review). Budoff, claiming to be influenced by the Luria (1961) paper, developed a pretest and posttest approach for use with mentally retarded children. Basically the child is tested for initial unaided competence. He is then taught systematically to solve problems of that kind and given a posttest. Posttest scores are a composite measure reflecting the initial starting level of competence, an effect due to practice, and an effect due to specific training. Budoff (1974) reports that, although low IQ children tend to gain little from mere practice without specific training,

> following suitable training, many low IQ children will function at a level similar to the child from more privileged circumstances. This posttraining score, regardless of pretraining level, represents the child's optimal level of performance following an optimizing procedure. It permits a comparison between his *presently* low level of functioning, as indicated by his IQ, and his *potential* level of functioning—the third score is the posttraining score adjusted for pretest level. This residual score indicates the child's responsiveness to training, and by extension to the classroom regardless of his pretraining level. It is hypothesized to indicate the student's amenability to training given suitable curricula and school experience. (p. 33)

Budoff's learning-potential approach is based on a conceptualization of intelligence that stresses instructability, or the ability to profit from learning experiences directly related to the task at hand. Improved performance after training indicates problem-solving capability is not evident when instruction is not provided as part of the test administration. Of interest is the way in which these training sessions were devised. Budoff concentrated on IQ-type tasks, such as Raven's matrices and block building. We will describe block building in some detail to provide an example of the general approach.

Following a pretest on several block designs, the subjects enter the training phase of the test-train-test assessment procedure. The initial stage consists of presenting the problem without aid and waiting until the children solve it or fail to solve it on their own. If a child fails, a series of more and more explicit prompts is given until solution is reached. A series of prompts for Kohs Block problems is illustrated in figure 1.

The first prompt is a presentation of only one row of the design. Initially the blocks in the row are not outlined. On succeeding presentations, if the subject fails to align the blocks correctly, the design is progressively outlined. On the prompt cards where the blocks are given in outline (B_3, C_2, F_3) and on the final card (H), subjects are required to check whether each block in their design corresponds exactly with the comparable block on the card. Throughout the training period the child is encouraged to check his or her construction block by block against the design card: to "actively point, block by block, to his constructed design and the corresponding blocks on the design card—it was hoped thereby to encourage a more planned and systematic work approach and to

FIGURE 1

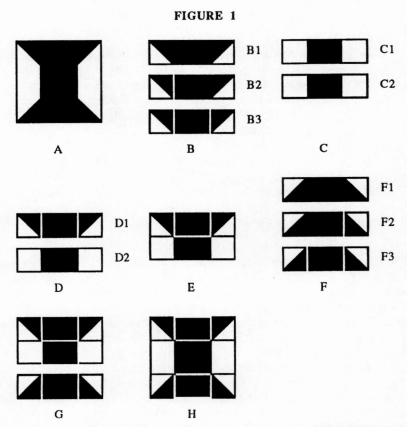

allow the subject to see concretely the success he is achieving" (Budoff 1974, 7). These procedures are strikingly similar to contemporary Soviet work (for a description, see Brown and French 1979), although the programs were developed independently.

Following training such as this on a variety of IQ-like test items, Budoff found three classes of children within his Educable Mentally Handicapped population: (a) subjects who demonstrate little or no gain following instruction (*nongainers*), (b) subjects who show marked gain (*gainers*), and (c) subjects who performed quite adequately on the pretest (*high scorers*).

Some problems are associated with Budoff's approach, notably the concentration on product rather than on process. For example, a gainer might be one who improved over pretest by four items, whereas a nongainer improved one item or less. Budoff was aware that this performance was difficult to interpret; the child who solved no blocks on pretest and five on posttest is difficult to compare with a child who solved, for example, three on the pretest and six on the posttest. Despite the difficulties, Budoff reports interesting correlates of the gainer/nongainer status. For example, middle-class children in special-education classes mainly tend to be nongainers, whereas lower-class children are more likely to be gainers. Learning-potential status also predicts performance on a variety of laboratory concept-learning tasks and a specially constructed math curriculum. It also predicts successful adaptation to mainstreaming, the ability to find and hold jobs during adolescence, the mother's perception of the child, and a variety of positive personality characteristics. Despite the vague specification of the particular effects of training, the importance of considering gainers and nongainers is clear.

More recently, Budoff (1987a) has abandoned this tripartite classification of gainers, nongainers, and high scorers in favor of a linear continuum of ability with essentially the same results (for details, see Budoff 1987a). Budoff's pioneering work has been influential in the field.

Carlson and His Colleagues

The approach of this group (Bethge, Carlson, and Wiedl 1982; Carlson and Dillon 1979; Carlson and Widaman 1986; Carlson and Wiedl 1978, 1979, 1980, 1988; Wiedl and Carlson 1985) differs from other dynamic assessment approaches in that they attempt to modify individual performance by varying the *method of intervention*. Their research has focused on the extent to which modifications in test performance brought about by varying the testing procedure result in more adequate descriptions of an individual's cognitive competence. Wiedl and Carlson (1985) refer to this approach to dynamic assessment as the *integration of specific interventions within the testing procedure*. Carlson and his colleagues have examined a variety of modifications in testing procedures to find out which procedures provide better estimates of an individual's upper limits of competence. They describe their approach as *testing the limits* of an individual's potentiality.

To sum up briefly this important body of work, Carlson's approach involves a pretest and posttest format, with special emphasis placed on the predictive validity of the posttest. Whereas studies of coaching have traditionally claimed that coaching destroys the validity of the score (Anastasi 1981), Carlson's data support the position that posttests after coaching may allow better estimates of competence (see also Embretson 1987). By testing the limits of a child's performance, we can better evaluate his cognitive competence.

To examine the limits of children's ability, Carlson and his colleagues compared standard administration of tests, such as the Raven, with five innovative testing procedures: (a) simple feedback (the child is informed following the solution of the problem if it is correct or not); (b) verbalization after solution; (c) verbalization during and after the solution (children describe the main stimulus pattern prior to searching for it and explain why they made a particular choice after choosing a particular distractor); (d) elaborated feedback (the child is provided with an elaboration of why a particular distractor is correct or incorrect, and the principles involved in the task are explicated for the child); and (e) elaborated feedback and verbalization during and after the solution.

The results of a series of such studies can be summarized as follows: (1) testing-the-limits procedures do yield higher estimates of children's ability than standardized tests; (2) testing-the-limits procedures result in better prediction than standardized tests; (3) testing-the-limits approaches work for children with *and* without learning handicaps and for white, black, and Hispanic populations; and (4) the more intensive the intervention, the greater the disparity between posttest and standardized tests. To recast this last finding, it appears that procedures that force the child to reflect, explain, and elaborate responses are the most effective interventions.

Like Feuerstein and Budoff, Carlson and colleagues also claim that their interventions affect noncognitive as well as cognitive factors of learning. For example, Bethge, Carlson, and Wiedl (1982) found that, compared to examinees receiving standard administration of tests, optimizing the testing conditions leads to reduced test anxiety, more positive attitudes toward the testing situation, and a reduction in impulsive responding.

Learning Potential Assessment in Germany

After we had prepared the major portion of this chapter, we learned of a summary of related research conducted in Germany and published only in German. That work has been reviewed and summarized by Guthke (1982), and here we outline his conclusions—needless to say, without going back to the original sources. It is both impressive and encouraging to note that the patterns of findings he reports are similar to those we have reported.

General Procedures

Several different paradigms have been used in the research, mapping quite well onto those we have already reviewed. Guthke discusses (1) *long-term learning tests*, which involve a test-train-test routine with multiple sessions; (2) *short-term learning tests*, which require a single session and feature attempts to optimize performance by providing feedback, prompts, and suggestions during test administration; and (3) *diagnostic programs*, designed around "a hierarchically arranged program using logical statement," in which "each instructional step is a test item." Like the short-term tests, these are administered in a single session. The long-term tests are akin to those described by Vygotsky, Budoff, and the Illinois group; the short-term tests are of the type used by Carlson and his colleagues. It is less clear that there are parallels between the diagnostic programs and any of the work we have reviewed.

Issues of Validity

As with much of the research we have already reviewed, the German work is conducted with IQ-type tests and with items drawn from IQ scales. The questions that Guthke addresses concern the extent to which the different test formats provide different pictures and, if they do, which ones provide the most interesting diagnostic information.

The first set of issues concerns comparisons between pretest and posttest scores and between normally administered and modified versions of a given test. Guthke evaluates the magnitude of the pretest-posttest and normal-assisted performance correlations. He reports that overall the correlations are not particularly high: tests given before or after instruction and tests given in canonical versus modified format do appear to provide different pictures of the relative abilities of individuals.

Given that the two do not overlap considerably, the question then becomes which sets of scores are more strongly related to criterion performance. Using as criteria school grades and teacher ratings, Guthke reports that scores obtained after instruction (posttest scores) are somewhat more predictive than pretest scores, although the data are not completely consistent. The same advantage is reported for modified testing procedures, as opposed to more traditional methods. Both advantages are more apparent for those scoring below average than those scoring above average on pretests. This is exactly what would be predicted by Vygotsky and Feuerstein, whose main point is that low scores on standard tests may underestimate the capabilities of those who have not had the kinds of experiences needed to acquire the skills and knowledge tapped on standard static tests of ability. Overall, the data Guthke reviews accord well with the findings we have outlined and reinforce the view that dynamic measures of learning potential provide a clearer picture of individual capabilities than do more traditional static indexes.

Instructional Effects

One of the assumptions that dominates the current literature on assessment is that a connection exists between assessment and instruction. Different forms of assessment are sensitive to different instructional regimes, and we need to understand this interdependency better if we are to be able to evaluate alternative programs. One of the most interesting findings Guthke recounts, attributed to Wiedl and Herrig (1978), is directly relevant to this issue. Wiedl and Herrig argue that conventional forms of ability testing map nicely in some way to standard instruction, whereas learning tests are more appropriate for informing the design of alternative learning environments. They investigated the sensitivity of a short-term learning test variant of the Raven Progressive Matrices and Cattell's Culture Free intelligence test to different forms of instruction. Lower-grade schoolchildren were taught set theory, "some of them in the conventional way, and the others in small groups" (Guthke 1982, 313). The tests administered in standard format more accurately predicted performance in the conventional program, whereas the learning test was a more accurate predictor for those in the small group curriculum. This general issue—the match between the form of assessment and the properties of alternative learning environments—is central to education and is one to which we will return in our discussions of current instructional research. The main point, of course, is that we cannot introduce new instructional programs unless we also develop methods for evaluating those programs: assessment cannot be considered independent of instruction (see also Resnick and Resnick, this volume). Guthke summarizes this point nicely: "Probably we will not be able to say anything definitive about the validity of learning tests until we manage, more effectively than hitherto, to add optimizing conditions of teaching to our optimizing procedures of test administration" (Guthke 1982, 313).

The Illinois Group

One of the more extensive programs of research on guided assessment is the "graduated prompts" method developed by the authors' research group (Brown and Ferrara 1985; Brown and French 1979; Bryant, Brown, and Campione 1983; Campione 1989; Campione and Brown 1984, 1987, in press; Campione, Brown, and Ferrara 1982; Campione et al. 1984; Campione et al. 1985; Day and Hall 1987; Ferrara 1987; Ferrara, Brown, and Campione 1986; French 1979).

Our own particular approach was influenced by (a) our interpretation of translations of Vygotsky's writings (notably *Mind in Society* 1978); (b) observations of Soviet clinicians' interpretations and implementations of Vygotskian ideas (Brown and French 1979); and (c) our own long-standing interest in learning and transfer processes as sources of differences between academically successful and less successful students (Brown 1974, 1978; Brown and Campione 1978, 1981, 1984; Campione and Brown 1977, 1978; Campione, Brown, and Ferrara 1982). Our idea was to assess the facility with which students learned from others and the flexibility with which they could use what they had learned. Our purpose was twofold. First, we wanted to test theoretical assumptions concerning underlying processes influencing learning efficiency. Second, we wanted to see whether indices of learning and transfer *under guidance* would provide important diagnostic information about individual students beyond that predicted by static tests.

Our approach is similar to that of others in that we adopted a pretest and posttest format. It is similar to Budoff in the attempt to specify and standardize the aid. Of course, because of the nature of social interaction, complete standardization is never possible or even desirable. Observers viewing videotapes of our testers, blind, are often surprised that they are following scripts. Our main contribution is that we concentrate on *how much help* is needed to achieve superior performance. But it is also essential to our procedure that we provide as little help as possible so that we can assess students' differential needs, their *readiness to learn*, if you will.

General procedure

Students of a wide range of ability (IQ 70–150) are *pretested* on their prior knowledge of the domain in question. To ensure that the tasks they are to learn are neither too hard nor too easy for them, the tasks are assigned to age groups such that most students can get easier items correct but do not perform well on harder items, the target of learning. The students then work collaboratively with a tester/teacher who provides a series of hints until the students can solve the problem. The tester estimates the level of hint required by a student, providing more or less help as needed. Early hints are general metacognitive prompts (to think of similar problems, to plan solution attempts, to look at only one line at a time), while later hints are much more specific, with the tester eventually providing a blueprint for solving a particular problem if the learner fails to catch on. This phase of the process continues until the student can solve an array of target problems without the teacher's help. The amount of help each student needs is taken as the estimate of her learning efficiency *within that domain* and *at that particular point in time*.

After achieving independent learning, students are given a series of *transfer problems*, varying in terms of their similarity to the items learned originally. The idea was to evaluate the extent to which individuals could use what they have learned on increasingly dissimilar tests. This introduces the notion of "transfer distance"; problems are classed as involving *near, far,* or *very far* transfer as a function of the number of transformations performed on the learning problems. The amount of help needed by the child to deal with each of the transfer problems is then used as an estimate of the student's "transfer propensity" (Campione and Brown 1984) *in this domain at this point in time.* Transfer performance is taken as an index of the extent to which the students *understand* the procedures they had been taught; that is, having learned the procedures, could they use and modify them in flexible ways? So far we have applied these general procedures to the domains of inductive reasoning and early mathematics learning, and work is now being conducted on reading.

Inductive Reasoning Tasks

Like many others in this field, we began our work on guided assessment using inductive reasoning tasks. We used the Raven Progressive Matrices and a letter-series completion task with older children (grade three and above). For younger ones (preschool and up), we invented similar, simpler tasks because existing IQ tests used with these younger children were not considered rule-based enough to provide a fruitful domain for learning; for example, the Raven test for younger children involves pattern matching on an item-by-item basis rather than the systematic application of a set of rules, such as rotation, addition, and so on.

An example of the series completion task used by Ferrara, Brown, and Campione (1986) with third-graders and sixth-graders is shown in table 1. The problem required children to complete a series in a letter string by determining the patterns and extrapolating upon them. Each pattern involved one or more of the following alphabetic relations: *identity* (I)—the repetition of a letter; *next* (N)—the appearance of letters in alphabetical order; and *backward-next* (B)—the appearance of letters in reverse alphabetical order. A pattern was defined not only by the types of relations among the letters, but also by the periodicity of those relations (that is, the number of letters between "related" letters, plus one). For example, in the series PZUFQZVF, the relations are those of next (P-Q, U-V) and identity (Z-Z, F-F), and periodicity is four. Transfer distance was graded so that maintenance items involved the pattern learned originally. Near transfer involved the same relations but in new combinations and far transfer introduced new relations or new periodicities. Finally, very far transfer items were selected from the Adult Binet scale; these require the children to decipher a secret code, involving backward-next as well as next relations between two rows of letters rather than within a single row.

Examples of the Modified Raven items used by Campione et al. (1985) with third-graders and up are shown in figures 2 and 3. Following French (1979), we selected three of the most common Raven rules: rotation, imposition, and subtraction. Examples of these problems are shown in figure 2. In the rotation problems, the left-most figure in each row is rotated 90 degrees to the right to obtain the figure in the center, and that figure is then rotated another 90 degrees to the right to obtain the right-most figure. In the imposition (addition) problems, the figures in the left and center positions of each row are superimposed to obtain the figure in the right position. In the subtraction problems, the figure in the center of each row is deleted from the figure in the left column of that row to obtain the entry in the extreme right column.

Transfer problems are illustrated in figure 3; they require the *simultaneous* application of two of the previously learned rules: rotation and subtraction (top example) and rotation and imposition (bottom example), again items from the Superior Adult Raven Scale.

In this particular study the problems were presented on a computer display; the children were required to construct the right answer. To do this, they made use of a touch-sensitive screen. An example of the screen arrangement is shown in figure 4. The essential features are (a) the problem to be solved; (b) a small control box featuring the commands; and (c) a practice box in which the students attempted to construct their answers.

TABLE 1
Examples of Learning Maintenance and Transfer Items

The letters themselves in the pattern notation refer to the alphabetic relations (that is,
N = next, I = identity, B = backward-next). The number of letters in each pattern notation equals the periodicity. (See the text.)

Problem Type and Pattern	Sample Problem	Correct Answer
Original learning:		
N N............................	N G O H P I Q J	_ _ _ _ (R K S L)
N I N I........................	P Z U F Q Z V F	_ _ _ _ (R Z W F)
Maintenance (learned pattern types: new instantiations):		
N N............................	H Q I R J S K T	_ _ _ _ (L U M V)
N I N I........................	T J F O U J G O	_ _ _ _ (V J H O)
Near transfer (learned relations and periodicities, but in new combinations):		
N I.............................	D V E V F V G V	_ _ _ _ (H V I V)
N N N N.......................	V H D P W I E Q	_ _ _ _ (X J F R)
Far transfer (new relation, backward-next; or new periodicity, three letters):		
B N............................	U C T D S E R F	_ _ _ _ (Q G P H)
N B N I........................	J P B X K O C X	_ _ _ _ (L N D X)
N I N..........................	P A D Q A E R A	_ _ _ _ (F S A G)

Very far transfer ("secret code" items embodying backward-next as well as next relations and "periodicity" of two letters, but relations must be sought between strings of letters rather than within a string)

Instructions

Pretend that you are a spy. You want to send the message on top in a secret code that only your friends will understand. Someone has begun coding the message for you on the second line. Try to figure out the secret code and finish coding the message by filling in the blanks with the letters that follow the code.

SIX SHIPS GONE
THY RIHQR _ _ _ _ (HNOD)

FIGURE 2

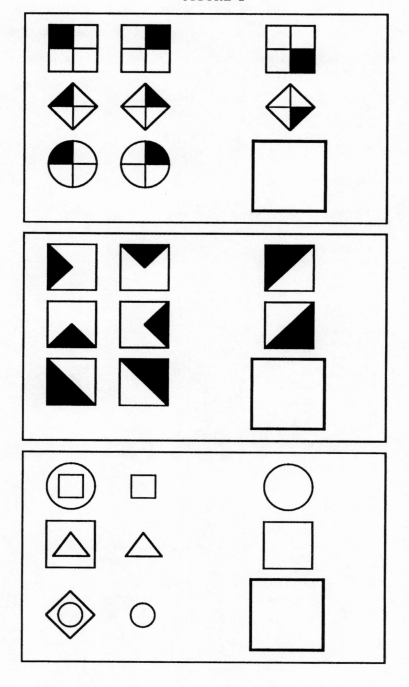

FIGURE 3

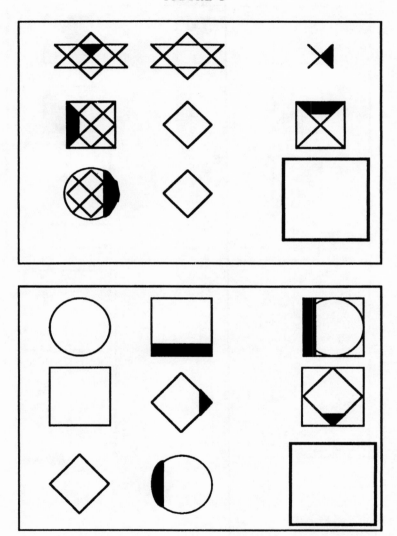

FIGURE 4

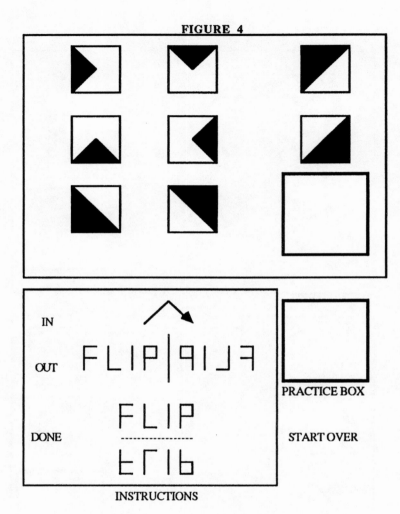

The IN command was used to place a pattern in the practice box. If the student touched IN and then touched one of the eight pictures in the matrix, that picture appeared in the practice box. Touching OUT followed by an item in the matrix would result in that pattern being deleted from the practice box. Note that all or part of the pattern in the practice box could be deleted, an important feature for trying out imposition and subtraction solutions. Pressing the ⋀⋀ command would result in the figure in the practice box being rotated 90 degrees to the right, essential for rotation problems. Finally, pressing one of the FLIP commands would result in the practice-box figure's being flipped on its vertical or horizontal axis. The FLIP commands were actually irrelevant transformations for the problems being worked: they served as distractor commands. When the subjects were sure they had constructed the right answer, they were told to press the DONE key. Pressing the DONE key resulted in the figure in the practice box being copied into the lower-right cell of the problem matrix (the answer slot).

The hints were also provided by the computer upon the child's request. An adult tester provided support, encouragement, and actually read the hints if the child could not. Children received a computer hint every time they pressed the help button. At a pre-specified point in the hint sequence, the computer provided an animated hint; for example, objects would physically rotate or subtract, thus illustrating the solution on a line-by-line basis. The hints ranged from very general (look at the top line only, can you see what's happening?) to the very specific (animations).

To summarize the main results: learning and transfer scores (as measured by number of hints needed to learn and transfer) possess reasonable psychometric properties, including both concurrent and predictive validity. In terms of *concurrent validity*, we found that grade-school children of higher academic ability, as compared with those of lower ability, required less help to learn sets of rules and principles and more readily transferred use of those rules to novel problems (Campione et al. 1985; Campione and Ferrara, in preparation; Ferrara, Brown, and Campione 1986). In addition, differences between ability groups were greater on transfer tests than on the initial learning problems, and group differences increased as transfer distance increased. Higher-ability students transferred their learning more broadly. It appears that academically weak children have particular difficulties applying what they have learned to novel but related situations. Also note that, like other research teams, we did find large effects due to the intervention, some third-graders and fifth-graders performing effortlessly on posttest items adapted from tests of adult intelligence.

To investigate predictive validity, we conducted a series of similar studies involving inductive reasoning tasks modified for use with young children. Preschool children were asked to solve either simple series-completion items or matrix problems with a format similar to that of the Raven Progressive Matrices but involving double classification problems. In these studies (Bryant 1982;

Bryant, Brown, and Campione 1983), children were given a series of pretests assessing both general ability (IQ measures, including subscales of the WPPSI and the Raven Coloured Progressive Matrices) and task-specific competence (unaided performance on the kinds of problems they were later to learn to solve). They were then given sets of learning and transfer sessions as described above and a final posttest on the kinds of problems they had been asked to learn. The transfer sessions included maintenance, near transfer, and far transfer problems as defined above. In these studies, we were particularly interested in the *change* from pretest to posttest performance, or the extent to which individuals had profited from the instructional sessions. We looked for the *best predictors* of this gain score: (a) static scores, that is, general ability or entering competence, or (b) dynamic scores, that is, learning and transfer measures.

The first point to note is that there were *large gains* from the pretest to the posttest. As all dynamic assessment teams agree, the initial unaided performance is a dramatic underestimate of the level of performance some children can achieve after receiving a little aid. Independent posttest scores indicated a great deal of hitherto unforeseen competence. There were sizable differences in the gain scores, and regression analyses were undertaken to determine the factors associated with those differences. The estimated IQ score and the Raven score together accounted for approximately 36 percent of the variance in gain scores. But even after the effects of the ability scores were extracted, the learning and transfer scores still accounted for significant additional portions of the variance in gain scores, an additional 39 percent in the matrices tasks and 22 percent in the series completion. Thus, taking the learning and transfer scores into account did provide further diagnostic information about individual children. Also of note, if one considers the simple correlations, the assisted learning and transfer scores were better predictors of gain than either of the static ability measures. Finally, within the set of dynamic measures, the tendency was for the transfer scores to be more strongly associated with gain than the learning index. This latter result is consistent with the earlier studies, where ability-group differences were larger on transfer than on learning. Even though students had learned the initial problem to the same criterion, they differed dramatically in how flexibly they could apply their newfound knowledge.

Summary

In short, dynamic assessment measures provide a different picture of individual competence than do traditional static measures. Static measures tend to underestimate many children's ability to learn in a domain in which they initially perform poorly. The estimates obtained under more favorable conditions provide greater insights into both their current competence and their learning potential. These findings were dramatic when IQ test items were the domain in question. We turn now to the case of mathematics.

Early Mathematics

A major issue for assessment practices is the extent to which the assessment procedure provides information that can be translated into suggestions for instruction. The data from these studies on inductive reasoning do not move us far toward that goal, but they were not really intended to. They established that the assisted learning and transfer scores did possess reasonable psychometric properties. The only suggestion for instruction that follows from these data, however, is that it is important to pay attention to learning readiness and transfer performance when designing instruction. Because of this limitation, we moved on from the domain of inductive reasoning and began situating our work in an area that was both richer and of more direct educational interest. We chose mathematics both for theoretical and practical reasons.

Theoretical

There are many who believe that individual and developmental differences can be explained largely in terms of variations in amount and quantity of *domain knowledge*. The strong interpretation of this position is that students equated for amount and quality of knowledge are equally ready to proceed within a domain and, therefore, should improve at comparable rates. In contrast, we emphasize the importance of *processing skills* underlying the acquisition and use of that knowledge, for how did individuals come to have different amounts of knowledge in the first place (Brown et al. 1983; Glaser 1988)? This contrasting, dynamic view holds that students may have taken different routes to acquire knowledge, and that predictions of future trajectories require an examination of individuals' learning efficiency as well as current knowledge levels. Although the results of inductive reasoning studies were consistent with the dynamic view, they do not provide a strong comparative test, since inductive reasoning tasks are featured on standard ability tests in large part because they *do not require* specific background knowledge. Students are thus equated for their lack of knowledge. Because mathematics understanding demands factual *and* process knowledge, we chose this domain for an extension of our assessment work.

Practical

As a long-term goal, we are concerned with integrating assessment and instruction. An assessment vehicle based on sound theoretical analyses of the skills and knowledge required for performance within some academically important domain has the potential of providing diagnostic information that *can* inform instruction. For example, if we know that a certain child is two grades behind on standardized achievement tests of mathematics, we know she needs additional instruction, but not of what kind. However, if we know that a particular child does not *now* have rapid access to number facts, does not *now* understand cardinality, but is *ready to learn* this information, we know a great deal about where to aim instruction. Thus, we believe that the best way to effect an assessment-instruction link is to situate the assessment within a particular academic domain rather than to target presumably general components of cognitive competence (Brown and Campione 1986; see also Glaser 1988).

Knowledge Assessment

So far only one completed study exists. In her doctoral thesis, Ferrara developed a theoretically rigorous test of kindergartners' knowledge about numbers (see Ferrara 1987, for details). Briefly, it consisted of eleven items that measured the child's knowledge of (a) basic principles of counting (Gelman and Gallistel 1978): specifically one-to-one correspondence, stable order, cardinality, and order-irrelevance principles; (b) facility with number-word sequences: the ability to count from a given number on, to count backward and so on; and (c) advanced counting: counting in novel contexts, such as haphazardly arranged items, generating sets of given numerosity, and so forth.

The validity of the knowledge test has been assessed by administering it to several samples of preschoolers with consistent results. The test does tap aspects of numerical understanding highlighted in cognitive developmental research. Factor analysis reveals three factors that correspond to the theoretical groupings suggested by Gelman and Greeno (1989). It is also of interest that performance on this theoretically based test correlates well with other standardized tests of mathematics ability. The measures were highly related (correlations of up to .71) to scores on the mathematics subtest (part A) of the Stanford Early School Achievement Test administered by school personnel. Thus, the knowledge test is related to widely normed standardized tests. The standardized test tells us only that a certain child is, for example, six months delayed compared with her peers. The theoretical knowledge test can tell us *why*: because the child does not understand cardinality, one-to-one correspondence, and so on. Practically speaking, one could test children on the simple-to-administer standardized test then give low scorers the Ferrara Knowledge test to help diagnose more specific problems.

Dynamic Assessment

The second phase of the research involved five-year-olds learning to solve addition and subtraction word problems. For each child, Ferrara obtained IQ scores, standardized math scores, and initial indexes of each subject's ability to solve the targeted problems, along with the knowledge scores derived from the new instrument.

During the initial learning sessions, the student and tester worked collaboratively, with the tester providing a series of gradually more explicit hints, to solve simple two-digit addition problems, for example, $3 + 2 = ?$, presented as word problems, such as:

Cookie Monster starts out with three cookies in his cookie jar, and I'm putting 2 more in the jar. Now how many cookies are there in the cookie jar?

The interaction continued until the student could solve a series of such problems without help, and Ferrara measured the amount of aid needed to achieve this degree of competence.

The hints used by the examiner were carefully worked out and were designed to counter some of the difficulties children might have solving these problems. One such sequence is shown in table 2. The hints both become progressively more specific and provide qualitatively different kinds of input, ranging from simple memory prompts through concrete aids to leading the child through the steps of a particular strategy for solving the problem.

Following this, a variety of transfer problems were presented in the same interactive, assisted format. These problems required the student to apply the procedures learned originally to a variety of problems that differed in systematic ways from those worked on initially. Some were quite similar. *Near transfer* problems involved new combinations of familiar quantities featuring different toy and character contexts. Others were more dissimilar; for example, *far transfer* problems involved three addends: $4 + 2 + 3 = ?$ And *very far transfer* problems involved a missing addend: $4 + ? = 6$. What was scored was the amount of help students needed to solve these transfer problems on their own. The aim of the transfer sessions was to evaluate *understanding of the learned procedures*. That is, the goal was both to program transfer and to use the flexible application of routines in novel contexts as the *measure of understanding*. Can students use only what they were taught originally, or can they go farther and apply their routines flexibly?

After these learning and transfer sessions were completed, a posttest was given to determine how much the student had learned during the course of the assessment/instruction: what was the gain from pretest to posttest? One main finding, in agreement with those from the inductive reasoning studies, is that the dynamic scores are better predictors of gain (mean correlation = −.57) than are the static knowledge and ability scores (mean correlation = .38). Further, in a hierarchical regression analysis, although the static scores when extracted first did account for 22.2 percent of the variance in gain scores, the addition of the dynamic scores accounted for an additional 33.7 percent of the variance, with transfer performance doing the majority of the work; it accounted for 32 percent of the variance.

This extension to math combines assessment with instruction. In addition to helping predict how well individuals may perform, it is highly desirable that the assessment process contribute directly to the instructional process. The approach we have taken does this automatically: instruction is an integral part of assessment. While students are being evaluated, they are also being taught

TABLE 2
Hint Sequence Scheme and an Instantiation for the Following Problem:

This time Miss Piggy is starting out with *4* pennies in her purse [briefly display to the child and then turn away], and I'm putting 3 *more* pennies into the purse. [Show them in the palm of your hand and then add them to the hidden display.] *Now* how many pennies are there *altogether* in the purse?

SIMPLE NEGATIVE FEEDBACK

Hint 1: [If child's response is incorrect but there seems some chance for self-correction, say the following:] That's a good try, but it's not quite right. Do you want to try again?

WORKING MEMORY "REFRESHERS"
Repeat starting quantity (x)

Hint 2: [Repeat parts of the problem verbatim if the child requests it or if he clearly was not attending originally. Wherever possible, phrase hint as a question first, for example, "How many pennies were in the purse to start with?"] Miss P had 4 pennies in her purse . . .

Repeat operation

2a: . . . and I put in some more pennies . . .

Repeat added quantity (y)

2b: . . . I put in 3 more pennies. So how many pennies does Miss P now have altogether in her purse?

NUMERALS AS MEMORY AIDS
Represent x numerically

Hint 3: [If child again forgets the "known" quantities, give the following two hints as necessary.] There were 4 pennies in the purse to start with this time. So why don't you put a number "4" right here [point] on the magnet board to remind yourself?

Represent y numerically

3a: And since I put 3 more pennies into the purse, why don't you put a number "3" right here [point] to remind yourself of that amount? [Assist, as necessary.]

"TRANSFER" HINT

Hint 4: Why don't you try playing this game like we played the other games? [Not relevant on first problem.]

Hint Sequence (continued)

ENUMERATIVE STRATEGY HINTS Suggest general strategy	Hint 5: Why don't you try pretending that each of these wooden knobs is a *penny* and act it out (like you did the other times)?
Instruct to make a set of size x	5a: Since Miss P had 4 pennies to start with this time, put 4 knobs here [point]. We'll pretend that those are the pennies she had to start with.
Correct set size	5b: [Correct quantity placed on board if necessary.]
Instruct to make a set size y	5c: And since I put 3 more *pennies* into the purse, put 3 more *knobs* over here [point].
Correct set size	5d: [Correct quantity added if necessary.]
Facilitate accurate set formation	5e: Count each knob as you put it out. [Demonstrate, if necessary.]
Facilitate accurate set formation	5f: If you leave a little space here between the old knobs and the new ones that you're adding, it's easier to keep track of how many new ones you're adding. [Demonstrate spacing.]
Facilitate accurate set formation	5g: If you place the knobs in a row, they're easier to count. [Assist.]
Facilitate accurate set formation	5h: If you spread the knobs out a little, they're easier to count. [Assist.]
Instruct to count all (of superset)	5i: So how many pennies does Miss P have altogether in the purse? You can figure it out by counting all the *pretend-pennies* here [point] in your working space—all these knobs.
Correct counting	5j: You counted wrong. [Describe error, if possible.] Try again more slowly and carefully.

Hint Sequence (continued)

Instruct on cardinality | 5k: [If child simply gives the count sequence as the solution . . .] So *how* many pennies are there altogether in the purse? Seven was the last number you counted, so 7 is the number of pennies there are altogether.

COMPLETE DEMON-
STRATION AND
RATIONALE

Hint 6: [If child has needed all of the instructions for implementing the target strategy as well as some strategy corrections or "facilitating tips," give a complete demonstration of the enumerative procedure with rationale.]

"STRATEGIC-
ORIENTATION" HINT

Hint 7: [If child did not attempt some reasonable strategy until prodded, say the following:] It's easy to figure out the right answer when you use your magnet board, isn't it? Next time, why don't you act it out with the magnets *right away while I'm showing you the pennies* so you don't forget the numbers? OK? . . . So clear the working space and get ready for the next game. Let's see if you can act out the next one *all by yourself.*

"ABANDON INEFFECTIVE
STRATEGY" HINT

Hint 8: [If child is using a different strategy that is not always effective, such as number fact retrieval, say the following:] Your way is very clever, but it doesn't always work for you. My way—with the knobs—always works if you do it carefully. So why don't you try it my way unless you're *absolutely positively* sure of the answer? OK?

something about the domain in question. The assessment involves testing skills that the students have not as yet mastered; they are asked to learn to solve problems that they cannot solve at the outset. And they show significant improvement in their ability to do just that. In the ideal case, the hints are based on a detailed task analysis of the components of competence within the domain and are intended to guide students through the problem-solving process. If the hints are appropriated by the students during assessment, the students will have begun to use those problem-solving routines independently.

In addition to signaling that a student may be in particular difficulty, it is also desirable that the assessment process provide specific information about the kinds of help that the student may need to advance more quickly. Our goal is to develop sequences of prompts that can be organized qualitatively as well as scored quantitatively so that, in addition to determining the number of hints individuals require, information about the specific kinds of hints they need would also be available. This information could then be used to devise more specific remedial instruction. For example, if the hint sequences suggested that a particular child's problem involved a misunderstanding of cardinal numbers, the implications for subsequent instruction would be obvious.

In summary of our work on dynamic assessment, in both domains of inductive reasoning and early mathematics, we have found that although static measures of general ability and task-specific competence do predict the amount of gain individuals achieve, the dynamic measures—learning and transfer scores— are better individual predictors of gain and account for significant additional variance in gain scores beyond ability and knowledge, and the transfer, or *understanding*, scores are significantly more diagnostic than learning scores. If the interest is in predicting the learning trajectory of different students, the best indicant is not their IQ or how much they know originally, or even how readily they acquire new procedures, but how well they understand and make flexible use of those procedures in solving novel problems. The extension of these dynamic measures to the domain of early mathematics has important implications for the link between assessment and instruction.

INTERACTIVE INSTRUCTION

Many of the research programs we have discussed have attempted to integrate assessment procedures and innovative instruction. In this section we will look more closely at several attempts in this direction.

Instrumental Enrichment

One of Feuerstein's major activities has been the development of a curriculum called Instrumental Enrichment (Feuerstein et al. 1979, Feuerstein 1980) for students deemed, on the basis of the LPAD, in need of further mediated learning experience. Incorporated in the curriculum is a series of exercises or instruments selected to provide the context for mediated learning. Originally these materials were specifically chosen not to represent traditional academic domains, such as reading and mathematics, precisely because Feuerstein believed that disadvantaged children had already experienced considerable school failure, and traditional materials were thought to be aversive for them. The instruments include such exercises as organization of dots, orientation in space, classification, and so on, which were intended as vehicles for improving student performance on the cognitive functions that Feuerstein believes are implicated in poor learning. Subsequently, the Vanderbilt group has adapted this approach to academic domains (see, for example, Bransford et al. 1988), and in so doing departed from the original Feuerstein agenda. Due to space limitations, we will consider here only the original and popular Instrumental Enrichment program.

In Instrumental Enrichment, each instrument is introduced to the class, then students work individually, and class discussions follow. Instruction focuses on strategic approaches, such as finding a starting point, performing a systematic search, planning, checking, and so on. More idiosyncratic to Feuerstein is that these familiar metacognitive activities are strategies specifically designed to remediate deficient cognitive functions noted on the LPAD, such as "projecting virtual relationships" (filling in lines with one's imagination) or performing "visual transport" (keeping the image of a figure in mind while moving it mentally to compare it with something else).

A crucial aspect of Instrumental Enrichment is bridging, which involves deliberate and intentional training for transfer. Students are encouraged to think of other examples in which a strategy or principle of organization would apply, in this way embedding a principle in multiple contexts to encourage understanding and transfer. This is an important aspect of the program, but it does lend itself to the interpretation that such metacognitive skills are very general, can be taught via "context-free vehicles" (by which Feuerstein means academically context-free), and transfer broadly. But it is yet to be proved that such transfer occurs readily, a point to which we shall return.

Reciprocal Teaching

It was because of our concern with the lack of broad lateral transfer, endemic in the history of instruction, that we decided to develop instructional procedures in the content areas of reading, science, and mathematics. Our program of research, referred to as Reciprocal Teaching, was also based on our interpretation of Vygotsky's theory. Because our goal is to integrate our assessment program with our instructional program, we will describe reciprocal teaching in some detail.

Reciprocal teaching of comprehension skills was originally developed for use with junior high school students who had experienced delays of from two to five years on standardized scores of reading comprehension. It was subsequently extended to listening comprehension with children as young as first grade. The method was based on Vygotsky's theory of a zone of proximal development being created, sustained, and extended in social settings. Reciprocal teaching was designed to provide a simple introduction to group discussion techniques aimed at understanding and remembering text content. To illustrate the procedure, consider the discussion below that took place between a group of first-graders at high risk for academic failure and their regular classroom teacher. The children have just been read a section of a story about aquanauts.

Student 1:	(question) My question is, what does the aquanaut need when he goes under water?
Student 2:	A watch.
Student 3:	Flippers.
Student 4:	A belt.
Student 1:	Those are all good answers.
Teacher:	(question) Nice job! I have a question, too. Why does the aquanaut wear a belt? What is so special about it?
Student 3:	It's a heavy belt and keeps him from floating up to the top again.
Teacher:	Good for you.
Student 1:	(summary) For my summary now: This paragraph was about what aquanauts need to take when they go under the water.
Student 5:	(summary) And also about why they need those things.
Student 3:	(clarify) I think we need to clarify gear.
Student 6:	That's the special things they need.
Teacher:	Another word for gear in this story might be equipment, the equipment that makes it easier for the aquanauts to do their job.
Student 1:	I don't think I have a prediction to make.
Teacher:	(prediction) Well, in the story they tell us that there are "many strange and wonderful creatures" that the aquanauts see as they do their work. My prediction is that they'll describe some of these creatures. What are some of the strange creatures you already know about that live in the ocean?
Student 6:	Octopuses.
Student 3:	Whales?
Student 5:	Sharks!

(Palincsar and Brown 1986, 771–72)

These students and their teacher are engaged in reciprocal teaching, a procedure that features guided practice in applying simple, concrete strategies to the task of text comprehension. An adult teacher and a group of students take turns leading a discussion on a text section that they have either read silently or listened to as the adult teacher reads aloud (depending on their reading skill level). The learning leader (adult or child) begins the discussion by asking a question on the main content and ends by summarizing the gist of the text. If there is disagreement, the group rereads and discusses possible questions and summary statements until they reach consensus. Questioning provides the impetus for the discussion. Summarizing at the end of a period of discussion helps students establish where they are before they tackle a new segment of text. Attempts to clarify any comprehension problems that might arise occur opportunistically when someone misunderstands or does not know the meaning of a word or phrase (as was the case with "gear" above). And, finally, the leader asks for predictions about future content.

The procedure is heavily dependent on social interaction within the group, which is jointly responsible for understanding and evaluating the text. All members of the group in turn serve as learning leaders, those responsible for guiding the dialogue, and as learning listeners (Yager, Johnson, and Johnson 1985), those responsible for encouraging the discussion leader to explain the content and help resolve misunderstandings. The goal is joint construction of meaning; the strategies provide concrete heuristics for getting the procedure going; the reciprocal nature of the procedure forces student engagement; and teacher modeling provides examples of expert performance (Brown and Palincsar 1989).

Questioning, clarifying, summarizing, and predicting were chosen because they are excellent self-testing mechanisms. They afford the learner an opportunity to monitor current understanding. For example, if one cannot summarize what one is reading, then comprehension is evidently not proceeding smoothly and some remedial action is required.

Also important is that these activities serve to structure individual as well as social dialogues. Reviewing content (summarizing), attempting to resolve misunderstandings (clarifying), anticipating possible future text development (predicting), and assessing the state of one's gradually accumulating knowledge (questioning) are all activities that an experienced learner engages in while studying independently, via an internal dialogue. The reciprocal teaching procedure was intended to make such internal attempts at understanding external, hence observable to all. Reciprocal teaching provides social support during the inchoate stages of the development of internal dialogues. In the course of repeated practice, such meaning-extending activities are gradually adopted (internalized) as part of the learner's personal repertoire of learning strategies.

Reciprocal teaching was designed to provoke a zone of proximal development within which novices could gradually take on greater responsibility for learning. The group cooperation ensures that a reasonable level of understanding is reached, even if individual members cannot achieve this unaided. It embodies a form of proleptic teaching (Wertsch and Stone 1979) that can best be understood by comparison to what it is not. The more traditional method of teaching (for example, reading skills) is to introduce a skill by starting out on a decontextualized, easy version of it. Upon success, a more difficult version is presented, and this step is repeated through gradually incrementing levels of difficulty until the learner is confronted with the "mature" version of the target task. Thus, one way of making the task easier is to divide it into manageable subcomponents and to provide practice on these, in isolation, until they are perfected. But it is usually the case in educational settings that the role of recombining the subcomponents or using them flexibly on an array of tasks of which they are elements is left up to the student, with disastrous results.

In proleptic teaching, by contrast, the integrity of the target task is maintained; components are handled in the context of the entire task; skills are practiced in context. For example, in reciprocal teaching, the aim of understanding the text remains as undisturbed as possible, but the novice's role is made easier by providing a supportive social context that does a great deal of the cognitive work until the novice can take over a greater degree of responsibility. But the task remains the same, the goal the same, the desired outcome the same.

The cooperative feature of the learning group in reciprocal teaching, in which everyone is seeking consensus about meaning, relevance, and importance, is an ideal setting for novices to practice their emergent comprehension skills. All of the responsibility for comprehending does not rest with one person, and even if a learning leader falters, the other members of the group, including the adult teacher, are there to keep the discussion going. Because the group's efforts are externalized in a discussion, novices can learn from the contributions of those more expert than they on any particular point. It is in this sense that reciprocal teaching dialogues create a zone of proximal development (Vygotsky 1978) for their participants, each one of whom may share in the co-construction of meaning to the extent that she or he is able. With its variety of expertise, engagement, and goals, the group collaborates to get the job done; the text gets understood. What changes over time is who has the major responsibility for the learning activities.

The adult teacher has an additional role over and above responsible group membership: to monitor the learning leaders, giving feedback tailored to their existing levels of competence. Because the students must participate when it is their turn to be the leader, the teacher can engage in on-line assessment of that competence. It is this aspect of reciprocal teaching that allows assessment to be an integral part of instruction: situations are created in which students exhibit their comprehension skills *in the actual context of reading for meaning,* allowing the teacher to evaluate their current competence. The teacher in this case serves the same function as does the tester in Feuerstein's assessment scheme. On the basis of this diagnosis, feedback is given and responsibility for the comprehension activities transferred to the students as soon as they can take charge of their own learning. Through interactions with the supportive teacher, the students are guided to perform at an increasingly challenging level. In response, the teacher gradually fades into the background and acts as a sympathetic coach (Binet 1909), leaving the students to handle their own learning. The teacher is always monitoring the discussions, however, and is ready to take control again when understanding fails.

In table 3 we illustrate the similarities and differences between our assessment (zone of proximal development) and instruction (reciprocal teaching) work. As can be seen, both approaches are loosely based on Vygotsky's theory (and Binet's, for that matter). Both involve guided learning sessions that feature on-line assessment and the provision of aid responsive to a student's needs. The procedures differ in that the goal of reciprocal teaching is to facilitate learning while the goal of the assessment procedures we have developed is to measure student readiness. Because of these different focuses, aid is given in standardized ways only if needed in assessment, while the assistance is provided clinically in reciprocal teaching.

Common to our work on diagnosis and instruction is the key notion of supportive contexts for learning. Four main principles are involved: (a) *understanding* of procedures, rather than just speed and accuracy of their execution, is the aim of assessment and instruction; (b) *expert guidance* is used to reveal as well as promote independent competence; (c) *microgenetic analysis* permits estimates of learning as it actually occurs over time; and (d) *proleptic teaching* (teaching in anticipation of competence) is involved in both assessment and instruction, for both aim at one stage beyond current performance, in anticipation of levels of competence not yet achieved individually but possible within supportive learning environments.

Reciprocal teaching has been used successfully as a reading-comprehension and listening-comprehension intervention by classroom teachers with academically at-risk children in grade school and middle school. These interventions were typically conducted by regular classroom teachers working with small groups (the ideal group size is six, but the teachers have handled much larger groups including whole classes). Students enter the study scoring approximately 30 percent correct on independent tests of text comprehension, and we count as successful any student who achieves an independent score of 75 to 80 percent correct on five successive days within a twenty-day period. With this as the criterion, approximately 80 percent of the students across ages are judged to be successful (six hundred experimental students have been exposed to this program). Furthermore, students maintain their independent mastery for six

TABLE 3
Assessment and Instruction Compared

<u>ZONE OF PROXIMAL DEVELOPMENT</u>

Collaborative assessment environments	Collaborative (reciprocal) teaching environments
Campione et al.	Brown and Palinscar

MAIN SIMILARITIES

1. Based (loosely) on Vygotsky's Learning Theory

2. Involve guided cooperative learning with expert feedback

3. Strategy modeling by experts (apprenticeship model)

4. Externalizing mental events via discussion formats

5. On-line assessment of novice status

6. Help given, responsive to student needs

7. Aimed at problem solving at the level of control structure (metacognition, intentional learning, learning to learn)

8. Understanding measured by transfer, flexible use of knowlege

MAIN DIFFERENCES

1. Goal:	individual assessment	1. Goal:	cooperative learning
2. Test:	knowledge and strategies	2. Teach:	knowledge and strategies
3. Aid:	standardized hints	3. Aid:	opportunistic
4. Hints:	hard to easy to measure students need	4. Hints:	easy to hard to scaffold student progress

months to a year after instruction ceases (Brown and Palincsar 1982; Brown, Palincsar, Slattery, and Ryan, work in progress); they generalize to other classroom activities, notably science and social studies; and they improve approximately two years on standardized tests of reading comprehension (Palincsar and Brown 1984).

After a brief period of instruction, some 40 percent of junior high school students are released from special educational placement in remedial reading groups. Similarly, students exposed to listening reciprocal teaching in grades one and two make the transition to reading reciprocal teaching well at third grade. Most children maintain their listening gains across grades one to two and two to three. Those that do not are quickly brought back to criterion after a few days of refamiliarization with the procedure (see Brown and Palincsar 1987, 1989; Palincsar and Brown, work in progress). In terms of research into practice, in one school district alone approximately fifty teachers and seven hundred students per year use the procedure as their regular reading-comprehension instruction.

Reciprocal Teaching and Learning Science

In the majority of our work on reciprocal teaching of reading comprehension, we have followed the typical pattern of "reading group," that is, each day the children read a text that is not related in any way to those that have gone before. Passage follows passage with no coherent link between them (a story about volcanoes follows one on dinosaurs, which followed one on aquanauts, and so on); there is little opportunity for cumulative reference. Such procedures positively encourage the child to acquire encapsulated "inert" knowledge (Whitehead 1916), knowledge learned but never used to acquire new knowledge.

We will give the details of just one study in which we bypassed this typical procedure; here "at-risk" minority third-grade children were trying to learn a coherent body of knowledge about animal defense mechanisms, including camouflage, mimicry, warning colorations, protection from the elements, extinction, parasites, and natural pest control. These themes repeat during the discussions and are also taken up in the daily independent tests of comprehension.

In the discussions, the students are forced to explain and justify their understanding to others, and in so doing, come to better understand the theme themselves. An example of this explanatory process can be seen in the dialogue in table 4 . The learning leader (S_1) does not fully understand the meaning of the term "camouflage" because she is unduly influenced by the inconsiderate text comment that "a chameleon can take on the color of its background." This she takes to mean any color whatsoever. The ensuing discussion forces the learning leader to reevaluate her understanding and come to terms with the constraints placed on the biological mechanism in question. Note Subject One's confusion and persistence. She attempts to understand by asking about special cases. She really wants to know, and eventually in her final summary she appears satisfied. It is also Subject One who sets up the motivation to find out how the mechanism works. Several days later, when discussing another instance of camouflage, the walking stick insect that disguises itself by changing its shape, Subject One shows she has mastered this idea:

> OK, it goes invisible because it looks like a twig. It's frozen and
> twig-like on the tree and on the ground. Some things change color,

to nature colors, green and brown; some things hold still, some things pretend to be twigs, I get it.

TABLE 4
The Meaning of Camouflage
(Third-Grade, High-Risk Children)

S_1:   (Question) What does camouflage mean?

S_2:   (Spontaneous analogy) It means you invisible like G. I. Joe.

S_1:   (Question) What color can it (the chameleon) be?

S_3:   Brown.

S_1:   No.

S_2:   Green?

S_1:   No.

All: What? (confusion)

S_1:   (Question) What color would it be if it was on a fire engine—red, right? And if it's on a car—black, right? And on a cab—yellow, right?

All: No! No!

S_4:   It can only be greenish or brownish, like in nature.

S_1:   (Indignant) It says (reading text), "A chameleon can take on the color of its background"—so it can be *any* color, right?

S_4:   (Spontaneous analogy) No, No! It can only be colors like brown earth and green trees and yucky color like mud—like G. I. Joe.

S_6:   So he matches.

T: (Scaffolding weaker student: repeating text line) Yes, he matches, he's almost invisible.

S_6:   He changes colors so his enemy won't get him.

T: Good. That's right.

S_1:   (Question—confused) But what if he's not in the grass, what if
he's   in a whitish kinda color?

S_6:   He would turn white?

All: No.

S_1:   (Question—still confused) But what if he doesn't have that color? What if he can't turn that color?

S_5:   He just moves on down to another spot that has his color.

S_4:   No, only green and brown and yucky.

S_1:   (Question, persistent) Can it be blue like water in the forest?

S_3:   Water in the forest isn't blue, its yucky colored, so chameleons
can   be yucky colored too.

S_1:   (Summary) OK. OK. I summarize, it change color.

T: What does?

S_1:   (Sigh) Chameleon change color to hide from its enemies. It can
be   green—umh brown—yucky color (pause) so it has to stay in the
         forest cause those colors are there.

S_1:   (Question) I have another question. How does it change color?

T: Good question. Anyone know?

S_6:   It don't say.

T: Do we really know how it changes?

S_1:   No.

T: Any predictions? No?

T: (Prediction) I think it might be a chemical in its body; let's read
to   find out.

Because the themes repeat, opportunities for extending and revising cumulative knowledge abound.

Twenty days of such discussions led to dramatic improvement in both comprehension processes and theme understanding. In terms of independent reading comprehension scores, students improved from a starting level of 30 percent correct to a level of 80 percent correct, a level that they maintained for a year. In terms of content knowledge, students came to recognize that themes repeated. They started off solving only a minority of problems on the basis of analogy to prior texts, but by the end of the training period, 80 percent of analogous problems were recognized and solved.

The students also made use of the analogous themes in their discussion. In table 5, a group of six children are discussing the critical paragraphs in passages about natural pest controllers. Note that the children readily hone in on the usefulness of ladybugs, remember ladybugs twelve days later when discussing the manatees, and finally, even a year later, discuss the analogy between ladybugs and lacewings.

Not only did the children remember how to conduct the reciprocal teaching dialogues and score well on independent tests, they also remembered the content. Asked to sort pictures of animals into the six themes, they scored 85 percent correct immediately after being in the study and 82 percent correct one year later. Scored as correct were responses in which the child could name the theme and justify why the animal in question was an exemplar of that theme. Finally, on both the long-term and short-term tests, the children were able to classify novel

TABLE 5
Repetitive Themes in Reciprocal Teaching Dialogues: Natural Pest Control
Third-Grade, High-Risk Children (N = 6)

Day 5 Ladybugs

S_1:   (Question) What do they eat?

T: What do what eat?

S_1:   (Question) The ladybugs. What do ladybugs eat?

S_2:   Aphids, little white bugs.

S_1:   (Question) Right. Why do farmers like them?

S_3:   Because they eat the little bugs off the farmers' plants.

S_1:   That's the answer I want. (pause)

S_1:   (Question) I have another question, where do they live? (overlapping discussion of potential places to live not accepted because they are not mentioned in the text)

S_4:   I know, they crawl on leaves and rosebuds as in the grass.

S_1:   (Summary) OK, it's about the ladybugs that crawl in the grass and help the farmer by eating bad little insects.

T: Good summary.

Day 17 Manatees

S_4:   (Question) How does the manatee clean up the river?

S_3:   By eating water plants?

S_4:   No, you missed one word.

S_3:   By eating water hedge-whatever.

T: Hyacinth.

S_4:   Yea, that's right.

S_4:   (Question) How many years—age people—moved some of the manatees from the sea in the inland river? Amelia?

S_6:   A few years.

T: (Scaffolding) Anne (S_4)—another way you could have asked that
        question would be—when did the people move the manatees.

S_4:   (Question) What did the people want the manatees to eat?

S_2:   The plants.

S_4:   I want the whole sentence.

S_2:   The people wanted the manatees to eat the water hyacinths that
        grow in the river.

S_4:   (Summary) OK, that's it; it tells where the people moved them
        and what they wanted them to eat, and why.

T: Good summary.

S_1:   (Noting analogy) The manatees went through and ate all the
        plants so that's helping like the ladybugs because they eat all the
        aphids, bad bugs.

Year Follow-up: Day 1 Lacewings

S_6:   (Question) OK, what do lacewings eat?

T: Good question.

S_5:   Bugs and insects.

S_3:   Aphids and other bugs.

S_2:   And they eat the farmers' crops.

All: No.

S_6:   (Clarification and question) No, the bad bugs eat the farmers'
        crops. OK, let me see (pause). Are insects nice to crops?

S_1:   Not always, some are.

S_6:   (Question, clarify) What's the story about, anyone need
        clarifying?

S_2:   It's about how the lacewing is destroying the insects that are in
        the fields trying to eat crops.

S_6:   OK, people often think of insects as just good-for-nothing bugs.

All: You told the answer. That's not a question.

S_6:   (Question) OK, let me see (pause). Why does the farmer like the
        (pause), oh yea, we already know this. I'll ask it anyway, Why
        does the farmer like the lacewing?

S_1:   (Analogy) Because they can stop other things from eating crops.
        I remember we read about farmers that don't want animals on
        their crops because they kill 'em.

S$_2$:   They put spray on it?

S$_1$:   No, ladybugs.

S$_4$:   The ladybugs ate them all up so they don't hurt no crops.

S$_6$:   So they quit messing up crops.

exemplars of the themes and place them in appropriate habitats. Reciprocal teaching experience enables the children not only to learn a coherent, usable, body of knowledge but also to develop a repertoire of strategies that will enable them to learn new content on their own.

Reciprocal Teaching and Mathematics Understanding

Reciprocal teaching of text-comprehension strategies was originally designed in response to the overwhelming evidence that many children fail to develop such skills on their own. Similarly, many educators agree that the way in which mathematics is taught in school leads to students' failure to understand what they are being taught. Many children master basic algorithms if provided with enough drill and practice, but they have difficulty achieving a robust understanding of the conceptual basis of these algorithms (Gelman and Greeno 1989; Resnick 1989). Students need practice connecting their fragmentary knowledge into systems of "meaningful mathematics" (Davis 1984; Noddings 1985). When this opportunity is provided by an expert classroom teacher, the results are quite dramatic (Lampert 1986; see also Hatano and Inagaki 1987). Lampert's students argue about the meaning of mathematical expressions and attempt to convince each other of the appropriateness of the algorithms they invent. They engage in lively discussions about the meaning of what they are doing, and it is these reflective processes that are largely absent from traditional mathematics classes (Schoenfeld 1985; Stodolsky 1988). Our goal then was to develop a procedure that would ensure such discussions even when regular teachers are engaged in teaching mathematics, that is, the equivalent of reciprocal teaching in reading.

Our first problem was to select appropriate strategic activities to scaffold the discussion because obviously the reading strategies could not be transported unchanged to the new domain. We decided to use the same selection criteria we had used in the case of reading. Questioning, summarizing, clarifying, and predicting were not randomly selected activities. We settled on them only after diagnosing that they were comprehension-monitoring activities rarely engaged in by weak students. They were also selected because they could be readily taught: the student could produce some questions or summaries right from the start, thereby assuring that a discussion of sorts got going. The activities were readily engaged in by inexperienced learners when instructions to "monitor your understanding" or "be strategic" provoked blank stares; and, most important, they were selected because a by-product of summarizing what one has just read, asking for clarification, and so on, is to force comprehension-monitoring.

In order to determine which comprehension activities needed to be practiced in mathematics, we again observed groups of children engaged in the target task, in this case sixth- to eighth-graders solving algebra word problems. We diagnosed six characteristic monitoring errors. The students had trouble (a) extracting relevant facts from the story, for example, the goal, the givens, the unknowns, relations among givens, and so on; (b) keeping track of the quantities that the algebraic expressions stood for (X = the number of marbles that Linda had); (c) estimating an approximate answer; (d) drawing visual representations when appropriate; (e) checking arithmetic facts; and (f) sensemaking.

Given this diagnosis, we asked what ritual activities comparable to questioning, summarizing, clarifying, and predicting could be used to (a) scaffold a discussion and (b) force reflection? Note that the choice of the activities was determined not by what experts would do to attack the problems but by what students were failing to do on their own.

Our first step was to introduce a reflection board on which the group externalized their problem-solving activities. All other aspects of the interactive learning environment remained the same. The students worked together with an instructor in small cooperative groups. The students and adult teacher again took turns being learning leaders responsible for leading a discussion aimed at understanding algebra word problems, while the others acted as supportive critics. The procedure embodied expert modeling, scaffolding, and coaching and on-line assessment on the part of the teacher; the method forced externalization of strategies, monitoring of progress, and attempts to impose meaning. What differed is that the strategies selected to scaffold the discussion were tailored to the domain.

The reflection board is illustrated in figure 5. It was designed to be directly responsive to the six characteristic monitoring errors of the target students. The board was designed to encourage problem solving and meaning imposition (Resnick 1989) rather than rote drill and practice. The solution path was made explicit, was in plain sight, and was the object of reflection. The repetitive use of the board both generated an external record of the group's problem-solving attempts and forced communal monitoring and reflection.

In this implementation, the solution path is parsed into four general categories: goal-setting, planning, problem solution, and sensemaking/checking. Goal-setting involves stating clearly the exact problem to be solved, along with identifying any unknown quantities that are relevant to the problem. Planning consists of having the student identify the quantities given in the problem, along with the relations between those quantities. If the students wish to do so, they can also draw a sketch representing the problem statement or come up with an estimate of what the answer might look like, that is, specify a range of possible solutions or constraints on the solution.

FIGURE 5

Problem: John has 4 marbles more than Karen, who has twice as many marbles as Linda. The 3 together have 24. How many does John have?

GOAL: STATE GOAL(S) Number of marbles that John has = X

STATE UNKNOWN(S) Y = number of marbles Karen has

Z = number of marbles Linda has

PLANNING

STATE GIVENS AND RELATIONSHIPS BETWEEN THEM

Z = 2Y (Karen has twice as many as Linda)

X = Y + 4 (John has 4 more than Karen)

X + Y + Z = 24 (all 3 together = 24)

(Error not noticed.)

PROBLEM SOLUTION

Tutor: You want to find the one unknown. (prompt)

Tutee: I know more about Y so let's get rid of the Z, can I?

Equation:

(Y + 4) + Y + Z = 24

Y + 4 + Y + 2Y = 24

4Y + 4 = 24

4Y = 20

Y = 5 = Karen

X = 9 = John

Z = 10 = Linda

(Error still not noticed.)

ESTIMATING, SKETCHING, ETC.

SENSEMAKING AND CHECKING

1) ANSWER MAKE SENSE?

2) COMPUTATIONS CORRECT?

3) REVIEW METHOD(S) OF SOLUTION

Checking:

1) 5 + 9 + 10 = 24

2) John = 9
Karen = 5, 9 - 5 = 4

3) Error accepted . . . :
Accept the answer without validating relation between Karen and Linda.

When the group is satisfied that they have extracted all the necessary information, the students proceed to the problem solution phase, where they attempt to generate their specific answer. Once an answer has been generated, the sensemaking/checking phase begins. This phase involves several related activities, including checking the actual computation for arithmetic errors and checking the answer against the problem statement or the estimation, if there was one, to see if the answer makes sense in the context of the actual problem. Finally, the group reflects on the overall problem-solving process to see if they want to make any changes or if there are any alternative methods of attacking the problem.

     An example of what a problem path might look like is given in figure 5. This represents an initial, unsuccessful attempt to solve the problem. This solution path was generated by an expert tutor and a naive tutee working collaboratively. They begin by stating the goal, the number of marbles John has, which they label X. They then go on to map out the givens and the relations among them, connecting X, Y, and Z with the quantities. Unfortunately, they confuse Karen and Linda, writing $Z = 2Y$, which means that Linda has twice as many as Karen, rather than the correct $Y = 2Z$ (a classic error in this type of problem). They do not detect the error but go on to the problem solution phase, lose track of the quantities again, and come up with an answer that satisfies one of the constraints of the problem; $5 + 9 + 10$ does add up to 24, which they note, and are duly satisfied, but they overlook the fact that Karen has half as many as Linda rather than the reverse. Happily, upon due reflection, the error was noted and the correct solution achieved.

     In this section we have reviewed our research program on reciprocal teaching, a procedure intended to provide supportive contexts for learning in a variety of domains. Based on our previous work in the reciprocal teaching of reading comprehension, we have attempted to transfer the philosophy behind the reading work to the new domains. In describing the similarities and differences between reading, science, and math, we illustrate the domain-specific nature of the activities that promote discussion, argumentation, explanation, and reflection, as well as the domain-independent philosophy of these interactive learning environments.

IMPLICATIONS FOR EDUCATIONAL POLICY

In the last part of the chapter, we have described progress toward an educational system in which assessment and instruction are integrated and support each other. Neither can be said to drive the other; the same theoretical constructs and understandings underlie both assessment and instruction. Ideally, children are not labeled and categorized by assessment; they are diagnosed and helped.

     Here we will begin by pointing out some major practical and social policy problems associated with the introduction of new forms of guided, interactive learning into assessment and instruction practices. We indicate where dynamic assessment approaches can play a role and where they would be inappropriate. We then discuss some of the problems that can result from nonoptimal use of the information these approaches can provide. And in the final section, we sketch some of the conditions that must be met if the implications of the research we have reviewed are to be given a serious test under school-like conditions.

Place for Dynamic Measures

Throughout this chapter, we have concentrated on only a portion of the various approaches to assessment. Our work, and that of the researchers we have reviewed, has centered on the performance of academically weak students. This emphasis has led us to focus on particular approaches to, and uses of, assessment. We have been concerned with assessment aimed at individual learners, and these procedures would clearly be inappropriate for policymakers wishing to compare districts and states. Methods designed for those purposes are the subject of other chapters in this series.

Further, within the realm of individual testing, we have been concerned with both selection and instruction. This has forced us to wrestle with the competing demands of (1) developing normative tests that can be used to identify those individuals who are to be provided additional services and (2) devising methods of assessment that can directly inform instructional approaches.

As long as there are limited resources available, with the accompanying need for fair and objective methods of deciding who is to receive them, this tension will continue. The decision to single out weaker students is based on the assumption that they will require more intensive and qualitatively different forms of instruction than more capable students will require. However, there are good reasons to question that assumption. Much of the work on interactive learning approaches has been with weak students, and the evidence emerging from that work suggests those approaches may work equally well with students of varying abilities. To the extent that we can develop truly diagnostic tests of competence in the main academic areas, and to the extent that we can provide more powerful learning environments capable of dealing with those individual differences, it should be possible to avoid the selection and labeling process altogether and instead concentrate on providing help to students when they encounter problems. This may appear unrealistic, but we are convinced that the field is making excellent progress toward that goal. There are also social and political forces at work that may force us toward that goal. As attempts to integrate the majority of students into regular classrooms (for example, the Regular Education Initiative) gain momentum, the development of methods to deal with diversity in classroom settings will take on even more importance.

Problems with Dynamic Measures

Danger of Reification of "Scores" into Cognitive Entities

We have carefully spelled out our understanding of notions like the Zone of Proximal Development in order that our quantification of various measures of learning potential would be seen for what it is—an attempt to investigate some psychometric properties of the methods. However, we realize that there is a danger such quantification will invite the creation of a static "score" from some aspect of a dynamic assessment, such as the number of hints needed to solve a problem, thus reifying it as a cognitive entity with the same properties as traditional IQ measures.

Indeed, we have already come across just such propensities in clinical and educational personnel. The education department of a large city we have worked with was very interested in using a form of the Illinois group's early work as an alternative to IQ tests. They saw that work as suggesting that children can be divided into four types: (a) fast learners, far transferrers (really good); (b) slow learners, narrow transferrers (bad); (c) fast learners, narrow transferrers (quite bad); and (d) slow learners, far transferrers (pretty good). Each child would be given two scores, a learning and a transfer score, instead of the one received on an IQ test.

Obviously, scores like these would have all the same problems of misuse as those gleaned from traditional IQ tests, no matter how dynamically they were obtained. Similarly, use of any such number, such as the mean number of hints needed in a specific dynamic assessment (a "1" needs only a suggestion; a "10" needs lots of help) would doubtless provoke the same kinds of self-fulfilling prophecies as the knowledge that a child "has" an IQ of 70 versus 120. A numerical measure of general learning efficiency across content and even time would then be achieved, no different from an IQ measure.

Interpretation of Dynamic Measures as Static

In the same vein, critics have argued that a particularly problematic aspect of standardized forms of dynamic assessment is the pretest and posttest methodology, added by Luria to the Vygotsky method (Minick 1987) and used extensively by American and German researchers. Critics see the measurement of performance both before and after intervention as an open invitation to reintroduce a static-like notion of competence rather than one of continuously evolving development. Situating a dynamic testing session between a static pretest and posttest gives the impression that one can freeze development in time. This does not sit well with Vygotsky's theory of development, which stresses spirals of continuous dialectic growth, the social and personal interacting fluidly and continuously. Of course, the much-quoted passage from Vygotsky, in which he compares the academic trajectories of the two fictitious eight-year-olds (see p. 16) is open to misinterpretations of considerable importance to social policy issues. One eight-year-old is characterized as "having" a ZPD of plus one, and the other of plus four (Minick 1987). Obviously, these quantitative terms, one and four, are meant merely as analogy. But analogies are potentially dangerous. Suppose an assessment revealed that two eight-year-olds could be classified such that the first has a chronological age of eight and a mental age of eight (IQ=100) while the second has a chronological age of eight and a mental age of twelve (IQ=150). Is this comparison any less potentially dangerous than classifying two eight-year-olds as having ZPDs of "plus one" or "plus four?" Taken this way, the dynamic measures offer no improvement whatsoever over standardized tests of traditional types, for both statements could be interpreted to mean that one child is superior intellectually to the other across domains and across time.

Our interpretation of dynamic (for example, learning and transfer) scores is that they provide estimates of current readiness, capable of predicting performance in the domain assessed at that particular time. There is no implication that a score obtained in domain A at a given time will necessarily predict performance in domain A at some later time or in domain B at any time. Individuals' capabilities can vary both across content areas and across time.

Not Easily Quantifiable

Those who adopt primarily a qualitative approach to assessment must solve the problem of how to specify that change has occurred. For example, Feuerstein assumes that social interaction plays a key role in the processes of cognitive development and change, but Feuerstein's understanding of the mechanisms of change is implicit and intuitive (Minick 1987), as it often is in the hands of expert clinicians (Bandler and Grinder 1975). Thus, for those approaches to dynamic assessment that easily afford the development of a scoring procedure, we have noted the problem of reification and classification. For those approaches that primarily consist of clinical interviews and intensive, individually determined interventions, we see the opposite problem. That is, it is very difficult to quantify measures of change without the use of pretest baseline measures and standard assessment protocols. But such quantification may be needed if we are to compare the effectiveness of different types of dynamic assessment. For example, it is difficult to evaluate the claim that the assessment process results in the identification of optimal individually tailored remediation programs. Vye et al. (1987) provide evidence that, following mediated dynamic assessment, different children were seen to have different types of problems, and that instruction based on that information resulted in clearly improved performance, that is, the assessment procedure did appear sensitive to individual differences and did lead to an effective teaching approach. The problem is that we have no way of knowing whether an alternative instructional avenue would have produced equal or better learning. But it can clearly be claimed, and to some this is the only issue, that a responsive clinician, familiar with the domain in question and working one-on-one with a student, can help him learn. And this, in collaboration with informed teachers, has a beneficial effect on the learning trajectories of disadvantaged children.

Not Easily Reproducible or Trainable

These criticisms notwithstanding, it should be clear that Feuerstein has made a major contribution to assessment and instruction. His work has clearly helped to shift the goal of special education in the United States from an emphasis on selection and labeling to one of amelioration and instruction. His gifts as a clinician are in no small measure determinants of his contribution. However, these gifts highlight still another problem. Most would agree that Feuerstein is a gifted clinician. But many would add that the open-ended flexibility of the LPAD device does raise questions about how it would fare in the hands of those less gifted. And if widespread implementation of the procedure is the goal, it will be overworked practitioners in the field who must diagnose meaningful conceptual change in their clients. Pragmatically, too, the cost of such training and the time it takes to admininster such an assessment should not be forgotten.

Linking Assessment with Instruction

One major goal of the principal workers in the field is the integration of assessment with instruction. Diagnostic insights gleaned from assessment are intended to be implemented in the classroom or clinic. However, another concern is that the emphasis on very general skills in programs that use IQ-like inductive reasoning problems leads to an enormous transfer problem. Assessment often takes place with specially developed materials that intentionally bear little relation to school-like tasks, and it is possible for students to improve the ability to deal with those tasks and yet show no appreciable gains in any academic discipline. For Feuerstein, assessment and even some instructional materials are *intentionally* divorced from the actual contents and contexts of schooling. Feuerstein believes that after several years of schooling, his clients are so "turned off" by traditional academic content areas that they respond to them with passive aggression. The introduction of neutral, novel contexts is intended to engage the students' interest, which is difficult to do with, say, the arithmetic problems or reading lessons on which they have repeatedly failed. As Bransford, Arbitman-Smith, et al. (1985) point out, many of the gains achieved by those who have participated in the Instrumental Enrichment program (Feuerstein 1980) have been on standardized ability tests that feature items similar to those found on the LPAD.

Feuerstein is not unaware of this problem. He points out that major attempts at "bridging" experiences from the Instrumental Enrichment classroom back to the "real world" and to regular classrooms will be needed to overcome this transfer problem. The success of such bridging ventures is critical for the practical use of this program. There is some evidence that this transfer is most likely to occur if the Instrumental Enrichment teacher also teaches the students in a content area (Bransford, Arbitman-Smith, et al. 1985), a condition that makes bridging much easier and more natural. The teacher learns and teaches the strategies in Instrumental Enrichment and then introduces them, often unknowingly, into regular classroom activities.

Toward an Implementation

So where does our brave new world fit into the universe of testing purposes? What would such an implementation look like, and where might there be room and reason to try it out on a large scale?

Curriculum Base

Much of the work discussed above focuses on inductive reasoning and performance on tasks that are divorced from the major literacies taught in schools (reading, writing, numeracy, and, more recently, computer literacy). But the initial success with reading and mathematics programs, both in assessment and instruction, encourages us to suggest a large-scale implementation of dynamic assessment and interactive instruction only in the content areas of the curriculum. There are two reasons for this. First, if we are to discover how powerful these notions can be in changing instruction, and if we are to develop the link between assessment and instruction, it is essential that we develop our program in the literacies that constitute the principal areas of the curriculum. We believe that if we are to take up a considerable portion of the school day from students who desperately need enabling literacy skills, instruction should enhance exactly those skills.

Second, we take seriously the danger of reification of test scores into fixed cognitive entities. It is for these reasons of interpretation that, once we had established that guided learning and transfer measures were valid and of theoretical importance, we switched to embedding such methods in contexts like early mathematics. If it were possible to develop several assessment units (per grade) and link them with instructional units, we could bypass the labeling problem altogether. Then, rather than trying to measure a child's "general" learning potential, we would measure readiness to learn about the properties of zero, negative numbers, and so on. Similarly, rather than measuring only how much help a particular child needs, we wish to be able to specify "what kind of help on what kind of problem" so that diagnosis can truly inform instruction.

It is important to note that measuring "readiness" in this context is intended simultaneously as an evaluation of that which has previously been "learned." We see guided assessments as affording both predictions about future performance and, as outcome measures, evaluations of the fruits of previous teaching. Those who score poorly on dynamic tests, that is, those who learn some new things only with considerable difficulty or who cannot readily use those new acquisitions, are likely to be those who have not *understood* what they have been taught previously. It is a sign not only that the student may have difficulty with upcoming lessons, but also that it may be prudent to review past lessons. The idea is to minimize the likelihood that students will proceed from one component of the curriculum to the next without having understood the earlier portions. This attempt, to assess understanding of routines rather than simply their execution, is not unique to guided assessment research—it is the touchstone of most current attempts at revising assessment—but we believe that observing students as they are learning new skills and being asked to apply them may be the best way to accomplish this goal.

Emphasis on K–4 Curriculum

Although consternation about our schools exists throughout the kindergarten through twelfth-grade spectrum and beyond, we believe strongly that an implementation of integrated dynamic assessment and interactive instruction must focus first on the years from kindergarten through fourth grade. A firm conceptual grasp of, for example, place value notation and basic processes of listening and reading comprehension, are prerequisite to all that follows. If a child can understand and do these basic things by fourth grade, the child has the option to continue in the school system. If not, the child faces remedial intervention, with the accompanying stigma of labeling and all its attendant problems (Brown, Palincsar, and Purcell 1985). The longer these problems go unchecked, the more likely it is the student will build up both serious misconceptions about the basic literacies and a deep-grained aversion to schooling itself. In this light, it would not make sense for us to focus first on the higher grades. If dynamic assessment used diagnostically in classrooms is really to demonstrate its worth, it should do so in a way that will provide a launching pad for later stages of learning.

Artificially Intelligent Tutors/Testers

One obvious concern with the use of some forms of guided assessment is that they require time and effort. In our own work, assessment involves several one-on-one sessions. We can try to justify some of the cost on the grounds that students are being taught new skills as they are being assessed, skills presumably central to the school curriculum; as such, assessment does also involve relevant instruction. But the amount of work required is still daunting. It is possible, of course, to reserve in-depth assessment for those having particular difficulties in the subject matter. For example, students having difficulty on a standardized math test could be singled out. Students so identified could be given a more detailed and theoretically based test, such as the one developed by Ferrara

(1987), to pinpoint more precisely the nature of their problems.[4] Only after that diagnosis would we proceed to more in-depth dynamic assessment.

But a better solution would be to use computer technology in this enterprise. We are convinced that in assessment of this complexity, the logical objective is to develop computerized support for the professionals charged with carrying out the assessments. It is clearly possible to conduct some forms of guided assessment via computer, as we have done so ourselves (Campione et al. 1985). Further, intelligent tutoring systems capable of incorporating guided assessment have been developed by others (for example, Fredericksen and White 1988), and there is every reason to believe that advances in computer technology will make additional development easier in the near future. Our emphasis in the early grades suggests a further need for advanced speech technologies because many of our students will not yet be readers. But this is again an area in which rapid strides have been made.

The First Stage

We assume that our plans will go through a lengthy first stage of relatively small-scale development. Eventually, we hope to see our integrated system more widely distributed. Here we will discuss the focal areas in which decisions will have to be made at the first stage.

Agreement on Key Units

Let us assume that one of the domains in which we want to develop intelligent tutor/dynamic assessment is place value. We will need a detailed analysis of the content of that domain, an understanding of its development, and a description of the problems that students may encounter. This would require a tremendous amount of basic research, but we do have promising beginnings here, since many of the leading researchers in cognition and instruction, child development, and artificial intelligence are currently working on such issues (Brown and Burton, VanLehn, Resnick, Gelman, Case, and others). But extensive basic research programs will be needed for each area of the curriculum from which we select key units. One advantage, of course, is that a detailed study of a particular content area provides insights into both testing and teaching.

Such a tremendous cost and effort obviously entails agreement on key units in order to avoid dilution of effort and resources. This would require a core group of teachers, researchers, administrators, and interested others to agree on some of the critical elements of the kindergarten through fourth-grade curriculum. Of course, this does not mean that nothing else would be covered in the school day, only that key areas would be developed for intelligent tutor/testing units.

This in itself raises another issue. If such a scheme were adopted on a relatively large scale, it would raise the specter of a partial national curriculum, something that has been at least officially avoided for many years. Yet many assert that the achievment tests created by national testing companies come very close to instituting a national curriculum, so perhaps this would be less of an obstacle than one would think.

Model Teaching Schools

The ideal implementation sites we imagine would be model laboratory teaching schools similar to the medical teaching hospitals where future doctors learn their specialties by means of mentor and apprenticeship methods. Similarly, model schools could be just such places of apprenticeship training for teachers and school psychologists. Innovative assessment and instruction methods that have been proven effective on a small scale would be demonstrated and practiced at these model schools, where teachers, like doctors, would intern as part of their training. These schools need not be run by schools of education or by ordinary school districts. They might be designated as special state-funded sites where associations of researchers, teachers, administrators, parents, and children could collaborate in providing a site for the development of teaching professionals and a testing ground for innovative methods in education.

Another advantage of such special schools is that it might be possible to impose a moratorium on standardized accountability testing. In order to have the time to develop curriculum that would instantiate our goals, we would need to give teachers, parents, and students "time off" from the demands of satisfying district and state test-score expectations while they attempt an innovative look at assessment and instruction.

An Exercise for the Reader

The approaches we have reviewed in this chapter can contribute in several ways to improving the practice of assessment and instruction, along with their integration. Both guided instruction and assessment are based on the same in-depth analyses of the skills involved in different academic domains. In either case, these skills are made overt and modeled by the teacher or tester, maximizing the likelihood that students will come to adopt them. Guided assessment techniques can hence reinforce directly the instructional innovations we have argued for here. By concentrating on the processes responsible for change and learning within academic domains, rather than on the products of past experience, guided assessment approaches focus attention directly on the critical skills schooling is designed to foster. Also, the skills and activities that are the targets of assessment are evaluated in the intended context of their use, that is, while students are reading a text for meaning or solving a mathematics problem. Thus, the match between assessment and use of skills is much closer than in more typical testing situations, where skills are tested in relative isolation from each other and from the larger academic context. In addition, the guided, interactive nature of the assessment both leads students to learn new skills during the assessment process and enables a more thorough evaluation of those students.

These strengths, however, come at some cost, and guided assessment approaches can form only a portion of an overall testing system. The majority of guided assessment approaches feature labor-intensive protocols aimed at the evaluation of individual learners. And this is not surprising; the developers of the procedures were in general concerned with the evaluation and remediation of students with learning problems. One consequence of this emphasis is that guided assessment is less well adapted to large-scale testing and issues of accountability, at the school, district, or state level. And it is also in this area that there are clear needs for improvement. While there are many reasons for concern, we will note only two here. First, as the goals of instruction have changed, the emphasis on thinking and reasoning processes has reappeared. As Resnick and Resnick (this volume) point out, standard assessment vehicles are not sensitive to the kinds of thinking processes that are the focus of the new "thinking curriculum." In fact, by directing attention to the products (facts, algorithms,and so on) of critical thinking activities, rather than those activities themselves, standard approaches may actually inhibit the development of the kinds of instructional programs we wish to create. Second, it is frequently argued that one desired outcome of schooling is the ability of students to work collaboratively; yet traditional assessment taps only individual performance. These concerns, among others, have led to calls for radically different approaches to assessment (see Gardner, this volume).

Although it was not our charge to to deal with these issues in this chapter, we would like to reinforce the arguments made by Resnick and Resnick, and Gardner. To illustrate some of the problems arising from a mismatch between standard assessment practices and alternative learning environments, we conclude with a brief description of a recent instructional program we have begun to implement (see Brown and Campione, in press, for additional details), and raise the question of how one might proceed to evaluate its effectiveness. The project involved three fifth- and sixth-grade classrooms, each including thirty students, who participated for three fifty-minute periods a week for the school year. At one level, the context was introductory biology, with an emphasis on interdependence in nature. At another level, we wanted our students to learn something about systems in general: the fact that in a functioning ecosystem, change in any element of the situation (an animal becomes extinct, there is an overall cooling or warming trend, man intervenes, and so on) reverberates throughout the entire system. Finally, and most important, we were interested in teaching skills of critical thinking and scientific inquiry.

Students were involved in designing the specifics of their own curriculum units. The curriculum was divided into three units (Protection from Predators; Systems and Cycles—Adaptation; and Systems and Cycles—Ecosystems and

Interdependence), and each unit was further subdivided into five topics (for example, in the Ecosystems and Interdependence unit—Oceans and Spills; Garbage and Hazardous Waste; Global Warming; Food Chains and Animal Habitats: Food Chains and Human Populations). Students worked cooperatively in both research and learning groups. The basic idea, illustrated in figure 6, is adapted from *The Jigsaw Classroom* (Aronson 1978). Students formed *research* groups covering the five subunits of each topic. We provided them with suitable materials: texts, articles, magazines, videos, and access to a library, plus adult guidance upon request. They prepared a booklet on their research (using a simplified version of Hypercard on Mac IIs), and then reassembled into *learning* groups that consisted of one member from each of the original research groups. It was the expert from each research group who was responsible for teaching other members of her learning group about that topic. Thus, the choice of a learning leader became based on expertise rather than random selection, as was the case in the original reciprocal teaching work. All children in the learning group were expert on one part of the material, taught it to others, and prepared questions for the test that all had to take on the complete unit. The students were in this way involved in: (a) *extensive reading* in order to research their topic; (b) *writing and revision* to produce booklets from which to teach and to *publish* in class books covering the entire topic; and (c) *computer use* to publish, illustrate, and edit their booklets. They were reading, writing, and using computers in the service of learning.

Figure 6

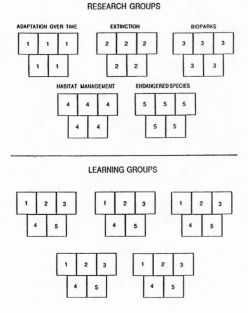

A Community of Learners

This social structure was devised to overcome some of the limitations inherent in more traditional instruction. For example, consider how this collaborative classroom (see table 6) differs from traditional practice in "reading group." In more traditional reading groups, teachers rely heavily on giving students assigned

Table 6
Reading Group vs. Research Teams

READING GROUPS	RESEARCH TEAMS
Organization	
Reading assigned text	Write own text
Doled out in pieces	Extended work on common themes: Long term projects
No right to put work aside	Set own agenda within time and social constraints
Read in order to answer questions	Answer own questions
	Accountability for quality of questions
Teacher knows more than reader	Teachers do not always know answer
Read to prove you have read	Read and write to teach, to publish, to understand, to learn, etc.
No other reader but teacher	Read and comment on each other's work
Individual accountability	Community of learners sharing common data base
Goals	
Reading qua reading	Reading in the service of learning
Writing qua writing	Writing in the service of learning
Computing qua computing	Computing in the service of learning
Method	
Direct teaching	Advising/Coaching
'Big heads to little heads'	By experts (children or adults)
	On a need-to-know basis, as in an intellectual community
	Children's expertise fostered and valued
	Adults as facilitators
Outcomes	
Misconceptions about reading, etc.	Community of discussion
	Distributed expertise

text, they dole out reading in small pieces, and students have no right to put the task aside. This is in sharp contrast to how literate events evolved and are maintained in the "real world." So too this practice is in contrast to our learning environment where children write the texts, working at their own pace, with extended involvement in personally chosen projects. Another strange aspect of reading lessons is that students read in order to prove to the teacher that they have read; to answer questions posed by the teacher, who, clearly, already knows the answer. The teacher is also the primary consumer of any written products. But in this classroom, students answer their own questions and are accountable for the quality of the questions asked. Teachers do not always know the right answer. Students read in order to communicate, teach, write, persuade, understand. The goal is reading, writing, thinking in the service of learning about something. Teaching is on a need to know basis, with experts (be they children or adults) acting as facilitators. Student expertise is fostered and valued by the community. A community of discussion is created with distributed expertise. We argue that this contrasts sharply with what usually goes on in reading, and in elementary science lessons, and that this change can result in significant improvements in *both* the students' thinking skills and in the domain-specific knowledge about which they are reasoning.

Evaluation. As we were responsible for grading the students—this was their social science course—we administered standard knowledge tests at the beginning and end of each unit and at the end of the year. And, indeed, students came to understand the material quite well. But that information provided by far the least, and least interesting, information about what had happened over the year. Major additional data sources included, but were not restricted to: (a) the booklets each research *group* prepared for teaching their subunit -- they were free to update them whenever they wanted throughout the year; (b) a book on each unit, prepared by the *class* as a whole; (c) *individual* research and writing on each unit; (d) a year-end "habitat design"—they were to build an imaginary animal and then design an optimal habitat in which the animal could live; and (e) on-line tests of computer use—they were seated in front of the computer and asked to accomplish varying goals, with hints provided when necessary. In addition, (f) all the learning-group discussions were audiotaped (some were videotaped) and then transcribed for further scoring.

The question, of course, is how does one summarize what happened during the year—what are the appropriate means of assessment? It seems clear that simple tests of factual information would not provide a good summary. It is quite possible, given that we chose to explore one topic, (interdependence in nature) in depth, that the students would fare more poorly on a standardized test of biological knowledge than would a control class afforded more typical instruction. In the latter case, the students would have been exposed to many more topics than were our students (introductory biology texts emphasize breadth over depth), and would have had a chance to acquire a larger fact repertoire (thereby making them more biologically literate?).

We do not propose to answer the assessment question here, rather to indicate some of the results that convinced us that the project was a success. In our view, one of the most impressive outcomes of the collaborative classroom is the development of a community of learners acquiring and sharing a common knowledge base. The nature of the reading/learning discussions and the writing samples all reflect higher levels of reasoning skills that are apparent in most classroom contexts, including the original reciprocal teaching dialogues.

Classroom discussions. Although there were many changes in the dialogues, the easiest to score is the *length* of the discussions—transcriptions of the lessons more than tripled over the course of the year, as the discussions became more extended. For the early sessions, on protection from predators, the transcripts ranged from six to eight pages; whereas for the later sessions, the transcripts ran over twenty pages.

The *content* of the discussions also changed. Although children in the collaborative classroom were all trained in the comprehension-monitoring strategies (question, clarify, summarize, predict) of reciprocal teaching, those activities took on less and less importance as the argument and explanatory structure of the teaching sessions developed. Over time we saw an increasing incidence of comprehension-extending activities, such as *deep analogies*, occurring in the teaching dialogues. A surface analogy is one where students notice similarities across incidents but do not use them as explanatory devices; in contrast, deep analogies involve students not only noticing systematic relations but also using deep structural similarity to explain mechanisms. Similarly, *causal explanations* became more evident, again increasing in explanatory precision and coherence over time. *Explanations* were more often supported by warrants and backings (Toulmin 1958). The nature of what constitutes *evidence* was discussed, including a consideration of negative evidence. A variety of *plausible reasoning* strategies (Collins et al., 1975) began to emerge. *Argumentation* formats developed, comparing different points of view and defensible interpretations. And finally, the nature and importance of *prediction* evolved, with students going beyond predictions of simple outcomes to considering possible worlds and engaging in thought experiments.

Writing Examples. Over time the writing samples produced by the research groups changed in a number of interesting ways. Consider first the content of the texts. At the outset, students were more attracted by the graphics capabilities of the computer than they were interested in producing informative texts. For example, the text segment shown in figure 7 includes impressive graphics but little in the way of text; the text is simply cut and pasted from other readings. In contrast, the segment in figure 8, while still incorporating impressive graphics, includes considerably more text. The *structure* of the texts also changed considerably, revealing increasingly sophisticated use of argument

structure, compare and contrast modes, and hierarchical structuring of the
content. The students progressed from producing a book that contained a
perfectly linear structure of twenty-two paragraphs about twenty-two animals
(such as figure 7) to books with a recognizable and complex hierarchical
organization. By the end of the year, the best class books consist of three types
of organization. As shown in figure 9, one example included a hierarchy, a
compare and contrast section, and an exemplar-based section. This mixed model
is difficult for even college students to handle. These are our very best examples;
not all students showed such progress. But, comparing the microgenetic change
over a year with existing cross-age norms for writing, we estimate that the best
students progressed from poor grade-school level to a writing level more typical
of young adults. It is clear that, over the course of the year, the students became

Figure 7

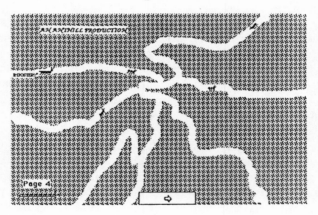

much more capable of working together to produce texts that afforded and supported their teaching of the content to their classmates. Although we do not have space to deal with the issue here, it was also interesting to trace how the nature of the collaboration changed, with different students taking on different portions of the overall responsibility, small groups (usually pairs) working on different segments, and then the group coming together to edit the final product.

Not all students were individually capable of such sophistication, of course, but most showed progress, perhaps the most dramatic progress coming from the initially weaker writers. Consider just one example. Tom, a learning-disabled, sixth-grade student reading at the second-grade level, was involved in producing figure 7. He spent the lion's share of his effort initially on graphics and had to be "persuaded" to provide any text at all, and this he "borrowed" from

Figure 8

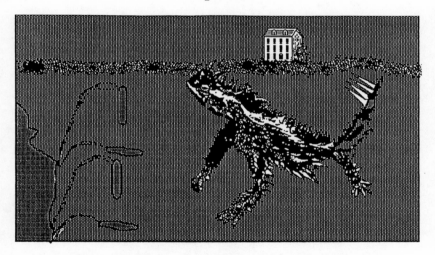

(My animal eats) Most insects some small fish and a canal rat her and thereand some crafish There are small spikes all over the body and 4 long poison stingers on it tail that they are amun to so when they eat it they do not get poisined like there pray. It has a very strong noise and very sharp eye sight .no because its mean.

(It defends itself) There are small spikes all over the body and 4 long poison stingers on it tail that they are amun to so when they eat it they do not get poisined like there pray. It has a very strong noise and very sharp eye sight . Yes they are very aggersive if you bother it would try very hard to hurt you.

On the avarge year the female will have about 60 babys a year. they are born under ground and the mother will get as many worms as possable.
If not for the very strange way of protection prey coule wipe out the whole litter in one atack. this strang way of proction is when they are born they do not have legs yet and it has allmost the exact pattern of a full groun corba.

Figure 9

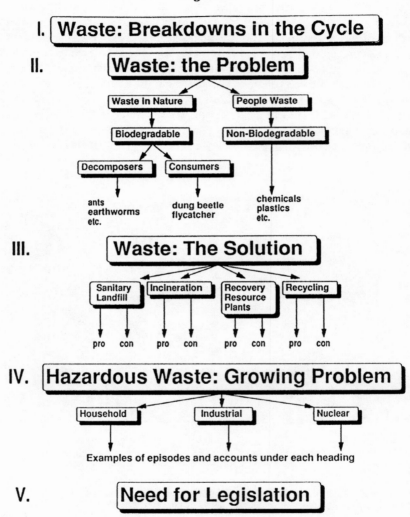

a book. He refused to provide an independent hand written sample, and both teacher and student agreed that he "couldn't write." At the end of the year, he was asked to design an animal on Hypercard that would be well adapted to a certain habitat, in this case a swamp. Tom showed no hesitation in attacking this problem, even though there were strange adults (the first two authors) watching him. He began with his favorite, graphics, and drew a splendid creature; but then he calmly added "created" text, a thing he would never do at the beginning of the year. The text was as follows:

> (My animal eats) Most insects some small fish and a canal rat her and thereand some crafish There are small spikes all over the body and 4 long poison stingers on it tail that they are amun to so when they eat it they do not get poisined like there prey.It has a very strong noise and very sharp eye sight . It doesn't depend on other animals because its mean.

> (It defends itself) There are small spikes all over the body and 4 long poison stingers on it tail that they are amun to so when they eat it they do not poisined like there pray.It has a very strong noise and very sharp eye sight . [If you have already written something relevant, why not just reuse it?] Yes they are very aggersive if you bother it would try very hard to hurt you.

> On the average the female will have about 60 babys a year. they are bord under ground and the mother will get as many worms as possable.

> If not for the very strange way of protection prey coule wipe out the whole litter in one atack. this strang way of proction is when they are born they do not have legs yet and it has allmost the exact pattern of a full groun corba

This text took about one-half hour to complete. The spelling and punctuation are weak, but Tom introduced several sophisticated biological themes. For example, he incorporated the notions of poisoned spikes to which the host is immune (amun) and mimicry—the litter have no legs and look like full-grown (groun) cobras (corba), thus mimicking dangerous snakes for protection. Tom's progress from a nonwriter to a writer was particularly pleasing.

Computer Use. Students acquired considerable facility using the computers. By the end of the year, quite a few were more accomplished than either their teacher or our research staff (not to mention ourselves). They came to understand the notion of a computer as a tool for accomplishing other tasks. For example, after a while, they were frustrated by the limitations imposed by the particular software we had provided for them (Hypercard), and several students essentially asked for a word-processing package they could use (they were not unimpressed by the power of spellchecking features). Beyond that, having seen some of the texts we provided for their research, they became interested in how they could include some of the same features in their own work. This led to our providing them with the more powerful software that resulted in the text shown in figure 8.

Summary. The students in these classes showed many accomplishments during the year. Their written samples, both resulting from collaborative efforts in research groups and individual undertakings, improved significantly. The discussions occurring in the learning groups became more extended; they were also more clearly focused on a deeper understanding of the material under consideration. In part because of these discussions, and in part because of the need to teach their peers, the students continued to go back and revise their texts over the year. Their computer usage became more sophisticated as they came to appreciate the ways in which the computer could facilitate their work. Finally, they acquired a considerable, and relatively deep, knowledge of specific biological principles and the nature of systems in general. Many of these attainments, however, would not be detected in assessments based on standard tests. To the extent that these curricular innovations are accomplishing their intended goals, it is essential that we also develop alternative assessment methods that are sensitive to those goals. Without some capability for documenting the outcomes, the programs will almost certainly die. At least as important, appropriate methods of assessment would help pinpoint areas in which the curriculum is failing to accomplish some of its goals. It is only when we are armed with information about both successes and failures that it is possible to determine intelligently which elements of the curriculum should be maintained and which should be modified (for some examples, see Brown and Campione, in press). The more precise the assessment, the greater the likelihood that it will lead to specific insights about how these modifications should be done. The considerations involved in instruction and assessment are thus the same, featuring as they do detailed analyses of the knowledge and processing skills necessary for performance within a domain. It is in this area that recent research has made impressive advances in the last decade. These discoveries, along with heightened attention to the features of novel learning environments, have laid the groundwork for exciting changes in the way education is practiced. The more recent focus on innovative assessment procedures, including those reviewed here and elsewhere in this series, complement that work in many important ways. The fact that similar theoretical views are being brought to bear on the instruction an assessment endeavors increases the likelihood that instruction and assessment can be integrated and gives us confidence that we, as a field, are making progress.

NOTES

1. The characterization that follows is not meant as an indictment of the field of psychometrics and educational measurement. Many measurement professionals have labored to find ways to improve the fairness and usefulness of assessments of ability and aptitude. Moreover, the view we are characterizing here is not the sophisticated view held by theoreticians in the field but an attempt to distill the essence of a perspective partially or completely held by many test consumers and laypersons. Although there has been little work that investigates the "common wisdom" or "folk models" of intelligence and IQ measurement among teachers and laypersons, our experiences in the field of special education have shown us that the traditional assumptions we outline are held by numerous individuals who are responsible for sorting and placing children in a wide variety of educational settings. Our experiences, which echo those described by Mehan (1985) and others, have convinced us that it is not sufficient merely to suppose that these assumptions are disappearing. Thus, while we intend no attack on the psychometric and measurement community, we ask the reader to understand our distillation in this section as an idealization of sorts, but an idealization that is substantially veridical in many communities.

2. However, see our discussion in the next section regarding the controversy in traditional psychological theories of mental measurement about the relationship between IQ and learning.

3. We are, of course, aware that IQ tests were never intended to be used as a means for teachers to diagnose and prescribe specific educational treatments. Our point is that the notions of intelligence and learning that underlie the measurement of IQ are conceptually quite different from the notions of learning potential and ability that we will describe here. The latter ideas provide the opportunity to reopen the question of how ability assessments may be used to improve educational development.

4. Although we have emphasized dynamic assessment here, we do not mean to suggest that this is the only approach to improving assessment. There are many research programs whose goal is the development of more sophisticated and theoretically based static tests designed to capture student understanding. These are thoroughly treated in other chapters in this series.

REFERENCES

Anastasi, A. 1981. Coaching, test sophistication, and developed abilities. *American Psychologist* 36:1086–93.

Aronson, E. 1978. The Jigsaw Classroom. Beverly Hills, CA: Sage Publications

Ballester, L. 1984. Feuerstein's model of cognitive functioning applied to preschool children: A study of the relationship between the specific cognitive strategies and learning. Ph.D. diss. Temple University, Philadelphia, PA.

Bandler, R., and J. Grinder. 1975. *The structure of magic.* Palo Alto, CA: Science and Behavior Books.

Bethge, H. J., J. S. Carlson, and K. H. Wiedl. 1982. The effects of dynamic assessment procedures on Raven matrices performance, visual search behavior, test anxiety and test orientation. *Intelligence* 6:89–97.

Binet, A. 1903. *L'étude experimentale de l'intelligence.* Paris: Schleicher Frères.

Binet, A. 1909. *Les idées modernes sur les infants.* Paris: Ernest Flammarion.

Binet, A. [1911] 1962. The nature and measurement of intelligence. In *Psychology in the making: Histories of selected research problems,* trans. R. D. Tuddenham; ed. L. Postman. New York: Knopf. (Originally published, Paris: Ernest Flammarion)

Binet, A., and T. Simon. 1908. Le développement de l'intelligence des enfants. *L'Année Psychologique* 14:1–94.

Binet, A., and T. Simon. 1916. *The development of intelligence in children (The Binet-Simon scale).* Trans. Elizabeth S. Kite from articles in *L'Année Psychologique* from 1905, 1908, and 1911. Baltimore: Williams and Wilkins.

Borkowski, J. G. 1985. Signs of intelligence: Strategy generalization and metacognition. In *Development of reflection in children,* ed. S. R. Yussen, 105–44. New York: Academic Press.

Bransford, J. D. 1979. *Human cognition: Learning, understanding, and remembering.* Belmont, CA: Wadsworth.

Bransford, J. D., R. Arbitman-Smith, B. S. Stein, and N. J. Vye. 1985. Improving thinking and learning skills: An analysis of three approaches. In Vol. 1, *Thinking and learning skills,* ed. J. W. Segal, S. F. Chipman, and R. Glaser, 133–206. Hillsdale, NJ: Erlbaum.

Bransford, J. D., V. R. Delclos, N. J. Vye, M. S. Burns, and T. S. Hasselbring. 1985. Improving the quality of assessment and instruction: Roles for dynamic assessment. Working Paper No. 1, Vanderbilt University, John F. Kennedy Center for Research on Education and Human Development.

Bransford, J. D., V. R. Delclos, N. J. Vye, M. S. Burns, and T. S. Hasselbring. 1986. Improving the quality of assessment and instruction: Roles for dynamic assessment. Paper presented at American Psychological Association, Washington, DC.

Bransford, J. D., V. R. Delclos, N. J. Vye, M. S. Burns, and T. S. Hasselbring. 1987. Approaches to dynamic assessment: Issues, data and future directions. In *Dynamic assessment: Foundations and fundamentals,* ed. C. S. Lidz, 479–96. New York: Guilford Press.

Bransford, J. D., T. S. Hasselbring, B. Barron, S. Kulewicz, J. Littlefield, and L. Goin. 1988. Use of macro-contexts to facilitate mathematical thinking. In *Research agenda for mathematics education: Teaching and assessment of mathematical problem solving,* ed. R. I. Charles and E. A. Silver, 125–47. Hillsdale, NJ: Erlbaum.

Brown, A. L. 1974. The role of strategic behavior in retardate memory. In Vol. 7, *International review of research in mental retardation,* ed. N. R. Ellis, 55–111. New York: Academic Press.

Brown, A. L. 1975. The development of memory: Knowing, knowing about knowing, and knowing how to know. In Vol. 10, *Advances in child development and behavior,* ed. H. W. Reese, 103–52. New York: Academic Press.

Brown, A. L. 1978. Knowing when, where, and how to remember: A problem of metacognition. In Vol. 1, *Advances in instructional psychology,* ed. R. Glaser, 77–165. Hillsdale, NJ: Erlbaum.

Brown, A. L. 1985. Mental orthopedics: A conversation with Alfred Binet. In Vol. 2, *Thinking and learning skills: Current research and open questions,* ed. S. Chipman, J. Segal, and R. Glaser, 319–37. Hillsdale, NJ: Erlbaum.

Brown, A. L., and J. C. Campione. 1978. Permissible inferences from cognitive training studies in developmental research. *Quarterly Newsletter of the Institute for Comparative Human Behavior* 2 (3): 46–53.

Brown, A. L., and J. C. Campione. 1981. Inducing flexible thinking: A problem of access. In *Intelligence and learning,* ed. M. Friedman, J. P. Das, and N. O'Connor, 515–30. New York: Plenum Press.

Brown, A. L., and J. C. Campione. 1984. Three faces of transfer: Implications for early competence, individual differences, and instruction. In Vol. 3, *Advances in developmental psychology,* ed. M. Lamb, A. Brown, and B. Rogoff, 143–92. Hillsdale, NJ: Erlbaum.

Brown, A. L., and J. C. Campione. 1986. Psychological theory and the study of learning disabilities. *American Psychologist* 41 (10): 1059–68.

Brown, A. L., and J. C. Campione, In press. Communities of learning and thinking, or a context by any other name. *Human Development.*

Brown, A. L., and R. A. Ferrara. 1985. Diagnosing zones of proximal development: An alternative to standardized testing? In *Culture, communication and cognition: Vygotskian perspectives,* ed. J. Wertsch, 273–305. New York: Cambridge University Press.

Brown, A. L., and L. A. French. 1979. The zone of potential development: Implications for intelligence testing in the year 2000. *Intelligence* 3:253–71.

Brown, A. L., and A. S. Palincsar. 1982. Inducing strategic learning from texts by means of informed, self-control training. *Topics in Learning and Learning Disabilities* 2 (1): 1–17.

Brown, A. L., and A. S. Palincsar. 1987. Reciprocal teaching of comprehension strategies: A natural history of one program for enhancing learning. In *Intelligence and exceptionality: New directions for theory, assessment, and instructional practices,* ed. J. D. Day and J. G. Borkowski. Norwood, NJ: Ablex.

Brown, A. L., and A. S. Palincsar. 1989. Guided cooperative learning and individual knowledge acquisition. In *Knowing, learning, and instruction: Essays in honor of Robert Glaser,* ed. L. B. Resnick. Hillsdale, NJ: Erlbaum.

Brown, A. L., and R. A. Reeve. 1987. Bandwidths of competence: The role of supportive contexts in learning and development. In *Development and learning: Conflict or congruence?,* ed. L. S. Liben, 173–223. Hillsdale, NJ: Erlbaum.

Brown, A. L., A. S. Palincsar, and L. Purcell. 1985. Poor readers: Teach, don't label. In *The academic performance of minority children: A new perspective,* ed. U. Neisser, 105–43. Hillsdale, NJ: Erlbaum.

Brown, A. L., J. D. Bransford, R. A. Ferrara, and J. C. Campione. 1983. Learning, remembering, and understanding. In *Handbook of child psychology*. 4th ed., ed. P. H. Mussen. Vol. 3, *Cognitive development*, ed. J. H. Flavell and E. M. Markman, 515–29. New York: Wiley.

Brown, A. L., J. C. Campione, R. A. Reeve, R. A. Ferrara, and A. S. Palincsar. In press. Interactive learning, individual understanding: The case of reading and mathematics. In *Culture, schooling and psychological development*, ed. L. T. Landsmann. Hillsdale, NJ: Erlbaum.

Bryant, N. R. 1982. Preschool children's learning and transfer of matrices problems: A study of proximal development. Master's thesis, University of Illinois.

Bryant, N. R., A. L. Brown, and J. C. Campione. 1983. Preschool children's learning and transfer of matrices problems: Potential for improvement. Paper presented at the Society for Research in Child Development meetings, April, Detroit.

Buckingham, B. R. 1921. Intelligence and its measurement: A symposium. *Journal of Educational Psychology* 12:271–75.

Budoff, M. 1974. Learning potential and educability among the educable mentally retarded. Final Report Project No. 312312. Cambridge, MA: Research Institute for Educational Problems, Cambridge Mental Health Association.

Budoff, M. 1987a. The validity of learning potential assessment. In *Dynamic assessment: An interactional approach to evaluating learning potential*, ed. C. S. Lidz, 52–81. New York: Guilford Press.

Budoff, M. 1987b. Measures for assessing learning potential. In *Dynamic assessment: An interactional approach to evaluating learning potential*, ed. C. S. Lidz, 173–95. New York: Guilford Press.

Burns, M. S. 1985. Comparison of "graduated prompt" and "mediational" dynamic assessment and static assessment with young children. Tech. Report No. 2, Vanderbilt University, John F. Kennedy Center for Research on Education and Human Development.

Burns, M. S., V. R. Delclos, and N. J. Vye. In press. Brief mediated assessment with young children: Principles and scripts. Tech. Report No. 5, Vanderbilt University, John F. Kennedy Center for Research on Education and Human Development.

Burns, M. S., N. J. Vye, J. D. Bransford, V. R. Delclos, and T. Ogan. 1987. Static and dynamic measures of learning in young handicapped children. Tech. Report No. 8, Vanderbilt University, John F. Kennedy Center for Research on Education and Human Development.

Campione, J. C. 1989. Assisted assessment: A taxonomy of approaches and an outline of strengths and weaknesses. *Journal of Learning Disabilities 22:151–65*.

Campione, J. C., and A. L. Brown. 1974. The effects of contextual changes and degree of component mastery on transfer of training. In Vol. 9, *Advances in child development and behavior*, ed. H. W. Reese, 69–114. New York: Academic Press.

Campione, J. C., and A. L. Brown. 1977. Memory and metamemory development in educable retarded children. In *Perspectives on the development of memory and cognition*, ed. R. V. Kail, Jr., and J. W. Hagen, 367–406. Hillsdale, NJ: Erlbaum.

Campione, J. C., and A. L. Brown. 1978. Toward a theory of intelligence: Contributions from research with retarded children. *Intelligence* 2:279–304.

Campione, J. C., and A. L. Brown. 1984. Learning ability and transfer propensity as sources of individual differences in intelligence. In *Learning and cognition in the mentally retarded,* ed. P. H. Brooks, R. Sperber, and C. McCauley. Baltimore: University Park Press.

Campione, J. C., and A. L. Brown. 1987. Linking dynamic assessment with school achievement. In *Dynamic assessment: An interactional approach to evaluating learning potential,* ed. C. S. Lidz, 82–115. New York: Guilford Press.

Campione, J. C., and A. L. Brown. In press. Guided learning and transfer: Implications for approaches to assessment. In *Diagnostic monitoring of skill and knowledge acquisition,* ed. N. Fredericksen, R. Glaser, A. Lesgold, and M. Shafto. Hillsdale, NJ: Erlbaum.

Campione, J. C., and R. A. Ferrara. In preparation. Ability-related differences in the learning and transfer of inductive reasoning principles.

Campione, J. C., A. L. Brown, and N. R. Bryant. 1985. Individual differences in learning and memory. In *Human abilities: An information processing approach,* ed. R. J. Sternberg, 103–26. New York: W. H. Freeman.

Campione, J. C., A. L. Brown, and M. L. Connell. 1988. Metacognition: On the importance of understanding what you are doing. In *Research agenda for mathematics education: Teaching and assessment of mathematical problem solving,* ed. R. I. Charles and E. A. Silver, 93–114. Hillsdale, NJ: Erlbaum.

Campione, J. C., A. L. Brown, and R. A. Ferrara. 1982. Mental retardation and intelligence. In *Handbook of human intelligence,* ed. R. J. Sternberg. New York: Cambridge University Press.

Campione, J. C., A. L. Brown, R. A. Ferrara, and N. R. Bryant. 1984. The zone of proximal development: Implications for individual differences and learning. In *New directions for cognitive development: The zone of proximal development,* ed. B. Rogoff and J. Wertsch, 77–91. San Francisco: Jossey-Bass.

Campione, J. C., A. L. Brown, R. A. Ferrara, R. S. Jones, and E. Steinberg. 1985. Breakdown in flexible use of information: Intelligence-related differences in transfer following equivalent learning performance. *Intelligence* 9:297–315.

Carlson, J. S., and R. Dillon. 1979. Measuring intellectual capacities of hearing-impaired children: Effects of testing-the-limits procedures. *Volta Review* 80: 216–24.

Carlson, J. S., and K. F. Widaman. 1986. Eysenck on intelligence: A critical perspective. In *Hans Eysenck: Consensus and controversy,* ed. S. Modgil and C. Modgil, 103–32. Philadelphia: Falmer Press.

Carlson, J. S., and K. H. Wiedl. 1978. The use of testing-the-limits procedures in the assessment of intellectual capabilities in children with learning difficulties. *American Journal of Mental Deficiency* 82:559–64.

Carlson, J. S., and K. H. Wiedl. 1979. Toward a differential testing approach: Testing-the-limits employing the Raven matrices. *Intelligence* 3:323–44.

Carlson, J. S., and K. H. Wiedl. 1980. Applications of a dynamic testing approach in intelligence assessment: Empirical results and theoretical formulations. *Zeitschrift fur Differentielle und Diagnostische Psychologie* 1, Heft 4:303–18.

Carlson, J. S., and K. H. Wiedl. 1988. The dynamic assessment of intelligence. In *Interactive assessment,* ed. H. C. Haywood and D. Tzuriel. Hillsdale, NJ: Erlbaum.

Collins, S., E. Warnock, N. Aiello, and M. Miller. 1975. Reasoning from incomplete knowledge. *In Representation and understanding: Studies in cognitive science,* D. G. Bobrow and A. Collins, ed. 383–415. New York: Academic Press.

Colvin, S. S. 1921. Intelligence and its measurement: A symposium. *Journal of Educational Psychology* 12:136–39.

Cronbach, L. J. 1967. How can instruction be adapted to individual differences? In *Learning and individual differences,* ed. R. M. Gagne, 23–44. Columbus, OH: Merrill Books.

Davis, R. B. 1984. *Learning mathematics: The cognitive science approach to mathematics education.* Norwood, NJ: Ablex.

Day, J. D., and L. K. Hall. 1987. Cognitive assessment, intelligence, and instruction. To appear in *Intelligence and exceptionality: New directions for theory, assessment and instructional practices,* ed. J. Day and J. G. Borkowski. Norwood, NJ: Ablex Press.

Dearborn, W. F. 1921. Intelligence and its measurement: A symposium. *Journal of Educational Psychology* 12:210–12.

Embretson, S. E. 1987. Improving the measurement of spatial aptitude by dynamic testing. *Intelligence* 11:333–58.

Ferrara, R. A. 1987. Learning mathematics in the zone of proximal development: The importance of flexible use of knowledge. Ph.D. diss., Department of Psychology, University of Illinois at Urbana-Champaign.

Ferrara, R. A., A. L. Brown, and J. C. Campione. 1986. Children's learning and transfer of inductive reasoning rules: Studies in proximal development. *Child Development* 57: 1087–99.

Feuerstein, R. 1969. The instrumental enrichment method: An outline of theory and technique. Jerusalem: Hadassah-Wizo-Canada Research Institute.

Feuerstein, R. 1979. *The dynamic assessment of retarded performers: The learning potential assessment device, theory, instruments, and techniques.* Baltimore: University Park Press.

Feuerstein, R. 1980. *Instrumental enrichment: An intervention program for cognitive modifiability.* Baltimore: University Park Press.

Feuerstein, R., Y. Rand, M. Hoffman, M. Hoffman, and R. Miller. 1979. Cognitive modifiability in retarded adolescents: Effects of instrumental enrichment. *American Journal of Mental Deficiency* 83:539–50.

Feuerstein, R., Y. Rand, M. R. Jensen, S. Kaniel, and D. Tzuriel. 1987. Prerequisites for assessment of learning potential: The LPAD model. In *Dynamic assessment: An interactional approach to evaluating learning potential,* ed. C. S. Lidz, 35–51. New York: Guilford Press.

Flavell, J. H., and H. M. Wellman. 1977. Metamemory. In *Perspectives on the development of memory and cognition,* ed. R. V. Kail, Jr., and J. W. Hagen, 3–33. Hillsdale, NJ: Erlbaum.

Frankenstein, C. 1979. *They think again: Restoring cognitive abilities through teaching.* Hillsdale, NJ: Erlbaum.

Fredericksen, J., and B. Y. White. 1988. Implicit testing within an intelligent tutoring system. *Machine-Mediated Learning* 2:351–72.

French, L. A. 1979. Cognitive consequences of education: Transfer of training in the elderly. Ph.D. diss., University of Illinois.

Gagne, R. M. 1965. *The conditions of learning.* New York: Holt, Rinehart & Winston.

Gelman, R., and C. R. Gallistel. 1978. *The child's understanding of number.* Cambridge, MA: Harvard University Press.

Gelman, R., and J. G. Greeno. 1989. On the nature of competence: Principles for understanding in a domain. In *Knowing, learning, and instruction: Essays in honor of Robert Glaser,* ed. L. B. Resnick. Hillsdale, NJ: Erlbaum.

Gould, S. J. 1981. *The mismeasure of man.* New York: Norton.

Griffin, P., and M. Cole. 1984. Current activity for the future: The Zo-ped. In *Children's learning in the "zone of proximal development,"* ed. B. Rogoff and J. V. Wertsch. San Francisco: Jossey-Bass.

Guthke, J. 1982. The learning test concept—An alternative to the traditional static intelligence test. *The German Journal of Psychology* 6:306–24.

Haggerty, M. 1921. Intelligence and its measurement: A symposium. *Journal of Educational Psychology* 12:212–16.

Hatano, G., and K. Inagaki. 1987. A theory of motivation for comprehension and its application to mathematics instruction. In *The monitoring of school mathematics: Background papers.* Vol. 2, *Implications from psychology, outcomes of instruction,* ed. T. A. Romberg and D. M. Steward, 27–66. Program Report 87. Madison: Wisconsin Center for Educational Research.

Haywood, H. C., J. W. Filler, Jr., M. A. Shifman, and G. Chatelanat. 1975. Behavioral assessment in mental retardation. In Vol. 3, *Advances in psychological assessment,* ed. P. McReynolds, 96–136. Palo Alto, CA: Science and Behavior Books.

Henman, V. A. C. 1921. Intelligence and its measurement: A symposium. *Journal of Educational Psychology* 12:195–98.

Hobbs, N. 1980. Feuerstein's instrumental enrichment: Teaching intelligence to adolescents. *Educational Leadership* 37:566–68.

Jensen, A. R. 1980. *Bias in mental testing.* New York: Free Press.

Lampert, M. 1986. Knowing, doing, and teaching multiplication. *Cognition and Instruction 3* (4): 305–42.

Lidz, C. S. 1987. Cognitive deficiencies revisited. In *Dynamic assessment: An interactional approach to evaluating learning potential,* ed. C. S. Lidz, 444–78. New York: Guilford Press.

Luria, A. R. 1961. Study of the abnormal child. *American Journal of Orthopsychiatry* 31:1–16.

Mehan, H. 1973. Assessing children's language-using abilities: Methodological and cross cultural implications. In *Comparative social research: Methodological problems and strategies,* ed. M. Armer and A. D. Grimshaw. New York: Wiley.

Meltzer, L. 1984. Cognitive assessment in the diagnosis of learning problems. In *Middle childhood: Developmental dysfunction,* ed. M. D. Levine and P. Satz, 131–52. Baltimore: University Park Press.

Minick, N. 1987. Implications of Vygotsky's theories for dynamic assessment. In *Dynamic assessment: An interactional approach to evaluating learning potential,* ed. C. S. Lidz, 116–40. New York: Guilford Press.

Narrol, H., and D. G. Bachor. 1975. An introduction to Feuerstein's approach to assessing and developing cognitive potential. *Interchange* 6:2–16. New York: Guilford Press.

Noddings, N. 1985. Formal models of knowing. In *Learning and teaching the ways of knowing: Eighty-fourth yearbook of the National Society for the Study of Education. Part II,* ed. E. Eisner. Chicago: University of Chicago Press.

Palincsar, A. S., and A. L. Brown. 1984. Reciprocal teaching of comprehension-fostering and comprehension-monitoring activities. *Cognition and Instruction* 1 (2): 117–75.

Palincsar, A. S., and A. L. Brown. 1986. Interactive teaching to promote independent learning from text. *The Reading Teacher* 39 (8): 771–77.

Peterson, J. 1925. *Early conceptions and tests of intelligence.* Yonkers-on-Hudson: World Book.

Pintner, R. 1921. Intelligence and its measurement: A symposium. *Journal of Educational Psychology* 12:139–43.

Resnick, L. B. 1989. Teaching mathematics as an ill-structured discipline. To appear in *Research agenda for mathematics education: Teaching and assessment of mathematical problem solving*, ed. R. Charles and E. A. Silver. Hillsdale, NJ: Erlbaum.

Schoenfeld, A. H. 1985. *Mathematical problem solving*. New York: Academic Press.

Spearman, C. 1904. "General intelligence," objectively determined and measured. *American Journal of Psychology* 15:206–19.

Spearman, C. 1923. *The nature of intelligence and principles of cognition*. London: Macmillan.

Spearman, C. 1927. *The abilities of man*. New York: Macmillan.

Sternberg, R. J. 1984. Mechanisms of cognitive development: A componential approach. In *Mechanisms of Cognitive Development*, ed. R. J. Sternberg, 163–86.

Stodolsky, S. 1988. *The subject matter: Classroom activity in math and social studies*. Chicago: University of Chicago Press.

Toulmin, S. 1958. *The uses of argument*. New York: Cambridge University Press.

Thorndike, E. L. 1926. *Measurement of intelligence*. New York: Teachers College Press.

Thorndike, E. L., and R. S. Woodworth. 1901. The influence of improvement in one mental function upon the efficiency of other functions. *Psychological Review* 8: 247–61, 384–95, 553–64.

Vye, N. J., M. S. Burns, V. R. Delclos, and J. D. Bransford. 1987. Dynamic assessment of intellectually handicapped children. In *Dynamic assessment: Foundations and fundamentals,* ed. C. S. Lidz. New York: Guilford Press.

Vygotsky, L. S. 1978. *Mind in society: The development of higher psychological processes,* ed. M. Cole, V. John-Steiner, S. Scribner, and E. Souberman. Cambridge, MA: Harvard University Press.

Vygotsky, L. S. 1986. Thinking and speech. In Vol. 1, *Collected works: Problems of general psychology*. Trans. N. Minick. New York: Plenum. Translation of V. V. Davydov, ed. [1934] 1982. *L. S. Vygotskii: Sobranie sochinenii* [L.S. Vygotsky: Collected works] *Vol. 2*. Moscow: Pedagogika.

Wertsch, J. V. 1984. The zone of proximal development: Some conceptual issues. In *Children's learning in the "zone of proximal development,"* ed. B. Rogoff and J. Wertsch, 7–18. San Francisco: Jossey-Bass.

Wertsch, J. V., and C. A. Stone. 1979. *A social interactional analysis of learning disabilities remediation*. Paper presented at the International Conference of the Association for Children with Learning Disabilities, San Francisco.

Whitehead, A. N. 1916. The aims of education. Address to the British Mathematical Society, Manchester, England.

Wiedl, K. H., and D. Herrig. 1978. Okologische validitat und schulerfolgsprognose im lern-und inteligeenstest: Eine exemplarische studie. *Diagnostica* 24:174–86.

Wood, D., and D. Middleton. 1975. A study of assisted problem-solving. *British Journal of Psychology* 66:181–91.

Woodrow, H. 1917a. Practice and transference in normal and feeble-minded children: 1. Practice. *Journal of Educational Psychology* 8:85–96.

Woodrow, H. 1917b. Practice and transference in normal and feeble-minded children: 2. Transference. *Journal of Educational Psychology* 8:151–65.

Woodrow, H. 1938a. The relation between abilities and improvement with practice. *Journal of Educational Psychology* 29:215–30.

Woodrow, H. 1938b. The effect of practice on groups of different mental ability. *Journal of Educational Psychology* 29:268–78.

Woodrow, H. 1946. The ability to learn. *Psychological Review* 53:147–58.

Yager, S., D. W. Johnson, and R. T. Johnson. 1985. Oral discussion, group to individual transfer, and achievement in cooperative learning groups. *Journal of Educational Psychology* 77:60–66.

Yerkes, R. M. 1921. Psychological examining in the United States Army. *Memoirs of the National Academy of Sciences,* vol. 15.

CAT: A Program of Comprehensive Abilities Testing

Robert J. Sternberg

INTRODUCTION

If you decided to invest in the stock market, your first goal might be to look at various indicators of stock market performance. You would be unlikely to make a large investment based on a single indicator, such as the company's profits or debit position, because a company's performance depends on many variables. People are the same way. Their future performance depends on a number of variables, and any one indicator would be incomplete and probably misleading. Yet we make predictions about people's performance on the basis of small numbers of indicators, sometimes a single one. This single indicator usually goes under the name of "an intelligence test," "a test of mental abilities," or "a scholastic aptitude test."

This proposal for a Comprehensive Abilities Test (CAT) includes assessments that go well beyond those found in conventional ability tests and testing batteries. The proposed system involves both intelligence (broadly defined) and intellectual styles, which involve how intelligence is used. The system of testing also takes into account the context in which these aspects of mentation manifest themselves. Through the CAT system, it should be possible to understand abilities in a way that takes into account their depth and breadth, rather than in a way that is narrow and unrepresentative of the full range of human performance.

The chapter is divided into four parts. The first part deals with intelligence, the second with intellectual styles, and the third with context. The final part integrates the discussion that precedes it.

INTELLIGENCE

Basic Issues in Theories of Intelligence

The thesis of this section is straightforward: Because theorists of intelligence have dealt with different aspects of the phenomenon of intelligence without acknowledging that they are dealing only with *aspects* of the whole, and because they have failed to separate differences in methods from differences in substance, artificial competitions have been set up among theories that are not competitive at all. This unfortunate turn of events dates back to the beginnings of modern theorizing with Galton and Binet. If we go to the trouble to resolve these artificial competitions, we can construct a theory that encompasses the entire range of human intelligence, understood at multiple levels of information-processing.

In his seminal work on intelligence, Galton (1883) proposed to view intelligence in terms of basic psychophysical abilities like various kinds of sensory acuities and discriminations. Many of his measures, such as strength of grip, probably had nothing to do with intelligence, but others, such as various measures of reaction time, probably did relate to intelligence in some way. More important than the particular measures Galton chose to use was his conception of intelligence in terms of very basic, "bottom-up" kinds of psychophysical, and especially mental, skills. Because Galton's measures were inadequate, initial tests of his theory yielded disappointing results (Wissler 1901, for example). But there may well have been more to his basic theoretical view than his measures, because Galton's ideas about intelligence have been revived and rejuvenated in recent times (Carroll 1976; Hunt, Frost, and Lunneborg 1973; Jensen 1982). For example, most contemporary theorists of intelligence agree that mental speed has something to do with intelligence, although there is considerable disagreement as to just what this something is, and how it relates to measurements of mental speed.

The theories of Binet and Simon (1916) represented a more "top-down," judgment-based view of intelligence. They held that intelligence is best understood in terms of one's ability to comprehend, evaluate, and act upon the world. Binet and Simon's tests of reasoning, problem solving, and judgment proved to be more highly correlated with external criteria, such as school performance and career attainments, than did Galton's.

The respective approaches to intelligence of Galton and Binet were never incompatible. Galton's measures were almost certainly inferior to Binet's, and even if Galton had used more refined tests, the importance of his measures for predicting everyday competencies would almost certainly have been lower than that of Binet's measures. However, intelligence almost certainly involves the interaction of both bottom-up, basic processes and top-down, high-level processes. For example, reading comprehension depends upon and interacts with perception of the written word. Listening comprehension depends upon the rate at which one can take in information. If one is too slow in comprehending, the words will pass by before one is able fully to encode them, and the stream of thought the speaker is attempting to convey may be lost. Reasoning under any kind of time pressure at all—whether internally or externally imposed—requires speed as well as high levels of judgment.

Intelligence can only be understood fully at *multiple levels of the processing of information*. Any approach to understanding intelligence based solely upon individual differences in test performance may miss this important fact. Certain kinds of tests may swamp others in accounting for observed variation in test scores among individuals. But a process analysis of test performance should reveal the importance of multiple levels of processing. In fact, not all process analyses will reveal all levels of processing, because task analyses typically are constructed to decompose stimulus variance only at a single level of processing. For example, typical decompositions of analogy test performance (such as that of Sternberg 1977) deal with processes more at the level studied by Binet than at the level studied by Galton. The processes not isolated by a given task analysis are lumped into an undifferentiated "regression constant." Perhaps because so much of the richness of information-processing is typically lumped into the constant, such residual components have often shown high correlations with external measures of intellectual abilities (Mulholland, Pellegrino, and Glaser 1980; Sternberg 1977).

It is important to note also that the contributions of various levels of processing may differ over an individual's life span. For adults who have largely automatized bottom-up information processing, top-down processes may contribute most of the variance both to person and to task differences. For children who have not fully automatized the basic processes, such processes may appear statistically to be more important. Thus the effects of age can lead to confusion in understanding mental phenomena. For example, reading disabilities, which are almost inevitably multifaceted, have appeared to be more bottom-up in origin in some studies and more top-down in others. A review of the literature suggests, however, that the bottom-up processes contribute more at earlier ages, and the top-down processes contribute more at later ages (Spear and Sternberg 1987). Hence, limitations in ranges of ages studied can lead to systematic misinterpretations of the loci of reading difficulties.

Conflicts among factor theorists of intelligence followed that between Galton and Binet. In an attempt to place the study of intelligence on a more solid and scientific footing, theorists used factor analysis to help identify what they believed would be fundamental latent sources of individual differences in intelligence. These "factors of the mind" were essentially structural in nature, although what these structures were remained something of a mystery. Spearman (1927) proposed a "two-factor" theory, according to which the intellect comprises a general factor common to all intelligent performances and a set of specific factors, each of which is limited to influencing performance on a single test. Thurstone (1938) proposed a theory of primary mental abilities, according to which abilities such as verbal comprehension, verbal fluency, number, spatial visualization, and inductive reasoning are viewed as central to the intellect. Guilford (1967) proposed an elaborated version of Thurstone's theory, according to which the mind comprises 120 factors that differ in the processes, products, and contents involved.

Although the debates among factor theorists were always lively and at times acrimonious, they were probably not well-founded. These theorists were debating over different and ultimately isomorphic interpretations of the same basic data.[1] The question was not who was right, but rather who was right for what purpose. As theories of intelligence, most of the factor theories, with the possible exception of Guilford's, are structurally isomorphic. Again, in the history of theorizing about intelligence we see the emergence of ill-motivated conflicts.

The conflicts that have emerged about intelligence are not limited to the psychometric approach. Information-processing psychologists have renewed the conflict between Galton and Binet in a modern-day guise. For example, in the 1970s, an apparent competition arose among advocates of the "cognitive-correlates" approach, on the one hand, and of the "cognitive-components" approach, on the other. Advocates of the former approach (Hunt 1978; Jensen 1979) believed that intelligence should be studied in terms of basic, low-level processes of cognition, such as speed of lexical access or choice-reaction speed. Advocates of the latter approach (Sternberg 1977; Pellegrino and Glaser 1979; and Snow 1980) believed that intelligence should be studied in terms of higher processes, such as those contributing to performance on psychometric tests of intelligence. Examples of such processes would be inferring relations and applying relations. As time went on, it became progressively clearer that these two approaches were no more in conflict than were those of Galton and Binet. Rather, they dealt with different levels of processing in the same cognitive system, in which all levels are consequential for intelligent performance.

The disputes among theorists of intelligence have occurred not only within paradigms, but between paradigms as well. In the 1970s, attempts to integrate psychometric and information-processing theorizing tended to be at the expense of psychometric theorizing. Sternberg (1977), for example, expressed considerable skepticism regarding the role of factor analysis in theory and research on intelligence. It later became clear, however, that the two approaches are complementary: Factors and components of information-processing are two different ways of parsing essentially the same mental phenomena. Both are useful for different purposes, depending upon whether one wishes to concentrate upon structure or process (Sternberg 1980).

Yet another conflict was that between Piaget (1972) and proponents of psychometrics. Piaget developed his theory partly in response to his dissatisfaction with the procedures of Binet. He saw Binet as interested primarily in why children answer problems correctly, whereas Piaget was also interested in why they answer problems incorrectly. Piaget's theory focused upon the roles of maturation and experience in intelligence. In particular, he discussed stages of development and mechanisms by which this development might take place. This kind of theorizing is actually complementary to psychometric and information-processing theorizing, in that either kind of theory needs to consider development as well as end states.

Perhaps the most significant conflict has been that between cognitivists, broadly defined, and contextualists. Cognitivists, including all of the theorists so far mentioned, have stressed the importance of understanding intelligence in terms of the mental mechanisms of mind. Contextualists, such as Berry (1972) and the members of the Laboratory of Comparative Human Cognition (1982), have emphasized the importance of contextual factors in understanding intelligence. Berry suggested a radical contextualist view, according to which intelligence probably means a somewhat different thing in each culture. Cole and his colleagues in the Laboratory of Comparative Human Cognition have suggested that there may be no fundamental universals in intelligence, although they have not taken a position as radical as Berry's.

In some respects, the conflict between cognitivists and contextualists has not been as apparent as that between, say, various psychometricians or between these psychometricians as a group, on the one hand, and information-processing psychologists, on the other. This is because the two camps have more or less ignored each other. The cognitivists, especially, often have seemed unaware of cross-cultural work being done, or its implications for their own theory and research. Again, this conflict is misguided. Irvine (1969, 1979) was among the first to note that a rapprochement between the two views is not only possible but desirable. He has combined psychometric, factor-analytic methodology with sensitivity to cultural differences in cognitive task performance, with the result that it has been possible to go beyond merely saying that intelligence is all relative or all universal. One of his main goals has been to specify just what is relative and what is universal. More recently, Goodnow (1976) and Sternberg (1984) also have attempted to specify which aspects of intelligence might be universal, and which might not. Once again, an integrative rather than segregative view of perceiving the differences between positions has been more useful.

These debates, which are representative but not exhaustive of those that have occurred among theorists of intelligence, illustrate the importance of considering complementarity as well as conflict among theories and approaches. The appearance of difference has stemmed largely from two confusions.

The first confusion is over domain of discourse. Some theories, such as the psychometric and information-processing theories, have emphasized the role of internal mental mechanisms in intelligence. Other theories, such as the contextualist ones, have emphasized the role of external context. Still other theories, such as that of Piaget (1972), have emphasized the role of experience. The theories have differed primarily in terms of universe of discourse, rather than in empirical or theoretical claims within any one domain. The theorists have been talking not against each other, but past each other. A full theory of intelligence would interrelate and integrate the role of intelligence as it occurs in each of these three domains.

A second source of confusion has been with respect to methodology, or the kind of information used to draw theoretical inferences. Some theorists, especially the psychometric ones, have emphasized "between subjects," or individual-difference variation. Others, especially information-processing theorists, have emphasized "main effect," or stimulus variance. The two sources of variance are not in conflict: They are independent. A full theory of intelligence, again, would have to take into account the role of both sources of variance in intelligence, and interactions among "main effects." The triarchic theory presented below attempts to provide these various kinds of integration.

Before considering the triarchic theory of intelligence, consider three profiles of intelligence that serve to motivate the theory.

Three Profiles of Intelligence

Alice was the admissions officer's dream. She was easily admitted to our graduate program at Yale. She came with stellar test scores, outstanding college grades, excellent letters of recommendation, and, overall, close to a perfect record. Alice proved to be, more or less, what her record promised. She had excellent critical and analytical abilities, which helped her earn outstanding grades during her first two years at Yale. When it came to taking tests and writing course term papers, she had no peer among her classmates. During her first couple of years in the graduate program, she was an outstanding success. But after the first two years, Alice no longer looked quite so outstanding. In our graduate program, as in most, emphasis shifts after the first couple of years. It is not enough just to criticize other people's ideas or to study concepts that other people have proposed. You must start coming up with your own ideas and proposals for implementing them. Alice was "IQ-test" smart, but she was not equally intelligent in the synthetic or practical areas of intelligence. This could not have been predicted from the evidence in her admissions folder. Although conventional measures can give us a good reading on analytic abilities, they give virtually no reading on synthetic abilities.

People like Barbara are the admissions officer's nightmare. When she applied to Yale, she had good grades, but abysmal aptitude test scores, at least by Yale standards. Despite these low scores, she had superlative letters of recommendation, which described her as an exceptionally creative young woman, who had designed and implemented research with only the most minimal guidance. Moreover, her resumé showed that she had been actively involved in important research. Unfortunately, people like Barbara are rejected from many graduate programs, and must either enter a less competitive program or a different field altogether.

This pattern is not limited to graduate school. Thousands of people like Barbara are rejected by law schools, medical schools, business schools, and education schools. Some never even get to this point, having been rejected earlier from competitive colleges. But the exceptions like Barbara often prove to be fine students possessing excellent research abilities. These students may not excel in course performance, although they might do much better than test scores predict. But when the demands of the graduate program shift, for example, to an emphasis on synthetic abilities, people like Barbara are in their element. They may not have Alice's analytic abilities, but they greatly surpass Alice in synthetic abilities.

Celia, on paper, appeared to be somewhere between Alice and Barbara in terms of suitability for admission to the graduate program. She was good on almost every measure of success, but not truly outstanding on any of them. We admitted her, expecting her to come out near the middle of the class. Instead, Celia has proved to be outstanding, although in a way quite different from Alice or Barbara. Celia's expertise is in figuring out and adapting to the demands of the environment. Placed in a new setting, she determines what is required and then does it just right. She knows exactly how to get ahead. In conventional parlance, Celia is "street-smart": she excels in practical intelligence.

Clearly, Alice, Barbara, and Celia are all exceedingly intelligent, although in very different ways. People like Alice excel in conventional academic, or analytic, intelligence. To the extent that one seeks to understand intelligence in terms of the conventional factors or information-processing components that researchers have used to characterize intelligence, individuals such as Alice would be viewed as very smart. Thus, if one looks at the relationship between intelligence and the internal world of the individual, people like Alice excel. Individuals like Barbara do not look nearly as intelligent in terms of conventional notions of academic intelligence. They excel in synthetic ability, or the ability to deal with novelty—to view new things in old ways or old things in new ways. Hence, these people come out as looking extremely intelligent if one looks at the relationships of intelligence to experience, and particularly, novel experience. People like Celia have neither Alice's nor Barbara's patterns of strength. Instead, they excel in terms of the relationship between intelligence and the external world of the individual. Their excellence is in practical intelligence, or in applying their mental abilities to everyday kinds of situations. Their "street smarts" are not measured by conventional tests, but quickly show up in their performance in real-world settings.

The Triarchic Theory of Human Intelligence

The triarchic theory of human intelligence seeks to explain in an integrative way the relationship between (a) intelligence and the internal world of the individual, or the mental mechanisms that underlie intelligent behavior; (b) intelligence and the external world of the individual, or the use of these mental mechanisms in everyday life to attain an intelligent fit to the environment; and (c) intelligence and experience, or the mediating role of one's passage through life between the internal and external worlds of the individual. Consider some of the basic tenets of the theory.

Intelligence and the Internal World of the Individual

Psychometricians, Piagetians, and information-processing psychologists have all recognized the importance of understanding what mental states or processes underlie intelligent thought. In the triarchic theory, this understanding is sought through the identification and understanding of three basic kinds of information-processing components: metacomponents, performance components, and knowledge-acquisition components.

Metacomponents. Metacomponents are higher-order, executive processes used to plan what one is going to do, to monitor the process, and to evaluate it afterward. These metacomponents include (a) recognizing the existence of a problem, (b) deciding upon the nature of the problem, (c) selecting a set of lower-order processes to solve the problem, (d) selecting a strategy for combining these components, (e) selecting a mental representation upon which the components and strategy can act, (f) allocating one's mental resources, (g) monitoring one's problem solving as it is happening, and (h) evaluating one's problem solving after it is done.

Deciding upon the nature of a problem plays a prominent role in intelligence. For example, with young children as well as older adults, their difficulty in problem solving often lies not in actually solving a given problem, but in figuring out what exactly the problem is (see, for example, Flavell 1977; Sternberg and Rifkin 1979). A major feature distinguishing retarded from nonretarded persons is the retardates' need to be instructed explicitly and completely as to the nature of the particular task they are solving and how it should be performed (Butterfield, Wambold, and Belmont 1973; Campione and Brown 1979). The importance of figuring out the nature of the problem is not limited to retarded persons. Resnick and Glaser (1976) have argued that intelligence is the ability to learn from incomplete instruction.

Selection of a strategy for combining lower-order components is another critical aspect of intelligence. Early information-processing research on intelligence, including my own (for example, Sternberg 1977), placed primary emphasis on what subjects do when confronted with a problem. What components do subjects use, and in what strategies? Soon, however, researchers of information-processing began to ask why subjects choose particular strategies. For example, Cooper (1982) has reported that in solving spatial problems, and especially mental-rotation problems, some subjects seem to use a holistic strategy of comparison, while others use an analytic strategy. She has sought to understand what leads to the choice of a strategy. Siegler (1986) has proposed a model of strategy selection in arithmetic computation problems that links strategy choice to both the rules and mental associations one has stored in long-term memory. MacLeod, Hunt, and Mathews (1978) found that high-spatial subjects tend to use a spatial strategy in solving sentence-picture comparison problems, while high-verbal subjects are more likely to use a linguistic strategy. In my own work, I have found that subjects tend to prefer strategies for analogical reasoning that place fewer demands upon working memory (Sternberg and Ketron 1982). Similarly, subjects choose different strategies in linear-syllogistic reasoning (spatial, linguistic, mixed spatial-linguistic), but in this task they do not always choose the strategy most suitable to their respective levels of spatial and verbal abilities (Sternberg and Weil 1980). In sum, the selection of a strategy seems to be at least as important for understanding intelligent task performance as how well the chosen strategy is implemented.

Intimately tied with the selection of a strategy is the selection of a mental representation for information. Early literature on mental representations emphasized how information is represented. For example, can individuals use imagery as a form of mental representation (Kosslyn 1980)? In more recent research, investigators have realized that people are quite flexible in their representations of information. The most appropriate question seems to be not "how is information represented?" but "which representations are used in what circumstances?" For example, Sternberg (1977) found that analogy problems using animal names can draw upon either spatial or clustering representations of the animal names. The researchers of strategy choice mentioned above found that subjects can use either linguistic or spatial representations in solving sentence-picture comparisons (MacLeod et al. 1978) or linear syllogisms (Sternberg and Weil 1980). Sternberg and Rifkin (1979) found that the mental representation of certain kinds of analogies can be either more or less holistic, depending upon the age of the subjects.

As important as any other metacomponent is the ability to allocate one's mental resources. Hunt and Lansman (1982), for example, have concentrated upon the use of secondary tasks in assessing information-processing, and have proposed a model of attention allocation in problem solving that involves both a primary and a secondary task. In my work, I have found that better problem solvers tend to spend relatively more time in global strategy planning (Sternberg 1981). Similarly, in solving analogies, better analogical reasoners seem to spend relatively more time encoding the terms of the problem, but relatively less time in operating upon these encodings than do poorer reasoners (Sternberg 1977; Sternberg and Rifkin 1979). In reading as well, better readers are more able than poorer readers to allocate their time across reading passages as a function of the difficulty of the passages and the purpose for which they are being read (compare Brown et al. 1983; Wagner and Sternberg 1987).

Finally, the monitoring of solution processes is a key aspect of intelligence (see also Brown 1978). Consider, for example, the "missionaries and cannibals" problem, in which the subjects must transport a set of missionaries and cannibals across a river in a small boat without allowing the missionaries to be eaten by the cannibals, which will occur if the cannibals outnumber the missionaries on either side of the riverbank. The main errors made in solving the problem are returning to an earlier state in the problem space for solution, or making an impermissible move (Simon and Reed 1976; see also Sternberg

1982b). Neither of these errors results if the subject closely monitors his or her solution processes. For young children learning to count, a major source of errors is counting an object twice, which again can result from a failure in solution monitoring (Gelman and Gallistel 1978). The effects of solution monitoring are not limited to one kind of problem. One's ability to use the strategy of means-ends analysis (Newell and Simon 1972), that is, the reduction of differences between where one is in solving a problem and where one wishes to go in solving that problem, depends upon the ability to monitor just where one is in problem solution.

Performance Components. Performance components are *lower-order* processes that execute the instructions of the metacomponents. These lower-order components solve the problems according to the plans laid out by the metacomponents. While the number of metacomponents used in the performance of various tasks is limited, the number of performance components is probably quite large. Many of these performance components are relatively specific to narrow ranges of tasks (Sternberg 1979, 1983, 1985a).

One of the most interesting classes of performance components is found in inductive reasoning of the kind measured by tests such as matrices, analogies, series completions, and classifications. These components are important because of the tasks into which they enter: Induction problems of these kinds show the highest loadings on the so-called *g*, or general intelligence factor (Jensen 1980; Snow and Lohman 1984; Sternberg and Gardner 1982). Thus, identifying these performance components can help us understand the nature of the general factor. [2]

The main performance components of inductive reasoning are encoding, inference, mapping, application, comparison, justification, and response. They can be illustrated with reference to an analogy problem, such as lawyer : client :: doctor : (a) patient, (b) medicine. In encoding, the subject retrieves potentially relevant semantic attributes from semantic memory. In inference, the subject discovers the relation between the first two terms of the analogy, here, lawyer and client. In mapping, the subject discovers the higher-order relation that links the first half of the analogy, headed by lawyer, to the second half of the analogy, headed by doctor. In application, the subject carries over the relation inferred in the first half of the analogy to the second half, generating a possible completion. In comparison, the subject compares each of the answer options to the mentally generated completion, deciding which, if any, is correct. If none of the answer options matches the mentally generated solution, the subject decides which, if any, of the options is close enough to constitute an acceptable solution to the examiner.

Two fundamental issues have arisen regarding the nature of performance components as a fundamental construct in human intelligence. The first, mentioned briefly above, is whether their number keeps expanding indefinitely. Neisser (1983), for example, has suggested that it does. As a result, he views the construct as of little use. But this expansion results only if one considers seriously those components that are specific to small classes of problems or to single problems. If the more important, general components of performance are studied, the problem simply does not arise, as shown in Sternberg and Gardner's (1982) analysis of inductive reasoning, or in Pellegrino and Kail's (1982) analysis of spatial ability. The second issue is one of the level at which performance components should be studied. In "cognitive-correlates" research (Pellegrino and Glaser 1979), theorists emphasize components at relatively low levels of information-processing (Hunt 1978, 1980; Jensen 1982). In "cognitive components" research (Pellegrino and Glaser 1979), theorists emphasize components at relatively high levels of information-processing (Mulholland, Pellegrino, and Glaser 1980; Snow 1980; Sternberg 1977). Because of the interactive nature of human information-processing, it would appear that there is no right or wrong level of analysis. Rather, all levels of information-processing contribute to both task and subject variance in intelligent performance. The most expeditious level of analysis depends upon the task and the subject population: Lower-level performance components might be more important, for example, in studying more basic information-processing tasks, such as choice-reaction time, or in studying higher-level tasks, in children who have not yet automatized the lower processes for these tasks.

Knowledge-Acquisition Components. Knowledge-acquisition components are used to *learn how to do* what the metacomponents and performance components eventually do. Three knowledge-acquisition components appear to be central in intellectual functioning: selective encoding, selective combination, and selective comparison.

Selective encoding involves sifting out relevant from irrelevant information. When new information is presented in natural contexts, information relevant to one's given purpose is embedded in large amounts of purpose-irrelevant information. A critical task for the learner is to sift the "wheat from the chaff" (see Schank 1980).

Selective combination involves forming an integrated, plausible whole from pieces of selectively encoded information. Simply sifting out relevant from irrelevant information is not enough to generate a new knowledge structure (see Mayer and Greeno 1972).

My emphasis upon components of knowledge acquisition differs somewhat from the emphasis of some contemporary theorists in cognitive psychology upon what is already known, and the structure of this knowledge (Chase and Simon 1973; Chi 1978; Keil 1984). These emphases are complementary. For example, if one is interested in understanding differences in performance between experts and novices, clearly one would wish to look at the amount and structure of their respective knowledge bases. But if one wishes to understand how these differences came to be, one would also have to look at differences in how the knowledge bases were acquired. It is here that understanding knowledge-acquisition components will be most relevant.

We have studied knowledge-acquisition components in the domain of vocabulary acquisition (Sternberg 1987; Sternberg and Powell 1983). Difficulty in learning new words can be traced, at least in part, to the application of components of knowledge acquisition to context cues stored in long-term memory. Individuals with higher vocabularies tend to be those who are better able to apply the knowledge-acquisition components to vocabulary-learning situations. Given the importance of vocabulary for overall intelligence, almost without respect to the theory or test used, utilization of knowledge-acquisition components in vocabulary-learning situations appears to be critically important for the development of intelligence. Effective use of knowledge-acquisition components can be taught. I have found, for example, that just forty-five minutes of training in the use of these components in vocabulary learning can significantly improve the ability of adults to learn vocabulary from natural-language contexts (Sternberg 1987).

To summarize, the components of intelligence are an important part of the intelligence of the individual. The components work together. Metacomponents activate performance and knowledge-acquisition components, which in turn provide feedback to the metacomponents. Although one can isolate various kinds of information-processing components from task performance using experimental means, in practice, the components function together in highly interactive, and not easily isolable, ways. Thus, diagnoses and instructional interventions need to consider the interaction of all three types of components. However, there is more to intelligence than a set of information-processing components. One could scarcely understand why a person is more intelligent than another person by understanding the components of processing on, say, an intelligence test. The other aspects of the triarchic theory address some of the other aspects of intelligence that contribute to individual differences in observed performance, both inside and outside testing situations.

Intelligence and Experience

Components of information-processing are always applied to tasks and situations with which one has some level of prior experience (including the null level). Hence, these internal mechanisms are closely tied to experience. According to the experiential subtheory, the components are not equally good measures of intelligence at all levels of experience. Assessing intelligence requires study of both the components and the level of experience at which they are applied.

During recent years, there has been a tendency in cognitive science to study script-based behavior (for example, Schank and Abelson 1977), whether under the name of "script" or "schema" or "frame." Although much of our behavior is scripted in some sense, from the standpoint of the present subtheory, such behavior is not optimal for understanding intelligence. Typically, one's actions at a restaurant or a doctor's office or a movie theater do not provide good measures of intelligence, even though they provide good measures of scripted behavior. What, then, is the relation between intelligence and experience?

According to the experiential subtheory, intelligence is best measured at those regions of the experiential continuum that involve tasks or situations that are either relatively novel or in the process of becoming automatized. As Raaheim (1974) pointed out, totally novel tasks and situations provide poor measures of intelligence: One would not want to administer trigonometry problems to a first-grader. But one might administer problems that are just at the limits of the child's understanding, to test how far this understanding extends. Related is Vygotsky's (1978) concept of the zone of proximal development, in which one examines a child's ability to profit from instruction in solving novel problems. To measure automatization skill, one might wish to present a series of problems—mathematical or otherwise—and to observe how long it takes for solution of them to become automatic, and how automatized performance becomes. Thus, both slope and asymptote (if any) of automatization are of interest.

Ability to Deal with Novelty. According to three sources of evidence, the ability to deal with relative novelty is a good measure of intelligence. First, we have conducted several studies on the nature of insight in children and adults (Davidson and Sternberg 1984; Sternberg and Davidson 1982). In the studies with children (Davidson and Sternberg 1984), we separated three kinds of insights: selective encoding, selective combination, and selective comparison. Use of these knowledge-acquisition components is referred to as insightful when they are applied in the absence of existing scripts, plans, or frames. One must decide what information is relevant, how to put the information together, or how new information relates to old without any obvious cues on how to make these judgments. A problem is insightfully solved at the individual level when a given individual lacks such cues. A problem is insightfully solved at the societal level when no one else has these cues. In these studies, our hypothesis was that intellectually gifted children are gifted in part by virtue of their insight abilities, which represent an important part of the ability to deal with novelty.

Children were administered quantitative insight problems, of the kinds found in puzzle books, that measured primarily skills of selective encoding, selective combination, or selective comparison. We manipulated the need for such insights experimentally. Problems were either administered uncued (standard format) or precued. The form of precueing depended upon the kind of insight being assessed. For selective encoding, we highlighted all information relevant to solving each problem. Thus, we eliminated the need for selective encoding by pointing out to the children just what information was relevant for a given problem. In the selective-combination condition, precueing consisted of telling the children how to combine the given information selectively. For example, a table might be drawn showing how the various terms of the problem interrelated. In the selective-comparison condition, the examples in the introduction to the problems were varied. Precued conditions ranged from one in which examples were given but their relevance to the later problems not pointed out, to examples that were explicitly stated to be relevant for solution of the later problems, to examples that were indicated as relevant to designated problems in the set of problems that needed to be solved. The basic design, therefore, was to test both children identified as gifted and those not so identified, and to administer problems that either required one of the three kinds of insights or that did not require such insights because they were provided to the children.

The critical finding was that providing insights to the children significantly benefited the nongifted but not the gifted children. (None of the children performed anywhere near ceiling, so that the interaction was not due to ceiling effects.) In other words, the gifted children spontaneously had the insights and hence did not benefit from having them provided. The nongifted children did not have the insights spontaneously, and hence did benefit. Thus, the gifted children were better able to deal with novelty spontaneously.

In a very different paradigm, adult subjects were given what I call conceptual projection problems (Sternberg 1982a). In these problems, one must make predictions about future states of objects based upon incomplete and sometimes partially faulty information about the current states of the objects. These problems generally employ a science-fiction type of scenario. For example, one might be introduced to four kinds of people on the planet Kyron: One kind of person is *born young and dies young*, a second kind of person is *born young and dies old*, a third kind is *born old and dies old*, and a fourth kind is *born old and dies young*. Given incomplete information about the person in the present, one must figure out what kind of person the individual is (names such as "kwef," "pros," "balt," and "plin" were used) and determine what his or her appearance would be twenty years later. Performance on the conceptual-projection task was experimentally decomposed, and the mathematical model of task performance accounted for most of the stimulus variance (generally 90 percent or above) in task performance.

Each of these component scores was then correlated with performance on a variety of psychometric tests, including tests of inductive reasoning ability, which are primary measures of general intelligence. The critical finding was that the correlation of overall response time[3] with psychometric test scores stemmed from those performance components that tap the ability to deal with novelty. In this paradigm, for example, the subject must change conceptual systems from a familiar one (born young and dies old) to an unfamiliar one (born old and dies young). These correlations held without regard to the particular surface structure of the problem. Thus, it was the ability to deal with novelty, rather than other abilities involved in solving the problems, that proved to be critical to general intelligence.

A third source of evidence for the proposed hypothesis derives from the substantial literature on fluid intelligence, which in part involves dealing with novelty (see Cattell 1971).[4] Snow and Lohman (1984; see also Snow, Kyllonen, and Marshalek 1984) have analyzed a variety of such tests and found that those tests that best measure the ability to deal with novelty are more similar to tests of general intelligence than are tests in which the assessment of the ability to deal with novelty is more attenuated. In sum, research supports the idea that the components of intelligence involved in dealing with novelty provide particularly apt measures of intellectual ability.

Ability to Automatize Information-Processing. Although we are only now testing the second aspect of the experiential subtheory—the ability to automatize information-processing—several converging lines of evidence in the literature support the claim that it is a key aspect of intelligence. For example, Sternberg (1977) found that the correlation between People-Piece (schematic-picture) analogy performance and measures of general intelligence increased with practice, as performance on these items became increasingly automatized. Skilled reading is heavily dependent upon automatization of bottom-up functions, and the ability to read well is an essential part of crystallized ability, whether from the standpoint of theories such as Cattell's (1971) or Vernon's (1971), or from the standpoint of tests of crystallized ability, such as the verbal portion of the Scholastic Aptitude Test. Poor comprehenders often are those who have not automatized the elementary, bottom-up processes of reading, and hence do not have sufficient attentional resources to allocate to top-down comprehension processes.

Some theorists (Jensen 1982; Hunt 1978) have attributed the correlation between tasks such as choice-reaction time and letter matching to the relation between speed of information-processing and intelligence. Although there is almost certainly some relation, I believe it is much more complex than these theorists seem to posit. A plausible alternative hypothesis is that at least some of that correlation results from the effects of automatization of processing: The simplicity of these tasks probably enables them to become at least partially automatized fairly rapidly, and hence they can measure both rate and asymptote of automatization of performance. In sum, although the evidence is far from complete, there is at least some support for the relationship between rate and level of automatization and intellectual skill.

The abilities to deal with novelty and to automatize information-processing are interrelated, as shown in the example of reading above. If one can automatize well, one has more resources remaining to deal with novelty. Similarly, if one can deal with novelty well, one has more resources left for automatization. Thus, performance at the various levels of the experiential continuum are related.

These abilities must be viewed in combination with the componential subtheory. The components of intelligence are applied to tasks and situations at various levels of experience: The ability to deal with novelty can be understood in part in terms of the metacomponents, performance components, and knowledge-acquisition components involved in it. Automatization, when it occurs, is of these components. Hence, the two subtheories considered so far are closely intertwined. We need now to consider the application of these subtheories to everyday tasks, in addition to laboratory ones.

Intelligence and the External World of the Individual

Intelligence is not aimless or random mental activity that happens to involve certain components of information-processing at certain levels of experience. According to the contextual subtheory, intelligent thought is directed toward one or more of three behavioral goals: *adaptation to an environment, shaping of an environment,* or *selection of an environment.* All of these goals have specific and concrete instantiations in people's lives.

Adaptation. Most intelligent thought is directed toward the attempt to adapt to one's environment. However environments are defined (families, jobs, subcultures, cultures), the requirements for adaptation can differ radically from one environment to another. Hence, although the components of intelligence required in these various contexts may be the same or quite similar, and although all of them at some point may involve dealing with novelty and automatization of information-processing, the concrete forms that these processes and levels of experience take can differ substantially across contexts. This fact is important to our understanding of the nature of intelligence. According to the triarchic theory in general, and the contextual subtheory in particular, the processes and experiential facets and functions of intelligence remain essentially the same across contexts, but the particular forms of these processes, facets, and functions differ radically. Thus, the content of intelligent thought and its manifestations in behavior will bear no necessary resemblance across contexts. As a result, although the mental elements that an intelligence test should measure do not differ across contexts, the vehicle for measurement may have to differ. A test that provides an adequate measure of processes, experiential facets, or intelligent functions in one context may not do so in another context. What is viewed as intelligent in one culture may be viewed as unintelligent in another.

The work of Cole et al. (1971) provides an example of this variation. These investigators asked adult Kpelle tribesmen to sort twenty familiar objects into groups of things that belong together. Their subjects separated the objects into functional groupings (such as a knife with an orange), as children in Western societies would do. This pattern of sorting surprised the investigators, who had expected to see taxonomic groupings (tools sorted together and foods sorted together) of the kind that would be found in the sortings of Western adults. Had the investigators used the sorting task as a measure of intelligence in the traditional way, they might well have labeled the Kpelle tribesmen as intellectually inferior to Western adults. Through persistent exploration, however, they found that the Kpelle considered functional sorting to be the intelligent form of sorting. When the tribesmen were asked to sort the way a stupid person would, they had no trouble sorting taxonomically. In short, they differed not in their intellectual competence vis à vis Western adults, but in their conception of what was functionally adaptive. Indeed, it is easy to see the practicality of sorting functionally: People do, after all, use utensils frequently with particular foods.

The particular difference illustrated by the Kpelle is in what is considered to be adaptive, rather than in the ability to act adaptively. But different contextual milieus may result in the development of different mental abilities. For example, Puluwat navigators must develop their large-scale spatial abilities for dealing with cognitive maps to a degree that far exceeds the adaptive requirements of contemporary Western societies (Gladwin 1970). Similarly, Kearins (1981) found that aboriginal children probably develop their visuo-spatial memories to a greater degree than do Anglo-Australian children, who are more likely to apply verbal strategies to spatial memory tasks. In contrast, members of Western societies probably develop their abilities for thinking abstractly to a greater degree than members of societies in which concepts are rarely dealt with outside their concrete manifestations in the objects of the everyday environment.

One of the most interesting differences among cultures and subcultures in the development of patterns of adaptation is in the matter of time allocation, a metacomponential function. In Western cultures, in general, time is budgeted and carefully allocated. Our lives are largely governed by careful scheduling. There are fixed hours for certain activities, and fixed lengths of time for completing these activities. Indeed, the intelligence tests we use show our esteem for time allocation to the fullest. Almost all of them are timed to make completion of the tests a significant challenge. A slow or very cautious worker is at a distinct disadvantage.

Not all cultures and subcultures view time the same way we do. For example, among the Kipsigi, schedules are much more flexible, and hence these individuals have difficulty understanding Western notions of the time pressure under which people are expected to live (Super and Harkness 1980). In Hispanic cultures, it has been my experience that the press of time is taken much less seriously than in typical Anglo cultures. Even within the continental United States, there can be major differences in the importance of time allocation. Heath (1983) describes young children brought up in the rural community of "Trackton," where there is very little time pressure, and things get done when they get done. These children can have great difficulty adjusting to the demands of school, where they may experience severe time pressures for the first time in their lives.

These examples illustrate how differences in environment and people's conceptions of what constitutes an intelligent response to it can influence what is considered to be adaptive behavior. To understand intelligence, one must understand it not only in relation to its internal manifestations in mental processes, and its experiential manifestations in facets of the experiential continuum, but also in how thought is intelligently translated into action in different contextual settings. The differences in what is considered adaptive and intelligent can extend even to different occupations within a given cultural milieu. For example, Sternberg (1985b and see below) has found that individuals in different occupations (art, business, philosophy, physics) view intelligence in slightly different ways that reflect the demands of their respective fields.

Shaping. Shaping of the environment is often used as a backup strategy when adaptation fails. If one is unable to change oneself to fit the environment, one may attempt to change the environment to fit oneself. For example, repeated attempts to adjust to the demands of one's romantic partner may eventually lead to attempts to get the partner to adjust to oneself. But shaping is not always used in lieu of adaptation. In some cases, shaping may be used before adaptation is ever tried, as in the case of the individual who attempts to shape a romantic partner with little or no effort to adjust to the partner's wants or needs.

In the laboratory, examples of shaping behavior can be seen in strategy selection situations where one molds the task to fit one's preferred style of dealing with tasks. For example, in comparing sentence statements to pictures that either do or do not accurately represent these statements, individuals may select either a verbal or a spatial strategy, depending upon their pattern of verbal and spatial abilities (MacLeod, Hunt, and Mathews 1978). The task is "made over" to conform to what one does best. Similarly, I find that in multivariate statistics, my graduate students tend to view problems either algebraically or geometrically, depending upon their pattern of abilities and preferences. My own presentation of the subject is, again, "made over" to conform to their needs and desires.

Because people operate in groups as well as in isolation, group members' shaping efforts can result in products that either profit or lose from the group effort. My collaboration with one of my graduate students is an example of productive group effort. In research, I tend to be a "selective comparer," seeking to relate new theories and facts to old ones. I am probably less careful, however, about "selective combination," that is, about fitting together the various facts at my disposal. As a result, I may neglect to deal with those facts that do not quite fit into the framework I establish for them. My graduate student tends to be more a selective combiner than a selective comparer. She is less concerned with relating new facts to old facts or theories, and more concerned with making sure that the various new facts can be fitted together into a coherent account that deals with them all. In our research collaborations, each of us attempts to shape the research in accordance with our preferred style of working. In this case, the two styles complement each other, as one individual makes sure that the research is not conducted in isolation from past research or ideas, while the other makes sure that inconvenient experimental results are not overlooked. Thus, attempts to shape the environment in two different ways can result in a healthy tension that improves rather than harms the final outcome. Indeed, such efforts may produce true breakthroughs in research.

In some respects, shaping may be seen as the quintessence of intelligent thought and behavior. One essentially makes over the environment rather than allowing oneself to be made over. Perhaps it is this skill that has enabled humankind to reach its current level of scientific, technological, and cultural advancement (for better or for worse). In science, the greatest scientists are those who set the paradigms (shaping), rather than those who merely follow them (adaptation). Similarly, in art and in literature, the individuals who achieve greatest distinction are often those who create new modes and styles of expression, rather than merely following existing ones. It is not their use of shaping alone that distinguishes them intellectually, but a combination of their willingness to do it with their skill in doing it.

Selection. Selection involves renunciation of one environment in favor of another. In terms of the rough hierarchy established so far, selection is sometimes used when both adaptation and shaping fail. After attempting to adapt to or shape a marriage, one may decide to "deselect" the marriage, and choose the environment of the newly single. Failure to adjust to or change the demands of a work environment to make it fit one's interests, values, expectations, or abilities may result in the decision to seek another job. But selection is not always used as a last resort. Sometimes one attempts to shape an environment only after attempts to leave it have failed. Other times, one may decide almost instantly that an environment is simply wrong, and feel that one need not or should not even try to fit into or to change it. For example, we occasionally get a new graduate student who quickly realizes that he or she came to graduate school for the wrong reason, or that graduate school is not what he or she expected. In such a case, the intelligent thing to do may be to leave the environment as soon as possible to pursue activities more in line with one's goals in life.

Environmental selection is not usually directly studied in the laboratory, although it may have relevance for certain experimental settings. Perhaps the most salient research example of its relevance has been the experimental paradigm created by Milgram (1975), who, in a long series of studies, asked subjects to "shock" other subjects (confederates who were not actually shocked). The finding of critical interest was how few subjects either shaped the environment by refusing to shock their victims, or employed the device of selection by simply refusing to continue with the experiment and walking out of it. Milgram has drawn an analogy to the situation in Nazi Germany, where obedience to authority created an environment whose horrors will always amaze us.

To conclude, adaptation, shaping, and selection are functions of intelligent thought as it operates in context. They may, although they need not, be employed hierarchically, with one path followed when another one fails. It is through adaptation, shaping, and selection that the components of intelligence, as employed at various levels of experience, become actualized in the real world.

Because the modes of actualization can differ widely across individuals and groups, intelligence cannot be understood independently of the ways in which it is manifested.

The goal of the triarchic theory is not to replace previous theories of intelligence but to incorporate them, particularly their best aspects. I argued earlier that most theories of intelligence are intercompatible, and this argument also applies to the triarchic theory vis à vis other theories of intelligence.

The Sternberg Triarchic Abilities Test

I am developing the Sternberg Triarchic Abilities Test, which is currently in a trial version for research use. The test will be divided into multiple levels suitable for students in kindergarten through college, as well as for adults. The test differs from conventional tests in its scope. For one thing, it yields separate scores for componential information-processing, coping with novelty, automatization, and practical-intellectual skills. Thus, the scores provided by the test correspond strictly to the aspects of intelligence specified by the triarchic theory. Crossed with these scores are scores for three content areas: verbal, quantitative, and figural. Thus, each kind of processing is measured in each of the three content domains. In this way, it is possible to diagnose strengths and weaknesses not only in processing, but also in various kinds of representation of information. The test is a group test, and can be administrable in two class periods. Two forms of the test will be available.

What actual item types will appear on the Sternberg Triarchic Abilities Test? Subject to modification, they are as follows:[5]

Componential: Verbal. Verbal comprehension abilities are traditionally measured by vocabulary tests, taking such forms as synonym or antonym questions. While these items have been shown to correlate highly with overall IQ (see Sternberg and Powell 1983), they seem to measure achievement more than ability, that is, to emphasize the products of learning over the processes of learning.

In the Sternberg test, verbal comprehension abilities will be measured by items assessing ability to learn from context. The underlying notion is that vocabulary is a proxy for the ability to pick up information from relevant context. We believe that most vocabulary is learned through context. An example of a learning-from-context item is (grades 10–12 level):

> The Depression did not happen suddenly with the 1929 stock market crash, although the *laz* that preceded it seemed carefree and spendthrift. The twenties saw homeless workers beginning to wend their way across the country, and small businesses going bankrupt.

Laz most likely means:

a. economy

b. years

c. history

d. lifestyles

Componential: Quantitative. Quantitative componential abilities are measured by number series items. These items measure inductive reasoning ability in the numerical domain. They require the examinee to extrapolate a sequence of numbers. An example is (grades 10–12 level):

1, 3, 6, 8, 16, __.

a. 18

b. 24

c. 32

d. 48

Componential: Figural. Figural componential abilities are measured by figure classifications in the primary grades (K–3) and by figure analogies at all remaining levels. Classifications are used for the youngest children because they can be made more easily than analogies. These items, like number series, measure inductive reasoning ability. An example of a figure classification is (kindergarten level):

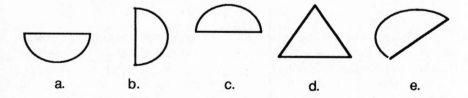

a.   b.   c.   d.   e.

The examinee must indicate which figure does not belong with the others. An example of a figure analogy is (grades 4–5 level):

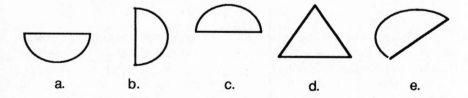

Coping with Novelty: Verbal. These items measure, within the verbal domain, the ability to think in relatively novel ways. Two kinds of items are used, both requiring hypothetical thinking with counterfactuals. The first item type asks the examinee to imagine a counterfactual situation, and then to draw an inference based on it. An example is (grades 8–9 level):

If dogs laid eggs, which of these would most likely be true?

a. Dogs would fly.
b. Puppies would have feathers.
c. Eggs would have tails.
d. Puppies would hatch.
e. Chickens would bark.

A second kind of item is the novel verbal analogy, which also requires counterfactual reasoning. An example is (grades 6–7 level):

Assume: Snowflakes are made of sand. Which solution is now correct, given this assumption?

Water is to *drop* as *snow* is to

a. storm
b. beach
c. grain
d. ice

Coping with Novelty: Quantitative. These items measure coping with novelty skills in the context of the quantitative domain. Examinees receive number matrix items, but with an element of novelty beyond the numerical-matrix format: A symbol is used in place of certain numbers in the item, and the examinee must make a substitution. An example of a numerical matrix item is (grades 6–7 level):

*	3	9
1 2	*	?

* = 6

a. 1 5
b. *
c. 1 8
d. 9

Coping with Novelty: Figural. These items are like figure completion items, except that they are novel in requiring examinees to complete the series in a domain different from the one in which they have inferred the rule. An example is (grade 1 level):

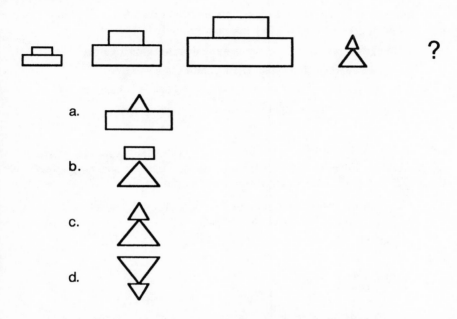

Automatization: Verbal. The items in this and the other automatization subtests are the only ones that are highly speeded. Subjects must make rapid decisions as to whether two letters are both of the same category (vowel or consonant) or of different categories (vowel-consonant or consonant-vowel). For example, the pairs "f n" and "e a" would both be "sames," whereas the pairs "f e" and "n a" would both be "differents."

Automatization: Quantitative. The items in this subtest require the examinee to make rapid judgments as to whether two numbers are the same (both odd or even) or different (one odd and the other even). For example, "2 6" and "3 9" would both be "sames," and "2 3" and "9 6" would both be "differents."

Automatization: Figural. The items in this subtest require the examinee to judge whether two figures have the same or different numbers of sides. For example, " △▽ " and " □▭ " both have the same number of sides, whereas " □△ " and " ◁ ▯ " both have a different number of sides.

Practical: Verbal. Practical verbal items require examinees to answer everyday inferential reasoning problems. In other words, the test taker must reason informally rather than formally, as would usually be the case for such items. An example of a practical verbal item is (grades 8–9 level):

Johnson's service station makes good on its claim that "We will not be undersold." Which of these is most likely to be true?

1. Garcia's service station charges more than Johnson's garage.

2. No other garage charges less than Johnson's garage.

3. The owner of Johnson's garage has a good head for business.

4. Johnson's garage is the busiest garage in town.

Practical: Quantitative. These items require the examinee to reason quantitatively with practical problems of the kind he or she might face in everyday life. An example of part of a problem is (grades 10–12 level):

You plan to make some cookies for your club's bake sale. The recipe calls for the following ingredients:
    1 stick butter
    1 cup sugar
    1 egg
    1 cup flour
    1 cup pecans
    Yield: 24 cookies

You have the following ingredients: 4 sticks of butter, 5 cups of sugar, 1/2 dozen eggs, 7 cups of flour, 2 eight-oz. bags of chocolate chips, and 3 cups of pecans. If you decide to make pecan cookies, what is the largest number of cookies you can make, using the ingredients you already have?

a. 3 dozen

b. 4 dozen

c. 6 dozen

d. 8 dozen

Practical: Figural. Items in this subtest require route planning, or the ability to plan a route efficiently, given the information in a map or diagram. The examinee might be shown a map of part of a town and asked which of several routes from one location to another is the most efficient.

Do test items such as those in the Sternberg Triarchic Abilities Test actually work? Many of the item types have been explored in my research on the triarchic theory of human intelligence, and only items yielding favorable outcomes have been used in the test. We have just completed a pilot testing of figural items for the componential and coping-with-novelty sections, with favorable results across grade levels. Some of the main findings were that subtests were generally reliable (Cronbach's coefficient alpha), scores on a given subtest increased across successive grade levels, subtest correlations for componential and novel items were only moderate (which is what we hoped for, as the two types of items are supposed to measure somewhat different abilities), and scores from conventional figural items generally showed higher correlations with scores on a standard intelligence test than did scores from novel figural items (which are supposed to measure abilities somewhat different from those measured by the conventional tests). Thus, the preliminary results look favorable for the test.

The main idea in this program of testing is to extend the testing of intelligence substantially beyond the conventional boundaries. If we want to measure intelligence, we can and should measure it broadly rather than narrowly.

The Sternberg Triarchic Abilities Test is not immune to effects of prior learning, nor is it culture-free. It is impossible, I believe, to test intelligence outside the boundaries of a culture. Intelligence is always used—and must be measured—in some context. The proposed test, however, seems broader and more comprehensive than existing tests, and hence allows for more diversity in backgrounds than typical tests.

Conclusions and Implications

The triarchic theory consists of three interrelated subtheories that attempt to account for the bases and manifestations of intelligent thought. The componential subtheory relates intelligence to the internal world of the individual. The experiential subtheory relates intelligence to the individual's experience with tasks and situations. The contextual subtheory relates intelligence to the external world of the individual.

The elements of the three subtheories are interrelated: The components of intelligence are manifested at different levels of experience with tasks and in situations of varying degrees of contextual relevance to a person's life. The components of intelligence are posited to be universal: Thus, the components that contribute to intelligent performance in one culture do so in all other cultures as well. Moreover, the importance to intelligence of dealing with novelty and the automatization of information-processing is posited to be universal. But the manifestations of these components in experience are posited to be relative to cultural contexts. What constitutes adaptive thought or behavior in one culture is not necessarily adaptive in another culture. Moreover, thoughts and actions that would be appropriate to shape behavior in one context might not be appropriate in another context. Finally, the environment one selects will depend largely upon which environments are available, and upon the fit of one's cognitive abilities, motivations, values, and affects to the available alternatives.

The triarchic theory has certain implications for the assessment and the training of abilities. A full assessment battery would necessarily tap all of the abilities specified by the triarchic theory, which no existing test can do. I am pursuing the development of a triarchic test of intelligence. However, even a test explicitly designed to measure intelligence according to the triarchic theory can only approximate an ideal test, if only because the relativity of the contextual subtheory limits the adequacy of any one test to a limited population. Similarly, I have developed a training program for understanding and improving intellectual skills based on the theory (Sternberg 1986a). However, the training program could not possibly develop all of the skills posited by the theory because of the variability of contextual skills across environments.

In conclusion, the triarchic theory offers a relatively complete account of intelligent thought that draws upon and partially subsumes many existing theories. This new theory, like all other theories, is only an approximation, which will serve a constructive purpose if it, too, is eventually subsumed by a more complete and accurate theory of human intelligence. It does not deal with styles in the way intelligence is actually used. For such an issue, one needs a separate theory of intellectual styles.

INTELLECTUAL STYLES

Three Profiles of Styles

Throughout my college years, my two roommates and I remained together. The roommates—Alex, Bob, and Cyril (only one of these names is unchanged)—seemed remarkably similar intellectually when they entered college. All had high Scholastic Aptitude Test (SAT) scores, excellent grades in high school, and similar intellectual strengths and weaknesses. In terms of standard theories of intelligence, the three roommates had similar intellectual abilities. Moreover, today, all three are successful in their jobs and have achieved national recognition for their work, showing that they were similar in motivational levels as well. However, a look beyond the intellectual similarities reveals some salient differences among the roommates that have profoundly affected their lives.

Alex, a lawyer, is fairly conventional, rule-bound, and comfortable with details and structure. He does well what others tell him to do, as a lawyer must, and has described his idea of perfection as a technically flawless legal document or contract that binds those who sign on the dotted line to the terms of the contract without loopholes. In a nutshell, Alex is an accomplished follower of systems. He was a Rhodes scholar and today is a partner in a major national law firm. Alex can figure out a system and work excellently within it.

Bob, a university professor, has a different style than Alex. He is fairly unconventional, and unlike Alex, dislikes following or even dealing with other people's rules. Moreover, he has relatively few rules of his own. Although he has some basic principles that he views as invariants, he tends not to take rules very seriously, viewing them as conveniences meant to be changed or even broken as the situation requires. Bob dislikes details, and generally is comfortable working within a structure only if it is his own. The things he does well are usually the things he wants to do, rather than what someone else wants him to do. His idea of intellectual perfection would be the generation of a great idea and a compelling demonstration that it is correct or at least useful. In brief, Bob is a creator of systems, and has designed some fairly well-known psychological theories that reflect his interest in system creation.

Cyril, a psychotherapist, is also fairly unconventional. Like Bob, he dislikes others' rules, but unlike Bob, he has a number of his own. He tends to be indifferent to details. He likes working within certain structures, which need not be his own, but must have been adjudged by him to be correct and suitable. Cyril does well what he wants to do. His idea of perfection would be a difficult but correct psychological diagnosis, followed by an optimal psychotherapeutic intervention. In sum, Cyril is a judge of systems. His interest, perhaps passion, for judging was shown early in his career, when, as a college student, he constructed "Cyril Test" to give to others, especially to dates, to judge the suitability of their values and standards. As editor of the college course critique, Cyril was responsibile for judging and evaluating all undergraduate courses at the university.

Although Alex, Bob, and Cyril are all intellectually able and similarly competent, even these brief sketches illustrate that they differ in terms of their intellectual style, or ways in which they direct their intelligence. Alex is a follower or executor, Bob, a creator or legislator, and Cyril, a judge of systems. A style, then, is not a level of intelligence, but a way of using it—a propensity. When one is talking about styles rather than levels, one does not speak in terms of better or worse, but of better or worse "for what?"

The Model of Intellectual Styles as Mental Self-Government

I am proposing here a model of intellectual styles as mental self-government (Sternberg 1988). The basic idea is that governmental structures may be external societal manifestations of basic psychological processes that are internal and individual (see also Bronfenbrenner 1977). Seeds of this notion can be found in the writings of Plato, Hobbes, Locke, and Rousseau, whose political theories were based on psychological theories of what people are like. The difference here, perhaps, is that rather than attempting to understand governments in terms of the psychology of human beings, we try to understand the psychology of human beings in terms of governments. From this point of view, government in society is a large-scale, externalized mirror of the mind. People, like societies, are systems (Ford 1986), and they need to govern themselves just as societies do.

Mental incompetence results from a breakdown of self-regulating functions, and high levels of mental competence derive in part from superior self-regulation.

The mental self-government model focuses more on styles than on levels of intelligence. Standard theories of intelligence, including recent ones (Gardner 1983; Sternberg 1985a), emphasize levels of intelligence of one or more kinds. Measuring intelligence thus entails assessing each ability in an individual. In contrast, the self-government model leads to assessment of how intelligence is directed or exploited. Two individuals of equal intelligence by any of the standard theories might nevertheless be viewed by this theory as intellectually quite different because of the ways in which they organize and direct that intelligence. People do not have—exclusively—one style or another, but rather show preferences for styles that result in different preferred ways of using their intelligence. In the next section, the implications of the mental self-government model as a basis for understanding intellectual styles are explored in some detail.

The Functions of Government

Governments may be viewed as having three primary functions: legislative, executive, and judicial. The legislative style characterizes individuals who enjoy creating, formulating, and planning for problem solution. Such individuals, like Bob, the university professor described earlier, prefer to create their own rules, enjoy doing things their own way, prefer problems that are not prestructured or prefabricated, and like to build structure as well as content in deciding how to approach a problem. People with legislative tendencies prefer creative and constructive planning-based activities, such as writing papers, designing projects, and creating new business or educational systems. They tend to enter occupations that enable them to use their legislative style, such as creative writer, scientist, artist, sculptor, investment banker, policymaker, and architect.

Individuals with an executive style are implementers. Like Alex, the lawyer described earlier, they prefer to follow rules and work within existing systems on problems that allow them to fill in content within existing structures. They prefer predefined activities, such as solving algebra-word problems or engineering problems, giving talks or lessons based on others' ideas, and enforcing rules. Executive types gravitate toward occupations such as lawyer, law enforcement officer, builder (of others' designs), surgeon, soldier, proselytizer (of others' systems), and manager (lower echelon).

The judicial style, as shown by Cyril, the psychotherapist described earlier, involves judgmental activities. Judicial types like to analyze and criticize, preferring problems in which they evaluate the structure and content of existing things and ideas. They prefer activities that exercise the judicial function, such as writing critiques, giving opinions, judging people and their work, and evaluating programs. People with a primarily judicial style tend to choose occupations such as judge, critic, program evaluator, admissions officer, grant or contract monitor, systems analyst, and consultant.

People do not have one style exclusively—rather, they tend to specialize, some people more than others. For example, one individual might be strongly legislative and only weakly executive and judicial, while another might be more equally balanced among the three functions. Thus, people differ not only in their direction of specialization but also in the degree to which they specialize. People will gravitate toward problems whose solutions require their preferred styles of functioning. They may also use certain styles in the service of other styles. A primarily legislative type, for example, may use judicial functions primarily to further legislative ends.

We need to distinguish the proclivity toward a style from the ability to implement that style. Most people probably prefer styles that capitalize upon their strengths. But there is no logical or psychological reason why preferences and abilities will always correspond. Some people may prefer styles less suited to their abilities than others would be. In measuring styles, it is important to measure both predilections toward styles and abilities to implement them, to determine how well an individual's predilections and abilities match.

An important implication of these differences is that, although style is generally independent of level of intelligence, it probably is not independent of level of *perceived* intelligence within a particular domain. The same individual who might be thought to be a brilliant science student because he is a legislative type might be thought to be rather dull in business courses that emphasize executive skills.

Forms of Mental Self-Government

Four major forms of government are the monarchic, the hierarchic, the oligarchic, and the anarchic. Logically any form may be paired with any function, although psychologically certain pairings are more likely than others. People prefer to organize their experience in ways that correspond to the various forms of government.

People who exhibit a predominantly monarchic style tend to be motivated by a single goal or need at a time. Single-minded and driven, they often believe that the ends justify the means and attempt to solve problems full-speed ahead— damn the obstacles. They may oversimplify problems, often being more decisive than the situation warrants. Although they may be systematic in a limited sense, they may neglect variables not obviously pertinent to their goal.

Individuals preferring a hierarchic style tend to be motivated by a hierarchy of goals, with the recognition that not all goals can be fulfilled equally well and that some goals are more important than others. They take a balanced approach to problems, believing that ends do not justify means, and viewing competing goals as acceptable (although they may have trouble if they cannot form a hierarchy of the priorities). Hierarchic types seek complexity and tend to be self-aware, tolerant, and relatively flexible. They set priorities well and are usually decisive, unless priority-setting becomes a substitute for decision or action. They are systematic in problem solving and decision making.

Individuals preferring the oligarchic style tend to be motivated by multiple, often competing goals of equal perceived importance. They are often driven by goal conflict and tension arising from their belief that satisfying the constraints is as important as solving the problem itself. They usually believe that ends do not justify means, and find that competing goals and needs tend to interfere with task completion, because each goal and need is seen as of roughly equal importance. Oligarchic types seek complexity (sometimes to the frustration point), and are self-aware, tolerant, and very flexible. They tend to have trouble setting priorities because everything seems equally important, and thus they are rather indecisive, with many systems in competition because of the need to satisfy multiple, equally important goals.

Anarchic stylists tend to be motivated by a potpourri of needs and goals that are often difficult for them, as well as others, to sort out. They take a random approach to problems, driven by what seems to be a muddle of inexplicable forces. They may act as though ends justify means. They may believe that anything goes, and often have trouble setting priorities because they have no firm set of rules upon which to base them. They tend to be extreme, either too decisive or too indecisive, and are thoroughly asystematic.

Some general issues arise with regard to formal style of mental self-government. Monarchists may be too single-minded for the likes of most teachers and even social acquaintances. However, their single-minded zeal may make them highly successful entrepreneurs or goal-attainers. Often, their memories of school will not be fond because they believe that their talents went unrecognized. Monarchists can also be difficult to live with because of their single-mindedness.

Hierarchical types can probably solve the widest variety of problems in school life and beyond, because most problems are probably best conceived of hierarchically. They will generally achieve a good balance between thought and action, but they must remember that the existence of priorities does not guarantee that those priorities are right. When there is a pressing goal, hierarchists may get lost or sidetracked in their own hierarchies, while the monarchist may blitz through and attain the goal.

Oligarchists often frustrate themselves and others, in school and in careers, because of their indecision and hesitation. Their tendency to assign equal weights to competing means and goals may make them appear to be "lost in thought" and unable to act. They can act, but may need to have others set their priorities for them.

Anarchists are at risk of becoming educational as well as social misfits, and their talents may actually lead them into antisocial paths. Properly nurtured, they may have the potential for truly creative contributions to the world, if their anarchic style is combined with the necessary intellectual talents for creative performance. But proper nurturance may be quite a challenge because of the anarchists' unwillingness to work within existing systems in order to eventually go beyond them. Rather than working within systems, anarchists may end up attempting to destroy them.

Levels of Mental Self-Government

Globalists prefer to deal with relatively large, abstract issues. They tend to ignore or dislike detail, choosing instead to conceptualize and work in the world of ideas. They may be diffuse thinkers who can get lost on cloud nine, and they may see the forest but not always the trees within it.

In contrast, localists prefer concrete problems requiring detailed work and are often pragmatic. They may not see the forest for the trees.

In terms of the three individuals described earlier—Alex, Bob, and Cyril— Bob and Cyril tend to be globalists and Alex tends to be a localist. The local level is not, however, inextricably linked to the executive style Alex has shown. Some executive types may prefer to work only at a broader level, accomplishing the main tasks in a project while relegating the local details to others. Similarly, a legislative or judicial type could be more local than either Bob or Cyril.

Although most people prefer to work either at a more global or a more local level, a key to successful problem solving in many situations is the ability to move between levels. It is often helpful for a person who is weak within a given level to pair up with someone whose strengths are complementary. Although we often most value people who are like ourselves, we actually benefit most from people who are moderately unlike ourselves with respect to preferred level of processing. Too much overlap leads to some levels of functioning simply being ignored. Two globalists, for example, may form ideas well, but need someone to take care of the details of implementing the ideas. Two localists may help each other in implementation, but need someone to set down the global issues to be addressed. Too little overlap, however, can lead to a breakdown in communication. People who do not overlap at all in levels may not be able to understand each other well.

Scope of Mental Self-Government

Governments may be internally oriented and isolationist, or externally oriented and collaborative with other nations. Similarly, mental self-governments need to work both alone and with others.

Internalists tend to be introverted, task-oriented, aloof, socially less sensitive, and interpersonally less aware than externalists. They also like to work alone, applying their intelligence to things or ideas in isolation from other people.

Externalists tend to be extroverted, people-oriented, outgoing, socially more sensitive, and interpersonally more aware than internalists. They like to work with others, and seek problems that either involve working with other people or are about others.

Among the three individuals described earlier, Alex and Bob tend more toward the internal scope of mental self-government, while Cyril tends more toward the external. These proclivities fit with their jobs. Alex works in corporate law, dealing with legal principles and documents rather than with people; Bob works primarily with ideas and their experimental instantiation. Cyril, as a psychotherapist, is constantly working with people. It should be realized that there is some degree of situation-specificity involved. Bob, for example, works actively with students and frequently gives lectures on his work. At the same time, he shuns parties and prefers social interactions that involve at least some degree of task orientation. Moreover, he recognizes the importance of dealing with people on his job and makes sure that necessary interactions take place.

Regardless of their preference, most people are not strictly internalists or externalists, but alternate between the two as a function of task, situation, and the people involved. But it is important to realize in education and job placement that bright individuals forced to work in a mode that does not suit them may perform below their capabilities.

Leanings of Mental Self-Government

Governments can have various leanings. For present purposes, the two major "regions" of leanings will be designated as conservative and progressive.

Individuals with a predominantly conservative style like to adhere to existing rules and procedures, minimize change, and avoid ambiguous situations, preferring familiarity in life and work.

Individuals with a progressive style like to go beyond existing rules and procedures, maximize change, seek or at least accept ambiguous situations, and prefer some degree of unfamiliarity in life and work.

Although individuals may tend toward a more conservative or progressive leaning in their mental self-government, there is clearly some degree of domain-specificity involved. For example, a politically conservative individual will not necessarily be conservative in personal life. Thus, in evaluating styles, and especially leanings, tendencies within particular domains must be taken into account. Moreover, leanings may well change over time as people feel more or less secure in their environments. Thus, an individual who is new to an environment may tend to adapt conservatively, whereas an individual who has been in that environment longer may feel free to attempt to shape the environment progressively. This may be among the most mercurial of the aspects of style.

Development of Intellectual Styles

Where do these various modes of intellectual functioning originate? At least some portion of stylistic preference may be inherited, but I doubt that it is a large part. Styles, like intelligence, seem to be partly socialized constructs (Sternberg and Suben 1986). Certain modes of interaction are rewarded more than others, and from an early age we probably gravitate toward these modes, while our built-in predispositions determine how much and how well we are able to adopt these rewarded styles.

Consider some of the variables that are likely to affect the development of intellectual styles.

A first variable is culture. Different cultures tend to reward different styles. For example, the North American emphasis on innovation ("making the better mouse trap") may lead to relatively greater reward for the legislative and progressive styles, at least among adults. National heroes in the United States—Edison as inventor, Einstein as scientist, Jefferson as political theorist, Steve Jobs as entrepreneur, and Hemingway as author—are admired for their legislative contributions. Societies that value conformity and the following of tradition may be more likely to reward executive and conservative styles. A society that emphasizes conformity and tradition too strongly may stagnate because of the styles it promotes.

A second variable is gender. Traditionally, a legislative style has been more acceptable in males than in females. Men were supposed to set the rules, and women to follow them. Although this tradition is changing, the behavior of many men and women does not fully reflect the new values.

A third variable is age. Legislation is generally encouraged in the preschool young, who are encouraged to develop their creative powers in the relatively unstructured and open environment of the preschool and in some homes. Once the children start school, the period of legislative encouragement rapidly ends. Children are now expected to be socialized into the largely conforming values of the school. The teacher decides what the student should do, and the student does it, for the most part. Students who do not follow directions and the regimentation of the school are viewed as undersocialized and even as misfits. In adulthood, some jobs again encourage legislation, although training for such jobs may not. For example, presentation of high school physics or history is usually largely executive, with students answering questions or solving problems that the teacher poses. But the physicist and historian are expected to be more legislative. Ironically, they may have forgotten how. We sometimes say that children lose their creativity in school. What they may really lose is the intellectual style that generates creative performance.

A fourth variable is parenting style. What the parent encourages and rewards is likely to be reflected in the style of the child. Does the parent encourage or discourage legislation, or judgment, on the part of the child? The child tends to emulate the parent's style, and modeling is an important source of behavioral development. A monarchic parent, for example, will probably reward a child who shows the same single-mindedness, whereas an anarchic parent would probably try to suppress such monarchic style. Mediation also is a powerful source of development (Feuerstein 1980). Parents who mediate for their children in ways that point to larger rather than smaller issues underlying actions are likely to encourage a global style, while parents who do not themselves generalize are likely to encourage a more local style.

A last variable is type of schooling and, ultimately, of occupation. Schools and occupations reward different styles. An entrepreneur is likely to be rewarded for styles different from those for which an assembly-line worker is rewarded. As individuals respond to the reward system of their chosen life pursuit, various aspects of style will either be encouraged or suppressed.

Obviously, these variables are only a sampling of those variables that influence style. Any discussion such as this one inevitably simplifies the complexities of development, if only because of the complex interactions among variables. Moreover, styles interact with abilities. Occasionally one runs into legislative types who are uncreative, creative people who eschew legislation, hierarchists who set up misguided hierarchies, and so on. But for the most part, the interactions will be more synchronous in well-adjusted people. According to the triarchic theory of human intelligence (Sternberg 1986b), contextually intelligent people are those who capitalize on their strengths and remediate or compensate for their weaknesses. A major part of capitalization and compensation appears to be in finding harmony between one's abilities and one's preferred styles. People who cannot find such harmony are likely to be frustrated by the mismatch between how they want to perform and how they are able to perform.

If styles are indeed socialized, even in part, then they almost certainly can be modified, at least to some degree. Such modification may not be easy. We know little about how to modify intelligence and even less about how to modify intellectual styles. Presumably, when we learn the mechanisms that might underlie such attempts at modification, we will pursue a path similar to that used by some educators and psychologists in teaching intelligence (for example, Sternberg 1986a).

We need to teach students to make the best of their intellectual styles. Some remediation of weaknesses is probably possible. To the extent that it is not, mechanisms of compensation can usually be developed to narrow the gap between weak and strong areas of performance. For example, children with different preferred styles can be paired. Ultimately, a theory of intellectual styles may serve as a basis not only for a test of such styles, but for training that maximizes people's flexibility in dealing with their environment, society, and themselves. The main teaching method may well become role-modeling by teachers for learners.

Schools most reward executive types—children who work within existing rule systems and seek the rewards that the schools value. To some extent, the schools create executive types out of students who might have been otherwise. Whether the rewards will continue indefinitely for the executive types depends in part upon career path, which is why school grades are poor predictors of job success. One's ability to get high grades in science courses involving problem solving, for example, probably will not be highly predictive of one's success as a scientist, an occupation that rewards formulating the problems in the first place. Judicial types may be rewarded somewhat more in secondary and especially tertiary schooling, where at least some judgmental activity is required, as in paper writing. Legislative types, if they are rewarded at all, may not be rewarded until graduate school, where there is a need to come up with original ideas in dissertation and other research. However, some professors may not reward legislative types even in graduate school, preferring executive types who will carry out their research for them in an effective, diligent, and nonthreatening way.

The fit between student and teacher, as between principal and teacher, can be critical to the success of either system. A legislative student and an executive teacher, for example, may not get on well at all. A legislative student may not even get along with a legislative teacher if that teacher happens to be intolerant of other people's legislations. In my own career, I have found that although I can work with a variety of students, I probably work best with students whom I would classify as legislative. I also work reasonably well with executive types. I am probably weakest with judicial students, who seem to me to be more eager to criticize than to do research. The general point is that educators need to take their own styles into account in understanding the influence of these styles on their perceptions of and interactions with others. Clearly, certain children benefit from certain styles. A gifted executive-type student might benefit more from presentation of the same material at a more rapid pace. A gifted legislative-type student might benefit more from the opportunity to do creative projects consistent with the student's preferred style of working.

Schools need to take into account not only fit between teacher and student (or principal and teacher) styles but also the fit between the way a subject is taught and the way a student thinks. A given course often can be taught in a way that is advantageous (or disadvantageous) to a particular style. Consider, for example, an introductory or low-level psychology course. This course might stress learning and using existing facts, principles, and procedures (an executive style of teaching), or designing a research project (a legislative style), or writing papers evaluating theories, experiments, and the like (a judicial style). Little wonder that I received a grade of "C" in my introductory psychology course, taught in the executive style! In my own psychology courses, I have almost always made the final grade heavily dependent upon the design of a research project. As it does for others, my style of teaching has reflected my own style of thinking. The general principle of style of teaching reflecting the teacher's preference is not limited to psychology or even science. Writing, for example, might be taught in a way that emphasizes critical (judicial) papers, creative (legislative) papers, or expository (executive) papers.

Sometimes, there is a natural shift in the nature of subject matter over successive levels of advancement, as in jobs. In mathematics and basic science, for example, lower levels are more executive, requiring solution of prestructured problems. Higher levels become more legislative, requiring formulation of new ideas for proofs, theories, and experiments. Unfortunately, some of the students screened out in the earlier phases of education might have succeeded quite well in the later ones, while some students who readily pass the initial stages might be ill-suited to later demands.

Perhaps the most important point is that we tend to confuse level with style of intelligence. For example, most current intelligence and achievement tests reward the executive style by requiring solution of prestructured problems. One cannot create one's own problems, or judge the quality of the problems on the test (at least not at the time of test!). Judicial types get some credit for analytical items, but legislative types hardly benefit at all from existing tests, and may actually be harmed by them. Clearly, style will affect perceived competence, but as noted earlier, in general, style is independent of intelligence, although not within particular domains. Style ought to count as much as ability and motivation in recommending job placements, although probably not in making tracking decisions that deal with issues of ability rather than style.

The styles of intellect proposed here are not, of course, the only ones ever to have been proposed. Theories of intellectual styles abound, and I will cite some pertinent examples.

Myers (1980; see also Myers and McCaulley 1985) has proposed a series of psychological types based upon Jung's (1923) theory of types. According to Myers, there are sixteen types, resulting from all possible combinations of two ways of perceiving—sensing versus intuition; two ways of judging—thinking versus feeling; two ways of dealing with self and others—introversion versus extroversion; and two ways of dealing with the outer world—judgment versus perception.

Gregorc (1985) has proposed four main types or styles, based upon all possible combinations of just two dimensions—concrete versus abstract and sequential versus random.

Concrete-sequential refers to a preference for the ordered, the practical, and the stable. Individuals who are dominant concrete-sequentials tend to focus their attention on material reality and physical objects, to validate ideas via the senses, and to conform. Abstract-sequential refers to a preference for mentally stimulating environments. Individuals who are dominant abstract-sequentials tend to focus their attention on the intellect. They prefer logical and synthetic thinking and validate ideas via personal formulas. Abstract-random refers to a preference for emotional and physical freedom. Individuals who are dominant abstract-randoms tend to focus their attention on feeling and emotion. They also tend to validate ideas via inner guidance. Finally, concrete-random refers to a preference for a stimulus-rich environment free from restriction. Individuals who are dominant concrete-randoms tend to engage with the concrete world of activity and the abstract world of intuition. They prefer intuitive and instinctive thinking and rely on personal proof for validating ideas, rarely accepting outside authority.

Renzulli and Smith (1978) have suggested that individuals possess various learning styles, with each style corresponding to a method of teaching: projects, drill and recitation, peer teaching, discussion, teaching games, independent study, programmed instruction, lecture, and simulation. Holland (1973), from a job-related orientation, proposed six styles that are used to understand job interests as revealed by the Strong-Campbell Interest Inventory (1985). Holland's typology includes six "types" of personality: realistic, investigative, artistic, social, enterprising, and conventional.

Intellectual styles probably represent a way in which personality is manifested in intelligent thought and action. Attempts to understand academic or job performance solely in terms of intelligence or personality neglect the issue of intellectual style—the effect of intelligence and personality on each other. Thus, styles may represent an important "missing link" between intelligence, personality, and real-world performance.

The Intellectual Styles Questionnaire

Can intellectual styles be measured? Yale graduate student Marie Martin and I believe they can be. We are currently validating an inventory designed to measure intellectual styles, the Intellectual Styles Questionnaire, based on our theory of mental self-government.[6] The questionnaire contains 130 statements, ten for each of thirteen styles. Examinees rate each statement on a 1 to 9 scale, where 1 signifies that a statement does not characterize the examinee at all, and 9 signifies that a statement characterizes the examinee perfectly well. The following are typical items from the questionnaire. Although they are ordered by style here, they are in random order on the actual questionnaire.

Functions

Legislative
1. If I work on a project, I like to plan what to do and how to do it.
2. Coming up with my own way of doing things is something I like to do.
3. I feel happier about a job when I can decide for myself how to do it.

Executive

1. When I am interested in a problem, I like to find out what great thinkers have thought about it in the past.
2. I like situations in which it is clear what role I must play or in what way I should participate.
3. I like to follow instructions when solving a problem.

Judicial

1. I like to analyze people's behavior.
2. I like tasks that allow me to express my opinions to others.
3. I like situations that permit me to evaluate existing perspectives on issues that I am interested in.

Levels

Global

1. I like to avoid situations in which I am expected to be concerned with details.
2. In any written work I do, I like to emphasize the scope and context of my ideas, that is, the general picture.
3. I tend to pay little attention to details.

Local

1. I like problems that require engagement with details.
2. In carrying out a task, I am not satisfied unless even the nitty-gritty details are given close attention.
3. I find that the only way I am able to complete a project is by finding out all the details.

Leanings

Progressive

1. I like to avoid activities that expect me to follow or act according to approved rules.
2. When working on a project, I like to have the freedom to try to carry it out in whatever way I consider best, regardless of what others may think of such a way.
3. I like to do things in new ways, even if I am not sure they are the best ways.

Conservative

1. In my work, I like to keep close to what has been done before.
2. I like to do things in ways that have been shown in the past to be correct.
3. I dislike those problems for which it has not been shown how best to solve them.

Forms

Hierarchic
1. I usually make written or mental lists of things to do, including the order by which each thing will get done.
2. Before I start working on a project, I like to have an idea of the things I must do and in what order to do them.
3. I like having a planned-out order of things to do whenever there are a lot of things to get done.

Oligarchic
1. When I undertake some task, I am usually equally open to starting by working on one of several things.
2. When there are competing issues of importance to address in my work, I somehow try to address them simultaneously.
3. I sometimes have trouble setting priorities for multiple things that I need to get done.

Anarchic
1. When I have to start to do some task, I usually do not organize my thoughts in advance.
2. When working on a written project, I usually let my mind wander and my pen follow up on whatever thoughts cross my mind.
3. Whenever I have to get something done, I usually feel that there are an infinite number of ways of getting it done.

Monarchic
1. I like to devote all my time and energy to one project, rather than dividing my time and attention among others.
2. I like to complete what I am doing before starting something else.
3. I like to avoid being interrupted when working on a task or project.

Scope

Internal
1. I like to be alone when working on a problem.
2. When I undertake a task, I like to be independent of others in carrying it out.
3. I like to avoid situations in which I have to work in a group.

External
1. Before I start on a project, I like brainstorming ideas with some friends or peers.
2. I like to work with others rather than by myself.
3. I like to participate in groups in which all members contribute to the same project.

Marie Martin and I have collected some preliminary data, seeking to construct-validate the theory and the measure. The results are promising. Of the thirteen scales, five had internal-consistency reliabilities over .80, five between .70 and .80, two between .60 and .70, and one between .50 and .60. A factor analysis yielded a separate factor for scope and level, and a combined factor for leaning and function. Form was distributed across factors. The questionnaire scores were correlated with scores from the Myers-Briggs and Gregorc tests of styles, but generally were uncorrelated with academic measures, including IQ, GPA, and SAT scores. Thus, the questionnaire showed both convergent and discriminant validity. In sum, initial results for the construct validity of the theory and the questionnaire are promising.

CONTEXT AND ENVIRONMENT

In the science-fiction short story "Second Game" (De Vet and MacLean 1958), the Veldians judge the intelligence of members of their society by their ability to play a rather complicated, chess-like game. The ability to play this game determines not only the society's evaluation of one's intelligence, but also one's position in the society. Thus, the society chooses as its leaders those who play the game best, and fills slots at various levels of the job-skill hierarchy according to level of game performance. In sum, to be intelligent on Velda is to excel in a particular way.

A starkly contrasting view of intelligence is held on the planet Standard in Anthony's (1973) science-fiction novel, *Race Against Time*. Standard is actually Earth many centuries after wars, pollution, and plague have wiped out most of the original Earth population. The Standards, having learned the lessons of the past, no longer view traditional kinds of excellence as intelligent. Indeed, those excellences had decimated the human population through such clever inventions as bombs and man-made strains of disease for use in germ-warfare. The intelligent person on Standard conforms to "the standard," as average as a person can be. Such a person adapts perfectly to the Standard society, thus fitting the notion of intelligence as adaptation to the environment. To be intelligent on Standard is to excel in no way at all.

The Veldian and Standard conceptions of intelligence are certainly wrong or, at best, incomplete. In "Second Game", the protagonist, Robert Lang, a representative of the Galactic Federation, accomplishes his goal of finding out why Veldians resist contact with Federation planets by purposely losing the first of a two-game set and then winning the second game. He uses the first game in an intelligent strategy to determine the opponent's strengths and weaknesses. In *Race Against Time*, the protagonist, John Smith, is able to discover the sad history of Standard, and how he is different from the Standards by not conforming to the Standard norms and by outwitting the Standards and running away from them. For both protagonists, accomplishment of their goals requires an action-set that is unintelligent by planetary standards. In short, there is a sense in which intelligence is socioculturally defined and subject to society's dictates, and in another aspect, it is objective and immune to such dictates.

In the world of intelligence, we need to understand the rules of two games. While almost all of the scientists who study intelligence have studied the rules of the first game, this exclusive preoccupation has been a mistake. The rules of the first game are set by nature: The investigator needs to discover the latent mental structures and processes that underlie intelligence in an objective sense. This sense is the one that led Robert Lang to win his second game after losing his first, and the one that led John Smith to conform to the Standard in appearance, but not in reality. The rules of the second game are set by society: The investigator needs to discover the manifest behaviors that the society labels as intelligent and that underlie intelligence in a subjective sense. It will be argued that the rules of the first game are universal, whereas the rules of the second game are socioculturally specific.

Some might ask, Why study the rules of the second game at all? They might argue that any difference between what intelligence actually is and what it is thought to be merely represents human error. People's conceptions of intelligence, in this view, have no more claim to legitimacy than does phlogiston, an imaginary substance once believed to be responsible for fire. This point of view is wrong scientifically and pernicious educationally.

The science-fiction stories described above illustrate the importance of understanding intelligence in both its objective and subjective aspects. Each aspect addresses a different question with relation to the individual. The objective aspect addresses the relationship between intelligence and the internal world of the individual: What goes on "inside a person's head" that renders the mental functioning of that person more or less intelligent? The subjective aspect addresses the relationship between intelligence and the external world of the individual: What goes on in the society that judges the behavior of an individual as being more or less intelligent? To the extent that intelligence is defined in terms of adaptation to one's environment, both aspects of intelligence are important: The Veldians and the Standards might have been dead wrong in their conceptions of intelligence, but their conceptions had an extremely powerful influence upon a person's adaptation to those environments. A person who is thought by society and the schools to be intelligent—or unintelligent—will be treated in certain ways, regardless of his or her "actual" intelligence. In principle, the correlation between the behaviors that might emanate from intelligence, objectively defined, and intelligence, subjectively defined, might range anywhere from -1 to +1. In practice, the correlation will probably be positive, but almost certainly less than 1.

In education, the subjective aspect of intelligence is of paramount importance, because the conceptions of intelligence held and inculcated by the school—the school's-eye view of intelligence—will determine what is rewarded and what is punished, and ultimately, who garners society's rewards and who does not. People have long recognized the difference between the objective and subjective aspects of intelligence, and their importance for schooling. Indeed, Binet was commissioned to devise the first major intelligence test because teachers were not distinguishing between maladaptive performance resulting from mental retardation (in the objective sense) and maladaptive performance resulting from behavior problems. Thus, students from both groups were lumped together in classes for the retarded. Even then, the prevailing subjective view of intelligence resulted in many students being placed in classes in which they did not belong, and potentially, in their being deprived of the kind of station in life they might have attained, had they been perceived differently. Then, as today, the school's-eye view of intelligence played a major role in determining who succeeds and who fails, in school as well as in later life.

There is no single school's-eye view of intelligence. The view can vary depending upon the age of the children involved, the point of view (children, parents of school children, teachers, administrators), and the time and the place of the school under consideration. The remainder of this chapter will be devoted to elaborating what these various views are; how they coexist and, in some cases, clash with each other; and how they influence the schooling and later life of the child.

Intelligence as Perceived by Adults

The Structure of Implicit Theories

In a first series of studies on these issues, Sternberg, Conway, Ketron, and Bernstein (1981) sought to determine the structure and use of implicit theories of intelligence. In a first study, people entering a supermarket, commuters in a train station, and students in a college library were asked to list behaviors that they believed characterized an extremely intelligent, academically intelligent, or everyday intelligent individual. We then compiled a master list of behaviors, and asked new samples of subjects to rate how characteristic each behavior was of an "extremely intelligent person," "academically intelligent person," and "everyday intelligent person." A separate set of samples was asked to rate how important each behavior was to defining intelligence, academic intelligence, and everyday intelligence. We were particularly interested in two particular samples: laypersons and experts (well-known university professors in psychology and education) in the field of intelligence, broadly defined. From these studies we learned some interesting facts about people's implicit theories of intelligence.

First, laypersons (as represented by the shoppers, commuters, and students) have well-defined implicit theories of intelligence. Three factors emerged clearly from their rating data: practical problem-solving ability (reasons logically and well, identifies connections among ideas, sees all aspects of a problem, gets to the heart of problems), verbal ability (speaks clearly and articulately, is verbally fluent, converses well, reads with high comprehension), and social competence (accepts others for what they are, admits mistakes, displays interest in the world at large, is on time for appointments).

Second, there is a high correlation between lay and expert views of intelligence: The median correlation between the response patterns of university professors specializing in the study of intelligence and those of laypersons was .82. There were, however, two main differences between the two groups. The first was that experts considered motivation to be an important ingredient in academic intelligence, whereas no motivation factor emerged for the laypersons. Behaviors central to the motivation factor for experts included, for example, "displays dedication and motivation in chosen pursuits," "gets involved in what he or she is doing," "studies hard, and is persistent." The second difference was that experts placed somewhat less emphasis on the sociocultural aspects of intelligence than did the laypersons. Behaviors such as "sensitivity to other people's needs and desires" and "is frank and honest with self and others" showed up in the social-competence factor for laypersons but not for experts.

To get a better sense of just how experts and laypersons differ in their views of intelligence, I went back to the original ratings of the importance of the various behaviors to people's conceptions of intelligence. I was particularly interested in behaviors that received higher ratings from laypersons than from experts, and in those that received higher ratings from experts than from laypersons. The pattern was clear. Consider first some of the behaviors that laypersons emphasized more in defining intelligence: acts politely, displays patience with self and others, gets along well with others, is frank and honest with self and others, and emotions are appropriate to situations. These behaviors clearly show an emphasis on *inter*personal competence in a social context. Consider next some of the behaviors that professors emphasized more in defining intelligence: reads with high comprehension, shows flexibility in thought and action, reasons logically and well, displays curiosity, learns rapidly, thinks deeply, and solves problems well. These behaviors clearly show an emphasis on *intra*personal competence in an individual context. To the extent that there is a difference, therefore, it is clearly in the greater emphasis among laypersons on intelligence as an interpersonal and social construct.

Third, the three kinds of intelligence are correlated, but differentially. Recall that we asked the subjects to rate how characteristic certain behaviors are of a person who is generally intelligent, academically intelligent, and "everyday" intelligent. For laypersons, the correlations between the ratings for the three types of intelligence were .75 between intelligence and academic intelligence, .86 between intelligence and everyday intelligence, and .45 between academic intelligence and everyday intelligence. For experts, the correlations were .83 between intelligence and academic intelligence, .84 between intelligence and everyday intelligence, and .46 between academic intelligence and everyday intelligence. Two conclusions emerge from these correlations. First, the professors view intelligence as closer to academic intelligence than do laypersons. Second, for the professors *and* the laypersons, academic and everyday intelligence are viewed as related but clearly distinct constructs.

Fourth, a fine-grained analysis of our data reveals not only differences between experts and laypersons, but also distinguishable subpopulations among laypersons. Students gave greater weight to academic ability as a component of general intelligence than commuters did. Commuters, on the other hand, considered everyday intelligence—the ability to function well in daily life—more important.

The experts in our initial studies were all college professors, almost exclusively in the fields of psychology and education. These professors had clear notions of what constituted intelligence in their students. But would these notions be the same across fields? Would professors of philosophy, for example, look for the same kinds of attributes as would professors of physics in evaluating the intelligence of a student? To address this question, I conducted a separate set of studies in which professors of art, business, philosophy, and physics were asked to list behaviors that were characteristic of highly intelligent individuals in their fields. Once the behaviors were compiled, new samples of professors in the same fields were asked to rate how characteristic each behavior would be of an extremely intelligent person (Sternberg 1985c). We found differences in emphasis across fields.

While professors of art emphasized knowledge and the ability to use that knowledge in weighing alternative possibilities and in seeing analogies, the business professors emphasized the ability to think logically, to focus on essential aspects of a problem, and to follow others' arguments easily and to see where these arguments lead. The emphasis on assessment of argumentation was much stronger in the business professors' implicit theories than in those of the art professors. The philosophy professors emphasized critical and logical abilities very heavily, especially the abilities to follow complex arguments, to find subtle mistakes in them, and to generate counter-examples to invalid arguments. The philosophers' view clearly emphasized those aspects of logic and rationality that are essential in analyzing and creating philosophical arguments. The physicists, in contrast, emphasized precise mathematical thinking, the ability to relate physical phenomena to the concepts of physics, and the ability to grasp quickly the laws of nature. In short, professors in different fields had a core view of the nature of intelligence, but with important and intuitively plausible differences among the fields in what kinds of behaviors were emphasized in the assessment of intelligence.

In the studies described above, all of the teachers taught at the undergraduate and graduate levels. One might wonder how teachers of younger students conceive of intelligence, and whether there are differences as a function of the grade level of the students whom the teachers teach. Fry (1984) addressed this question in a series of studies using the Sternberg et al. (1981) procedures with teachers whose students ranged from the elementary to the college level. Her results generally replicated those of Sternberg et al. (1981), but she found clear differences in emphasis as a function of the grade level at which the teachers taught. At the elementary level, teachers emphasized the social-competence aspects of intelligence in their evaluations. At the secondary level, teachers emphasized verbal skills. And at the college level, teachers emphasized problem-solving skills. These results have potentially important implications for understanding what is valued in the schools at different levels. In particular, they suggest that in the elementary school grades, noncognitive factors are important in teachers' conceptions of intelligence.

In sum, both laypersons and teachers at all levels have rather well-defined notions of intelligence. These notions display a common core, but are shaded according to the individual's walk of life. In particular, teachers' conceptions of intelligence vary as a function of the level of teaching and as a function of the field of teaching at the upper levels. There is not one "school's-eye" view of intelligence, but several such views, which color teachers' perceptions of the intelligence of their students.

Use of Implicit Theories

People have well-defined implicit theories of intelligence. But do they actually use these implicit theories in evaluating themselves and others? We sought to address these questions in our research. We sent lay subjects a series of personal sketches of fictitious people, employing behaviors taken from the master list. These sketches in some ways resembled brief and telegraphic letters of recommendation one might get if one sought written evaluations of people's intelligence. Consider two typical sketches:

Susan:
She keeps an open mind.
She is knowledgeable about a particular field.
She converses well.
She shows a lack of independence.
She is on time for appointments.

Adam:
He deals effectively with people.
He thinks he knows everything.
He shows a lack of independence.
He lacks interest in solving problems.
He speaks clearly and articulately.
He fails to ask questions.
He is on time for appointments.

The respondents' task was to rate the intelligence of each person on a scale from 1 (low) to 9 (high). Our task was to find out whether or not respondents' ratings were consistent with laypersons' conceptions of intelligence. If they were, then behaviors that were rated as being more characteristic of intelligence should lead to higher ratings of the intelligence of the fictitious persons.

For example, "keeps an open mind" had been rated 7.7 by laypersons, fairly characteristic of intelligence, whereas "shows a lack of independence" had been rated just 2.7. To get some idea of how our fictitious persons would rate on the laypersons' rankings, we averaged the ratings values for each of the given characteristics in our fictitious descriptions. We came up with scores of 6.0 for Susan and 4.3 for Adam. By comparison, our respondents (who were presented with the fictitious descriptions of Susan and Adam and asked to rate their intelligence) rated Susan's intelligence at 5.8 and Adam's at 4.3. Overall, when we calculated the correlation between the two sets of ratings (expected values on the basis of the average "characteristicness" ratings for the described persons, on the one hand, and actual ratings of the described persons, on the other), we obtained a coefficient of .96. In other words, laypersons' ratings of other people's intelligence were indeed firmly grounded in their implicit theories about intelligence.[7]

Do people use their implicit theories of intelligence in evaluating their own intelligence? To a limited extent, they do. Sternberg et al. (1981) found a moderate average correlation between individuals' self-descriptions and the descriptions elicited from other subjects of the prototypical intelligent person. The range of correlations, however, was quite wide.

To conclude, people use their implicit theories of intelligence in evaluating others. These implicit theories are important in the judgments both of laypersons and teachers. But how about the students? Do they have implicit theories, and if so, how do these theories match up with those of the schools? This question is addressed in the next section.

Children's Conceptions of Intelligence

Several studies have also been done on children's conceptions of the nature of intelligence. Three sets of studies are particularly relevant.

Yussen and Kane (1983) conducted a series of studies on children's conceptions of intelligence. In the first study, they interviewed children in the first, third, and sixth grades. All were lower-middle to middle-middle class. They found that younger children's conceptions of intelligence were less differentiated than those of older children. Older children were also more likely to characterize intelligence as an internalized quality of the individual. In other words, the younger children were more likely to believe that a person's level of intelligence could be assessed by things the person does or says than were the older children. These self-ratings tended to decline as grade level increased.

In a second study, Yussen and Kane asked first-graders and sixth-graders to imagine a child, who could be either smart or not smart, and to assess the performance of that child on various tasks. For example, suppose the hypothetical target child is Alice. Subjects would be asked questions such as: "Suppose Alice is having a jumping contest with her friends. How often will she jump the farthest and win the contest?" or "Suppose Alice hears a new song. How much of it will she remember the next day?" The questions were divided into four categories: physical, social, academic, and cognitive. The two sample questions above are physical and cognitive, respectively. In this second study, three clear-cut findings emerged. First, in all descriptive categories, smart children were judged as better than children who are not smart. Second, the gap between smart and not smart children is relatively small for the physical behaviors, but relatively large for each of the other kinds of behaviors. Third, the gaps are about the same for both first-graders and sixth-graders.

In a third study, children in grades three and six, as well as college-age adults, were asked to characterize an intelligent infant, ten-year-old child, adult, or older adult. The results of this study were complex and can only be presented here in barest outline.

Consider first the infant. Everyone agreed that gross and fine sensorimotor control, the tendency to do things without help, and precocious language acquisition are important indicators of intelligence. Both groups of grade-school children, but not the adults, also emphasized the importance of the infants' knowing what they should and should not do under particular circumstances. But only the adults mentioned motivation and curiosity as signaling infant intelligence.

Consider next the ten-year-old. All age groups agreed that superior school performance is typical of the intelligent child. Although everyone mentioned general kinds of knowledge and performance indicators, only the children emphasized excellence in the specific pursuits of reading and mathematics. All of the groups also mentioned such social skills as being helpful to others and being an adaptable member of a group. Only the children mentioned physical skills, such as in sports, as typifying the intelligent individual, whereas only the adults mentioned motivation, learning, thinking abstractly, showing interest in and affiliation with peers, independence, and creativity.

The greatest divergence between the children's and adults' characterizations was in their conceptions of the intelligent adult. The children emphasized the performance of specific tasks, such as managing the household, excelling at a job, earning money, and teaching children. They also valued the adult's ability to drive, perform in sports activities, and show manual skills. In contrast, adults stressed abstract qualities in their characterizations, such as independence, social adjustment, general cognitive abilities, and open-mindedness.

Finally, there were both similarities and differences between age groups in their characterizations of older adults. Children emphasized protecting oneself from and dealing with physical infirmities. They also emphasized amount of knowledge and the older adults' ability to find recreational outlets for themselves. The comments of the adults, on the other hand, stressed the importance of wisdom—its accumulation and its sharing with others.

To conclude, both children and adults have definable conceptions of intelligence for people of different ages. Although these conceptions overlap, there are notable differences as well. These differences may lead children to perform in ways that they believe distinguish them as intelligent, but that are not necessarily perceived in this way by adults. For example, the school-age children, but not the adults, viewed distinction in sports as typifying the intelligent ten-year-old. A study yet to be done is one of children's views of adults' perceptions of intelligence, and of adults' views of children's perceptions of intelligence. Such a study might directly indicate just how children and adults miscommunicate in attempting to show their intelligence to each other.

In a follow-up to the Yussen and Kane work, Alexander (1985) compared gifted versus nongifted children's perceptions of intelligence. Children in the sample ranged in age from twelve to seventeen years old. In general, gifted children tended to emphasize such cognitive attributes as understanding, reasoning, and problem solving in their conceptions. Nongifted students, on the other hand, emphasized social and academic attributes. Nongifted students were more likely to weigh physical attributes as important than were the gifted students. Thus, the conceptions of intelligence of gifted students seem to come closer to those of the adults studied by Yussen and Kane, while the nongifted students have perceptions more similar to those of the children in that study.

Dweck (see, for example, Dweck and Elliott 1983) has carried out some of the most interesting work on children's conceptions of intelligence. Dweck has suggested that children can be classified in one of two ways, depending upon their implicit theory of intelligence. "Incremental theorists" view intelligence as a repertoire of skills that increases through effort, and believe that effort is an investment that increases intelligence. In contrast, "entity theorists" view intelligence as a global, stable entity whose adequacy is judged through performance. They view effort as a risk that may reveal low intelligence. Thus, incremental theorists tend to stress learning and increasing competence through learning. Entity theorists tend to stress performance and the judgment of their competence through performance. For the incremental theorist, the optimal task maximizes one's learning, thus making one smarter. For the entity theorist, the optimal task maximizes one's looking smart. By late grade school, virtually all children understand aspects of both of these two views, but, independent of their actual level of intelligence, they tend to favor one view or the other. Incremental and entity theorists have very different views of what they should do in school to maximize their intelligence, and the appearance of it. In the short run, entity theorists may be benefited by their engagement in activities that make them "look smart." In the long run, however, they may be penalized by their reluctance to engage in tasks that, ultimately, will make them smarter.

Ethnographic Studies of the School's-Eye View of Intelligence

We have seen how laypersons, teachers, and students differ in their views of intelligence.[8] Moreover, there are differences within as well as between groups. What happens when a child, raised with one view of intelligence, goes to school and is confronted with another? The confrontation can be a recipe for disaster, as shown in the brilliant work of Shirley Heath (1983) on language development in three U.S. subcultures.

Heath studied language development in three communities in the Piedmont Carolinas: Trackton (lower-class black), Roadville (lower-class white), and Gateway (middle-class white). We present here only a fraction of her observations on the effects of match and mismatch between what constitutes intelligent behavior from the point of view of the school and from that of the community in which the child was raised.

One of the important mismatches Heath describes is that, in general, Trackton children do not expect adults to ask them questions. In Trackton, children are not seen as information-givers or as question-answerers. As a result, the very act of being asked a question is strange to them. When Heath asked Trackton children to do tasks she gave them or to do jobs she assigned them, the children often protested, seeing no reason why they should do these tasks. Trackton children particularly have trouble dealing with indirect requests, such as, "It's time to put our paints away now," because they may not even be perceived as requests. These children also have particular difficulty with "Why?" questions because adults in Trackton do not engage children in conversations in which such questions are asked, in stark contrast to typical middle-class upbringing.

In Roadville, as in Gateway, young children confront a very different situation. Adults see themselves as teachers, and thus ask and answer questions, including "Why?" questions. By the time they go to school, these children have had considerable experience with both direct and indirect requests. Unfortunately, parents in Roadville do not persist in this attitude. Once their children start school, they abdicate their roles as teachers, leaving it to the school to do the job.

Heath suggests that there is an implicit conflict in means of resource allocation across the three communities. One of the ways American schools prepare children for a schedule-dominated adulthood is through the expectation that the schools' fairly strict schedules will be observed. Place constraints are equally important. Things are expected to go in their proper place at the proper time. In Trackton, the flow of time is casual. There are no timed tasks at home, and few tasks are even time-linked. For example, people eat when they are hungry and there are few constraints on which parts of the meal come before or after other parts. There are few scheduled activities; and routines, such as going to bed, may happen at different times on different days. The children are accustomed to a flow of time in which their wants and needs are met as a function of whether someone is there to meet them, and whether the provisions needed are available. It is thus odd for the Trackton child to adhere to a schedule that appears to the child to be arbitrary and capricious. Timed tests, of course, seem even stranger than school schedules: Before entering school, the child may have had literally no experience with being timed in the performance of a cognitive task.

The Trackton child has similar difficulties with space allocation. Being told to put things in a certain place has little or no meaning to the Trackton child. He or she is used to putting things down when done, but the place may vary from time to time. The child has so few possessions that finding the object later will generally not be a problem. The Trackton child's relatively poor handling of time and space becomes a basis for teachers' unfavorable judgments almost from the start of school.

Children from Roadville and Gateway have a very different sense of time and place. Roadville parents want their children to grow up with a strict sense of everything having its time and place. In Roadville, even the stories maintain a strict chronological order, emphasizing sequences of events. In Gateway, life is strictly scheduled, and even babies are expected to adhere to this strict scheduling. Things have a time and a place, and children are expected to learn what these are, just as they will later be expected to do in school.

When they start school Trackton children are at a disadvantage from the standpoint of talking about (and perhaps understanding) similarities and differences between objects, a skill that is important in school and critical on typical intelligence tests. Trackton children never spontaneously volunteer to list similarities or differences between objects. Instead, they seem to view objects holistically, comparing the objects as wholes rather than attribute-by-attribute.

The situation is quite different in Roadville. Adults encourage children to label things, and they talk to children about the attributes of these things. A primary goal in adults' play with children is to encourage them to define the attributes of the play stimuli, and the toys given to the children encourage them to match such attributes as color, shape, and size. Gateway parents also give their children educational toys from an early age. Children are encouraged to note points of similarity and difference between objects, and to label these differences as they are encountered. Gateway parents talk to children about names of things in books as well as in the world, discussing matters of size, shape, and color as they arise.

Trackton children are disadvantaged by attitudes toward reading: In Trackton, reading is primarily a group affair. An individual who chooses to read on his or her own is viewed as antisocial. Solitary reading is for those who are unable to make it in the Trackton social milieu. Moreover, there are few magazines, books, or other reading material in Trackton, so that children have little opportunity to practice reading, or to be read to. While Roadville parents frequently read to their children, especially at night, such a practice would be most unusual in Trackton.

McDermott (1974) has noted that reading is an act that aligns the black child with the wrong forces in the universe of socialization. Reading is a part of the teacher's agenda and a game the teacher wishes the students to play, but it is not a part of the black students' agenda and the games they wish to play. Not reading is accepting the peer group's games over the teacher's games, and Trackton children are likely to make just this choice.

In Roadville, once children start school, parents generally stop reading to them, expecting the school to take on this task. Adults encourage children to watch "Sesame Street," one way for the children to pick up reading, but the adults themselves scarcely set examples to model. Heath notes that the two outstanding features of reading habits in Roadville are, first, that everyone talks about it but that few people do it, and second, that few take any follow-up action on the reading they do. Unlike in Trackton, Roadville homes do have reading matter, such as magazines. However, the magazines usually pile up unread, and are then thrown away in periodic cleanings.

Attitudes toward reading are different still in Gateway, where children are coached before they enter school both in reading and listening behaviors. Children are encouraged to read, to learn the structures of stories, and to use what they learn in their lives.

Another major difference among the communities is in preferred mode of communication. In Trackton, nonverbal forms of transmission of knowledge are heavily emphasized. Adults pay little or no attention to a baby's words. Even sounds that are clearly linked to objects are ignored. In contrast, adults pay careful attention to babies' nonverbal responses, and praise responses such as coos and smiles that seem appropriate to a situation. People talk about babies, but rarely to them. During the first six to twelve months of life, babies are not directly addressed verbally by adults. Signs of aggressive play in children are acknowledged, and generally encouraged. Babies sit in the laps of mothers and other adults frequently during the first year, and the child literally feels the nonverbal interaction of the conversationalist. Children are expected to pay close attention to nonverbal signals about the consequences of their actions, and to act accordingly. When older children show younger children how to do things, they do not generally use verbal descriptions. Rather, they exhibit the behavior and simply tell the younger child to do it in the way he or she sees it done. Watching and feeling how to do things are viewed as more important than talking about how to do them.

In Roadville, there is much more stress on verbal interaction and development. When babies respond to stimuli verbally, adults notice these responses, and ask questions and make statements in response that are directed at the baby. When the children start to combine words, usually between eighteen and twenty-two months, adults respond with expansions of these combinations. Children are encouraged to label things and, as importantly, to communicate their needs and desires verbally.

Habits of verbal learning in Roadville, despite these desirable features, do not very closely match what will later be expected in school. Home teaching and learning are modeled not upon modes of knowledge transmission in the schools, but upon those in the church. Children are expected to answer questions with prescribed routines. The measure of a child's understanding of things is his or her ability to recite back knowledge verbatim. The style of learning is passive: One listens, repeats back, and thereby is expected to learn. The sign of learning is memorization, not understanding. Even in their play, Roadville children use language in the same way as in more serious endeavors: They tell stories in strict chronological order, and do not embellish them either with evaluations or creative fictions.

In Gateway as in Roadville, early language use is encouraged and reinforced. Mothers talk to babies, and assume that the babies are listening to them and will want to respond. Parents believe that a child's success in school will depend, in part, upon the amount of verbal communication directed to the child and received from the child. But while Roadville parents discourage fantasy, Gateway parents encourage it, and praise children's imaginary tales. When children ask questions, adults answer at some length, and probe the children's knowledge to assess what is known and what needs to be known. The goal is to encourage understanding rather than verbatim recall.

When the goal of learning is verbatim recall, the techniques used by Roadville mothers are extremely effective. In Islamic cultures, for example, memorization of lengthy passages from the Koran is a goal unto itself. According to Cole and Scribner (1974), Nigerian children in Koranic schools are trained to memorize the Koran in Arabic, a language they do not speak or understand. In Nigeria, as in Roadville, the mode of learning is geared to what is to be learned; the result is perfectly acceptable in its immediate context, but may not be ideal in other situations.

Many of the issues that are featured in Heath's ethnography are echoed in the literature on the cross-cultural study of cognition. Cross-cultural studies of classification, categorization, and problem-solving behavior illustrate the effects of three processes I have labeled selective encoding, combination, and comparison (see Davidson and Sternberg 1984; Sternberg 1985a). *Selective encoding* is at issue in studies of attribute preference in classification tasks. In these tasks, a subject may be shown a red triangle, a blue triangle, and a red square, and asked which two things belong together. Western literature shows a consistent developmental trend, such that very young children choose color as the decisive (or relevant) stimulus attribute, whereas, by about age five, children shift their preference to form (see Suchmann and Trabasso 1966). Cross-cultural studies, on the other hand, often fail to show this color-to-form shift (Cole et al. 1971). Cole and Scribner (1974) suggest that the preference for form versus color may be linked to the development of literacy (where alphabetic forms acquire tremendous importance), which differs widely across cultures.

Luria (1976) provides an illustration of *selective combination* in a categorization task. Shown a hammer, a saw, a log, and a hatchet, an illiterate Central Asian peasant was asked which three items were similar. He insisted that all four fit together, even when the interviewer suggested that the concept "tool" could be used for the hammer, saw, and hatchet, but not for the log. The subject in this instance combined the features of the four items that were relevant in terms of his culture and arrived at a functional or situational concept (perhaps one of "things you need to build a hut"). In his failure to combine the "instrumental" features of the tools selectively into a concept that excluded the log, the subject was not performing intelligently—at least, from the perspective of the experimenter's culture.

In many of Luria's studies, the unschooled peasants have great difficulty in solving the problems given them. Often, they appear to be thrown off by an apparent discrepancy between the terms of the problem and what they know to be true. For example, take one of the math problems: "From Shakhimardan to Vuadil it is three hours on foot, while to Fergana it is six hours. How much time does it take to go on foot from Vuadil to Fergana?" The subject's response to this problem was, "No, it's six hours from Vuadil to Fergana. You're wrong . . . it's far and you wouldn't get there in three hours" (Luria 1976, 129). In terms of *selective comparison*, performance suffered precisely because the subject was comparing incoming data to what he knew about his world, which was irrelevant to the solution of the problem. As Luria put it, the computation could readily have been performed, but the condition of the problem was not accepted.

CONCLUSIONS AND IMPLICATIONS

In this chapter, I have argued that a program for complete abilities testing would be substantially broader than the testing we now do. It would take into account the broad definition of intelligence, intellectual styles, and the context of measurement. The program of testing I propose here differs also from most existing programs in being, for the most part, theory-based. We need not take a totally empirical, shotgun approach to the understanding and assessment of abilities: We can use psychological as well as measurement theory as a basis for testing.

The function of testing is conceived of differently here from the way it is often conceived of in psychometric testing. I do not view abilities as fixed. To the contrary, much of my work has been concerned with teaching intellectual and other skills to enhance people's abilities and their utilization of them (see, for example, Sternberg 1986a). I view a program of testing without one of teaching as somewhat futile: What good is a score to an individual if he or she does not have the possibility of modifying it? I have supported two forms of ability tests, for example, so that the two forms can serve as pretests and posttests in a comprehensive program of evaluation, training, and reevaluation. The goal of measuring abilities should be to assist people to capitalize upon their strengths and to remediate or compensate for their weaknesses.

There is no guarantee that the kinds of tests I propose here will be used appropriately. In a worst-case scenario, users would believe that they have a better than usual test, and hence can put complete confidence in the test results. No test is error-free, and the problems of test-anxiety, cultural difference, and inadequate education can cloud the interpretation of new tests as well as existing ones. We can work toward better tests, but we also must work toward more enlightened interpretation of test scores, no matter what the tests or test results may be.

I believe that the Sternberg Triarchic Abilities Test will prove useful for selection, placement, and diagnosis, both in school settings and on-the-job. With respect to selection, the test provides a broader basis for admissions and related decisions than do existing tests. The test measures not only the analytical abilities measured by traditional ability tests, but also synthetic and practical abilities that few of these tests even touch on. With respect to placement and diagnosis, the test provides a profile of nine scores covering three content domains and four process domains. The information it provides may be useful for making informed decisions regarding job and educational placement in a way that one or two scores from conventional tests could not. I believe that the Intellectual Styles Questionnaire, too, will be useful for placement and diagnosis, but it probably will not be useful for selection, as there are no right or wrong answers. In combination, the two kinds of tests can give a relatively comprehensive assessment of a person's intelligence and how the person chooses to use that intelligence.

NOTES

1. Differences in obtained factor structures depended largely upon rotations of axes in the factor space obtained for a given set of tests. There is no evidence that the factor spaces differed much: Rather, what differed among theorists was the way in which each chose to assign reference axes for interpreting the factors. But these various rotations of the given space are all mathematically equivalent with respect to the fit of the factor model to the data. Although some theorists, even to this day, argue that certain rotations of axes are psychologically superior to others (for example, Carroll 1980), I think it is becoming increasingly evident that assignment of axes is a matter of convenience, depending upon the expected use for factor-analytic data. If one wishes a global, parsimonious assessment of intellectual performance on a group of tests, the general factor obtained from an unrotated factorial solution is particularly useful. If one wishes a more differentiated, less parsimonious view of abilities, the simple structure of Thurstone may well be more useful. If one wishes to view abilities hierarchically, successively higher orders of

factors may be extracted to highlight the interrelations among factors at successive levels of generality (as in the hierarchical theories of Vernon 1971 or Cattell 1971).

2. I am not arguing for any one factorial model of intelligence (one with a general factor) over others: To the contrary, I believe that most factor models are mutually compatible, differing only in the form of rotation that has been applied to a given factor space (Sternberg 1977). The rotation one uses is a matter of theoretical or practical convenience, not of truth or falsity.

3. These correlations were generally at the level of about -.6. The correlations are negative because response times were correlated with numbers correct.

4. More specifically, Snow and Lohman (1984; see also Snow, Kyllonen, and Marshalek 1984) have multidimensionally scaled a variety of such tests and found the dimensional loadings to follow a radex structure. In particular, tests with higher loadings on g, or general intelligence, fall closer to the center of the spatial diagram. Those tests that best measure the ability to deal with novelty fall closer to the center, and tests tend to move away from the center as their assessment of ability to deal with novelty becomes more remote.

5. Items from Sternberg Triarchic Abilities Test, copyright © 1988, The Psychological Corporation, all rights reserved.

6. Items from Intellectual Styles Questionnaire, copyright © 1988, Marie Martin and Robert J. Sternberg, all rights reserved.

7. We also used multiple-regression techniques to determine the weights for each of the three factors in laypersons' implicit theories. As independent variables, we used approximation factor scores of each of the described individuals on each of the factors of the implicit theory (as well as on unintelligence). The multiple correlation was .97. The standardized regression (beta) weights for each of the three factors were .32 for problem-solving ability, .33 for verbal ability, and .19 for social competence. (There was also a weight for unintelligent behaviors of -.48.) These weights indicate the psychological importance assigned to each of these factors by the subjects in the study. All weights were statistically significant and all signs were in the predicted directions, with only unintelligent behaviors showing a negative weight. As expected, the unintelligent behaviors had the highest regression weight, because there was only one independent variable for such behaviors, as opposed to three for intelligent behaviors. Moreover, as anyone who has read letters of recommendation knows, even one negative comment can carry quite a bit of weight. Of the three kinds of intelligent behaviors, the two cognitive kinds (problem-solving and verbal ability) carried about equal weight, and the noncognitive kind (social competence) carried less weight.

8. This section of the report is based upon and condensed from Sternberg and Suben (1986), which discusses, among other things, the implications of Shirley Brice Heath's work for understanding the socialization of intelligence.

REFERENCES

Alexander, P. 1985. Gifted and nongifted students' perceptions of intelligence. *Gifted Child Quarterly* 29:137–43.

Anthony, P. 1973. *Race against time*. New York: Tom Doherty Associates.

Baltes, P. B. 1986. Notes on the concept of intelligence. In *What is intelligence? Contemporary viewpoints on its nature and definition,* eds. R. J. Sternberg and D. K. Detterman, 23–27. Norwood, NJ: Ablex.

Berry, J. W. 1972. Radical cultural relativism and the concept of intelligence. In *Mental tests and cultural adaptation,* ed. L. J. Cronbach and P. Drenth. The Hague, Holland: Mouton.

Berry, J. W. 1974. Radical cultural relativism and the concept of intelligence. In *Culture and cognition: Readings in cross-cultural psychology,* ed. J. W. Berry and P. R. Dasen, 225–29. London: Methuen.

Berry, J. W. 1980. Cultural universality of any theory of human intelligence remains an open question. *Behavioral and Brain Sciences* 3:584–85.

Binet, A., and T. Simon. 1905. Methodes nouvelles pour le diagnostic du niveau intellectuel des anormaux. *L'Annee Psychologique* 11:191–244.

Binet, A., and T. Simon. 1916. *The development of intelligence in children.* Baltimore: Williams and Wilkins.

Binet, A., and T. Simon. 1973. *Classics in psychology: The development of intelligence in children.* New York: Arno Press.

Blum, M. L., and J. C. Naylor, eds. 1968. *Industrial psychology: Its theoretical and social foundations.* New York: Harper and Row.

Bronfenbrenner, U. 1977. Toward an experimental ecology of human development. *American Psychologist* 7:513–31.

Brown, A. L. 1978. Knowing when, where, and how to remember: A problem of metacognition. In vol. 1, *Advances in instructional psychology,* ed. R. Glaser. Hillsdale, NJ: Erlbaum.

Brown, A. L., J. D. Bransford, R. A. Ferrara, and J. C. Campione. 1983. Learning, remembering, and understanding. In *Handbook of child psychology.* 4th ed., ed. P. H. Mussen. Vol. 3, *Cognitive development,* ed. J. H. Flavell and E. M. Markman, 77–166. New York: Wiley.

Butterfield, E. C., C. Wambold, and J. M. Belmont. 1973. On the theory and practice of improving short-term memory. *American Journal of Mental Deficiency* 77:654–69.

Campione, J. C., and A. L. Brown. 1979. Towards a theory of intelligence: Contributions from research with retarded children. In *Human intelligence: Perspectives on its theory and measurement,* ed. R. J. Sternberg and D. K. Detterman, 139–64. Norwood, NJ: Ablex.

Cantor, N., and W. Mischel. 1979. Prototypes in person perception. In *Advances in experimental social psychology,* ed. L. Berkowitz. New York: Academic Press.

Carroll, J. B. 1976. Psychometric tests as cognitive tasks: A new "structure of intellect." In *The nature of intelligence,* ed. L. B. Resnick. Hillsdale, NJ: Erlbaum.

Carroll, J. B. 1980. *Individual difference relations in psychometric and experimental cognitive tasks.* Final Report NR 150-406 ONR. Chapel Hill, NC: L. L. Thurstone Psychometric Laboratory, University of North Carolina.

Cattell, R. B. 1971. *Abilities: Their structure, growth, and action.* Boston, MA: Houghton Mifflin.

Chase, W. G., and H. A. Simon. 1973. The mind's eye in chess. In *Visual information-processing,* ed. W. G. Chase. New York: Academic Press.

Chi, M. T. H. 1978. Knowledge structure and memory development. In *Children's thinking: What develops?,* ed. R. S. Siegler. Hillsdale, NJ: Erlbaum.

Cole, M., and S. Scribner. 1974. *Culture and thought.* New York: John Wiley.

Cole, M., J. Gay, J. Glick, and D. W. Sharp. 1971. *The cultural context of learning and thinking*. New York: Basic Books.

Cooper, L. A. 1982. Strategies for visual comparison and representation: Individual differences. In vol. 1, *Advances in the psychology of human intelligence*, ed. R. J. Sternberg, 77–124. Hillsdale, NJ: Erlbaum.

Davidson, J. E., and R. J. Sternberg. 1984. The role of insight in intellectual giftedness. *Gifted Child Quarterly* 28:58–64.

DeVet, C. V., and K. MacLean. 1958. *Second game*. New York: Street and Smith Publications.

Dweck, C. S., and E. S. Elliott. 1983. Achievement motivation. In *Handbook of child psychology*, ed. P. H. Mussen, 643–91. New York: John Wiley.

Feuerstein, R. 1980. *Instrumental enrichment: An intervention program for cognitive modifiability*. Baltimore, MD: University Park Press.

Flavell, J. H. 1977. *Cognitive development*. Englewood Cliffs, NJ: Prentice Hall.

Ford, M. E. 1986. A living systems conceptualization of social intelligence: Outcomes, processes, and developmental change. In vol. 3, *Advances in the psychology of human intelligence*, ed. R. J. Sternberg, 119–71. Hillsdale, NJ: Erlbaum.

Fry, P. S. 1984. Teachers' conceptions of students' intelligence and intelligent functioning: A cross-sectional study of elementary, secondary, and tertiary level teachers. In *Changing conceptions of intelligence and intellectual functioning: Current theory and research*, ed. P. S. Fry, 157–74. New York: North-Holland.

Galton, F. 1883. *Inquiry into human faculty and its development*. London: Macmillan.

Gardner, H. 1983. *Frames of mind: The theory of multiple intelligences*. New York: Basic.

Gelman, R., and R. Baillargeon. 1983. A review of some Piagetian concepts. In *Handbook of child psychology*. 4th ed., ed. P. H. Mussen. Vol. 3, *Cognitive Development*, ed. J. H. Flavell and E. M. Markman, 167–230. New York: Wiley.

Gelman, R. S., and C. R. Gallistel. 1978. *The child's understanding of number*. Cambridge, MA: Harvard University Press.

Gentner, D., and J. Grudin. 1985. The evolution of mental metaphors in psychology: A 90-year retrospective. *American Psychologist* 40:181-92.

Gladwin, T. 1970. *East is a big bird*. Cambridge, MA: Harvard University Press.

Goodnow, J. J. 1976. The nature of intelligent behavior: Questions raised by cross-cultural studies. In *The nature of intelligence*, ed. L. B. Resnick. Hillsdale, NJ: Erlbaum.

Gregorc, T. 1985. *Inside styles: Beyond the basics*. Maynard, MA: Gabriel Systems, Inc.

Guilford, J. P. 1967. *The nature of human intelligence*. New York: McGraw Hill.

Gustafsson, J. E. 1984. A unifying model for the structure of intellectual abilities. *Intelligence* 8:279–303.

Heath, S. S. 1983. *Ways with words*. New York: Cambridge University Press.

Holland, J. L. 1973. *Making vocational choices: A theory of careers*. Englewood Cliffs, NJ: Prentice-Hall.

Horn, J. L. 1968. Organization of abilities and the development of intelligence. *Psychological Review* 75:242–59.

Horn, J. L., and J. R. Knapp. 1973. On the subjective character of the empirical base of Guilford's structure-of-intellect model. *Psychological Bulletin* 80:33–43.

Hunt, E. B. 1978. Mechanics of verbal ability. *Psychological Review* 85:109–30.

Hunt, E. B. 1980. Intelligence as an information-processing concept. *British Journal of Psychology* 71:449–74.

Hunt, E. B., and M. Lansman. 1982. Individual differences in attention. In vol. 1, *Advances in the psychology of human intelligence,* ed. R. J. Sternberg. Hillsdale, NJ: Erlbaum.

Hunt, E. B., M. Frost, and C. Lunneborg. 1973. Individual differences in cognition: A new approach to intelligence. In vol. 7, *The psychology of learning and motivation,* ed. G. Bower. New York: Academic Press.

Intelligence and its measurement: A symposium. 1921. *Journal of Educational Psychology* 12:123–47, 195–216, 271–75.

Irvine, S. H. 1969. Factor analysis of African abilities and attainments: Constructs across cultures. *Psychological Bulletin* 7:20–32.

Irvine, S. H. 1979. The place of factor analysis in cross-cultural methodology and its contribution to cognitive theory. In *Cross-cultural contributions to psychology,* eds. L. Eckensberger and Y. Poortinga. Lisse, Netherlands: Swets and Zeitlinger.

Jensen, A. R. 1979. *g:* Outmoded theory or unconquered frontier? *Creative Science and Technology* 2:16–29.

Jensen, A. R. 1980. *Bias in mental testing.* New York: Free Press.

Jensen, A. R. 1982. Reaction time and psychometric *g.* In *A model for intelligence,* ed. H. J. Eysenck, 93–132. Berlin: Springer-Verlag.

Jung, C. 1923. *Psychological types.* New York: Harcourt, Brace.

Kagan, J. 1976. Commentary on "Reflective and impulsive children: Strategies of information-processing underlying differences in problem solving." *Monographs of the Society for Research in Child Development* 41, no. 5, serial no. 168.

Kearins, J. M. 1981. Visual spatial memory in Australian aboriginal children of desert regions. *Cognitive Psychology* 2:434-60.

Keating, D. 1984. The emperor's new clothes: The "new look" in intelligence research. In Vol. 2, *Advances in the psychology of human intelligence,* ed. R. J. Sternberg, 1-45. Hillsdale, NJ: Erlbaum.

Keil, F. C. 1984. Mechanisms of cognitive development and the structure of knowledge. In *Mechanisms of cognitive development,* ed. R. J. Sternberg. San Francisco: Freeman.

Kogan, N. 1983. Stylistic variation in childhood and adolescence: Creativity, metaphor, and cognitive styles. In *Handbook of child psychology.* 4th ed., ed. P. H. Mussen. Vol. 3, *Cognitive development,* ed. J. H. Flavell and E. M. Markman, 630–706. New York: Wiley.

Kosslyn, S. M. 1980. *Image and mind.* Cambridge, MA: Harvard University Press.

Laboratory of Comparative Human Cognition. 1982. Culture and intelligence. In *Handbook of human intelligence,* ed. R. J. Sternberg, 642–719. New York: Cambridge University Press.

Luria, A. R. 1976. *Cognitive development: Its cultural and social foundations.* Cambridge: Harvard University Press.

MacLeod, C. M., E. B. Hunt, and N. N. Matthews. 1978. Individual differences in the verification of sentence-picture relationships. *Journal of Verbal Learning and Verbal Behavior* 17:493–507.

Maier, N. R. F., ed. 1970. *Problem solving and creativity in individuals and groups.* Belmont, CA: Brooks/Cole.

Mayer, R., and J. G. Greeno. 1972. Structural differences between learning outcomes produced by different instructional methods. *Journal of Educational Psychology* 63:165–73.

McDermott, R. P. 1974. Achieving school failure: An anthropological approach to illiteracy and social stratification. In *Education and the cultural process*, ed. G. Spindler. New York: Holt, Rinehart, and Winston.

Milgram, S. 1975. *Obedience to authority*. New York: Harper and Row.

Mulholland, T. M., J. W. Pellegrino, and R. Glaser. 1980. Components of geometric analogy solution. *Cognitive Psychology* 12:252–84.

Myers, I. B. 1980. *Gifts differing*. Palo Alto: Consulting Psychologists Press.

Myers, I. B., and M. H. McCaulley. 1985. *Manual: A guide to the development and use of the Myers-Briggs type indicator*. Palo Alto, CA: Consulting Psychologists Press.

Neisser, U. 1983. Components of intelligence or steps in routine procedures? *Cognition* 15:189–97.

Newell, A., and H. A. Simon. 1972. *Human problem solving*. Englewood Cliffs, NJ: Prentice-Hall.

Pellegrino, J. W., and R. Glaser. 1979. Cognitive correlates and components in the analysis of individual differences. In *Human intelligence: Perspectives on its theory and measurement*, eds. R. J. Sternberg and D. K. Detterman, 61–88. Norwood, NJ: Ablex.

Pellegrino, J. W., and R. Glaser. 1980. Components of inductive reasoning. In *Aptitude, learning, and instruction*. Vol. 1, *Cognitive process analyses of aptitude*, ed. R. E. Snow, P.-A. Federico, and W. E. Montague, 177–217. Hillsdale, NJ: Erlbaum.

Pellegrino, J. W., and R. Kail, Jr. 1982. Process analyses of spatial aptitude. In Vol. 1, *Advances in the psychology of human intelligence*, ed. R. J. Sternberg, 311–66. Hillsdale, NJ: Erlbaum.

Piaget, J. 1972. *The psychology of intelligence*. Totowa, NJ: Littlefield, Adams.

Raaheim, K. 1974. *Problem solving and intelligence*. Oslo: Universitetsforlaget.

Renzulli, J. S., and L. H. Smith. 1978. *Learning styles inventory*. Mansfield Center, CT: Creative Learning Press.

Resnick, L. B., and R. Glaser. 1976. Problem solving and intelligence. In *The nature of intelligence*, ed. L. B. Resnick. Hillsdale, NJ: Erlbaum.

Roediger, H. 1980. Memory metaphors in cognitive psychology. *Memory and Cognition* 8:231–46.

Schank, R. C. 1980. How much intelligence is there in artificial intelligence? *Intelligence* 4:1–14.

Schank, R. C., and R. P. Abelson. 1977. *Scripts, plans, goals and understanding*. Hillsdale, NJ: Erlbaum.

Siegler, R. S. 1986. Unities of thinking across domains. In *The development of intelligence: The 1984 Minnesota symposium on child psychology*, ed. M. Perlmutter. Hillsdale, NJ: Erlbaum.

Simon, H. A. 1976. Identifying basic abilities underlying intelligent performance of complex tasks. In *The nature of intelligence*, ed. L. B. Resnick, 65–98. Hillsdale, NJ: Erlbaum.

Simon, H. A., and S. Reed. 1976. Modeling strategy shifts in a problem-solving task. *Cognitive Psychology* 8:86–97.

Snow, R. E. 1979. Theory and method for research on aptitude processes. In *Human intelligence: Perspectives on its theory and measurement*, eds. R. J. Sternberg and D. K. Detterman, 105–38. Norwood, NJ: Ablex.

Snow, R. E. 1980. Aptitude processes. In *Aptitude, learning, and instruction*. Vol. 1, *Cognitive process analyses of aptitude*, ed. R. E. Snow, P.-A. Federico, and W. E. Montague, 27–63. Hillsdale, NJ: Erlbaum.

Snow, R. E., and D. F. Lohman. 1984. Toward a theory of cognitive aptitude for learning from instruction. *Journal of Educational Psychology* 75:347–76.

Snow, R. E., P. C. Kyllonen, and B. Marshalek. 1984. The topography of ability and learning correlations. In Vol. 2, *Advances in the psychology of human intelligence*, ed. R. J. Sternberg, 47–104. Hillsdale, NJ: Erlbaum.

Spear, L. C., and R. J. Sternberg. 1987. An information-processing framework for understanding reading disability. In Vol. 2, *Handbook for cognitive, social, and neuropsychological aspects of learning disabilities*, ed. S. Ceci, 3–31. Hillsdale, NJ: Erlbaum.

Spearman, C. 1923. *The nature of "intelligence" and the principles of cognition.* London: Macmillan.

Spearman, C. 1927. *The abilities of man.* New York: Macmillan.

Sternberg, R. J. 1977. *Intelligence, information-processing, and analogical reasoning: The componential analysis of human abilities.* Hillsdale, NJ: Erlbaum.

Sternberg, R. J. 1979. The nature of mental abilities. *American Psychologist* 34: 214–30.

Sternberg, R. J. 1980. Sketch of a componential subtheory of human intelligence. *Behavioral and Brain Sciences* 3:573–84.

Sternberg, R. J. 1981. Intelligence and nonentrenchment. *Journal of Educational Psychology* 73:1–16.

Sternberg, R. J. 1982a. Natural, unnatural, and supernatural concepts. *Cognitive Psychology* 14:451–58.

Sternberg, R. J. 1982b. Reasoning, problem solving, and intelligence. In *Handbook of human intelligence*, ed. R. J. Sternberg. New York: Cambridge University Press.

Sternberg, R. J. 1983. Components of human intelligence. *Cognition* 15:1–48.

Sternberg, R. J. 1984. Toward a triarchic theory of human intelligence. *Behavioral and Brain Sciences* 7:269–87.

Sternberg, R. J. 1985a. *Beyond IQ: A triarchic theory of human intelligence.* New York: Cambridge University Press.

Sternberg, R. J. 1985b. Human intelligence: The model is the message. *Science* 230:1111–18.

Sternberg, R. J. 1985c. Implicit theories of intelligence, creativity, and wisdom. *Journal of Personality and Social Psychology* 49:607–27.

Sternberg, R. J. 1986a. *Intelligence applied: Understanding and increasing your intellectual skills.* San Diego: Harcourt, Brace, Jovanovich.

Sternberg, R. J. 1986b. Intelligence is mental self-government. In *What is intelligence? Contemporary viewpoints on its nature and definition*, ed. R. J. Sternberg and D. K. Detterman, 141–48. Norwood, NJ: Ablex.

Sternberg, R. J. 1987. The psychology of verbal comprehension. In Vol. 3, *Advances in instructional psychology*, ed. R. Glaser, 97–151. Hillsdale, NJ: Erlbaum.

Sternberg, R. J. 1988. Mental self-government: A theory of intellectual styles and their development. *Human Development* 31:197–224.

Sternberg, R. J., and J. E. Davidson. 1982. The mind of the puzzler. *Psychology Today* 16 (June): 37–44.

Sternberg, R. J., and D. K. Detterman, eds. 1986. *What is intelligence? Contemporary viewpoints on its nature and definition.* Norwood, NJ: Ablex.

Sternberg, R. J., and M. K. Gardner. 1982. A componential interpretation of the general factor in human intelligence. In *A model for intelligence*, ed. H. J. Eysenck, 231–54. Berlin: Springer-Verlag.

Sternberg, R. J., and J. L. Ketron. 1982. Selection and implementation of strategies in reasoning by analogy. *Journal of Educational Psychology* 74:399–413.

Sternberg, R. J., and J. S. Powell. 1983. Comprehending verbal comprehension. *American Psychologist* 38:878–93.

Sternberg, R. J., and B. Rifkin. 1979. The development of analogical reasoning processes. *Journal of Experimental Child Psychology* 27:195–232.

Sternberg, R. J., and J. Suben. 1986. The socialization of intelligence. In *Perspectives on intellectual development.* Vol. 19, *Minnesota symposia on child psychology,* ed. M. Perlmutter, 201–35. Hillsdale, NJ: Erlbaum.

Sternberg, R. J., and R. K. Wagner, eds. 1986. *Practical intelligence: Nature and origins of competence in the everyday world.* New York: Cambridge University Press.

Sternberg, R. J., and E. M. Weil. 1980. An aptitude-strategy interaction in linear syllogistic reasoning. *Journal of Educational Psychology* 72:226–34.

Sternberg, R. J., B. E. Conway, J. L. Ketron, and M. Bernstein. 1981. People's conceptions of intelligence. *Journal of Personality and Social Psychology* 41:37–55.

Strong, E. K., Jr., D. P. Campbell, and J. C. Hansen. 1985. *Strong-Campbell Interest Inventory.* Palo Alto: Consulting Psychologists Press.

Suchmann, R. G., and T. Trabasso. 1966. Color and form preference in young children. *Journal of Experimental Child Psychology* 3:177–87.

Super, C., and S. Harkness. 1980. The infant's niche in rural Kenya and metropolitan America. In *Issues in cross-cultural research,* ed. L. L. Adler. New York: Academic Press.

Thurstone, L. L. 1938. *Primary mental abilities.* Chicago: University of Chicago Press.

Valsiner, J. 1984. Conceptualizing intelligence: From an internal static attribution to the study of the process structure of organism-environment relationships. In *Changing conceptions of intelligence and intellectual functioning: Current theory and research,* ed. P. S. Fry, 63–89. New York: North-Holland.

Vernon, P. E. 1970. *Creativity.* Harmondsworth, England: Methuen.

Vernon, P. E. 1971. *The structure of human abilities.* London: Methuen.

Vygotsky, L. S. 1978. *Mind in society: The development of higher psychological processes.* Cambridge, MA: Harvard University Press.

Wagner, R. K., and R. J. Sternberg. 1985. Practical intelligence in real-world pursuits: The role of tacit knowledge. *Journal of Personality and Social Psychology* 49:436–58.

Wagner, R. K., and R. J. Sternberg. 1987. Executive control in reading comprehension. In *Executive control processes in reading,* ed. B. K. Britton and S. M. Glynn, 1–21. Hillsdale, NJ: Erlbaum.

Wallach, M. A., and N. Kogan. 1965. *Modes of thinking in young children.* New York: Holt, Rinehart, and Winston.

Wechsler, D. 1950. *The measurement of appraisal of adult intelligence.* 4th ed. Baltimore: Williams and Wilkins.

Wissler, C. 1901. The correlation of mental and physical tests. *Psychological Review, Monograph Supplement 3,* no. 6.

Witkin, H. A. 1978. *Cognitive styles in personal and cultural adaptation: The 1977 Heinz Werner lectures.* Worcester, MA: Clark University Press.

Yussen, S. R., and P. T. Kane. 1983. Children's ideas about intellectual ability. In *The child's construction of social inequality,* ed. R. Leahy, 109–33. New York: Academic Press.

Zigler, E., D. Balla, and R. Hodapp. 1984. On the definition and classification of mental retardation. *American Journal of Mental Deficiency* 89:215–30.

Commentary:
Understanding What We Measure and Measuring What We Understand

James W. Pellegrino

INTRODUCTION

This volume has several goals, one of which is to consider some of the ways that contemporary views of intelligence and contemporary research in cognitive science can contribute to new approaches to assessment and instruction. On the positive side, the chapters represent excellent summaries of historical and contemporary issues relating to the uses, functions and limitations of traditional standardized testing procedures. They also provide important insights into new ways of approaching the task of assessment. Unfortunately, I must agree with Shepard (this volume) that the goal of making this information transparent to policy makers has probably not been met. It may well be the case that such a goal is unattainable for various reasons, one of which is the typical "rules" of academic discourse. It is highly likely that the present comments will suffer from the same academic opaqueness. Nonetheless, I will try to focus on some of the key issues facing educational researchers, teachers, test developers and policy makers regarding the whole enterprise of assessment.

I will not present a detailed review of each of the substantive chapters since much of that has already been accomplished in the chapters by O'Connor and Shepard in this volume. Rather, I will attempt to show what information may be needed to proceed further in thinking about problems of assessment and in taking some meaningful action. By meaningful action, I have in mind going beyond verbal statements of intent and hand waving about proposed solutions, to the business of hands-on research and development activities designed to start solving a problem. My intent, like the other authors in this volume, is to present some of the implications of contemporary work in the cognitive sciences for rethinking and resolving long-standing dilemmas within the field of assessment.

What can contemporary research and theory contribute to the process of test development, utilization and interpretation? How can contemporary research and theory enable test users to accomplish their real purposes, i.e. get the best information possible to meet the need for accountability, diagnosis and remediation, program evaluation, and so on? My own belief is that current research affords us the possibility of creating assessment devices that have substantially greater validity (see Pellegrino, 1988). Stated in ordinary language, this means several different things: it means that recent research and theory can give us a clearer picture of what it is that our tests are now measuring. More importantly, they can also give us a better understanding of what it is we really want to measure, and how to measure it.

I will argue that current cognitive theory and research can thus help us solve a central assessment problem: in the past we have often developed tests and assessments without an adequate understanding of the constructs we want to measure. These tests have then become simple stand-ins, substituting for a deeper understanding of a more complex construct. For example, lacking a complete theory of intelligence, tests that purport to measure intelligence become permanent proxies for investigations of individuals' intelligence. Furthermore, such tests come to play a role in defining what we mean by related notions such as "learning disability." I will argue that policy makers have a responsibility to think about issues of test meaning and test interpretation, and need to know how the current research base might be brought to bear on issues in test policy.

Understanding and measuring a construct: some background

Before I go on to talk about this in depth in the next section, I will briefly review a few aspects of assessment that I will rely on in making my argument. The arena of testing and assessment has always faced a number of difficult problems. On the one hand, tests are supposed to meet a variety of statistical criteria, including *reliability* of measurement. This seems reasonable since there is no point in measuring something if the measurement process or device can not be trusted. We would not use a thermometer if it produced widely varying results from one instant to the next when conditions had not ostensibly changed.

While tests are supposed to be reliable, they are also supposed to be *valid*. We would not use a thermometer to measure blood pressure. Probably no aspect of testing has been more debated than the validity issue (see e.g., Wainer & Braun, 1988). Many different forms of validity have been defined, but much of the controversy regarding tests has been focused on the topic of *construct validity*. Simply stated, if a test has construct validity, it means that the test does measure the underlying construct that it purports to measure: for example, a test of general intelligence should in fact be a measure of intelligence rather than something else. This sounds straightforward, but in fact it's very difficult to directly measure any of the traits or constructs we're interested in, from verbal intelligence to mathematics achievement. We must usually design indirect measures.

Thus, construct validity has proven elusive for many reasons, some of which are described below. Instead, tests have often been developed and evaluated in terms of a more practical standard, namely their *criterion* or *predictive validity*. Predictive validity is defined as how well a test administered at time A predicts some subsequent outcome or criterion further down the road at time B. For example, intelligence and scholastic aptitude tests are used for academic selection purposes because they "predict" the likelihood of success in a typical instructional environment.

Intelligence and aptitude tests, as well as achievement tests, are often criticized because they may lack construct validity even though they may have substantial predictive validity: an "aptitude test" may powerfully predict first year grades. But does it really tell us much about a person's aptitude—for example, how to foster it or expand it?

Some may wonder why we should care. If a test works and meets a pragmatic need then why worry about its construct validity? Unfortunately, too much of testing has opted for such an atheoretical, pragmatic approach. There have been a variety of consequences, not the least of which is that (a) tests, not theories of learning, frequently drive the instructional process, often to the detriment of effective instruction and learning, as noted by Resnick & Resnick (this volume), and (b) test information is of little practical assistance to teachers and other individuals involved directly in the instructional process.

So the technical problems of construct validity and predictive validity, which may sound abstract and theoretical, really lead to basic questions that policy makers can and should consider:

(1) Do we understand the traits we want to measure well enough to know how to go about measuring them? If not, how can we get a better understanding of these concepts and constructs?

(2) Since assessments are indirect measures of a trait, what meaning should we assign to the outcome of a test or assessment? What does it tell us about the underlying attribute?

(3) Do we know why we want to measure these things? Different purposes lead to emphasis on different aspects of a construct, and thus different ways of assessing it. Testing for accountability in language arts may lead to a very different picture of reading achievement than testing for diagnosis and instructional management in a particular reading class.

(4) Have we come to see the test as a definition of the attribute itself? For example, when we know a student's SAT score, do we assume that we know as much as we can or need to know about his or her scholastic aptitude?

To create a context for a broader discussion of the points raised above, I will start out by focusing on two "concepts" which are intimately linked to controversies in assessment: *intelligence* and *learning disability*. I have chosen to focus on these for several reasons. First, they are topics that policy makers, schools and the general public must deal with on a regular basis. Second, they very aptly illustrate some of the interpretive issues facing theorists, policy makers and practitioners. Specifically, they show why we should not lose sight of conceptual issues when we are pursuing functional goals. Third, they help focus on the reality that tests, particularly those used for selection and certification, frequently come to define constructs that have substantial policy implications. Fourth, the interpretive dilemma associated with these two constructs can also help us clarify our goals, and thus our policies, regarding educational assessment.

Implicit in the field of assessment itself, as well as in the terms *intelligence* and *learning disabilities*, is the idea of individual variation among learners. What has been problematic, however, is how to conceptualize such normal variation and what to do about it in the educational environment. As pointed out elsewhere in this volume, the goal of accommodating to individual differences led to the development of Binet and Simon's original tests of intelligence. This process of accommodation has never been easy, given the myriad demands of mass schooling. Consequently, we have historically opted for pragmatic solutions. This has led to operational classification, categorization and labeling schemes that frequently occur in the absence of any real understanding of the needs of individual children.

As a result of choosing pragmatic testing solutions in lieu of deeper diagnostic understandings, after 80 years of educational and psychological testing we still lack the understanding necessary to go beyond global, often poorly defined constructs. We are unable to use our assessments of global constructs such as intelligence or achievement to derive detailed representations of individuals' knowledge and cognitive skill. Thus, a primary goal for all parties concerned about issues of assessment should be to consider how contemporary thinking can provide for a richer understanding and analysis of individual differences in cognitive competence. We must also consider why that should be the focus of attention in assessment policy and practice.

There are four parts to this commentary. The first part deals with some of the conceptual and definitional problems surrounding the constructs of intelligence and learning disabilities and helps establish the agenda of interest. The second part then considers what our goals and strategies should be in light of the previously considered conceptual and pragmatic issues. The third part focuses on potential contributions of work in the cognitive sciences and provides an illustrative example drawn from the domain of elementary mathematics. The fourth part is a consideration of some issues in translating theory into practice.

PRETENDING THAT WE UNDERSTAND—
PROBLEMS OF DEFINITION VS. MEASUREMENT

We all recognize that part of the business of scientifically studying human behavior is achieving a balance between defining constructs at some conceptual level while at the same time providing ways of operationalizing those constructs. Operational definitions are essential to test our conceptual theories. However, operational and conceptual definitions need to be constantly evaluated lest they become disconnected, non-sensical and/or tautological. Consider the case of operational and conceptual definitions of intelligence and learning disabilities.

There has long been an implicit, if not explicit, assumption that the concept of intelligence is (or should be) of particular relevance to the concept of learning disabilities. Theory and research on intelligence and intelligence assessment should inform theory, research and policy on learning disabilities and vice versa. This seems a reasonable assumption on the surface, particularly since, historically, intelligence and learning disabilities have been inextricably tied together at the operational assessment level. Unfortunately, illustrating the relationships between *concepts* and *theories* of intelligence and learning disabilities, rather than just their *operational definitions*, remains problematic.

Consider first the conceptual level. It is a fact that people's conceptions of intelligence involve a variety of elements such as facility in reasoning and problem solving, verbal facility, and the ability to learn (e.g., Sternberg's chapter; Sternberg, Conway, Ketron & Bernstein, 1981). At the same time, learning disabilities are conceptually *and* operationally defined as a discrepancy between achievement (or school learning) and measured intelligence (PL 94-142). It seems more than just a bit anomalous to conceptually, operationally, and/or legally define learning disabilities as "a situation of normal intelligence but an inability to learn" when intelligence is, at least partly, conceived of as the ability to learn. The chapter by Brown, Campione, Webber & McGilly very nicely describes some of the additional history and controversy associated with the conceptual and operational linkages between the constructs of intelligence and learning.

There is thus a conflict between (poorly-defined) conceptual constructs such as intelligence and learning disabilities and operational definitions of those constructs. Particularly problematic is the lack of an adequate, agreed-upon conceptual definition of intelligence apart from the standard operational definition that intelligence is "what the tests test". It is this operational definition of intelligence, not the conceptual definition, that has become the central piece in our conceptual/operational definition of learning disabilities. These problems of relating conceptual and operational definitions within and across constructs seem inescapable and yet an awareness of them is central to issues of theory, research and practice in the field of assessment. An awareness of these problems is also central to policy concerns: the operational definitions of intelligence and learning disabilities have pragmatic, policy implications affecting the lives of individual children and the budgets of school districts.

Psychology's failure to conceptually define "intelligence"

This conundrum regarding the concept and definition of learning disabilities can be traced to psychology's general failure to conceptually specify what is meant by the term intelligence. Operational definitions have been developed, but no conceptual definition is uniformly accepted. To understand how we got to where we are now regarding conceptual and operational definitions of intelligence, it is useful to briefly consider some of the historical context. Again, I note that other chapters in this volume such as Sternberg's and Brown et al.'s provide a good discussion of some of the details.

The operational definition of intelligence was partly the product of an "apparent failure" to achieve conceptual consensus at a famous symposium on the nature of intelligence published in 1921 in the *Journal of Educational Psychology*. The 1921 symposium brought together leading theorists and researchers on intelligence and posed to each participant two general questions: (1) What did they conceive intelligence to be, and by what means could it best be measured by group tests? and (2) What were the most crucial next steps in research? Many interesting definitions were offered by individuals such as Thurstone, Terman, Thorndike and others. Unfortunately, most of that theoretical and conceptual discussion was subsequently ignored in favor of the operational definition offered in 1923 by E. G. Boring, namely that intelligence was what the tests test.

Sixty-five years later, in 1986, a similar symposium was published presenting the views of two dozen theorists in response to the same two questions (Sternberg & Detterman, 1986). The respondents represented the gamut from traditional psychometrics (e.g., Anastasi and Eysenck), to cognitive psychology (e.g., Hunt and Estes), to developmental psychology (e.g., Baltes and Zigler), to artificial intelligence (e.g., Schank), to individuals associated with the field of learning disabilities (e.g., Brown, Campione and Das). Just as in 1921, there was no consensus other than the agreement that a unidimensional, one-factor view of intelligence was untenable. Table 1 is a list constructed by Sternberg and Berg (1986) showing the various attributes provided by the 1921 and 1986 theorists and the percent occurrence of each attribute at each point in time. The attributes are ordered by frequency of occurrence within the 1986 sample.

Table 1

Attributes of intelligence mentioned in 1921 and 1986 symposia

	% Mentioned	
	1986	1921
Higher Level Processes	50	57
What is Valued by Culture	29	0
Executive Processes	25	7
Elementary Processes	21	21
Knowledge	21	7
Effective/Successful Responses	21	21
Metacognition	17	7
Process - Knowledge Interaction	17	0
Ability to Learn	17	29
Discrete Abilities	17	7
g	17	14
Not Easily Defined, Not One Construct	17	14
Adaptation to Environment	13	29
Speed of Processing	13	14
Automated Performance	13	0
Capacities Prewired at Birth	13	7
Physiological Mechanisms	8	29
Real World Manifestations	8	0
Restricted to Academic/Cognitive Abilities	8	14

There are some remarkable similarities between the two conferences as well as some interesting differences reflecting changing theoretical orientations. Most theorists in 1986 preferred a multidimensional, non-factorial view emphasizing general and specific knowledge, and cognitive processes applied within varying social contexts to achieve specific goals. The need to consider social context was partially reflected in the distinction between academic and practical intelligence (see also Sternberg's chapter for a discussion of this distinction). Furthermore, there seemed to be discomfort with use of the term intelligence and some agreement that the term may have become dysfunctional. For some theorists there is so much excess baggage associated with the term, mostly as a result of the history of the uses and abuses of tests, that it is sometimes difficult to separate out issues of scientific theory from issues of social justice (see e.g., Gould, 1981).

The results of the 1986 symposium reflect what has generally occurred as contemporary researchers and theorists have tried to grapple with issues concerning the nature and definition of intelligence (see for example, Kail &

Pellegrino, 1985; Resnick, 1976; Sternberg, 1985). There seems to be clear consensus that Boring was very wrong, intelligence is not just "what intelligence tests test". It is much more than the product of responses made to a limited set of items on a test. This consensus is certainly manifest in the chapters in this volume.

The rejection of Boring's conclusion has two major implications. The first implication is that a theory of intelligence must be composed of many elements and, most importantly, it must be grounded in a general theory of the nature of human cognition. This theory of human cognition must be oriented toward cognitive process and content, conceptualized in detail. It cannot be oriented, as past theories have been, toward "factors of intelligence," where factors are derived from correlational patterns found in individual difference data gleaned from performances on tests. (See also the discussion by O'Connor, this volume, on psychometric versus cognitive science views of intelligence.)

The second implication is more subtle, namely that we need not throw out the baby with the bathwater. Current tests of intelligence, aptitude and achievement need not be abandoned; they can provide potentially useful information about an individual's current levels of cognitive functioning. We need to better understand just what is being measured by conventional tests and then use that knowledge to help design better tests that are more useful for instructional decision making (see e.g., Embretson, 1985; Glaser, 1976; Pellegrino, 1988).

The Interpretive Dilemma

If there is no consensus with respect to conceptualizing and defining the nature of human intelligence (or learning, or learning disabilities) then where does that leave individuals such as parents, teachers and principals? There are many who would like to understand what it means to have children who score at or above the 50th percentile on conventional tests of intelligence and aptitude, and yet simultaneously score at the lowest percentile levels on conventional tests of achievement. Yet without independent conceptual and operational definitions of intelligence and learning disabilities, it is not clear what this pattern (or other patterns) might mean. This is what I call the interpretive dilemma.

Maybe we should ask whether we would be any better off in understanding this type of situation if we had better theories and definitions. An interpretive dilemma will always exist unless measures of an individual's cognitive competence are theory based, something that is not currently the case for most tests of either intelligence or academic achievement. Instead, contemporary tests are the product of a technology designed to maximize measurement principles rather than content and construct validity.

Furthermore, even though we have contemporary theories of intelligence, theories that are grounded in other theories of cognition and development (e.g.,

Gardner's theory of multiple intelligences and Sternberg's triarchic theories, this volume), we still have problems in dealing with the interpretive situation described above. Contemporary theories of intelligence are rather general, and only vaguely address the issue of learning disabilities (e.g., Kolligian & Sternberg, 1987; and Spear & Sternberg, 1986). In addition, they have yet to be translated into operational testing procedures. Sternberg's chapter presents an overview of his multifaceted theories of intelligence which serves as the basis for a new test. The translation of his theory into testing practice remains unspecified, however. It will be most interesting to see what happens when the theoretical constructs must be juxtaposed with some of the realities of standardized measurement. Equally problematic is how the information derived from such a test will assist in the design and delivery of instruction for individual children.

I can summarize much of the preceding discussion regarding conceptual and operational definitions in terms of the following set of problems.

    (1) Our current tests of intelligence (the operational domain) are not based in theory (the conceptual domain), i.e., they do not emanate from an explicit theory of intelligence and cognition.

    (2) Our current tests of achievement (the operational domain) are only weakly diagnostic relative to theories of content knowledge and expertise (the conceptual domain).

    (3) Current cognitive theories of general and specific abilities and domain specific knowledge (the conceptual domain) have yet to be translated into practical and prescriptive measurement devices (the operational domain).

WHAT DO WE WANT?—HOW DO WE GET THERE?

At issue is how contemporary cognitive theories and research can allow us to go beyond global concepts such as intelligence, achievement, learning disabilities and global test scores to get to an understanding of an individual's underlying cognitive competence. This is not a new idea, particularly as regards individual variation among learners vis-a-vis the goals of testing and assessment in the schools. "Teachers and schools need information on individuals that is oriented toward instructional decision rather than prediction. Tests in a helping society are not mere indexes which predict that the individual child will adjust to the school or which relieve the school from assisting the student to achieve as much as possible. The test and the instructional decision should be an integral event" (Glaser, 1981, p. 924).

If tests are to be used to devise instruction for the individual, rather than the more traditional emphasis on placing an individual in the appropriate niche in a fixed instructional system, then how should we proceed? One position is that tests should be able "to describe the initial state of the learner in terms of processes involved in achieving competent performance. This would then allow us to influence learning in two ways: (a) to design instructional alternatives that adapt to these processes, and (b) to attempt to improve an individual's competence in these processes so that he is more likely to profit from the instructional resources available" (Glaser, 1976, p. 14).

The sentiments just expressed regarding testing seem to fit squarely with the instructional management and monitoring functions discussed by Resnick & Resnick. They also are highly consistent with the goals of contemporary research on learning disabilities, public policy actions such as PL 94-142, and recent judicial decisions regarding test use. I think that thay are also at the heart of what is being attempted in the work described in this volume by Brown et al., and by Gardner. What all of these efforts seem to be pursuing is a better way of understanding and assessing what individuals do and do not know, and can and cannot do. They are also pursuing an understanding of how to go about adapting to and modifying the cognitive competence of the individual learner.

Pursuit of these goals is independent of the label attached to that learner, i.e., whether he or she is called learning disabled, EMR, gifted, mildly handicapped or normal. To achieve the goals, however, requires the existence of a body of knowledge that can serve as the foundation for Glaser's (1976) psychology of instruction, the elements of a "science of instructional design."

There are four components specified in Glaser's (1976) science of instructional design. These include:

(a) the analysis of competent performance
(b) description of the initial state of the learner
(c) conditions that foster the acquisition of competence
(d) assessment of the effects of instructional implementation.

The *analysis of competent performance* is concerned with a precise analytic description of what is to be learned. This requires detailed task analyses of the content domain as well as empirical and theoretical analyses of the elements of knowledge and skill that distinguish the "expert" from the "novice" within that domain and that characterize the transition from novice to expert. The domain can be reading, elementary mathematics, writing, physics problem solving etc.

The *description of the initial state of the learner* involves a number of features. One such feature is a description of the individual's current domain-specific knowledge. Instruction begins with the initial state of the learner and proceeds from this point toward the development of competent performance. Thus, it is essential that we have specific knowledge of what a given individual knows and does not know at particular points in his or her learning. Another critical aspect of the initial state of the learner is knowledge of general and specific abilities and strategies that can affect how and how readily an individual learns. Some of this is closely related to the dynamic assessment approach described by Brown et al. (this volume).

The third component, *conditions that foster the acquisition of competence*, involves knowledge of procedures that assist learning and optimize instructional outcomes. This knowledge can include the effects of different modes of presenting material, optimal presentation sequences, and processing strategies internal or external to the learner that are beneficial to learning.

Finally, instructional decision making and prescription obviously require *detailed assessment* of the effects of instructional implementation. In contrast to norm referenced assessment, what is needed is criterion referenced assessment. However, the criterion must be specified by a theory of competent performance, and the assessment techniques must be diagnostic relative to that same theory. Again, this is at the heart of the dynamic assessment approach exemplified in the Brown, Campione, Webber and McGilly chapter.

CONTRIBUTIONS FROM COGNITIVE SCIENCE— AN EXAMPLE FROM MATHEMATICS

Along with the other authors in this volume, I believe that contemporary theory and research in the cognitive sciences offer the conceptual and analytic tools for providing the body of knowledge prerequisite to developing a science of instructional design. Within that "science" is a key role for assessment and testing. However, I do not believe that the other chapters in this volume have provided sufficiently concrete examples, drawn from typical instructional content, to convince policy makers or the general public that such knowledge exists and/or how it might be useful for assessment and instruction. The one possible exception is the Brown et al. chapter.

There now exists an extensive body of cognitive science theory and research that is directly relevant to Glaser's four components of a psychology of instruction (see e.g., Glaser, 1978; 1982; 1986). Those interested in analyses of competent performance and the acquisition of competence in areas ranging from reading through mathematics and scientific reasoning should see articles and volumes such as Carpenter, Moser & Romberg (1982), Lesgold & Perfetti (1981), Perfetti (1985), Gentner & Stevens (1983), Samuels (1987), Lesh and Landau (1983), and Shoenfeld (1987).

Much of the work on the analysis of competence also relates very directly to the analysis of the initial state of the learner as regards domain specific knowledge and skill. With respect to the analysis of the initial state of the learner, a great deal of work has also been done on the cognitive analysis of general and specific aptitudes for learning (see e.g., Snow, Federico & Montague, 1980; Sternberg, 1982; 1984; 1986). The general processes of learning, domain-specific learning, and conditions that foster the acquisition of competence have also been the topic of considerable study (see e.g., Anderson, 1981). Finally, issues of theory-based, diagnostic assessment have been considered extensively in recent work such as Embretson (1985), Lidz (1987), and Fredericksen, Lesgold, Glaser and Shafto (1988).

Having sketched out the general character of this work, I will describe in the next section some specific research in a particular area that can support the general points made above. I will now focus on some contemporary theorizing and research from the area of mathematical cognition.

Cognitive science accounts of mathematical cognition

The literature on mathematical cognition and on its development covers a diversity of topics, ranging from geometry problem solving to infant perception of numerosity (e.g., Greeno, 1978; Starkey & Cooper, 1980). I have limited this discussion to current cognitive science accounts of performance on relatively basic aspects of mathematics, those that figure prominently in the early elementary school curriculum. These include single digit addition and subtraction and multicolumn addition and subtraction. The challenge to reader is to think about the relative match between what is now known about basic mathematics and the manner in which testing is currently conducted.

Adult competence in single digit addition For many basic mathematics skills, expertise is necessarily defined in terms of the knowledge, processing activities and performance of adults. Thus, to begin a discussion of cognitive analyses of basic mathematics we need to focus on theories of how adults do mental addition when faced with problems containing addends from 0-9 (e.g., Ashcraft, 1982; 1983; 1985). The theory assumes that adults have two basic types of mathematical knowledge. One type is an interrelated knowledge network containing the basic addition facts. Such knowledge is referred to as declarative knowledge, i.e., knowledge of things that are true or false, such as 2+3=5. The facts stored in this network have different *strengths* which determine how long it takes to activate a piece of information. Thus, if the fact 2+3=5 has greater associative strength than the fact 7+5=12, it will take less time to retrieve (activate) the answer 5 to the first of these two problems.

The theory also assumes the existence of a second type of knowledge, specifically, methods that can be used to derive answers for problems lacking prestored answers, e.g., 14 + 36 vs. 4 + 6. This is referred to as procedural knowledge, i.e., knowledge of "how to" do something. For single digit addition it might include procedures such as counting on from one of the addends an amount equal to the other addend. Adults actually have a variety of procedures for calculating answers, including shortcuts which make use of stored facts. An example is computing the answer to 28+25 by retrieving the sum of 25+25, and then adding 3 to the answer of the first computation, 50.

This theory may seem to be nothing more than a restatement of what is intuitively obvious to any adult. For most of us, the "process" of adding single digit numbers is essentially the automatic retrieval of specific facts from memory. This process is rapid, automatic, effortless, and largely errorfree. What is less obvious is that such a theory of stored knowledge and retrieval processes provides the basis for explaining several phenomena observed in adults' time to produce or verify basic addition facts. One such phenomenon is that adults produce answers very quickly, typically in less than a second (e.g., Ashcraft, 1985; Groen & Parkman, 1972). This can be attributed to the process of activating stored knowledge, a relatively rapid and automatic process, as opposed to computing answers by way of sequential procedures, a relatively slow and controlled process.

A second phenomenon is that the time to produce an answer systematically varies across problems. The slowest responses are for problems with "large" sums such as 9+8, with intermediate times for problems with "medium" sums such as 4+7, and relatively fast response for problems with small sums such as 2+1, 4+4, etc. These problems are relatively homogeneous in time to respond (Ashcraft & Battaglia, 1978; Ashcraft & Stazyk, 1981; Groen & Parkman, 1972). As noted earlier, such differences in retrieval time are attributed to differences in the strength of specific facts. Stronger associations in the knowledge network are faster to activate.

A third phenomenon is that the time to reject a fact such as 4+3=12 is substantially slower than the time for 4+3=10, even though the first "answer" is actually further from the correct answer (Winkelman & Schmidt, 1974). Such effects are attributed to associative confusions between addition and multiplication facts. (See Ashcraft, 1982; 1985 for a more comprehensive summary of basic results in mental addition and multiplication.)

The aforementioned theory of expert solution of simple addition problems relies heavily on the assumption of differential associative strengths across the "basic facts" formed by the digits 0-9. An obvious question is whether this assumption is arbitrary or whether the assumed pattern of strength differences can be related to experiential phenomena. According to the law of frequency, items accrue strength through use and practice. Analyses of problem presentation frequency in children's mathematics texts indicate that those "basic facts" assumed to be stronger in the network actually appear more frequently in the texts (Ashcraft, 1985). Furthermore, analyses of multicolumn addition reveal that the frequency of adding 1,2, or 3 is greater than that of adding 7,8, or 9, consistent with strength patterns in the network.

Children's competence in single digit addition Given that this theory is a plausible account of adult or expert performance, the question of developmental and instructional import concerns the nature of the progression from novice to expert. The acquisition of expertise in addition actually has its roots in the more general domain of number knowledge and quantitative understanding, acquisitions that are strongly tied to children's counting behavior (e.g., Gelman & Gallistel, 1978; Steffe, von Glaserfeld, Richards & Cobb, 1983). Prior to school entry most children have acquired relatively sophisticated counting sequences for the digits 1-20 (Fuson & Hall, 1983; Gelman & Gallistel, 1978).

Children also have a basic understanding of the "semantics" of addition and subtraction in terms of the combining and separating of quantities (e.g., Carpenter, 1985; Resnick, 1982). Their understanding of addition, in concert with their knowledge of counting, permits the solution of addition problems even in the absence of directly stored facts (e.g., Starkey & Gelman, 1982). Substantial evidence now exists that initial knowledge of addition consists of procedures for representing, combining and counting physical entities. Subsequently, addition can be performed as mental counting operations in the absence of physical objects. Such overt and covert operations constitute forms of procedural knowledge and processing that develop prior to and along with declarative knowledge and direct retrieval of addition facts (Fuson, 1982).

Evidence for an addition acquisition sequence of the sort described above is of several types. First, young children with primitive counting skills often cannot solve simple addition problems if the objects representing one of the addends are hidden (Steffe, Thompson & Richards, 1982). Second, children are often observed counting fingers when solving addition problems (Fuson, 1982). Third, the counting procedures used by children transition from counting up to the cardinal value of the first addend and then counting on an amount equal to the second addend, to simply counting on from the first addend (Carpenter, 1985; Fuson, 1982; Houlihan & Ginsburg, 1981). Fourth, the time to do addition problems is closely related to counting rates for young children but not for older children (Ashcraft, Fierman, & Bartolotta, 1984). Fifth, systematic differences in the time to answer problems are consistent with models that minimize the number of counts, i.e., use of a procedure of counting on from the larger addend (Groen & Parkman, 1972; Svenson, 1975). Sixth, even for young children, there are some "facts" that are directly retrieved such as ties and small sums (Groen & Parkman, 1972; Hamann & Ashcraft, 1985; Siegler & Shrager, 1984).

A developmental theory of the acquisition of expertise in addition includes specific assumptions about the state of both declarative and procedural knowledge at different points in time. It includes the assumption that there is a gradual acquisition and strengthening of the network structure of addition facts. There is also a gradual acquisition of counting procedures that permit the calculation of answers when "facts" are not of sufficient strength to be retrieved.

Preschoolers primarily depend on overt counting procedures to solve addition problems (Siegler & Shrager, 1984). Given instruction and practice in the early grades, there is a transition to more sophisticated and efficient counting procedures together with a transition from calculation via counting to direct retrieval. Thus, at any point in time from preschool age through at least fourth grade, a child will have some facts that can be retrieved and some that need to be calculated. From the fourth grade on through adulthood, simple addition problems are solved via retrieval with a continued strengthening of facts in the network resulting in further increases in the speed of retrieving all addition facts (Ashcraft, 1985).

Subtraction This discussion has concentrated on addition but the issues raised about the nature of expertise and its acquisition are equally applicable to simple subtraction problems. One can posit exactly the same type of theory of expertise for subtraction, with a network of stored facts of varying strength and a set of procedures for calculation in the absence of directly retrievable information. It is also reasonable to assume that subtraction facts vary in strength (speed of retrieval) although far less is known about the details of such differences and whether they parallel the results for addition.

With regard to procedural knowledge and the acquisition of expertise, there is ample evidence that preschoolers and children in the early primary grades solve subtraction problems by counting procedures, both overt and covert (Fuson, 1984; Svenson & Hedenborg, 1979; Woods, Resnick & Groen, 1975). Considerable research has been done on the use of different counting procedures to solve subtraction problems and the difficulties children sometimes experience in understanding and using such procedures (Fuson, 1984). One is a decrementing procedure in which the child counts down from the minuend an amount equal to the subtrahend. Another is an incrementing procedure in which the child counts on from the subtrahend until the minuend is reached. These procedures not only differ in ease of use but also in efficiency depending on problem characteristics. A decrementing procedure is more efficient when there is a large difference between the minuend and subtrahend (9 minus 2), while the converse is true for the incrementing procedure (9 minus 7). There is some evidence that older children select the optimal counting procedure given such differences in problem characteristics (Svenson & Hedenborg, 1979; Woods et. al., 1975).

A theory of expertise in subtraction and its acquisition is similar to the theory for addition. Both emphasize the gradual acquisition of declarative knowledge facts. These changes in knowledge and processing occur over a period of several years. The rate of change both within and between individuals will vary with the experiential history and learning rate of each person. Thus, one must consider the possibility that the difficulties in mathematics manifest by some children are partially attributable to problems with basic facts. The facts may be sufficiently weak such they can not be retrieved and must therefore be computed and the counting procedures for doing such computations may be slow and error prone.

Data on basic addition and subtraction performance suggest that children with mathematics difficulties often must compute rather than directly retrieve answers to problems (e.g., Connor, 1983; Russell & Ginsburg, 1984). Connor (1983) has reported results obtained by Fleishner and her colleagues from testing basic facts. Learning disabled students relied more on reconstructive counting strategies than the normal students who tended to rely on direct retrieval. This agrees with the results obtained by Russell & Ginsburg (1984) who compared a group of math disabled fourth graders to normally achieving third and fourth graders. They observed particular difficulties in retrieving addition facts by math disabled students, with the children performing at a level below the normal third graders. Svenson and Broquist (1975) have also reported results indicating that fifth grade children with low mathematics achievement are particularly slow at answering simple addition problems. Although available data are suggestive of difficulties in simple addition and subtraction, considerably more must be done to pursue these issues. The theory of expertise and its acquisition that has been outlined above provides a framework for systematically pursuing issues regarding both the assessment and instruction of basic skills.

Knowledge and performance in basic skills are particularly important when we consider more complex mathematical procedures that require facility in such skills. For example, the normal course of instruction is to progress from single column addition and subtraction problems to multicolumn problems of increasing difficulty. The ultimate objective is knowledge of complex procedures such that the individual can solve any addition or subtraction problem of any length. What do individuals know and do when they are "experts" in multicolumn addition or subtraction? There are now explicit theories of the knowledge underlying such complex skills, with primary attention given to subtraction (e.g., Brown & Burton, 1978; Young & O'Shea, 1981). Part of the emphasis on subtraction is attributable to the difficulties children often have in solving subtraction problems with borrowing, especially "borrowing from zero."

Knowledge of multicolumn subtraction can be conceptualized as a complex procedure with multiple parts, each of which represents a successive complication. The essential parts are (1) processing single columns in a right to left order, (2) borrowing when the bottom digit in a column is greater than the top digit, and (3) borrowing from zero. These three parts correspond to the typical sequence in learning how to subtract. The child first learns how to subtract a single column of numbers where the top number is always greater than the bottom number. Then this is expanded to multiple columns but in problems where borrowing is never needed. The assumption is frequently made that the child subtracts two numbers in a column by retrieving a "fact" from memory such as "7 minus 5 equals 2." However, a child might actually perform the subtraction for single digits by a counting procedure.

The next major stage is to introduce the borrowing part of the procedure. This involves a test to see if the top number is greater than the bottom number in a column. If it is, then borrowing is needed and the sequence of steps is taught. In beginning instruction this usually takes the form of crossing out the top digit in the column to the left, decrementing it by one then writing the new digit in the top of that column. The child then writes a 1 in front of the top digit in the original column and now goes on to do the column subtraction by retrieving a fact such as 17-9=8. Practice in borrowing is provided with a progression to problems with multiple columns which require borrowing.

The final stage of instruction is the procedure for borrowing from zero. The original borrowing procedure is now expanded to include a test for whether the column to the left contains a zero. If a zero is present then a new set of operations must be executed which include changing zero to 9 and moving one column to the left, testing for zero again etc.

The preceding is a superficial description of the overall procedure for doing multicolumn subtraction, its separate subprocedures and the general sequence for acquiring the subprocedures. Adults typically have procedural or "how to" knowledge of subtraction as well as declarative knowledge of the meaning (semantics) of individual actions such as borrowing or borrowing from zero relative to the base ten system. It is not clear, however, whether children comprehend the meaning of the procedures taught to them. Analyses of children's errors in subtraction suggest that they often follow faulty procedures that preserve "syntactic" aspects of subtraction procedures such as crossing things out or writing down a 1 while simultaneously violating the semantics of the procedures (see e.g., Resnick, 1982; 1984).

Expertise can be defined as being able to solve any subtraction problem, which minimally implies knowledge of all the elements of the subtraction procedure. Lower levels of expertise are defined by the probability that errors will occur. Errors in subtraction can imply (a) lapses of attention or memory, what have been termed slips (Norman, 1981), (b) the absence of a procedure or a step in a procedure, or (c) incorrect representation of a procedure or a step in a procedure. If errors are due to lapses of attention or memory failure such as retrieving 2 for 9-6, then there should be no pattern to the errors made by the child. However, if a child is lacking knowledge or has incorrect knowledge of a procedure then systematic error patterns should be observed within a child. To the extent that many children experience similar difficulty in acquiring and/or representing complex procedures, then one would expect to find consistent error patterns across children.

Considerable effort has been expended on analyzing children's errors on subtraction problems (Burton, 1981; Brown & Burton, 1978; Brown & VanLehn, 1980; Friend & Burton, 1981; VanLehn, 1982, 1990; Young & O'Shea, 1981). It is now apparent that errors are not just random, i.e., they cannot be attributed primarily to slips. Instead, errors tend to be systematic and the systematicity can be directly related to one or more of the elements of the major subprocedures of the complete subtraction procedure. As might be suspected, most of the systematic errors involve borrowing in general and borrowing from zero in particular. A common error is "smaller from larger" in which the child subtracts the smaller digit in a column from the larger regardless of which one is on top. This may be due to a child's lack of knowledge about how to borrow, a failure to incorporate a test for borrowing, or a carry over from simple subtraction where the smaller number is always "taken away" from the larger number and position doesn't matter.

Many common errors involve borrowing from zero. An example is changing zero to 9 but failing to decrement the column to the left of zero. A different type of error is borrowing across zero such that the column to the left of the zero is decremented by one but the zero is left unchanged. One final example involving borrowing from zero is to stop the borrowing process at zero. In this case the child correctly adds ten to the column where the top digit is less than the bottom digit but fails to make any change in either the column to the left containing zero or the column to the left of the zero. Another major set of errors involves the process of subtracting from zero within a column. In these cases the child fails to use any borrowing procedure, and instead writes 0 or n for the column 0 minus n. For example, if one column of the subtraction problem was 0 minus 4, the child would write 0, or 4. For a more complete discussion of the most frequently occuring errors in children's subtraction see Brown and Burton (1978), VanLehn (1982, 1990), and Young and O'Shea (1981).

One way to conceptualize the underlying source of these types of errors is in terms of slightly flawed procedural knowledge. The child has represented the procedures for performing subtraction but one or more of the elements is incorrectly represented, i.e., the child has a "bug" in his program for doing subtraction. The term "bug" is taken from computer programming and denotes an algorithm that contains an incorrect operation. A systematic error is produced each time the program is run on the particular class of problems that requires execution of that operation.

An alternative possibility is that the child is actually missing a piece of procedural knowledge, which is similar to a critical operation being omitted from a program. In a computer program, a missing operation will typically cause the program to "crash" and produce no output whatsoever. However, in the case of a child who knows that some response must be made, the child reaches an impass. In order to move on the child attempts to repair that impass by doing something. The something he or she does is an operation that may mimic syntactic but not semantic constraints of subtraction.

Given that children's errors in subtraction reflect slips, bugs, and impasses (VanLehn, 1982; 1990), there are several issues with respect to the applicability of such a theory of knowledge and performance. One issue is a diagnosis of a child's problem. It is a nontrival exercise to develop tests capable of isolating the many different types of procedural bugs and impasses that can occur, often in peculiar interaction, as well as a scoring procedure to do the diagnosis (Burton,

1981). Furthermore, multiple samples of performance are needed to determine if there is a stable pattern of bugs and/or impasses (see VanLehn, 1982). There are, however, some systematic efforts in this direction using instructional materials and computer based tests (VanLehn, 1982).

Other issues involve explaining how the child acquired flawed procedural knowledge, and developing instructional methods that minimize such outcomes. A missing procedure that gives rise to an impass in solution may result from a failure on the part of a student to represent a specific operation. Thus, the child attempts to repair the overall subtraction procedure when an impass is actually reached in solving a problem (Brown & VanLehn, 1980). If these repairs are practiced and fail to receive any corrective feedback they may become permanent bugs. Another possibility is that a child initially misrepresents a procedure and then subsequently practices that flawed procedure, again without corrective feedback.

Thus, bugs can arise from repairs to impasses, i.e., solution attempts for novel problems for which no procedure is represented. They can also arise from incorrect initial representations of correct procedures. In either case, the errors that children produce seem to follow many of the syntactic aspects of subtraction (crossing things out, writing 1 in a column , etc.) while violating some of the semantics of the procedures. Given this state of affairs, attempts have been made to investigate instructional methods that link more closely the semantics and syntax of complex procedures (Resnick, 1982, 1984). The hope is that such methods can minimize the development of flawed procedural knowledge.

It is almost a given that elementary school children experiencing difficulty in mathematics will demonstrate less than expert performance on problems requiring complex procedures. Our concern then turns to whether the errors they make can be understood in terms of the theory of knowledge and performance describe above. One possibility is that such children have all the correct procedures and that errors are due to slips and miscalculations associated with their weak "knowledge" of basic facts. This may be true in some cases (Russell & Ginsburg, 1984). A second possibility is that parts of the procedural knowledge are either missing or flawed, in which case the errors they make would be systematic. If there are systematic errors, then do these children exhibit "bugs" similar to those found in previous research or are their errors more bizarre?

There is little in the way of systematic data to address these questions. Russell & Ginsburg (1984) have reported limited data indicating that math disabled fourth graders have bugs similar to those exhibited by normal, younger children. They offer a hypothesis of "essential cognitive normality" in which math disabled children are at the lower levels of expertise representing the knowledge and performance of younger children. Considerably more needs to be done to explore such a hypothesis as it applies to complex procedural skills.

The theory of knowledge and performance described above provides the context for such an analysis.

TRANSLATING THEORY INTO PRACTICE

What purpose is served by the foregoing consideration of what we have learned about the knowledge and cognitive processing underlying basic mathematics tasks and skills? Hopefully, the preceding will help those outside the research arena understand that even the "simplest" cognitive acts and instructional domains imply complicated forms of knowledge that are slowly acquired through experience and instruction. Furthermore, just as knowledge is not random, neither is performance, especially errorful performance. In fact, some would argue that we can learn far more from mistakes than we do from correct answers.

Unfortunately, test content and test scores entail just the opposite view. For one thing, test items are often far removed from a theory of the knowledge underlying the performance of interest, and thus test scores provide little in the way of information that is directly useful to teachers to guide instructional decision making. In a typical test, the items are sampled from some universe of possibilities and the emphasis is not on the individual problem but the score derived by aggregating over problems. This leads to a situation where the same score can have very different meanings. There is no way of knowing what a score means, since the focus is on the total score rather than the way in which the score was produced.

If the research within cognitive science has told us anything it is that the process by which a response is produced is far more important than the product. The same products can often result from very different thinking processes and testing procedures are frequently insensitive to such differences. Consider, for example, a case where two children have systematic but different misconceptions involving borrowing in multicolumn subtraction. They might well achieve the same score by missing different problems. Even if they miss the same problem the nature of their errors might be different. Typical tests and test scoring procedures do not discriminate among these possibilities because they were not designed to do so nor do they provide any information about the incorrect choices that were made. A similar situation could arise with respect to tests of basic math facts. Tests of basic addition and subtraction facts are usually timed. What matters is the number of correct answers within the time period allotted. What is often ignored is how the number correct relates to the number attempted and the nature of the errors made on those attempted.

In this regard I am reminded of an actual situation that arose when one of my children brought home a test of addition and subtraction basic facts. All of the addition facts were correct but almost all of the subtraction facts were wrong. The note on the paper said that he should memorize his basic math facts. He was clearly distressed because he didn't know what the teacher meant. I examined his test and noticed that for all the subtraction fact answers that were incorrect they were off by 1. This suggested to me that he was not recalling his facts from memory but was using a counting scheme that had a systematic flaw or bug. I sat him down and got him to explain how he arrived at his answers and discovered that he was using a counting down procedure but with an extra count. I showed him how to correct his buggy procedure. He practiced the new one for awhile, and off he went content that he could now get the right answers. It was true that he still didn't "know" his subtraction facts but eventually he would because the counting procedure would yield the right answers and this in turn would give way to retrieval from memory once each of the facts was sufficiently strong to be associatively retrieved.

The point of this little example is that tests and testing procedures need to be brought into correspondence with current theories of the nature of expertise in the domain of interest, and the nature of the acquisition process. It is far less helpful to know that a child misses 70% of all his subtraction facts than it is to know that he understands what subtraction means and how to do it, despite low fluency in fact retrieval.

There is an obvious challenge in translating theories about content knowledge and the acquisition of expertise into acceptable and workable testing procedures. To think that this is an easy task is to seriously underestimate the practical problems of the translation and implementation process. On the one hand, researchers must be willing the expend the time and effort to articulate their theories and assessment procedures in ways that are operationally feasible. Test developers must be willing to adopt new measurement models, scoring and reporting procedures. Educational practicioners must be willing to articulate their needs regarding the instructional monitoring functions they would like to perform and then find ways to incorporate new teaching and assessment technologies into daily classroom practices.

Such a cooperative partnership is what is implied in the research described in several of the chapters in this volume. However, it is obvious that initial efforts of this type, such as those described in the chapters by Gardner and Brown et al., are still a long way from practical classroom application on a wide scale. Nevertheless, it is important that such attempts be made and documented so that a new model of assessment can be developed and nurtured. As pointed out by Resnick & Resnick, the current reality is that tests and the testing process frequently drive the instructional process. It would be far more useful if we could turn this around and have the goals of the instructional process driving the testing agenda with tests serving as an integral component of that process.

Before closing I will restate a critical theme of the Resnick & Resnick chapter. Specifically, policy makers and the general public need to understand that there are numerous purposes, goals and functions of assessment. Often this is overlooked, with the result that the interested parties have no basis for a meaningful exchange of ideas and perspectives. The Resnicks have done an excellent job of highlighting the very different functions of testing. As they point out, "discussions of testing that fail to specify clearly which function is under consideration, or that move from one function to another without clearly signalling the shift, are unlikely to help us reach clear, sensible decisions about testing policy." They specify three general functions: (a) public accountability/program evaluation, (b) student selection and certification, and (c) instructional management and monitoring. These three functions have implications in terms of who wants to know, what information they seek, and what they will do with the answers they obtain.

Much of the preceding has seemingly focused on only one of the assessment functions described by Resnick & Resnick in this volume—instructional management and monitoring. It is reasonable to ask whether developing tests that better meet this function will have any impact on the other two functions of assessment: public accountability/program evaluation and student selection and certification. Since these other two functions are rather distal from the world of the classroom it might be argued that different types of assessment instruments and procedures are needed (or can be used). One form of the argument is that we need (or can get by with) instruments with a coarser grain but wider breadth.

While it may be true that the picture we paint is on a different scale than the picture needed for instructional management and monitoring there is no reason that the instruments developed for a fine-grained analysis of an individual's cognitive competence can not serve the broader function. The issue may be one of how the data are aggregated rather than the data themselves. It seems that we would be on far more defensible grounds if we could always argue that we understand how the meaning of the scores were derived from tests. In other words, if we can start from a position of high construct validity, we will be in a far better position than if we are forced to say that we do not have a clearcut way to interpret the meaning of a given test score. In short, we always want to be in the position of understanding what we measure and measuring what we understand. Doing so requires an adequate theory of what individuals know and how they know it as well as a clearly articulated set of goals for what we expect them to learn.

REFERENCES

Anderson, J.R. (Ed.). (1981). *Coginitive skills and their acquisition.* Hillsdale, NJ: Lawrence Erlbaum Associates.

Ashcraft, M.H. (1982). The development of mental arithmetic: A chronometric approach. *Developmental Review, 2,* 213-236.

Ashcraft, M.H. (1983). *Simulating network retrieval of arithmetic facts* (Report No. 1983/10). Pittsburgh: University of Pittsburgh, Learning Research and Development Center.

Ashcraft, M.H. (1985). *Children's knowledge of simple arithmetic: A developmental model and simulation.* Unpublished manuscript, Cleveland State University.

Ashcraft, M.H. (1987). Children's knowledge of simple arithmetic: A developmental simulation. In J. Bisanz, C. Brainerd, & R. Kail (Eds.), *Formal methods in developmental psychology* (pp. 302-338). New York: Springer-Verlag.

Ashcraft, M.H., & Battaglia, J. (1978). Cognitive arithmetic: Evidence for retrieval and decision processes in mental addition. *Journal of Experimental Psychology: Human Learning and Memory, 4,* 527-538.

Ashcraft, M.H., & Fierman, B.A., & Bartolotta, R. (1984). The production and verification tasks in mental addition: An empirical comparison. *Developmental Review, 4,* 157-170.

Ashcraft, M.H., & Stazyk, E.H. (1981). Mental addition: A test of three verification models. *Menroy & Cognition, 9,* 185-196.

Boring, E.G. (1923). Intelligence as the tests test it. *New Republic,* June, pp. 35-37.

Brown, J.S., & Burton, R.R. (1978). Diagnostic models for procedural bugs in mathematics. *Cognitive Science, 4,* 379-426.

Brown, J.S., & Van Lehn, K. (1980). Repair theory: A generative theory of bugs in procedural skills. *Cognitive Science, 4,* 379-426.

Burton, R.B. (1981). DEBUGGY: Diagnosis of errors in basic mathematical skills. In D.H. Sleeman & J.S. Brown (Eds.), *Intelligent tutoring systems.* London: Academic Press.

Carpenter, T.P. (1985). Learning to add and subtract: An exercise in problem solving. In E.A. Silver (Ed.), *Teaching and learning mathematical problem solving: Multiple research perspectives.* (pp 17-40). Hillsdale, NJ: Lawrence Erlbaum Associates.

Carpenter, T.P., Moser, J.M., & Romberg, T.A. (Eds.). (1982). *Addition and subtraction: A cognitive perspective.* Hillsdale, N.J.: Lawrence Erlbaum Associates.

Connor, F.P. (1983). Improving school instruction for learning disabled children: The Teachers College Institute. *Exceptional Education Quarterly, 4,* 23-44.

Embretson, S.E. (1985). *Test design: Developments in psychology and psychometrics.* New York: Academic Press.

Fredriksen, N., Lesgold, A., Glaser., & Shafton, M. (Eds.). (1988). *Diagnostic monitoring of skill and knowledge.* Hillsdale, NJ: Lawrence Erlbaum Associates.

Friend, J., & Burton, R. (1981). *A teacher's manual of subtraction bugs* (working paper). Palo Alton, CA: Xerox Palo Alto Research Center.

Fuson, K.C. (1982). An analysis of the counting-on procedure in addition. In T.P. Carpenter, J.M. Moser, & T.A. Romberg (Eds.) *Addition and subtraction: A cognitive perspective* (pp. 67-81). Hillsdale, NJ: Lawrence Erlbaum Associates.

Fuson, K.C. (1984). More complexities in subtraction. *Journal for Research in Mathematics Education, 15,* 214-225.

Fuson, K.C., & Hall, J.W. (1983). The acquisition of early number word meanings: A conceptual analysis and review. In H.P. Ginsburg, (Ed.), *The development of mathematical thinking* (pp. 49-107). New York: Academic Press.

Gelman, R., & Gallistel, C.R. (1978). *The child's understanding of number.* Cambridge, MA: Harvard University Press.

Gentner, D., & Stevens, A.L. (Eds.). (1983). *Mental models.* Hillsdale, NJ: Lawrence Erlbaum Associates.

Glaser, R. (1976). Components of a psychology of instruction: Toward a science of design. *Review of Educational Research, 46,* 1-24.

Glaser, R. (Ed.). (1978). *Advances in instructional psychology.* (Vol. 2). Hillsdale, NJ: Lawrence Erlbaum Associates.

Glaser, R. (1981). The future of testing. *American Psychologist, 36,* 923-936.

Glaser, R. (Ed.). (1982). *Advances in instructional psychology.* (Vol. 2). Hillsdale, NJ: Lawrence Erlbaum Associates.

Greeno, J.G. (1978). A study of problem solving. In R. Glaser (Ed.) *Advances in instructional psychology* (Vol. 1) (pp.13-75). Hillsdale, NJ: Lawrence Erlbaum Associates.

Groen, G.J., & Parkman, J.M. (1972). A chronometric analysis of simple addition. *Psychological Review, 79,* 329-343.

Hamann, M.S., & Ashcraft, M.H. (1985). Simple and complex mental addition across development. *Journal of Experimental Child Psychology, 40,* 49-72.

Houlihan, D.M., & Ginsburg, H.G. (1981). The addition methods of first- and second-grade children. *Journal for Research in Mathematics Education, 12,* 95-106.

Kail, R., & Pellegrino, J.W. (1985). *Human Intelligence: Perspectives and prospects.* New York: Freeman.

Kolligian, J., & Sternberg, R.J. (1987). Intelligence, information processing, and specific learning disabilities: A triarchic synthesis. *Journal of Learning Disabilities, 20,* 8-17.

Lesgold, A., & Perfetti, C.A. (Eds.). (1981). *Interactive process in reading.* Hillsdale, NJ: Lawrence Erlbaum Associates.

Lesh, R., & Landau, M. (Eds.). (1983). *Acquisition of mathematics concepts and processes.* New York: Academic Press.

Lidz, D. (Ed.) (1988). *Dynamic assessment: Foundations and fundamentals.* New York: Guilford Press.

Norman, D.A. (1981). Categorization of action slips. *Psychological Review, 88,* 1-15.

Pellegrino, J.W. (1988). Mental models and mental tests. In H. Wainer & H.I. Braun (Eds.), *Test validity* (pp. 49-60). Hillsdale, NJ: Lawrence Erlbaum Associates.

Resnick, L.B. (Ed.). (1976). *The nature of intelligence.* Hillsdale, NJ: Lawrence Erlbaum Associates.

Resnick, L.B. (1984). Beyond error analysis: The role of understanding in elementary school arithmetic. In H.N. Creek (Ed.), *Diagnostic and prescriptive mathematics: Issues, ideas, and insight* (pp. 181-205). Kent, OH: Research Council for Diagnostic and Prescriptive Mathematics.

Russell, R.L., & Ginsburg, H.P. (1984). Cognitive analysis of children's mathematics difficulties. *Cognition and Instruction, 1,* 217-244.

Samuels, S.J. (1987). Information processing abilities and reading. *Journal of Learning Disabilities, 20,* 18-22.

Schoenfeld, A.H. (1985). *Mathematical problem solving.* Orlando, FL: Academic Press.

Siegler, R.S., & Shrager, J. (1984). Strategy choices in addition and subtraction: How do children know what to do? In C. Sophian (Ed.), *Origins of cognitive skills* (pp. 229-293). Hillsdale, NJ: Lawrence Erlbaum Associates.

Snow, R.E., Federico, P.A., & Montague, W.E. (Eds.). (1980). *Aptitude, learning, and instruction. Vol. 1: Cognitive process analyses of aptitude.* Hillsdale, NJ: Lawrence Erlbaum Associates.

Spear, L.C., & Sternberg, R.J. (1986). An information-processing framework for understanding learning disabilities. In S. Ceci (Ed.), *Handbook of cognitive, social, and neuropsychological aspects of learning disabilities* (Vol. 2, pp. 2-30). Hillsdale, NJ: Lawrence Erlbaum Associates.

Starkey, P., & Cooper, R.G. (1980). Perception of numbers by human infants. *Science, 210,* 1033-1035.

Starkey, P., & Gelman, R. (1982). The development of addition and subtraction abilities prior to formal schooling in arithmetic. In T. P. Carpenter, J.M. Moser, & T.A. Romberg (Eds.), *Addition and subtraction: A cognitive perspective* (pp.99-116). Hillsdale, NJ: Lawrence Erlbaum Associates.

Steffe, L.P., von Glaserfeld, E., Richards, J., & Cobb, P. (1983). *Children's counting types: Philosophy, theory, and application.* New York: Praeger Scientific.

Sternberg, R.J. (Ed.). (1982). *Advances in the psychology of human intelligence* (Vol 1). Hillsdale, NJ: Lawrence Erlbaum Associates.

Sternberg, R.J. (Ed.). (1984). *Advances in the psychology of human intelligence* (Vol 2). Hillsdale, NJ: Lawrence Erlbaum Associates.

Sternberg, R.J. (1985). *Beyond IQ: A triachic theory of human intelligence.* New York, Cambridge University Press.

Sternberg, R.J. (1986). *Advances in the psychology of human intelligence* (Vol 3). Hillsdale, NJ: Lawrence Erlbaum Associates.

Sternberg, R.J., & Berg, C.A. (1986). Qualitative integration: Definitions of intelligence: A comparison of the 1921 and 1986 symposia. In R.J. Sternberg & D.K. Detterman (Eds.), *What is intelligence?* (pp. 155-162). Norwood, NJ: Ablex.

Sternberg, R.J., & Conway, B.E., Ketron, J.L. & Bernstein, M. (1981). People's conceptions of intelligence. *Journal of Personality and Social Psychology, 41,* 37-55.

Sternberg, R.J., & Detterman, D.K. (Eds.). (1986). *What is intelligence?* Norwood, NJ: Ablex.

Svenson, O. (1975). Analysis of time required by children for simple additions. *Acta Psychologica, 39,* 289-302.

Svenson, O., & Broquist, S. (1975). Strategies for solving simple addition problems: A comparison of normal and subnormal children. *Scandinavian Journal of Psychology, 16,* 143-151.

Svenson, O., & Hedenborg, M.L. (1979). Strategies used by children when solving simple subtractions. *Acta Psychologica, 43,* 477-489.

Van Lehn, K. (1983). Bugs are not enough: Empirical studies of bugs, impasses and repairs in procedural skills. *Journal of Mathematical Behavior, 3,* 3-71.

Winkelman, H.J., & Schmidt, J. (1974). Associative confusions in mental arithmetic. *Journal of Experimental Psychology, 102,* 734-736.

Woods, S.S., Resnick, L.B., & Groen, G.J. (1975). An experimental test of five models for subtraction. *Journal of Educational Psychology, 67,* 17-21.

Young, R.M., & O'Shea, T. (1981). Errors in children's subtraction. *Cognitive Science, 5,* 153-177.

Commentary:
What Policy Makers Who Mandate Tests Should Know About the New Psychology of Intellectual Ability and Learning

Lorrie A. Shepard

This volume addresses itself to policy makers but is inaccessible to them. These chapters, written by some of the most prominent researchers in contemporary psychology, are long, dense, and complex. Can it be imagined that a state legislator, concerned about highway funding one day and re-election the next, would sit down some evening and digest the contents of this book? Does one imagine, even, that school board members whose purview is focussed on educational issues will read and reread these pages so as to reframe their conceptions of learning and assessment? And why should policy makers want to know about psychological theory or what psychologists think about assessment? Because, many educational policy decisions about categorical programs for handicapped children, compensatory education, grade-to-grade promotion standards, or mandated accountability tests are based implicitly on policy makers' own "theories" about what conditions of education will foster student learning. If they are unaware of new research findings about how children learn, policy makers are apt to rely on their own implicit theories which most probably were shaped by the theories that were current when they themselves attended school. Scientific knowledge about the development of intellectual ability and learning is vastly different today than what was known 40 or 50 years ago. Some things that psychologists can prove today even contradict the popular wisdom of several decades ago. Therefore, if policy makers proceed to implement outmoded theories or tests based on old theories, they might actually subvert their intended goal--of providing a rigorous and high quality education for all students.

The purpose of this commentary is to translate for policy makers the most important findings from the "new psychology" of intelligence and learning, and to summarize the implications of our current knowledge for assessment practices. The commentary is organized into three parts. In the first section are summaries and critiques of each chapter. In the second section consensus views are presented, summarizing across the chapters what cognitive science tells us today about the nature of intelligence and the nature of learning and achievement.

Finally, implications of the new psychology are considered for three assessment applications: classroom assessment, assessment for special placement and tracking, and accountability assessment.

CHAPTER SUMMARIES AND CRITIQUES

Each chapter summary is intended to provide an overview of important ideas and explanations for lay audiences. Because my aim is to arrive at consensus views, presented in the next major section of the commentary, I tend to give uneven treatment to key ideas in this section. Here I elaborate on unique aspects of each author's contribution and discuss my criticism of ideas that are excluded from the later consensus. The most important ideas, which form the basis of the later consensus, are mentioned here but are discussed in greater detail in later sections of the commentary.

The Resnicks' Chapter: Assessing the Thinking Curriculum: New Tools for Educational Reform

Lauren Resnick is an internationally recognized cognitive researcher whose work bridges the worlds of psychology and education. She is a past president of the American Educational Research Association and the founding editor of the journal, Cognition and Instruction. Daniel Resnick is an eminent historian of American education, with particular expertise in the history and social functions of testing. Thus Daniel Resnick broadens the perspective of the volume that is otherwise focused on cognitive psychology.

More than any of the other authors, the Resnicks address themselves to policy makers. Authors of the remaining chapters consider how assessment should be transformed based on current theories of learning and ability, but they are interested in making accurate decisions for individual test takers primarily for instructional purposes. The Resnicks talk directly to policy makers about accountability assessment, i.e., the kinds of tests that policy makers are responsible for. What kinds of measures should be given to groups of students to judge, in the aggregate, the quality of educational programs? They help policy makers see how the character of the mandatory, external assessments they choose will foster or hinder educational reform.

The Resnicks focus on the goal of education which is to teach students to think. Much of current educational practice derives from the mass-education system of the past century which was designed to teach rudimentary basic skills to the majority, reserving higher-order intellectual pursuits for an elite few. Today, educational reformers recognize that the current economic environment demands that all students, not just the elite, be taught to reason, adapt, and solve problems in an ever-changing work environment.

Unfortunately the mass-education system's emphasis on the basics is ill suited to helping students develop the ability to think. The most important contribution in the chapter and in the volume is the insight from contemporary research that all learning involves thinking. It is incorrect to believe, according to old learning theory, that the basics can be taught by rote followed by thinking and reasoning. As documented by the Resnicks, even comprehension of simple texts requires a process of inferring and thinking about what the text means. Children who are drilled on number facts, algorithms, decoding skills, or vocabulary lists without developing a conceptual model or seeing the meaning of what they are doing have a very difficult time retaining information (because all the bits are disconnected) and are unable to apply what they have memorized (because it makes no sense). These ideas from current learning theory are developed further in the consensus section.

Having described the kind of curriculum that must exist to foster thinking, the Resnicks turn to current testing practices which are inimical to the goal of teaching thinking. Key assumptions from out-moded learning theory, which the Resnicks refer to as the decomposability and decontextualization assumptions, are carried forward by present-day tests. Psychological theories of the 1920s assumed that learning of complex competencies could be broken down into constituent skills (into individual stimulus-response bonds) and learned one component at a time. The Resnicks use the metaphor of a machine that is put together after all the component parts have been manufactured. The old theory never specified, however, how the parts were to be assembled into thinking. Similarly according to the decontextualization assumption component skills are generic and do not depend on the context in which they are learned or applied.

One of the most useful and compelling parts of the Resnicks' chapter is their analysis of specific standardized tests in light of contemporary learning theory. The best multiple-choice tests are reading comprehension tests which nonetheless have students reading short passages and searching for right answers at a rate of one-per minute. Multiple-choice questions elicit superficial comprehension rather than deep reflection. (Given the rules of the test-makers art, they certainly never invite students to wrestle with ambiguity.) The nature of the test tasks is much worse in other skill areas, requiring recognition of errors and computational fluency rather than thinking. The character of test questions is particularly worrisome if one begins to ask not just how well the items measure what students know, but how well they serve as templates for instruction. "Children who practice reading mainly in the form in which it appears on the tests--and there is good evidence that this is what happens in many classrooms--would have little exposure to the demands and reasoning possibilities of the thinking curriculum." (p. 46) And again, "Students who practiced mathematics in the form found in the standardized tests would never be exposed to the kind of mathematical thinking sought by all who are concerned with reforming mathematics education..." (p. 47) (see also National Council of Teachers of Mathematics, 1988; National Research Council, 1989).

Next the Resnicks offer an analysis of the different functions of testing as a framework for their subsequent in-depth treatment of accountability assessment. The contrasts between what is needed for instructional tests and for accountability tests are taken up in later sections of the commentary. For example, instructional assessments must be much more frequent than accountability measures but do not require disinterested verification of teacher judgments.

Accountability assessment exerts a potent influence on school curriculum because of the importance attached to publicly reported test results. Tests are not unobtrusive measures like thermometers; they influence how educators behave. Many testing programs have been instituted intentionally to leverage school reform. What the Resnicks' analysis reveals, however, is that "measurement-driven instruction" will lead reform in the wrong direction if tests embody incomplete or low-level learning goals. They deduce three guiding principles for accountability assessments:

1. You get what you assess. "Educators will teach to tests if the tests matter in their own or their students' lives" (p.59).

2. You do not get what you do not assess. "What does not appear on tests tends to disappear from classrooms in time" (p.59).

3. Build assessments toward which you want educators to teach. "Assessments must be designed so that when teachers do the natural thing--that is, prepare their students to perform well--they will exercise the kinds of abilities and develop the kinds of skill and knowledge that are the real goals of educational reform" (p.59).

In the last section of the commentary I elaborate on the Resnicks' recommendations for performance assessments. In essence they have laid out what policy makers should do, in the name of accountability, if they are serious about reforming schools so that all students will be taught to think.

Gardner's Chapter: Assessment in Context: The Alternative to Standardized Testing

Howard Gardner is a famous Harvard psychologist who has popularized the concept of multiple intelligences. His chapter begins with a stark portrayal of the excessive reliance today on formal testing. Current testing practices derive both from out-moded theories about human capacities and the cult of efficiency in U.S. society. Gardner then offers explicitly a summary of contemporary scientific knowledge that should serve more appropriately as the basis for new approaches to assessment. Key points, especially the variety of intelligences and the influence of context, are discussed in a later section of this chapter regarding the nature of intelligence.

The spirit of Gardner's recommendations for alternative assessments is captured by his envisioning of an apprenticeship model. The novice should be evaluated from the all-knowing, teaching perspective of the master rather than by a remote and decontextualized test. New approaches to assessment should be a natural part of the learning environment and should preserve "ecological validity." Assessments should tap the full range of intelligences, using multiple measures. Assessors should be responsive to individual differences and use materials that are intrinsically interesting and motivating. The purpose of assessment should be to help individual students.

Gardner then goes on to describe in considerable detail two assessment projects based on these principles. The first is a preschool program with activities designed to measure a broad array of cognitive strengths as well as children's styles in approaching various tasks. The second is a secondary school arts project intended to assess intellectual competence in creative writing, graphic arts, and musical performance. The final portion of the chapter is devoted to Gardner's conception of the ideal school which would feature assessment specialists, student-curriculum brokers, and school-community brokers.

In my opinion, the details of Gardner's assessment examples provide two powerful insights: 1. It is possible, although exceedingly difficult, to implement complex, broad, performance-based assessments in real learning environments. (I return to Gardner's development of domain-projects and process-folios of students' work later, in the context of discussing "authentic" assessments for educational accountability.) 2. It is impossible to assess aptitudes for as yet undeveloped intelligences without providing instruction. Thus, Gardner and his associates found they could not maintain a distinction between developing assessment and developing curriculum. In the preschool setting, "our approach has been to expose students to rich experiences in the particular domain of interest and to observe the way in which they become engaged in that domain. The ensuing record provides a powerful indication of how much talent or potential such students exhibit in the domain of interest" (p.96). In the arts project, students are provided with instruction and exercises. Assessment of students' talent is based as much on progress in response to instruction as on the technical quality of finished products. These examples, where students do not have to have had enriched prior experiences to fare well on the assessments, are more compelling to the reader than merely asserting the conclusion of contemporary psychology that "IQ is developed." Furthermore, they convey concretely how extensive efforts must be really to provide opportunities to develop an array of aptitudes.

Having praised Gardner's insight, I nonetheless have the following criticisms of his chapter: 1. He is too quick to turn brilliant and promising research into practice, without validity evidence and without an appreciation of negative side-effects in real school contexts. 2. Gardner's very broad conception of intelligence unwittingly preserves a very narrow and elite view of the two academic intelligences. 3. His ideal school with separate assessment and curriculum specialists recreates all the mistakes of Special Education, especially it errs by separating assessment from instruction and disempowering teachers. In the following paragraphs I explain these points briefly.

Gardner himself mentions the potential risk of early labelling. Nonetheless he is willing to send preschool profiles home to parents with the caveat that a child's strengths and weaknesses may not be stable over time. Gardner's assessment exercises are highly experimental. He does not know whether they are reliable or predictive of adult profiles. He has not examined whether children's apparent talents and interests are "real" (i.e., hold true across all of the tasks in a given domain) or depend on idiosyncratic features of selected activities. It is not known whether the game-like activities are differentially attractive to children because of race or gender stereotypes. The effect of training strengths or of training weaknesses following assessment has not been investigated systematically. Given a history where lay persons are likely to over-interpret "scientifically" derived test scores, and a climate where "yuppie parents" may well feel compelled to instruct their child's strengths or weaknesses, it seems irresponsible to release the results of preschoolers' profiles. The entire history of intelligence testing, which Gardner recounts derisively, might have been different if researchers making the first tentative efforts to understand human intelligence had not been so eager to turn their fallible measuring devices into practical applications like army selection and school placement tests.

A fundamental question regarding Gardner's work is the appropriateness and timing of specialization. If a child has potential talent to be a dancer, at what time should development of "bodily-kinesthetic intelligence" be at the expense of the other intelligences? Because Gardner's contribution has been to focus on talents missed by traditional schools and tests, he tends to ignore the possibility explained by the Resnicks that academic intelligences have been underdeveloped by opportunities in schools, especially for some groups of students. Consider the following statements:

In truth, I do not worry about those students who are excellent in linguistic and logical pursuits. They will likely find their rewards within the school, in standard gifted programs, or in special advanced sections or honors group. The educational challenge is to provide correlative kinds of opportunities for students who have cognitive and personal strengths which, however, are not well addressed by the standard curriculum in school (p.111).

I believe that, especially when resources are scarce, every individual ought to have the opportunity to show his or her strength. There is no objection to a "high scorer" being able to show off his string of 800s to a college admissions staff; by the same token, individuals with other cognitive or stylistic strengths ought to have their day as well (p.114).

Although Gardner's own analysis can be used to argue that there are individuals with potential strengths in linguistic and logical-mathematical intelligences who do not do well on decontextualized tests or in school, he proceeds as if individuals with strengths in these areas were well assessed and well served. In contrast to the Resnicks who propose more rigorous academic opportunities for all students, there is the dangerous inclination in Gardner's work to give up on those who are not already accomplished academically and focus on "vocational training" (albeit of an intellectual sort).

Gardner's ideal for the future is an individual-centered school that would differentiate instruction according to individual assessed strengths and weaknesses. While Gardner's motive is to develop talents that have hitherto been ignored, there is reason to fear, given a realistic understanding of the sociology of schools, that these ideas could foster tracking and denial of opportunities. Curiously, the extent of differentiation among students that Gardner has in mind causes him to propose separate assessment specialists and curriculum brokers as well, leaving teachers free to teach subject matter. He thus abandons his own apprenticeship model where the master-teacher knows intimately the development and learning style of the apprentice. His own assessment projects suggest that the observer learns more from interacting with students than can be summarized in a set of scores, yet he proposes to separate the roles of teacher and assessor (presumably because students will be tracked into such different curricula that they cannot be served by a common set of teachers). Special Education is replete with examples of what happens when valid clinical assessment procedures are institutionalized and bureaucratized. Not only are the resulting student placements often inaccurate by scientific criteria, but costly assessment procedures are reported by teachers to serve no instructional purpose except to justify placement (Shepard, 1983). Gardner's school of the future is hypothetical, based on many idealized assumptions, including the assumptions that a huge cadre of highly trained assessors would be available, that assessments would be sufficiently accurate not to risk misclassifying students on the basis of past opportunities, and that teachers and assessors would always act in the best interests of students rather than the efficiency of the school. If one is imagining an ideal, however, why not imagine teachers with the training of Gardner's assessors and a system of instruction that is so effective in developing all the intelligences in all individuals that there is no need to differentiate for specialization until very late in individuals' school careers?

Brown, Campione, Webber, and McGilly's Chapter: Interactive Learning Environments: A New Look at Assessment and Instruction

Ann Brown and Joseph Campione are two of the most eminent cognitive researchers in the United States today. Although perhaps unknown to policy makers, they and their colleagues are highly esteemed in the academic world for

their exhaustive research on the development of intelligent thought processes--
e.g., how learning, remembering, and understanding occur. Unlike most
laboratory scientists, they have managed to make significant contributions to
both psychological theory and educational practice. For example, based on what
is known about how higher-order thinking processes are developed, Palincsar and
Brown (1984) were able to improve remarkably the reading comprehension
strategies of poor junior-high-school readers who had not been helped up to that
time by years of remedial instruction.

Brown, Campione, Webber, and McGilly's chapter is the individual
assessment companion to the Resnicks' accountability assessment chapter. The
two chapters share a common view of learning and the type of instructional
environment essential to teaching children to think. What Brown et al. provide is
a detailed picture of the kinds of instructional efforts that could ensue in
classrooms if teachers had to answer to the Resnicks' kind of accountability
measures rather than to standardized tests. Brown et al. are interested in
developing dynamic assessment techniques, closely tied to instruction, that
would help a teacher see how a student is learning and what new understandings
and insights are just next within the student's reach. As can be seen in the
structure of the chapter, the chronology of their work has two distinct phases.
Early on, Brown and Campione were interested in assessment procedures that
would permit a more accurate determination of learning potential. Insights from
these studies have moved them more and more to focus on instructional methods
that actually change children's ability to learn.

Brown et al. begin with a history of the concept of intelligence. There is
no better way to see the import of current research understandings than to
contrast them with old beliefs. In the past, IQ was seen as a highly stable and
generalized trait. This view made it reasonable to believe that static, one-time
tests could locate students accurately on a continuum of teachability.
Accordingly tests were used to make permanent placement and selection
decisions, in keeping with the student's relative standing, rather than attempting
to disrupt or alter the student's existing capacity to learn. Problems that persist
today in tracking and labelling students can be linked back to traditional theories
of intelligence.

Next Brown et al. summarize the seminal theories of Vygotsky and
Feuerstein--in a way very helpful to the uninitiated reader. Both theorists saw
intellectual abilities as malleable and explained the development of cognitive
processes in terms of highly interactive, social experiences. Both were clinicians
dealing with individuals from severely deprived learning environments, Vygotsky
with children raised after the dislocation of the Russian Revolution, and
Feuerstein with refugees from World War II. If individuals have had markedly
limited opportunities to learn, it is clearly not possible to assess from what they
know what their capacity to learn might be. Therefore, both Vygotsky and
Feuerstein, like Brown and Campione after them, developed assessment

techniques based on focused intervention so that they could learn something from how students responded to instruction. If static assessment is inaccurate, better to draw conclusions about capacity to benefit from instruction by staging real instructional experiments. It is impossible to distinguish whether each of these theories is a developmental theory, an assessment model, or an instructional paradigm--all are entwined. If the reader has never heard of Vygotsky, this portion of the Brown et al. chapter deserves careful attention. Presently there is an enormous resurgent interest in Vygotskian theory--focused on the social construction of meaning--affecting research and reform in every curricular area from reading comprehension to science concepts.

Guided assessment is the term Brown et al. use to refer to techniques based on observing students in the process of learning. The most lengthy section of the chapter is devoted first to describing a taxonomy of approaches to guided assessment followed by a review of the major programs of research and clinical intervention programs. All but the most diligent students and scholars will be tempted to skip this section. However, it is worthwhile for the reader to pick any one of the research programs and follow the arguments and evidence presented in detail. Understanding the kinds of investigations undertaken and their extent helps one to appreciate that assertions about helping students to "learn to learn" are not mere rhetoric. Evidence to support what Brown et al. call the corrigibility of intelligence is substantial. Furthermore, when guided assessment approaches are compared to traditional measures, it is demonstrated repeatedly , as often claimed by political groups, that traditional measures dramatically underestimate the learning potential of some children.

The authors' own version of guided assessment, called "dynamic assessment," is based on Vygotskian theory. The assessment-teaching effort begins with a pretest of what the child already knows. The assessor-teacher has to judge where the child is ready to begin. Then the child and teacher work cooperatively with the teacher providing increasingly more specific hints until the child learns to solve the assessment problems of a certain type independently. (Measurement of the child's ability is based on the number and specificity of hints required.) The process continues with the teacher providing support and hints to aid transfer of the student's learning to more and more different problem types. Thus children learn in the course of being assessed. After their initial studies aimed at assessing-teaching general inductive reasoning skills, Brown and her colleagues directed their efforts toward assessing thinking skills in subject-matter contexts. They did this to ensure that assessment would contribute directly to the instructional process.

The great promise of dynamic assessment poses a considerable practical dilemma, however. Because the procedures require labor-intensive protocols administered by well-trained assessors, the demands of the program seem to be nothing less than full-time one-on-one tutoring by expert teachers. At different points in their discussion, Brown et al. consider three possible resolutions to the dilemma: assess only children with seriously learning difficulties (the Special Education model), develop intelligent computer programs to conduct the assessments, or develop instructional programs where the assessment steps are implicit.

Along with many other cognitive psychologists, Brown et al. see the computer as a means to help teachers with the impossible logistical demands of individual diagnostic assessment. If it were possible to develop a formal model of expert understanding of a subject area and to model developmental stages as well as typical missteps in acquiring mastery, then the computer could be used to conduct dynamic assessments, providing hints and giving instantaneous feedback. Examples of such intelligent tutors have already been tried out in very circumscribed instructional domains; for example, Brown et al. use the example of teaching place value. Perhaps these endeavors hold promise for the distant future. However, the cognitive mapping of most subject matter areas is still too primative to lend itself to computerized teaching. Furthermore, even in the future, it remains to be seen whether the efficiency and immediacy of computerized tutoring can substitute for the social aspects of meaning-making that students gain when they interact with teachers and peers. Reliance on computers is the only part of Brown et al.'s brave-new-world image of the future that I find disquieting. The branch in their work toward computers seems not to have preserved the integrity of Vygotskian social-constructivism as well as the path toward instructional paradigms, which we consider next. In any case, an appropriate way to evaluated the effectiveness of computerized assessments would be to compare their cost against an equal investment spent to train teachers to think about student thinking.

In the penultimate section of the chapter, Brown et al. make the shift from interactive assessment (of learning potential) to instruction. Although Brown and her colleagues embark on this course so as to integrate assessment and instruction, the reader will note that the transformation in their work in really more profound that this. As they undertake real and extensive instructional programs, assessment disappears. The Reciprocal Teaching model provides a format for instruction so that students will have extensive guided practice with the kinds of thinking skills that are most valued. In the case of reading comprehension, students are trained explicitly to use strategies of questioning, summarizing, clarifying, and predicting, when discussing the meaning of a text they have read with their peers. In mathematics, students are explicitly taught the strategies of problem identification, assembling relevant information, problem representation and problem solving, and checking. The instructional programs that Brown et al. describe share several features derived from cognitive-constructivist research. In each application, the reasoning skills that are taught explicitly are those that good students tend to develop implicitly. The instructional activities are interactive and egalitarian providing for social, co-construction of meaning. And, in keeping with the Resnicks' and Gardner's arguments against decontextualized skill development, their teaching activities preserve the integrity of the target task by handling component skills in the context of larger tasks. Their instructional programs are aimed at developing higher-order thinking in subject matter domains because reasoning ability depends on domain-specific knowledge and because it is indefensible to divert so much instructional time unless the content is useful.

In the end, Brown et al. give very little advice to policy makers because their interest is the assessment and guided instruction of individual learners. Stated or unstated, however, the insights in their chapter have tremendous policy implications. First, it should be clear that the kind of <u>assessment</u> that will genuinely improve student learning and thinking cannot be conducted from the statehouse. Second, large-scale implementation of the kind of <u>instruction</u> that Brown et al. have described would make it increasingly unnecessary to select and assign students to a separate place for special education or remedial help.

Sternberg's Chapter:
CAT: A Program for Comprehensive Abilities Testing

Robert Sternberg is a Yale psychologist famous for his research on intelligence. As can be seen from his reference list, he has conducted empirical studies on components of intelligence, but he is best known for his efforts to produce a grand, synthesizing framework to conceptualize all aspects of mental ability.

In the first part of his chapter, Sternberg recapitulates the history of conflicting views of intelligence, and presents his integrative theory--called the triarchic theory because of its tripartite structure. In addition to <u>internal</u> mental processes, such as knowledge-acquisition components and the ability to monitor one's own problem solving efforts, Sternberg's theory acknowledges the effects of <u>prior experience</u> and <u>contextual demands</u> on an individual's manifest intelligence.

Sternberg's triarchic theory exemplifies contemporary psychological thought about the nature of intelligence. Especially, he explains that intelligence is multidimensional (thus, individuals are likely to have very different profiles of strengths and weaknesses) and hierarchical (higher-order processes direct the use of lower-order processes). Mental ability is also developed, rather than fixed, and the use of intelligence is dependent on context. It is these themes in Sternberg's work that I rely on to develop the consensus view of ability in the discussion that follows.

After the triarchic theory, Sternberg's chapter becomes problematic. He offers a new test to measure intellectual abilities and a new theory about intellectual styles. While these contributions are inventive and likely to lead appropriately to a further broadening of our understandings of intelligence if used for research purposes, they are too avante guarde and speculative to be relied on in practice.

The Sternberg Multidimensional Abilities Test is based on the triarchic theory. It is necessarily, however, a limited approximation of the theoretically ideal assessment. The available empirical data in support of the test (p.236) are "favorable" but wholly inadequate if this test were being proposed as a substitute for the WISC-R in Special Education placements. Is the new test intended to select children for special programs? Or are classroom teachers supposed to assess and then train mental abilities? Sternberg is annoyingly vague about the purpose of the test except to say that it "will be suitable for students in Kindergarten through college, as well as adults," and that it is a group test to be administered in two class periods. Yet, test validity depends on the intended use. In later sections on assessment for special placements and for classroom instruction, I consider the type of evidence that would be required to support the use of a test for these purposes.

Intellectual style is proposed as an attribute independent of one's level of intelligence but which determines how intelligence is applied. For example, a scientist and a doctor might be equally bright, but one likes to solve novel problems and the other does not. Sternberg uses a governmental model to describe various styles. The scientist has a legislative style and likes to construct things and make rules, whereas the doctor has an executive style and likes to implement and follow rules. Similarly, styles can be distinguished as global or local, monarchic, hierarchic, oligarchic, or anarchic, and so forth. When all of the dimensions of the model are considered, one individual could be said to have a judicial, oligarchic, global, external, and conservative style of self-government. ("Bob" is at least correct when he portrays himself as one who likes to build systems.)

The governmental model of intellectual styles is an interesting metaphor. Although Sternberg posits style as if it were distinct from personality, the most useful aspect of the exposition is that it illustrates how intelligent behavior is mediated by personality. Whether this theory has something to offer apart from traditional theories of personality remains to be seen. This avenue of Sternberg's work does not have immediate implications for practice except to alert us to the danger that traditional assessments of ability might be biased toward one style, thereby underestimating the intelligence of individuals governed by other styles.

Lastly Sternberg considers the extent to which intelligence is socio-culturally defined. This is a key idea, essential to an understanding of how current scientific views have changed compared to historic theories of intelligence. The social construction of intelligence is considered further in the section on ability. Sternberg's explication of these issues has some troublesome features, however. First, he creates a false dichotomy between objective intelligence, which refers to the mental structures set by nature, and subjective, socially-defined perceptions of intelligence. Philosophers of science reject the positivist notion that there is such an objective, discernible truth independent of the scientist's subjective framework, constructs, and choice of instruments.

Earlier, Sternberg himself acknowledged that an attempt to assess intelligence from the perspective of the triarchic theory could not be made culture-free. In the main, Sternberg fails to draw the connections between his discussion of cultural definitions of intelligence in the last section and his earlier contextual subtheory; thus he allows for the influence of culture on the judgment of intelligence but not on its development.

CONSENSUS VIEWS: THE NEW PSYCHOLOGY OF INTELLECTUAL ABILITY AND LEARNING

In this section, consensus conclusions derived from the contributions in this volume and from cognitive psychology more generally are presented as summary statements followed by brief explanatory discussions. The stipulative summaries describe first the nature of intelligence and then the nature of learning and achievement according to contemporary psychological theory.

The Nature of Intelligence

Intelligence is not an inborn, permanent lump in each person's head. Intellectual ability can be developed to a great extent by opportunities to learn and think. The nature-nurture controversy has been prominent in public debates about intelligence for 20 years. Most educated individuals believe that intelligence is influenced by both heredity and environment. Nevertheless, lay conceptions of intelligence have not kept up with findings from developmental and cognitive psychology about the extent to which thinking ability is learned. Laymen tend to credit environment for the amount of school-relevant information an individual has been exposed to and for attitudinal differences caused by one child's family valuing education while another's does not. But lay views generally do not acknowledge that the mechanisms of intelligent thought are actually created as children are guided through their interactions with the environment by adults who model and explain things to them.

This is not to say that the authors in this volume dispute a genetic contribution to manifest intelligence. Rather, they deny that differences among individuals as presently observed are largely attributable to genetics and are therefore unalterable. The best example of the practical significance of this claim is offered by Brown et al.'s citation of Budoff's (1974) efforts to test the instructability of intelligence. As might be predicted by prior differences in opportunities to learn, Budoff found that among Educable Mentally Retarded subjects lower-class children were more likely to gain from instruction on concept-learning tasks than were middle-class children. Thus we make a mistake if we conclude that children who have not learned cannot learn.

In practice individuals who do not fully appreciate that children can learn to learn, are more willing than is warranted to assign individuals to different opportunity tracks, like special education classes for the mildly handicapped or average instead of gifted programs, on the basis of what Brown et al. call "static" measures of ability. We have also found that school board members and educators may be willing to act on nativist beliefs regarding cognitive abilities when the policy decision appears in a guise different from IQ testing (Shepard & Smith, 1985; Smith & Shepard, 1988). For example, an estimated 20% of school districts nationally use some kind of "readiness" measure to determine which children may enter kindergarten or first grade. An environmental perspective would suggest that children who score poorly should be in school to have access to learning opportunities that will develop language and learning concepts, whereas the nativist position supporting these policies argues that biological readiness cannot be hurried and therefore low scoring children are better off waiting a year to allow these abilities to emerge spontaneously. Because the tests associated with readiness policies are not called ability tests, decision makers may not even realize that what they have learned about the heritability of "intelligence" is pertinent.

Intelligent thought involves "metacognition" or self monitoring of learning and thinking processes. If policy makers wanted to learn one piece of scientific jargon that best summarizes the contribution of cognitive psychology to today's understanding of intelligence, they would learn the term "metacognition." Whereas earlier generations of psychologists had treated internal brain processes as if they were unknowable black-box mechanisms, the goal of cognitive science has been to examine and model these internal processes. What they have learned is that intelligence is a set of hierarchically organized mental activities that enable the individual not only to solve problems but to monitor and direct problem solving.

Metacognition is the general term referring to the next level of thinking, or thinking about thinking, which includes a variety of self-awareness processes. Intelligent though involves these higher-order processes identified by Brown et al. as "the ability to allocate one's mental efforts efficiently, to plan, monitor, oversee, orchestrate and control one's own learning." Sternberg is talking about the same sorts of things with the metacomponents and knowledge-acquisition components in his internal subtheory. Sternberg called his metacomponents of intelligence "executive processes" which include: (a) recognizing the existence of a problem, (b) deciding upon the nature of the problem, (c) selecting a set of lower-order processes to solve the problem, (d) selecting a strategy to combine these components, (e) selecting a mental representation of the problem, (f) allocating one's mental resources, (g)monitoring one's problem solving as it is happening, and (h) evaluating problem solving after it is done.

In practical terms, metacognition is important because it is the development of metacognitive abilities, rather than lower-order skills, that is more likely to make an individual more intelligent. When cognitive psychologists say that intelligence is developed, they mean most significantly that these learning-to-learn processes are acquired through experience. Furthermore, when an individual fails to learn these abilities "naturally" through their own powers of reflection, they can be instructed explicitly. For example, Brown has been able to teach children how to comprehend better and Sternberg has trained adults how to learn vocabulary in natural-language contexts.

Intelligence is socially and culturally constructed. The more scientists learn about the mental mechanism we call intelligence, the less sense it makes to think of them as content-free processes. Intelligence is socially developed in the same way that language, gestures, interpersonal behaviors, manners, tastes, etc., are shaped by a child's interactions with family and community. According to Sternberg, the mental process that constitute intelligence may be the same across cultures but their instantiations will be radically different in different contexts. Culturally determined conceptions of intelligence not only govern want is valued in a society but actually shape the development of different mental abilities, as in the example cited by Sternberg where aboriginal children have more highly developed spatial memory strategies than do Anglo-Australian children who rely on verbal strategies for the same memory tasks.

This insight from cognitive psychology--that metacognitive processes are developed by one's culture in the same way that language structures and concepts are developed--has profound implications not only for the assessment of intelligence but for the provision of learning opportunities to children with different cultural experiences. This research changes the meaning of terms like "culturally deprived" and "culturally disadvantaged." Feuerstein's work, cited in the Brown et al. chapter, allows for the possibility that children could be culturally deprived if their interactions with adults are so limited that they are never socialized into their own culture. Except for extreme cases however of parent absence or apathy, it is not true to say that poor and minority children in the United States do not have a culture or that they have not developed intelligent thought processes according to the constructs of their culture. These children are not culturally deprived or disadvantaged, they are culturally different. The insights offered by cognitive psychology jibe with those of numerous sociological studies which suggest that children of diverse cultural backgrounds do poorly in American schools not because they have no culture but because of the mismatch between their frame of reference and that of the dominant culture. If teachers could engage students in learning in ways more compatible with their own cultural patterns, fewer students would appear to be unable to learn.

Although Sternberg discusses Shirley Brice Heath's work extensively to illustrate the influence of community modes of discourse and learning on the development of thought processes, even he does not see the full implications of Heath's findings. In recounting Heath's descriptions of child rearing practices in a black working-class community she called Trackton, Sternberg emphasizes the lack of academic preparation of these children rather than their competence within their own culture. The tone of Sternberg's rendition preserves the idea that children from lower socio-economic circumstances come from deficient cultures. He does not suggest how they can use their community-specific intelligence to learn in school or even whether he thinks this is possible. A more careful reading of Heath's original work (Heath, 1982), reveals that many of the school language expectations that put poor black children at a disadvantage are arbitrary, determined by the pattern of discourse familiar in middle-class homes, and not fundamental to legitimate academic goals. For example, Heath documents how pervasive the use of questions is in classroom language routines. Often white middle-class teachers address questions to children even when they mean to make a declarative statement. They also require children to demonstrate comprehension by asking them to name discrete objects removed from their natural context whereas Trackton children would be more comfortable retelling about things in a story context. Ironically requiring children to enumerate things, rather than relating meaning and connecting meaning to their own experiences, is not consistent with sound learning theory for any children and needlessly places culturally different children at a disadvantage. When Heath worked with teachers to try to adapt initial instruction to language forms more familiar to Trackton children, they found they could elicit far more energetic talk and lesson participation by asking higher-order "probing question" than by asking for naming of objects. They also found that they could teach children explicitly about the kinds of questions and answers that were expected in school rather than presuming that the children were deficient if they did not come to school already knowing these conventions.

Intelligence is multifaceted. Individuals have not one but several intelligences of different degrees of strength and development. Although psychologist would not all agree on the specific subtypes of intellectual ability, there is much wider agreement that intelligence is indeed differentiated. An individual can be very "smart" in one type of endeavor and quiet dull in another. Even individuals who are regarded as generally very bright show great differences among their own strengths and weaknesses and retarded individuals, except for those who are profoundly disabled, have profiles showing varying degrees of competence in different areas. Again, intelligence is not an undifferentiated lump of a certain size that governs the amount of a person's ability for all time and all tasks.

Evidence to support the multidimensional nature of intelligence comes from several lines of inquiry including the componential analyses exemplified by Sternberg's earlier work. Gardner based his conclusions about the existence of multiple intelligences on the fact that normal children are not equally accomplished in all areas and the finding that brain-damaged individuals may lose function in specific areas without harm to their other abilities. Cross-cultural research, demonstrating that different mental abilities are developed to a greater or lesser degree in different cultures, also supports the idea that individuals have different kinds of intelligence not just different amounts of "it". In fact, the argument that intelligence is multifaceted overlaps with the previous point that intelligence is socially constructed, except that additionally individuals within a culture will nonetheless show different patterns of strengths and weaknesses. Although Gardner casts a very broad net, including bodily-kinesthetic thinking and interpersonal knowledge as types of intelligence, the idea of multiple dimensions of thinking ability has important educational consequences even if one focuses only on the more traditional academic abilities of linguistic intelligence, logical-mathematical ability, and spatial reasoning. To the extent that individuals have different patterns of strengths and weaknesses in these areas, they will be helped or hurt by modes of instruction that presume only one approach or one pathway to understanding. For example, statistics is a quantitative subject that draws heavily on one's logical-mathematical ability. However, I have found that graduate students in education and psychology, who tend to be verbal learners, can develop sophisticated conceptual understanding of statistical methods if relations are explained verbally rather than expecting that they are "obvious" from the equations.

Also, in practical terms, the existence of multiple intelligences means that individuals cannot be reliability ranked on a single continuum. Therefore, school placement practices that separate children for differently paced instruction according to one dimension of ability (usually verbal-reading ability) will clearly misassign children according to their other abilities.

The Nature of Learning and Achievement

There is not a neat and tidy distinction between developing intelligence and learning to think about subject matter. To organize this commentary, I have adopted the traditional distinction between intelligence and achievement because these are the terms familiar to laymen. (If one of the learning principles offered in this section is that new learning ought to build on students' background knowledge, then it seems advisable to start with what is known.) A careful reading of these chapters, however, should make it difficult to maintain the separation. The development of metacognitive or self-monitoring processes resembles very closely the critical thinking processes that the Resnicks discuss in the context of subject matter expertise. Is the ability to analyze and comprehend what one reads a sign of intelligence or reading achievement?

Of course, a distinction can still be made at the extremes between general cognitive strategies that could be applied in several learning contexts and domain specific knowledge. But there is considerable overlap between the constructs of intelligence and achievement, when one is talking about conceptual understanding and ability to apply knowledge of subject matter. One pragmatic consequence of the blurred distinction between developed learning ability and higher-order learning of subject matter, is the conclusion arrived at by Brown et al., the Resnicks, and implicitly by Gardner: the development of critical thinking can be accomplished in the context of important substantive topics. There is no reason to digress and practice thinking about puzzles that bear no relation to real experiences. Note that many of Sternberg's ability tasks run contrary to this principle. For purposes of measuring one's ability to cope with novelty it might make sense to pose problems based on counterfactuals. It does not follow, however, that instruction based on these types of tasks would have the desired amount of transfer, i.e., would help the individual become better at solving anything other than this particular type of problem.

By-rote sequential instruction does not foster critical thinking or meaningful learning. To be perfectly clear about how revolutionary and important the findings from current psychological research are to the future of education, it is useful to explain what the "outmoded learning theory" is, how it is carried forward in numerous public policies, and why it does harm to student learning. The Resnicks provide a succinct summary of what scientists believed about learning 50 years ago. The decomposability assumption refers to the idea that learning can be taken apart into its constituent bits and transmitted to the new learner bit by bit. The real spirit of the old theory, sometimes referred to as behaviorist or associationist theory, is captured best by a couple of popular analogies. According to the old view, sometimes called the "bean-jar theory of learning," the student is an empty vessel into which knowledge is poured, one bean at a time. Others prefer the tower of blocks metaphor--learning occurs by stacking blocks of information one on top of the other--because it also implies that there is a prescribed sequence for acquiring bits of knowledge. The old theory made no provision for how insight or conceptual understanding was to take place, nor did it admit that there needed to be any organization in the mind to comprehend or use information.

As illustrated graphically by the Resnicks and Gardner, the old learning theory is enforced in present day practice by standardized tests. If tests administered for accountability purposes exert pressure on classroom teachers, then implicitly day-to-day instruction is governed by the old learning theory underlying tests even if teachers nominally have a more up-to-date understanding of how children learn. Specifically, when teachers drill on facts, use worksheets resembling standardized tests, substitute multiple-choice items over essay tests for their own classroom evaluation, and reduce the amount of time spent on activity-based learning and problem solving, the old learning theory can be said to have driven out good instruction.

In addition, educational policies that determine what should be done when students are doing poorly in school almost invariably enforce implementation of the old theory. For example, the back-to-basics movement not only stresses the importance of basic academic skills but assumes a sequential bit-by-bit learning model. If students have not mastered the basics, such as number facts in mathematics, they cannot go on to conceptual problems. From the vantage point of current research discussed in the next section, we see that children who are behind are then doubly disadvantaged because they are denied any kind of context that would make the number skills more meaningful and easier to learn. Grade-to-grade promotion tests, grade retention, and skill-drill remediation programs are all educational policies premised implicitly on the outmoded theory of learning. Ironically, the sequential, bit-by-bit learning model does the most harm to slow learners because it postpones sometimes indefinitely opportunities for these children to learn things that are intrinsically interesting and connected to their own real-life experiences.

Learning is a constructive process. The learner must build a schema in her own head to understand a body of knowledge. Many people have had the experience of failing to learn the directions to a distant destination if each time they visit it they travel as a passenger; but they learn the directions well as soon as they drive to the destination themselves. Learning is an active process. Rather than passively receiving information (without noting landmarks or changes in direction), the learner must actively make sense of new knowledge and decide how to integrate it with previously held concepts and information. The learner must make meaning. Many metaphors have been used to describe the constructive nature of learning, including the idea that mastery occurs as an individual develops their own conceptual map of a knowledge domain.

The Resnicks make the important point that students must think and interpret even to learn simple reading and math skills, otherwise they perceive only disembodied and nonsensical strings of words and numbers. To comprehend a reading passage, the reader develops a mental image or outline of key points. Good readers ask questions of the text and reread when they don't understand. Children learning mathematics must invent mental models to represent arithmetic operations. If, by dint of extraordinary effort, children only memorize rules without understanding, the "knowledge" is of no use because it can't be retrieved, applied, or generalized. Meaning makes learning easier, because the learner knows where to put things in her mental framework, and meaning makes knowledge useful because likely purposes and applications are already part of the understanding.

Effective instruction helps students to use what they already know to arrive at new understandings. If real learning requires the student to make sense of things, then teachers telling the answers will often fail to produce student learning. Instead, good teachers stage activities that allow students to make connections and gain insight for themselves. This does not mean that students are allowed to wander aimlessly. Instructional opportunities must be carefully guided, to use Brown's term, i.e., tailored to the student's level of readiness and monitored to ensure that learning occurs. Instruction designed to make students do the mental work is often referred to as scaffolded instruction. The teacher provides the external support--not unlike an adult holding out two fingers to support an infant's first steps--until the student can perform the conceptual task independently.

Effective instruction also focuses on making meaning by engaging students in purposeful tasks, eliciting student background knowledge, and teaching students explicitly about learning strategies. If a goal of teaching mathematics is for students to be competent at everyday tasks, like making change or buying the right amount of paint to apply two coats to a 10' by 12' room, then these are the types of experiences that young children should have as the context for learning addition and subtraction facts, the decimal system, and multiplication. Their intuitions about how to solve simple problems should be the basis for eliciting and discussing their mental models; the goal of teaching is to help students extend their conceptual understanding rather than telling them the rules. By explicitly teaching metacognitive activities such as Brown et al.'s strategies of questioning, summarizing, clarifying, and predicting, students receive permission not to know "the answer" immediately and learn that there are intermediate steps to understanding. Without this explicit modeling students who don't "get it" easily are apt to gaze at the ceiling hoping that a ready-made answer will pop into their heads. In essence, if you want students to be able to think when they're finished, teach them to think every day in each school subject.

IMPLICATIONS FOR ASSESSMENT

What's wrong with traditional tests?

All of the authors in this volume have explained the important features of their own work in contrast to traditional test theory, which has been harmful because of its oversimplified and distorted assumptions about human learning. Traditional efforts to measure intelligence have erred by assuming that learning potential could be assessed by static, one-dimensional, culturally neutral instruments. Traditional achievement tests have suffered from the behaviorist notion that learning can be carved up into discrete instructional objectives and from psychometric reliance on a correlational model. According to the latter theory, tests are considered to be adequate measures of a knowledge domain if they are highly correlated with more in-depth assessments of that domain. This is the (concurrent validity) argument used, for example, to substitute short tests for long tests and, many years ago, to substitute multiple-choice tests for essay tests (see Coffman, 1971). Now we see in a different political context that the adequacy of multiple-choice tests as proxies for more in-depth assessments of student learning is seriously in doubt--both because we distrust the accuracy of the data (do the scores really tell us what students know?) and because of the influence of politically important tests in redirecting what is taught.

Policy makers are undoubtedly tired of hearing complaints about standardized tests. Unless one is persuaded about the seriousness of harm that can be done by ill-conceived tests, the criticisms sound like so much whining from educators who don't want to be held accountable. The incessant repetition of what's wrong with testing is useful in two respects: 1) although there is some movement to adopt assessment programs more conducive to student learning, most policies and practices have not changed--suggesting that the insights offered in this volume are not yet widely understood; and 2) measurement specialists and cognitive psychologists alike know better what is wrong with the old tests than precisely how to make the new assessments. Thus the complaints help to clarify the principles that should guide the reform of assessment practices. What is sketched in the following sections, in broad outline, is the character to be aimed for if assessments are shaped by current perspectives on learning potential and learning progress.

Assessments tailored to educational purposes

To translate important discoveries from cognitive psychology into recommendations for assessment requires an understanding of purpose. The Resnicks explain how the features of testing programs must necessarily vary with function. They identify several dimensions of variation: the audience for test results; the extent to which information is needed for individual students; the need for independence from teacher's judgments; how quickly the data must be available; and the level of detail required in the test results. For example, teacher observations of reading performance are the most detailed and most timely way to inform day-to-day instructional decisions but are not trusted as objective evidence for accountability purposes.

Similarly it has also always been the case that psychometric criteria for judging the adequacy of measuring instruments depend on purpose. Two dimensions govern the stringency of technical requirements for reliability and validity evidence. First, is the test to be used to make individual or group decisions? Group data can tolerate less precise measurement because, statistically speaking, group means are stable even when individual scores are not. Second, will test results be used to make crucial decisions, like placing a student in Special Education or a school district in receivership, or not so important decisions, like counseling a student about career options or planning curriculum improvement for the next year? Tests used to make irreversible, important decisions about individual pupils require the greatest degree of technical accuracy. In addition, the type of validity evidence sought depends on the particular use made of the test results. For example, an early childhood measure involving language concepts and gross motor skills might be very useful to kindergarten teachers for planning instruction but invalid for screening children into transitional first grade classrooms because the test is not accurate enough to categorize children as "ready" and "unready" and because the placement itself (the transition grade) does not have validity evidence of effectiveness (Graue & Shepard, 1989). Implications from cognitive learning theory for assessment are therefore considered separately for each of several educational purposes.

Implications for Classroom Assessment

Gardner and Brown et al. talk about assessment intended to assist the individual learner. If we have an image of the teacher guiding the student just as a parent guides a child, to try new things just within his reach of understanding, the teacher has need of constant information both about what the student knows and the strategies being used to process and comprehend new concepts. For purposes of instruction, the ideal assessment instrument is the mind of the teacher so that decisions and correctives can occur "on the fly" as Garner put it. By imbedding diagnostic assessments in instructional activities, teachers can preserve the integrity of assessment tasks (the wholeness of tasks and natural learning context) and protect instructional time that would otherwise be diverted to testing.

Although it is very clear that informal day-to-day assessment is essential to effective teaching, it is also painfully clear that teachers presently do not have the training to carry out assessments of mental processes with the kinds of insights envisioned in this volume. Rather, teachers have been trained in a "follow the book," test-teach-test approach (Calfee & Hiebert, 1988) which identifies missing facts but not specifics about failures in a student's thinking. Nonetheless, it is my position here that there are no viable alternatives except to train teachers better.

There is general agreement that external, packaged tests will not solve the problems of what teachers need to know about student learning. Most external tests such as state-administered criterion-referenced tests or commercially published diagnostic batteries are simply too cumbersome, as well as sharing the conceptual limitations of other multiple-choice tests. Important instructional decisions are made every day. It is simply impossible for formal, uniform tests (where every student in a grade takes the same test) to inform these decisions unless teachers spend as much time testing as teaching. The divisions of assessment purposes made by the Resnicks imply critically important policy choices. Decision makers cannot imagine that they can mandate a single test to serve both accountability and instructional purposes. Any test tells only what students know on the day of the test, and once the data are removed from the context of observation, it tells very little even about how they know what they know. Therefore, accountability tests would be minimally useful to instruction only on the day after testing. Furthermore, if tests are broad enough to cover the full range of what students know, they cannot possibly be detailed enough to be diagnostic about the comprehension of individual students. When the Resnicks discuss the instructional importance of thinking tasks in accountability assessments they are not interested in the data that will be reported back about individual pupils, they are interested in the symbolic importance of assessment tasks in shaping what teachers throughout the system chose to teach their students.

Finally, an important implication for classroom assessments pertains to the choice between teaching thinking in the context of subject matter or teaching thinking with novel cognitive tasks. In the past, Special Education in particular has had some bad experiences when models of internal brain processes were turned into instructional programs intended to fix the brain. Years later research summaries confirmed that training on underlying process tasks improved scores on those tasks but did not transfer improvement to target academic tasks (Arter & Jenkins, 1979). As a result time spent in Special Education training actually diverted time from academic work rather than improving it. Feuerstein specifically used non-school tasks because he wished to avoid topics for which deficient students had already developed a considerable aversion. Obviously, then, there are arguments on both sides. Given the risk that "training abilities" without transfer can divert attention from school topics that are relevant and useful, the burden of proof should rest with those who want to train students with exotic tasks that are unfamiliar and bear no relevance to everyday problem solving. When Brown et al. propose to work with very young students on academic tasks they have the best of both worlds, i.e., to intervene and teach thinking in the context of school subjects before students have had negative experiences with school content.

Implications for Placement and Tracking

The traditional view of intellectual ability as a generalized, fixed trait led to a convenient model for assigning individuals to their permanent place in the educational system. Individuals could be tested and located on a continuum describing their ability to learn and hence the pace at which they should receive standard instruction. Those at the very lowest end of the scale were placed in Special Education, and the next-lowest into low-ability tracks. Those at the top end of the scale were placed in high-ability tracks or gifted and talented programs. This model has never admitted the possibility that instruction could be aimed at developing the capacity to learn nor that an individual's location on the continuum might be inaccurately assessed. Despite three decades of research on the negative effects of tracking, this model still dominates much of educational practice (Oakes, 1985; Slavin, 1987).

On the face of it, the authors in this volume do not address themselves to problems of Special Education diagnosis, or assessment for purposes of remedial instruction or class placement. In fact, however, the evidence they have amassed speaks directly to the matter--leading unequivocally to a rejection of the fixed-ability special-assignment model. First, it should be clear from the extensive research recapitulated in the chapters that traditional, static measurements of learning ability are inaccurate for individuals who have had inadequate opportunities to learn. Second, the instructional treatments given to individuals in Special Education and low ability tracks can be expected to be ineffective because they are based on an outmoded learning theories--that emphasize by-rote learning of skills and that intentionally postpone opportunities to learn to think until after basic skills have been mastered.

Educational researchers and sociologists have for years documented the negative effects of tracking, Special Education placement for mildly handicapped children (Carlberg & Kavale, 1980; Madden & Slavin, 1983), and grade retention (Shepard & Smith, 1989). These separate research literatures have several key features in common. Although each educational "treatment" is intended to improve academic achievement by putting at-risk students in a place where instruction will be aimed more closely to their learning level, controlled studies show that members of each poor achieving group learn more when placed with regular students than when they are separately placed and get a special treatment. Research also consistently finds that each type of special placement carries a negative social stigma and, in each case, that the intended individualized instruction is not accomplished by the special placement.

Insights from cognitive psychology are able to provide a much more concrete explanation as to why at-risk students would consistently learn less from the kinds of basic-skills remediation they typically receive. In the past, sociologists have documented that children in Special Education and low ability tracks are given a "watered-down" curriculum. However, because the public shares with most educators the linear-learning idea that students can't learn "hard" things until they know the basics, policy makers have not been able to see concretely what instructional alternatives exist to the go-slow model. The Resnicks, Gardner, and especially Brown et al. in this volume provide a rich description of the kind of instruction students should receive if we want to improve student learning dramatically. Ironically, in today's schools only gifted children regularly enjoy opportunities to develop thinking skills by working on contextualized problems and extended projects, by having critical thinking and questioning modeled for them, and by trying out and practicing their own reasoning efforts in social settings.

The authors in this volume do not tell how to make special placement assessments more accurately. Instead they offer a view of learning and effective instruction that recommend against special placements for all but the most severely handicapped students.

Policy makers endorse and perpetuate a fixed-ability tracking model of education when they make decisions to require nonpromotion of students who are deficient in basic skills, exclude children from kindergarten or first grade who are "unready to learn," require that at-risk or remedial students be in self-contained programs to receive funding, and forbid the co-mingling of Special Education funds to support instruction of handicapped children in the regular classroom.

Therefore, the understandings of learning offered in this volume would have a profound effect if they could alter the fixed-ability special-assignment view of education that is still so powerful in the public mind.

Implications for Accountability Assessment

Following the advice of the Resnicks, state legislators and school board members should be mindful of the effects mandated accountability tests will have on what is taught in schools. In the current political climate of intense attention to test scores, standardized multiple-choice tests have become templates for instruction. Whatever can be said about the adequacy or efficiency of multiple-choice tests as indicators of student achievement, multiple-choice tests cannot be defended as good curriculum. "Teaching to the test" as practiced by most educators is not the same as cheating, which would involve practicing on the exact questions from the test or giving students answers to test questions. "Teaching to the test" means letting the content of the test and even the types of questions on the test become the exclusive focus of instruction. As a consequence teachers stop giving essay tests or having students work on projects and instead spend the year on fill-in-the-blank worksheets. Although accountability pressure is intended to improve the quality of education, it may actually worsen student achievement by driving out opportunities that develop thinking and reasoning abilities.

If accountability measures determine what is taught and we want students to learn to think, then assessment exercises must be devised to be much more ambitious and extended tasks requiring students to demonstrate the kinds of reasoning and problem solving that are the real goals of education. The point is not just to ensure more valid measurement but to redirect instruction toward more challenging learning goals. The Resnicks describe several types of performance assessments as alternatives to traditional tests. The key is to capture in the assessment tasks demonstration of the specific performances, reasoning abilities, oral and written communication skills, etc., that we wish students to acquire as outcomes of education. Various efforts to reform assessment use terms such as "authentic" (Wiggins, 1989), "direct" (Frederiksen & Collins, 1989), and "performance" assessment to convey the idea that assessments must capture real learning activities if they are to avoid distorting instruction. Proxy measures like standardized tests invite distortion because it is possible to raise test scores without genuinely improving student achievement (Shepard, 1989).

Performance measures are much more difficult to develop and score than conventional tests. Nonetheless the examples reviewed by the Resnicks suggest that such measures can be scored reliably enough to provide accurate accountability evidence. Generally authentic or performance assessments use one of two strategies. Either tasks are constructed, like writing prompts or science experiments, that can be administered under standardized conditions, or work products are collected from the students' on-going instruction, such as portfolios of writing assignments or math papers. To permit aggregation and comparison of results scoring rules must be developed for rating written products or the quality of students' responses when interviewed after a science experiment. When portfolios are used, safeguards such as occasional audits are required to ensure that students submit their own work and that instruction is not distorted by spending all year polishing a single assignment.

Scoring by human judges rather than optical scanning machines costs more. The reason policy makers should be willing to invest in performance assessment is, again, not just because it will yield more valid data but because with the right kinds of tasks, it will lead educational reform in the right direction. Given the current negative effects of testing on instruction, the urgency for reform of assessment is great. Performance assessments could be undertaken without increasing the budgets currently spent on state and local testing if policy makers were willing to trade off and test fewer students, using scientific sampling procedures, or fewer grades and subject areas (Resnicks, this volume; Shepard, 1989). The idea that accountability requires testing every pupil in every grade in every subject has to be given up to make it feasible to institute performance assessments.

It should be clear for logistical reasons that the same assessment cannot be used for instructional purposes and for accountability to external audiences. The views offered by Brown et al. and the Resnicks as to how assessment should be undertaken at these two levels are compatible but not the same. They are informed by the same learning theory and would engage students in the same kinds of activities aimed at developing their ability to think about subject matter. But in classrooms the teacher should be the one who assesses and guides instruction. Conversely for accountability purposes, teachers can be trained to score assessment responses but should not be responsible for judging their own students. A collateral benefit of large-scale performance assessments, in fact, is the amount of professional development that occurs during training and scoring when teachers see student efforts from other classrooms and are asked to reflect on their own goals and criteria for judging the quality of student work.

CONCLUSION

Since the time that most of today's policy makers were in school, our research-based understandings of human intelligence and learning have changed profoundly. Two of the most important findings from cognitive psychology are: 1) that intelligence is developed, and 2) that all learning requires thinking. Furthermore, activities and socially-supported interactions that develop intelligence are virtually indistinguishable from the kinds of instruction that enable students to think critically about subject matter.

Unfortunately much of educational practice, most especially traditional standardized tests, carry forward the assumptions of psychological theories that have since been disproven. Students are still placed in special educational programs, low-ability tracks, readiness rooms, and the like on the basis of static measurements that do not take account of opportunity to learn in calculating ability to profit from instruction. A linear, bit-by-bit skills model of learning is enforced so that students are not allowed to go on to thinking until they have mastered the basics. In the name of accountability and educational reform teachers are forced to spend so much time on the multiple-choice format curriculum that they provide students few of the opportunities that would teach them to think.

What the insights in this volume offer is a reconceptualization of instruction to teach thinking and a commensurate reformulation of assessment to help not hinder that effort.

REFERENCES

Arter, T.A., and J.R. Jenkins. 1979. Differential diagnosis--prescriptive teaching: A critical appraisal. Review of Educational Research, 49:517–555.

Budoff, M. 1974. Learning potential and educability among the educable mentally retarded. Final Report Project No. 312312. Cambridge, MA: Research Institute for Educational Problems, Cambridge Mental Health Association.

Calfee, R., and E. Hiebert. 1988. The teacher's role in using assessment to improve learning. In Assessment in the service of learning: Proceedings of the 1987 ETS Invitational Conference. Princeton, NJ: Educational Testing Service.

Carlberg, C., and K. Kavale. 1980. The efficacy of special versus regular class placement for exceptional children: A meta-analysis. Journal of Special Education, 14:295–309.

Coffman, W.E. 1971. Essay examinations. In R.L. Thorndike (Ed.), Educational Measurement, Second Edition. Washington, DC: American Council on Education.

Frederiksen, J.R., and A. Collins. 1989. A systems approach to educational testing. Educational Researcher, 18:27–32.

Graue, M.E., and L.A. Shepard, 1989. Predictive validity of the Gesell School Readiness Tests. Early Childhood Research Quarterly, 4:303–315.

Heath, S.B. 1982. Questioning at home and at school: A comparative study. In G. Spindler (Ed.), Doing the ethnography of schooling: Educational anthropology in action. New York: Holt, Rinehart and Winston. Madden, N.A., and Slavin, R.E. (1983). Mainstreaming students with mild handicaps: Academic and social outcomes. Review of Educational Research, 53:519–569.

National Council of Teachers of Mathematics. 1989. Curriculum and evaluation standards for school mathematics. Reston, VA: Author.

National Research Council. 1989. *Everybody counts--A report to the nation on the future of mathematics education.* Washington, D.C.: National Academy Press.

Oakes, J. 1985. Keeping track. New Haven, CT: Yale University Press.

Palincsar, A.S., and Brown, A.L. 1984. Reciprocal teaching of comprehension-fostering and comprehension monitoring activities. Cognition and Instruction, 1(2):117–175.

Shepard, L. 1983. The role of measurement in educational policy: Lessons from the identification of learning disabilities. Educational Measurement: Issues and Practice, 2:4–8.

Shepard, L.A. 1989. Why we need better assessments. Educational Leadership, 46:4–9.

Shepard, L.A., and M.L. Smith. March 1985. Boulder Valley kindergarten study: Retention practices and retention effects. Boulder, CO: Boulder Valley Public Schools.

Shepard, L.A., and M.L. Smith. 1989. Flunking Grades: Research and Policies on Retention. New York: The Falmer Press.

Slavin, R.E. 1987. Ability grouping and student achievement in elementary schools: A best-evidence synthesis, Review of Educational Research, 57:293–336.

Smith, M.L., and L.A. Shepard. 1988. Kindergarten readiness and retention: A qualitative study of teachers' beliefs and practices. American Educational Research Journal, 25:307–333.

Wiggins, G. 1989. Teaching to the (authentic) test. Educational Leadership, 46:41–47.

INDEX

330